Advance Praise for *Trauma Through A Child's Eyes*

"This work is the most valuable method I have found to help children reclaim their vitality, alleviate symptoms, and develop resiliency to future threats ... I only wish I had possessed these skills when the American Red Cross assigned me to the Pentagon Special Response Team in DC after 9/11."

– *Lisa R. LaDue, MSW, LISW, senior advisor, co-founder, and former director of the National Mass Fatalities Institute, University of Iowa*

"This book is one of the most valuable gifts one can give to friends, colleagues, parents, relations, and all other people who care about children; it is our choice for the book of the year."

– *The International Society for the Scientific Prevention of Violence*

"Finally, a comprehensive and inspiring book that will change your understanding of what it takes to raise healthy children. Peter Levine and Maggie Kline open our eyes and our hearts for healing our families, our schools, and our failing health-care system by addressing the most pervasive problem of our times. It is a must read."

– *Ray Castellino, DC, director of Building and Enhancing Bonding and Attachment*

"What could be more empowering than teaching our children how to unlock their innate resiliency, release trauma, and return to calm? I am thankful to the authors for the lives of the children they touch by their good work."

– *Pepper Black, program director of the Office of Student Development, University of California, Berkeley*

"The focus on the trauma work presented here has been necessary (and missing) for years. As young people experience more overwhelm, we need to offer more to help them build the resources needed to respond. This book provides both insight and strategy for educators to support the children of this millennium. I applaud the foresight and the effort."

– *Tiffany Brown, EdD, senior psychologist, Long Beach Unified School District elementary schools, and professor of educational psychology, Chapman University*

"This book is *the essential emotional first-aid guide* to help children of all ages ... empowering everyone to effectively support children using these easy-to-use steps!"

– *Wendy Anne McCarty, PhD, RN, author of* Welcoming Consciousness: Supporting Babies' Wholeness, *and founding chair of the Prenatal and Perinatal Psychology Program, Santa Barbara Graduate Institute*

Trauma Through A Child's Eyes

Awakening
the Ordinary Miracle
of Healing

Infancy through Adolescence

PETER A. LEVINE, PhD

MAGGIE KLINE, MS, MFT
(Marriage & Family Therapist)
and School Psychologist

North Atlantic Books
Berkeley, California

ERGOS Institute Press
Lyons, Colorado

Published by   and
North Atlantic Books   ERGOS Institute Press
P.O. Box 12327   P.O. Box 110
Berkeley, California 94712   Lyons, Colorado 80540

Cover and book design © Ayelet Maida, A/M Studios
Printed in the United States of America

Trauma Through A Child's Eyes: Awakening the Ordinary Miracle of Healing is sponsored by the Society for the Study of Native Arts and Sciences, a nonprofit educational corporation whose goals are to develop an educational and crosscultural perspective linking various scientific, social, and artistic fields; to nurture a holistic view of arts, sciences, humanities, and healing; and to publish and distribute literature on the relationship of mind, body, and nature.

North Atlantic Books' publications are available through most bookstores. For further information, call 800-733-3000 or visit our Website at www.northatlanticbooks.com.

Library of Congress Cataloging-in-Publication Data
Levine, Peter A.
   Trauma through a child's eyes : awakening the ordinary miracle of healing / by Peter A. Levine and Maggie Kline.
      p. cm.
Includes bibliographical references and index.
   ISBN-13: 978-1-55643-630-7 (pbk.)
   ISBN-10: 1-55643-630-0 (pbk.)
   1. Child mental health—Handbooks, manuals, etc. 2. Child psychology—Handbooks, manuals, etc. 3. Stress (Psychology)—Handbooks, manuals, etc. 4. Post-traumatic stress disorder—Patients—Handbooks, manuals, etc. I. Kline, Maggie. II. Title.
   [DNLM: 1. Stress Disorders, Traumatic—prevention & control. 2. Stress Disorders, Traumatic—therapy. 3. Stress, Psychological—prevention & control. 4. Stress, Psychological—therapy. 5. Child. WM 172 L6643t 2006]
   RJ499.3.L48 2006
   618.92'89—dc22
      2006011307

3 4 5 6 7 8 9 10 United 14 13 12 11 10 09 08

Dedication

We dedicate this book to all children everywhere, whether already here or yet to be born. May their lives be a little easier, may they suffer less, because they have grown up unencumbered by the shadow of trauma. May they be blessed with resilience, inner peace, and the joy of living fully imbued in the richness of their instinctual wisdom. And may we all be blessed, as they are our hope for the future.

– Peter and Maggie

Acknowledgments

From Peter A. Levine

Of my teachers, none have been as important as the children I have worked with over the years. They have shown me, through their courage, enthusiasm, spontaneity, vitality, and transparent spirits, how to evoke the ordinary miracle of healing. I thank Maggie, for her steadfast collaboration and enduring creative partnership, and for her passionate dedication to children's healing and welfare. Thanks also to Lorin Hager for his help developing the rhythms used in the later sections of the book and for Juliana DoValle who, at age eleven, drew the illustrations for those poems. Professionally, I want to acknowledge Richard Grossinger, the entire creative staff at North Atlantic Books, and especially Kathy Glass and Shannon Kelly for their talented and diligent editorial work. Finally, I acknowledge myself for trusting my dreams and intuitions; and my parents who, though flawed from their own pain, have always done the best that they could and have supported my growth and education, and fostered the gifts of curiosity and creativity.

From Maggie Kline

First, I wish to acknowledge Peter Levine, my mentor since 1994, who has been my inspiration and unwavering guiding light. He taught me how to access my own instinctual wisdom and creative juices. His gifts to me have been passed on one hundred–fold to children and families that I serve and to the professionals whom I teach. I thank my parents, Marge and Jim, for giving me these gifts: my father modeled that work is another way to love; my mother told me that I was a writer. Next, I'd like to express my gratitude to the courageous children who have taught me so much with their candor, curiosity, courage, and spontaneity, and gave me permission to write their stories so others would benefit. I would be remiss not to thank their parents as well, who are willing to grow side-by-side with them. I consider it a blessing to have worked in the inner-city schools of Long Beach, California, the most ethnically diverse city in the nation. I drew strength from witnessing my students overcome obstacles that no child should ever have to endure. I am blessed to have encountered so many dedicated teachers, counselors, and principals who made my job a joy. I am grateful that I was able to bring Beijo, my therapy dog, to school to comfort teens torn apart by gang violence. I wish to thank Kathy Glass, our editor, for her talent, tenacity, and diligence in making this book shine with her lovely polish. I am grateful to the many professionals to whom I have taught the principles of Somatic Experiencing® for their heartfelt enthusiasm, talent, and wisdom that have enhanced my learning. I thank my many friends for their support and good humor, especially Carolyn for sharing her story that became "The Power of Cool" in these pages. There are many SE® friends I'd like to thank in particular—Alexandre Duarte, Patti Elledge, and Karen Schanche for their direct contributions to the book; Abi Blakeslee, Sara Petit, Melinda Maxwell-Smith, and John Amodeo for their astute editorial suggestions; and the assistants in my SE® trainings who have dedicated themselves to healing trauma. Last, but not least, I wish to express my deepest appreciation to my son, Jake, for demanding of me to be my best, having patience, and forgiving my shortcomings. He showed me what a child needs and taught me how to be a better parent. I would also like to thank him for his "Guy Friday" errand running, cooking, and technological support during my computer crises on any given day of the week over the course of the writing of this book.

Contents

Foreword

Each year more than four million children in the United States are exposed to a traumatic event.[1] That figure is an underestimation, valid only if we narrowly restrict our definition of trauma to self-evident adverse circumstances such as sexual or physical abuse, serious injury, or the loss or death of a loved one. As Peter Levine and Maggie Kline show in this groundbreaking volume, trauma resides not in the external event but in how the child's nervous system processes that event. Based on Dr. Levine's decades of pioneering work, they make clear that it's the storage and freezing of unresolved emotions triggered by adverse events that create the long-term negative impact.

As a physician whose current work is with drug addicts, I see daily how early traumatic experiences are stored in people's brains and bodies and are daily "acted out" in the form of violence towards others or "acted in," in the form of self-harming beliefs and behaviors.

The prevention or compassionate and astute handling of potentially traumatic influences is essential. We now know that negative experiences do far more than form bad memories or unconscious negative dynamics: they can cause lifelong alterations in brain chemistry and body physiology. Such experiences can act even on the unborn child. A recent study found that, at one year of age, the infants of women traumatized during their pregnancies by the 9/11 tragedy had abnormal blood levels of the stress hormone, cortisol.[2] According to numerous human and animal studies, adverse early experiences may lead to permanent imbalances of essential brain chemicals that modulate mood and behavior.

Many "ordinary," everyday happenings that we take for granted as inevitable facts of life can become traumatic, and the younger the child, the less obviously harmful those occurrences need be in order to leave a traumatic impact. A "minor" fall, for example, can become traumatic if the child is not supported in processing it in a healthy way and especially if she is shamed for "over-reacting" or labeled as "too sensitive." An elective medical procedure can also have long-term negative effects if the child is not adequately supported and prepared, and if his reactions are not empathically received. As Levine and Kline convincingly argue, our culture imposes trauma upon children in many unwitting ways, from unnecessarily intrusive birth practices and institutionalized and mechanical pedagogic techniques, to divorce cases in which the child's emotional needs are lost amidst the parents' mutual anguish.

The positive message of this book is that many of these traumas can be prevented, and where the events themselves are unavoidable their traumatic impact can be avoided or, at least, minimized. The key is allowing and encouraging children to flow through the natural trajectory of their emotional shock reactions to difficult events without attempting to censor or control these reactions, preaching to our children, or projecting our own fears and anxieties.

The foundational truth imparted by the authors is that the adult's first task is to attend to his or her own emotional state, since it's only in the adult's calm, competent, and reassuring presence that children find the space to resolve their tensions. Who we are being is more important than what we are doing. More accurately, who we are being when facing an upsetting situation will dictate both the form and the impact of what we do. Levine and Kline allow us to practice for our role as trauma healers by using the best possible coaches: our own bodies and feelings.

The "trauma proofing" techniques Levine and Kline outlined in this book are masterful in their wisdom and simplicity, in their step-wise attention to detail, and in the clear rationale for their application. The authors take care to apply their principles in practical ways to the specific needs of the different stages of childhood, from infancy to adolescence.

Trauma Through A Child's Eyes is neither an academic textbook—although it could usefully replace many—nor a how-to-deal-with-trauma self-help tome. It's a teaching written to awaken the loving discernment of the nurturing adult, whether as parent or professional, and a handbook to guide us in supporting children through difficulties that, absent our compassionate and skillful intervention, could leave them scarred for life.

I wouldn't know what other work to compare this book to. Some books are said, in their originality, to "break the mold." *Trauma Through a Child's Eyes* goes one further: it creates its own mold in a way that everyone concerned with the health and happiness of children will be grateful for.

– Gabor Maté, MD

Author of Hold On To Your Kids: Why Parents Need to Matter More Than Peers *and* When The Body Says No: Understanding the Stress-Disease Connection

Introduction

This book is intended to be an accessible, concrete guide for
the prevention and healing of childhood trauma. This illustrated volume includes essential tools for parents, caregivers,
and professionals of various disciplines who have dedicated themselves to working with children in such everyday settings as schools,
hospitals, medical facilities, and therapy offices. In addition to
easy-to-follow suggestions for making life a little easier and safer
for everyone in these troubled times, abundant case examples are
included from the vast experience of both authors.

Dr. Peter A. Levine's work is informed by his background in
medical biophysics, psychophysiology, and psychology, with his
innovative theories coming from his keen observation of the instinctual behavior of wild animals in their natural environments. He
noticed their inborn immunity to traumatic symptoms and spent
thirty-five years developing and refining a method called Somatic
Experiencing® (SE) based on his discoveries in the natural world.

Dr. Levine's unique approach to trauma receives widespread
national and international recognition in both lay and professional
circles. His best-selling book *Waking the Tiger: Healing Trauma* has
been published in eighteen languages (originally published in English by North Atlantic Books, 1997). He has also published *Healing Trauma: A Pioneering Program in Restoring the Wisdom of Your
Body* (a book/CD); and *It Won't Hurt Forever: Guiding Your Child
Through Trauma* and *Sexual Healing: Transforming the Sacred
Wound,* both audio programs from Sounds True. Dr. Levine is a

sought-after speaker, teacher, and advisor. He serves as a consult-ant to The Meadows, a leading residential addiction recovery cen-ter in Arizona. He has provided leadership in grassroots efforts with communities that have been traumatized by war and natu-ral disasters. His professional training program has been growing rapidly throughout the world.

Maggie Kline, MS, MFT, has devoted herself to helping chil-dren of all ages for nearly thirty years as a teacher, psychothera-pist, and school psychologist. What she learned from Dr. Levine over a decade ago supplied the missing piece to the puzzle of effec-tive yet gentle trauma resolution that crosses cultural, ethnic, reli-gious, and socio-economic barriers. She creatively integrates art, play, poetry, and story with Somatic Experiencing®. Maggie uses the knowledge she has acquired from SE® in her private practice, the public school system, and with parents. She also provides train-ings in Somatic Experiencing® as a senior faculty member for Dr. Levine's Foundation for Human Enrichment (FHE) Professional Certification Program. In addition, Maggie participated in the trauma relief effort in Thailand after the devastating tsunami of 2004. She collaborated with Peter Levine in his Sounds True audio learning programs and co-authored with him "It Won't Hurt For-ever—Guiding Your Child Through Trauma," which appeared in the January/February 2002 issue of *Mothering* magazine.

Both Peter and Maggie have been moved by their hearts' desire to relieve the unnecessary suffering of so many children through-out the world whose precious young lives have been shattered by experiences too shocking and overwhelming to be handled by most adults. Understanding that trauma begets violence and violence begets trauma, the authors' intention is to provide information, examples, and activities that will break this vicious cycle. Children are free to develop a strong sense of self when inner turmoil is transformed into inner peace, setting the stage for them to be all they can be. In this comprehensive guide, the authors entice you to build "communities of caring" that foster and amplify the natural resiliency of children. Neighborhoods, schools, hospitals, and clinics are guided to bring the "ounce of prevention" necessary to turn the current tide of despair in a new direction.

This book offers a hopeful alternative to the "acting in" (on oneself) in the form of anxiety and illness and/or the "acting out" (on others) as hyperactivity and violence that is painfully prevalent today in the wake of so much traumatic stimulation. Peter and Maggie graciously invite you to join them in a collective dream of weaving a new social fabric through the powerful trauma intervention tools offered here so that children throughout the world can be truly free to be children.

The Website of the Foundation for Human Enrichment is www.traumahealing.com.

Overview of This Book

Trauma Through A Child's Eyes outlines step-by-step the practical application of "emotional first aid" to children in the aftermath of injury and emotional overwhelm. It is written for a general audience, with specific chapters that will be of special interest to parents, educators, and health care providers.

Trauma can result not only from catastrophic events such as child abuse and violence, but from incidents that generate effects that are often minimized, such as minor auto accidents, invasive medical and surgical procedures, divorce, separations, and falls—even from something as seemingly benign as a bicycle! These common experiences are often dismissed as ordinary events without considering the possibility of traumatic consequences. Regardless of the cause, the good news is that not only can trauma be healed, but oftentimes also prevented by using the skills you will learn in this book.

This book has grown out of the authors' desire to reduce unnecessary suffering by providing concrete methods that can be used by concerned adults to both prevent and heal the effects of trauma in children. Drawing on nearly forty years of research and experience in the field, Dr. Levine asserts that the basis of trauma is physiological. Simply put, this means that because there is often no time to think when facing threat, our primary response is instinctive. We are born with specific survival mechanisms. This perspective derives to a large degree from Dr. Levine's background in the biological sciences, but the uniqueness of his approach comes from the study of the behavior of animals in the wild. Discussed in detail in *Waking the Tiger: Healing Trauma* (North Atlantic Books, 1997), this information is summarized in Chapter One.

The link between animal behavior and the phenomenon of human trauma was first discovered by Dr. Levine in the late 1960s, when he observed that prey animals in the wild, though threatened routinely, are rarely traumatized. Further research on this phenomenon led him to the discovery of a built-in ability in animals to literally "shake off" the consequences of life-threatening encounters without lingering after-effects. Research on the human brain led him to wonder if people possess the same innate ability as animals, but somehow they aren't utilizing (or they override) this capacity. Extensive clinical practice strongly suggested that this theory is correct. Dr. Levine found that with appropriate guidance human beings could also "shake off" the effects of potentially overwhelming events and return to their normal lives. He found that if these events were left unresolved, the debilitating symptoms of trauma would accumulate over time, often not surfacing until long after an overwhelming incident is forgotten. He noticed that this situation often manifests as a slow but steady undermining of a child's sense of power and well-being. By understanding and working with the physiological (and, to a lesser degree, psychological) aspects of trauma, harmful events that often limit children's potential for fulfillment can be transformed into experiences that expand their ability to obtain a sense of mastery, resilience, power, and possibility.

The need for this book is reinforced by the fact that in professional circles the understanding that the cumulative effect of unresolved "ordinary" events can be as damaging as catastrophic ones is not fully appreciated and all too often disregarded. Although there are a few volumes on medical first aid for children, there are none that deal with "emotional" first aid for potentially traumatic occurrences. *A Parents' Guide to Medical Emergencies: First Aid for*

Your Child, by best-selling authors Zand, Walton, and Roundtree (Avery Publishing Group, 1997), contains one chapter entitled "Understanding Childhood Trauma," written by Dr. Levine.

Although several books have been written for the general public that deal with childhood loss, divorce, bereavement, and accompanying emotional reactions, there are no comprehensive handbooks available to teach parents and professionals how to gently guide children through the initial shock experienced in the aftermath of a wide range of overwhelming life events. Even the volumes written for professionals over the past two decades have overlooked the essential nonverbal physiological component that makes Dr. Levine's work (and this manual) unique. Healing the wounds of trauma from a physiological perspective moves the emphasis away from the story surrounding the event to the previously ignored "story" in the body itself.

The book informs by using case illustrations of traumatic occurrences that are a part of everyday life. Common situations that can be traumatizing are discussed in terms of symptom prevention. Falls, automobile accidents, surgical and dental procedures, near-drowning, abrupt separation (e.g. divorce, death, getting lost), natural disasters, and witnessing violence all have the potential to traumatize children. Although some of these ordinary events are not usually traumatic, concerned adults need to know when a child is indicating that he or she has been overwhelmed by what may appear to be a "minor" mishap. With this information, adults can help guide "at risk" children through their own built-in healing process. Extensive information on how to reduce children's vulnerability to sexual assault is also included.

In addition to case examples, exercises have been designed to give readers and their children a first-hand experience of the concepts discussed. They are meant to give the sense of the freedom and power that comes from being able to "tune in" to your own internal states and feel how real change occurs. Once adults understand the mechanism by which the shift out of shock, fear, and constriction can happen, it is easy to guide children.

The adult's role in helping children is similar in many ways to a Band-Aid. The Band-Aid doesn't heal the wound but it protects it, supporting the wisdom of the body to do what it is designed to do. Since children are highly attuned to the emotional states of adults, it is very important for adults to stay relatively calm and collected so that they may be present to the needs of their children. This book outlines step-by-step procedures to enable parents to be good "Band-Aids."

Trauma Through A Child's Eyes is also interactive, with an illustrated section that employs rhymed verses that can be read to young children by parents, teachers, social workers, nurses, and other medical and mental health professionals. It can be used to help children prepare for necessary medical procedures, as well as to recover after overwhelming or injurious events, in order to prevent traumatic reactions from developing. The activities can be used one-on-one, with small groups, or with an entire classroom of children.

Children have a vibrant and innate resiliency and are able to rebound from "overwhelm" and injury. With the support and guidance provided by this book, parents and other adults can help children prevent traumatic reactions from developing. In addition, the book can be used to help children resolve residual effects of trauma from past events, both known and unknown. The prevention and resolution of trauma, past and present, will increase the natural resiliency of children, allowing them to be more resourceful and successful in future potentially harmful situations. When symptoms don't readily resolve with parental support, it is advised that professional help be sought.

PART I

UNDERSTANDING
TRAUMA

CHAPTER ONE

What Is Trauma?
A Working Definition

The striving and territorial protectiveness of the reptile,
the nurturing and family orientation of the early mammal,
the symbolic and linguistic capacities of the neocortex
may multiply our damnation or grace our salvation.

– Jean Houston[1]

W hat is trauma? Everywhere we look these days, the word "trauma" pops up. Titles such as "Unlocking Trauma" and "In the Aftermath of Abuse" are featured headlines of both professional journals and mainstream magazines. Popular TV shows such as *Oprah Winfrey* try to bring understanding to millions of viewers regarding trauma's gripping effect on body and soul. Today it is finally becoming common knowledge just how devastating trauma's impact can be to children's emotional and physical well-being, cognitive development, and behavior. For professionals, there is no dearth of forums available that highlight statistics regarding trauma's effects on our young. Since September 11, 2001, there has been an information blitz on how to cope in the aftermath of catastrophe.

Despite the focus on scanning and studying the traumatized brain, little has been written regarding the common causes, much less the prevention and treatment of trauma. Focus instead has been on the diagnosis and the medication of its various symptoms. "Trauma is perhaps the most avoided, ignored, belittled, denied, misunderstood, and untreated cause of human suffering."[2]

3

Fortunately you—the parents, educators, and health professionals who serve children—are in a position to prevent the perilous
effects of trauma and do the most good with those in your care.

With the increasing occurrence and witnessing of disturbing
local and world events, it's clear that parents, educators, medical
professionals, and therapists cannot wait another moment to learn
how best to prevent trauma. It is essential to recognize the root of
this problem in order to restore the natural resiliency of the growing numbers of children already suffering. In this chapter we hope
to close the information gap as we take a closer look at trauma—
its myths and realities.

Trauma Is in the
Nervous System—Not in the Event!

Trauma happens when *any* experience stuns us like a bolt out of
the blue; it overwhelms us, leaving us altered and disconnected
from our bodies. Any coping mechanisms we may have had are
undermined, and we feel utterly helpless and hopeless. It is as if
our legs are knocked out from under us.

Trauma is the antithesis of empowerment. Vulnerability to
trauma differs from person to person depending on a variety of
factors, especially age and trauma history. The younger the child,
the more likely she is to be overwhelmed by common occurrences
that might not affect an older child or adult.

It has been commonly believed that traumatic symptoms are
the result of and equivalent to the type and enormity of an external event. While the magnitude of the stressor is clearly an important factor, it does not define trauma. That is because *"trauma is
not in the event itself; rather, trauma resides in the nervous system."*[3]
The basis of "single-event" trauma (as contrasted to ongoing neglect and abuse) is physiological rather than psychological. Because
there is no time to think when facing threat, our primary responses
are instinctual. Our brain's main function is survival! We are wired

for it. At the root of a traumatic reaction is our 280-million-year heritage—a heritage that resides in the oldest and deepest structures of the brain known as the reptilian brain.

When these primitive parts of the brain perceive danger, they automatically activate an extraordinary amount of energy—like the adrenaline rush that allows a mother to lift the auto her child is trapped beneath and pull him to safety. This in turn elicits a pounding heart along with more than twenty other physiological responses designed to prepare us to defend and protect ourselves and our loved ones. These rapid involuntary shifts include the redirection of blood flow away from the digestive and skin organs and into the large motor muscles of flight, along with fast and shallow respiration and a decrease in the normal output of saliva. Pupils dilate to increase the ability of the eyes to take in more information. Blood-clotting ability increases, while verbal ability decreases. Muscle fibers become highly excited, often to the point of trembling. Or alternatively, our muscles may collapse in fear as the body shuts down in overwhelm.

Fear of Our Own Reactions

When a person does not understand what is happening internally, the very responses that are meant to give a physical advantage can become downright frightening. This is especially true when, due to size, age, or other vulnerabilities, one is either unable to move or it would be disadvantageous to do so. For example, an infant or young child doesn't have the option to run. However, an older child or an adult, who ordinarily could run, may also need to keep very still, such as in the case of surgery, rape, or molestation. There is no conscious choice. We are biologically programmed to freeze (or go limp) when flight or fight is either impossible or *perceived* to be impossible. Freeze is the last-ditch, "default" response to an inescapable threat, even if that threat is a microbe in our blood. Infants and children, because of their limited capacity to defend themselves, are particularly susceptible to freezing and therefore are vulnerable to being traumatized. This is why adult support is so crucial in preventing trauma and helping our youngsters heal.

Underneath the freeze response is a variety of physiological effects. What must be understood about the freeze response is that although the body looks inert, those physiological mechanisms that prepare the body to escape may *still* be on "full charge." The sensory-motor-neuronal blueprint that was set into motion at the time of threat is paradoxically thrown into a state of immobility or "shock." When in shock the skin is pale and the eyes appear vacant. The sense of time is distorted. Underlying this situation of helplessness there is an enormous vital energy. This energy lies in wait to finish what has been started. In addition, very young children tend to bypass active responses and go right to shutdown. In either case they need our guidance to come fully back into life. Furthermore, many young children protect themselves not by running away, but by running towards the adult attachment figure. Hence to help the child resolve a trauma, there needs to be a safe adult available.

How does this outpouring of energy and multiple changes in physiology affect us in the long run? The answer to this question is an important one in understanding trauma. The answer depends on what happens *during and after* the potentially overwhelming event. The catch is that to avoid being traumatized, the excess energy evoked in our defense must be "used up." When the energy is not fully discharged, it does not simply go away; instead it stays trapped, creating the potential for traumatic symptoms.

The younger the child, the fewer resources she has to protect herself. For example, a preschool or primary school child is unable to escape from or fight a vicious dog, while infants are unable even to keep themselves warm. For these reasons the protection of respectful adults who perceive and meet children's needs for security, warmth, and tranquility is of paramount importance in preventing trauma. Additionally, adults often can provide comfort and safety by introducing a stuffed toy animal, doll, angel, or even a fantasy character that can act as a surrogate friend. These objects can be especially consoling when children must be temporarily separated from their parents, and as sleeping aids when they are alone in their room at night. Resources such as these may seem unremarkable for an adult but may prove vital to the young child in preventing overwhelm.

Adults who received this type of secure connection when frightened as children may call the above information "common sense." This implies that children's needs are commonly noticed and attended to. Historically, however, the needs of children have been disgracefully minimized, if not overlooked entirely. Developmental psychiatrist Daniel Siegel, author of the acclaimed book *The Developing Mind*, provides a synthesis of the neurobiological research underscoring exactly how crucial the safety and containment provided by adults is to infants and children. The early brain develops its intelligence, emotional resilience, and ability to self-regulate by the anatomical-neuronal shaping and pruning that takes place in the context of the face-to-face relationship between child and caregiver. When traumatic events occur, the imprinting of neurological patterns is dramatically heightened. Thus when adults learn and practice the simple emotional first aid tools we offer, they are also making a pivotal contribution to healthy brain development and behavior in their children.

The Recipe for Trauma

The likelihood of developing traumatic symptoms is related to the level of shutdown as well as to the undischarged survival energy that was originally mobilized to fight or flee. This self-protective process has now gone haywire. Children need support to release this highly charged state, given how susceptible they are to trauma's effects. The myth that babies and toddlers "are too young to be affected" or that "it won't matter because they won't remember" can be laid to rest. What was not so obvious becomes apparent as we learn that prenatal infants, newborns, and very young children are the *most* at risk to stress and trauma due to their undeveloped nervous, motor, and perceptual systems. This vulnerability also applies to older children who have limited mobility because of permanent or temporary disabilities, such as having a splint, brace, or cast due to an orthopedic injury or correction. Let's look at a real-life example.

The Case of Jack

Jack, an eleven-year-old Boy Scout and straight-A student, developed "school phobia" shortly after a minor earthquake—a tiny tremor by California standards. His parents didn't make the connection between the quake and the phobia, finding his symptoms rather mysterious. Jack was also puzzled by his extreme fear of school. He explained that he had recently undergone back surgery and was grateful to be free of pain and was eager to return to school to be with his friends. However, he could literally not get up out of bed because the "butterflies in his stomach" were so intense. He lay frozen under his covers as he endured his panicky feelings. During the first of three sessions an amazing story unfolded as we worked with these "butterflies"—focusing on Jack's scary sensations (as well as his resources). What emerged was a terrifying image of his bookcase shaking during the tremor. Still, since the bookcase did not topple, what made Jack's experience so traumatic as to keep him away from his friends at school? As we continued to work together, it soon became clear.

When Jack first felt the tremor, he was unable to predict the accurate level of danger; the only thing that registered in his reptilian brain was the "red flag" of threat. His nervous system responded to the perceived danger with full alert, and he continued to feel panicky well after the brief "shaker" was over. The severity of his response becomes demystified when we learn that as a young child Jack had been confined to a body cast for several weeks following an earlier back surgery. Frightened by the procedure and then immobilized by the cast, he was powerless to respond to the dangers he perceived lurking all around him, as young children do after such a scary event. The normal impulse to flee could not be acted upon; he was in fact paralyzed. In Jack's case, the hard confines of the cast prevented movement.

When the brain sets a sensory-motor impulse into motion but the limbs cannot move (or if the movement itself could be dangerous, such as with molestation or surgery), symptoms are likely to develop. Discomfort can be experienced as irritability, anxiety, "butterflies," numbness, etc. When the body can no longer bear the overwhelming feelings, it collapses into fearful resignation ("learned helplessness")—which is what any animal does in a situation where active escape from threat is impossible. As Jack grew older, what had been a terrifying experience in his early childhood appeared long "forgotten" at eleven.

The problem is that although the event may have disappeared from conscious memory, the *body* does not forget. There is a physiological imperative to *complete* the incomplete sensory-motor impulses that were activated *before* the body is able to return to a state of relaxed alertness. Therefore, even after Jack's cast was removed, the undischarged energy and the neurological "imprint" of restriction remained present in his nervous system.

The Reason Our Bodies Don't Forget: What Brain Research Has Taught Us

Why is it that once the threat is over we are not free of it? Why are we, unlike our animal friends, left with anxiety and vivid memories that alter us forever if we don't get the help that we need?

The highly regarded neurologist Antonio Damasio, author of *Descartes' Error* and *The Feeling of What Happens*, discovered that emotions literally have an anatomical mapping in the brain necessary for survival.[4] That is to say the emotion of fear has a very specific neural circuitry etched in the brain corresponding to specific *physical sensations from various parts of the body*. When something we see, hear, smell, taste, or feel signals the original threat, the experience of fear helps the body to organize a "flee or freeze" plan to remove us from danger quickly. The trigger produces more than a memory (in fact many times there is no conscious memory of the origin, only a physical response). The heart rate rapidly escalates, sweat is produced, and the anguish occurs because the body is totally re-engaged *as if* the threat is still happening. The strong emotion of the original event left an equally strong imprint to teach us a survival lesson. This is all well and good in the face of the next danger. But why does this response become maladaptive, occurring even when there is no actual danger? Let's look again to the research.

Bessel van der Kolk, a leading trauma researcher at Boston University, has studied the fear response via MRI (magnetic resonance imaging).[5] A small almond-shaped structure in the midbrain called the amygdala is responsible for activating quickly when threat is perceived. It is highly responsive to sights and sounds, and it recruits many areas of the brain to deal with the situation. Joseph LeDoux of New York University, author of *The Emotional Brain,* likens it to an early warning system that alerts and prepares the body for danger.[6] That is why muscles begin to tense and hormones (designed to aid our survival) are released, flooding our body and brain. The frontal cortex, which thinks and reasons, then plays a critical role in sorting out whether or not the barking dog is friend or foe, the shadow is a stalker or a friendly stranger, or the object in your path is a snake or a stick. If the dog turns out to be friendly, the message the cortex then sends back to the amygdala quiets the fear response.

Unfortunately, in the traumatized person, the cortex is unable to allay the fear response. With this "cortical bypass" we cannot reason away the fear and inadvertently are left either to act it out on others with extreme emotion, suffer silently from overwhelming feelings, or blank out from the distressing fear-response signals. Or as Bessel van der Kolk put it, "In PTSD [post-traumatic stress disorder] the frontal cortex is held hostage by a volatile amygdala. Thinking is hijacked by emotion. People with PTSD are very sensitively tuned to respond to even very minor stimuli as if their life is in danger."[7]

Back to the Story of Jack

The preceding scientific explanation makes it easy to understand how it was possible that years later when Jack was lying in bed shortly after his second surgery, the minor quake triggered sensations (recalled by the body consciousness) of helplessness from the traumatic residue of his previous surgery. His body responded to the present danger as though he were still confined in a cast. With his body at the mercy of an overly sensitive amygdala, the extra burst of adrenaline set off a cascade of reactions that was as overwhelming as the original feelings of terror. These anxious feelings prevented Jack from going out into the world, though they made no sense on the surface. However, the newly activated sensations from the "old" event, when he was unable to protect himself, had been etched into his "body memory," undermining his self-confidence. Not being able to sort out the source of these crippling internal sensations, Jack became panicked.

What looked like school phobia was really the "fear of" the rush of disturbing sensations caused by a flood of newly released stress hormones triggered by the earlier "imprint" when Jack was immobilized and unable to run to safety. Fortunately, as Jack learned how to "befriend" his scary feelings in small increments, his body made the connection to the past and discharged the paralyzing sensations in his legs as they began to tremble. Then, almost miraculously, Jack felt his legs wanting to run as fast as they could carry him! This was precisely what his sensory-motor system was "programmed" to do at the time of his first surgery—but was unable to.

Most of us have had some sort of "ordinary" frightening event from which we have not fully rebounded. And some of these "long forgotten" experiences have formed the bedrock of various emotional and physical symptoms, and even our dislikes and "preferences." The following example illustrates how we ordinarily do not question them.

Henry

Four-year-old Henry's mother became concerned when he refused to eat his (previously) favorite foods: peanut butter and jelly with a glass of milk. When his mother placed them in front of Henry, he would get agitated, stiffen, and push them away. Even more disturbing was the fact that he would start shaking and cry whenever the family dog barked. It never occurred to her that this "pickiness" and fearfulness of the barking were directly related to an "ordinary" incident that had occurred almost a year before, when Henry was still using a high chair.

Sitting in his high chair, devouring his favorite foods—peanut butter, jelly, and milk—he had proudly held out his half-empty glass for his mother to fill. As things like this happen, Henry lost his grip and the glass fell to the ground with a crash. This startled the dog, causing it to jump backward, knocking over the high chair. Henry hit his head on the floor and lay there, gasping, unable to catch his breath. Mother screamed and the dog started barking loudly. From his mother's perspective Henry's food aversion and apparent fear of the dog made no sense. However, from the vantage of trauma, the simple association of having milk and peanut butter right before the fall and the wild barking of his dog, in a Pavlovian response, conditioned his fear and food aversion.

Once Henry had "practiced" controlled falling onto pillows (with the suggestions detailed in this book) he learned to relax his muscles as he gradually surrendered to gravity. Before this, he "simply" would not eat those foods and had trouble sleeping when dogs barked in the neighborhood. Fortunately, after a couple of play sessions this little boy was once again devouring his favorite foods and barking back at the dog in playful glee.

Lessons Learned from the Animals

Why is it that non-domesticated prey animals are rarely traumatized? Although animals in their natural surroundings do not experience surgical procedures and casting as Jack did, their lives are threatened routinely—often many times a day. Yet, they are rarely traumatized when in the wild. Observations of wild animals in their natural environments led to the premise that animals have a built-in ability to rebound from a steady diet of danger.[8] They literally "shake off" the residual energy through trembling, rapid eye movements, shaking, panting, and completing motor movements. As the body is returning to equilibrium, the animal can be observed "taking" deep spontaneous breaths. Actually, when watching carefully, one realizes that the breath is being infused into the animal from deep within its organism. This is all part of the normal mechanism of self-regulation and homeostasis. The good news is that we share this same capability with our animal friends.

Why then do humans suffer from trauma symptoms? There are several answers to this vital question. First of all, we are more complex than other creatures. Endowed with a superior rational brain, simply put, we think too much. Thinking is all too often paired with judgment. Animals do not have words to judge their feelings and sensations. There are no guilt trips, shame or blame games.

The end result is that they do not impede the healing process of returning to balance and homeostasis like we do. Another reason is that we are not accustomed to such strong physical responses. Without skill to guide rather than impede these involuntary reactions, the instincts that animals take for granted can be frightening, both to children and adults. In addition, our young are dependent on us for their safety and protection much longer than the young of other species remain dependent. Children need the security of a caregiver to rebound.

Most young mammals, and that of course includes human children, rather than running away from threat will run towards a source of adult protection, usually to the mother (or to other adults). Similarly human babies, infants, and toddlers will cling to their attachment figures when they feel threatened. In fact humans of *all* ages seek the comfort of others when fearful or stressed. (This is what happened in New York after 9/11, with people spending hours on the phone talking to their families and friends.)

We think it is apparent how a dilemma of profound consequences is set up if the people who are supposed to love and protect us are also the ones that have hurt, humiliated, and violated us. This "double bind" undermines a basic sense of self and trust in one's own instincts. In this way one's whole sense of safety and stability becomes weakened. For this reason if you have a child with attachment problems (such as may occur in adoptions, foster families, and when there has been separation or abuse), help and support from a trained professional is generally advisable if not essential.

Fortunately, this book will teach you how to help children feel and move through sensations without undue distress—just as the animals do! Your new knowledge will help take the fear out of the experience of these involuntary reactions. Whether you are a parent, teacher, counselor, or nurse—through play, art, games, and activities you will be guided to help your own children and others like Jack and Henry. Simple rhymes are included that use animal imagery (see Chapter Five). Since animals are nonjudgmental and instinctual, they can be powerful resources in helping children connect directly with their own innate healing process.

Many real-life examples are included to illustrate how you can support children in recovering from frightening and overwhelming experiences. Although many are from private practice sessions and others are from counseling in school settings, the basic principles are meant to be applied as "emotional first aid" by conscientious caregivers. This book is written to aid therapists in their efforts. It is also meant to assist parents and other guardians of children, such as medical personnel, to recognize the signs of trauma while learning simple skills to alleviate or prevent trauma symptoms after a frightening mishap. There are situations, of course, as mentioned earlier, when professional counseling is highly recommended.

—————————— 🌿 ——————————

CHAPTER TWO

Trauma's Scope—
Sources Ranging from
the Ordinary to the Extraordinary

On and on the rain will fall . . .
like tears from a star . . . like tears from a star.
On and on the rain will say,
how fragile we are . . . how fragile we are.

– "Fragile" by Sting

We will now explore the triggers of trauma—some conspicuous, even palpable, while others are ordinary occurrences. These common triggers have been largely overlooked by most people, including professionals. Our examples will help shed light on the importance of helping youngsters get through the everyday mishaps, as well as the more extraordinary events.

Many parents and professionals would define trauma as an unexpected horrific event that is relatively rare, affecting only a few unlucky individuals. We [the authors] would venture to say that no one totally escapes the long reach of trauma's shadow to some degree, at some time or another, during their lifespan. And those who are traumatized in the fragile period during infancy carry the burden of trauma's imprint as a lifelong struggle that seems to add a murky layer over ordinary existence.

Some events are overwhelming to almost any child. These include exposure to violence, events surrounding robbery, school shootings, kidnapping, as well as physical and sexual abuse. Sadly, these kinds of events are a reality for far too many children. Other events may not appear traumatizing from an adult's perspective. However, to a child, many "ordinary" events can have lasting effects.

Common Causes of Childhood Trauma

The most universal sources of possible traumatic reactions, including falls, accidents, and invasive medical/surgical procedures, occur with such frequency that a conscious link between later symptoms and a precipitating incident is rarely made. Often these events have no lasting ill effects. Having said this, the wisdom of "an ounce of prevention being worth a pound of cure" could not be truer when startling things happen. Prevention of ill effects after frightening occurrences is often simple, as you will learn in Part II. In order to give you a better sense of how common events can affect children adversely, let's look at a variety of typical scenarios that happen to children on any given day in any city or town.

Real-Life Examples of Children We Have Known

By taking a peek into the worlds of five different children, you will have a better sense of the scope of trauma that can occur at any age. One or two of the situations described may even remind you of someone you know! After you read the dilemmas of the youngsters below, the source of their painful symptoms will be revealed.

Lisa cries hysterically every time the family prepares to get into the car.

Carlos, a painfully shy fifteen-year old, is chronically truant. "I don't want to feel scared all the time anymore," he says. "All I want is to feel normal."

Sarah reports dutifully to her second-grade class on time every morning; invariably, by 11 a.m., she is in the nurse's office complaining of a stomachache, although no medical reason can be found for her chronic symptoms.

Curtis, a popular, good-natured middle school student, tells his mother that he feels like kicking someone—anyone! He has no idea where this urge is coming from. Two weeks later he starts behaving aggressively toward his little brother.

The parents of three-year-old Kevin are concerned about his "autistic-like" play. He repeatedly lies on the floor and stiffens his body, pretending he is dying and slowly coming back to life, saying, "Save me ... save me!"

What do these youngsters have in common? How did their symptoms originate? Will their symptoms disappear or grow worse over time? To answer these questions for concerned parties such as teachers, health professionals, and parents, let's look at the source of their troubles.

We'll begin with Lisa, the hysterical crier. When she was three years old, she had been strapped into her car seat when the family's van was rear-ended. There were no physical injuries to her or her mom, who was driving. In fact, the car was barely scratched and the accident was considered a minor "fender bender." Little Lisa's crying was not associated with the accident, because it was a delayed reaction. It took several weeks before the numbing impact of the collision wore off. Her symptoms of quiet behavior coupled with a poor appetite changed to fearful tears when approaching the family van.

While Lisa experienced a one-time episode, Carlos' "injury" developed over time. He had been physically intimidated for more than five years by an emotionally disturbed adolescent step-brother. No one intervened. No adult in the house saw it as anything more than "normal" sibling conflict. Carlos was terrified, not only by the brother, but by fears that his parents would be furious with him for not having more empathy for his mentally ill brother. He had tried to express his dread to his mother but his feelings were dismissed; he was, instead, asked to be more tolerant.

No one except Carlos' older sister, who was in distress herself due to the family dynamics, saw his pain or predicament. Meanwhile, Carlos fantasized night and day about being a professional wrestler, but he had barely enough strength or confidence to get out of bed to come to school each day, let alone become part of a high school sports team. It wasn't until Carlos revealed a plan for suicide that his parents finally recognized the profoundly detrimental impact that the repeated physical and emotional harassment was having on their son.

The next youngster mentioned above was Sarah, who had been very excited about starting second grade. After a fun shopping trip to pick out brand-new clothes for school, she was told, abruptly and unexpectedly, that her parents were getting divorced and her father would be moving out in two weeks! Her joy for school became paired with panic and sadness as the aliveness in her tummy changed into tight twisted knots. No wonder she was the nurse's most frequent visitor!

While waiting for the school bus one morning, Curtis witnessed a drive-by shooting that left the victim dead on the sidewalk. He was with a small group of classmates at the bus stop, and all received some counseling when they arrived at school. Curtis, however, continued to look disturbed and agitated as the days passed.

The last youngster described was Kevin. He had been delivered by emergency cesarean and had a lifesaving surgery within twenty-four hours of his birth. He was born with anomalies requiring immediate intestinal and rectal repair. Often, medical and surgical procedures *are* required and do make life possible. Amidst the relief and celebration of a saved life, it is easy to overlook the reality that these same procedures can inflict trauma that may leave emotional and behavioral effects long after the surgical wounds have healed.

Except for the shooting witnessed by Curtis and the major surgery performed on Kevin at birth, the situations above are not extraordinary; in fact, they are typical. Although each "event" was very different, what these youngsters have in common is that each experienced feelings of overwhelm. Each youngster was traumatized by what happened and how they experienced what happened. How do we know? The answer is quite simple. Each child carried on in life, some way, as if the event were still happening. They were "stuck" or fixated in time, as their bodies responded to an alarm that was set at the traumatic moment. Although memory may not be consciously connected to the event, the children's play, behavior, and physical complaints reveal their struggle to deal with internal turmoil.

Ideally, the above examples give you a concept of the breadth and depth of common situations that can be overwhelming to children. To help broaden your awareness of a wide variety of "traumatic triggers," samplings of potential causes are separated into five categories in the discussion below. While some are obvious, others you may find surprising. They are: 1) accidents and falls, 2) medical and surgical procedures, 3) violent acts and attacks, 4) grief and loss, and 5) environmental stressors. Throughout this book, case examples and first-aid suggestions will be given on how to work with a variety of situations from each of the categories.

Accidents and Falls

Falls are commonplace as infants become toddlers, negotiating the unforgiving forces of gravity for the first time. Learning to walk on unstable, wobbly legs is a challenge. Generally, these small falls are innocuous both physically and emotionally. This trial-and-error learning of motor skills, in fact, helps kids develop competence and confidence. However, infants and children, in an unguarded moment, occasionally fall down stairs, off beds, and out of high chairs. With these types of falls, both physical and emotional repercussions are more likely.

A Cautionary Note

In infants and toddlers, *symptoms of concussion* can include continual crying, crankiness, and inability to be calmed. Other possible signs are a change in play habits, loss of interest in favorite toys or foods, loss of balance, and/or loss of newly acquired skills such as toilet training, walking, or language. Even though these can readily be signs of trauma, they can also be an indication of a concussion. If you notice any of the above signs persisting or worsening, particularly if the child's head may have taken an impact, it is essential to get professional medical assistance as soon after the incident as possible.

As children mature, they have an appetite for testing their limits in sports, dance, and gymnastics. Often, because a child does not want to appear weak in front of parents or peers, she will suppress crying. This bravado of "keeping a stiff upper lip" often interferes with the release of both emotional and physiological stress. Another common effect in many children's lives is being involved in a motor vehicle accident, as was the case with little Lisa.

Another potentially significant mishap for children of all ages involves near-drowning. This can happen in bathtubs, swimming pools, backyard ponds, lakes, or at the ocean. Parents who look away briefly can find their child choking on water, or worse—that the child has disappeared, momentarily, under the water. Older children and adolescents can get pulled under by "rip tides" or pounded by waves. Near-drowning is a form of suffocation, which can be terrifying. Other ways that children get feelings of suffocation include getting tangled under covers or squashed by pillows, falls where the "wind is knocked out" of them, pets lying across the throat or chest, rough play with older siblings, aggressive tickling, and the medical procedure of intubation, which blocks air passages. The following table summarizes these situations.

ACCIDENTS AND FALLS

- Falls (stairs, beds, and high chairs)
- Sports injuries (from team sports, spills from bicycles, skateboards, skis, etc.)
- Auto accidents (even at low speeds)
- Near-drowning and near-suffocation

Medical and Surgical Procedures

This category is perhaps the most overlooked and potentially problematic, particularly with modern life-saving technologies, as we have seen with Kevin (who had surgery immediately following birth). These traumatic effects seem to be intrinsic to hospitalizations and invasive medical procedures. Such trauma is more likely when children have been separated from their parents, frightened, restrained against their will, and unprepared for what will happen to them.

Dr. David Levy, a psychiatrist and medical researcher, noted in his observational studies (1944) that the symptoms displayed by children hospitalized for "routine" medical procedures were little different than those displayed by "shell-shocked" (traumatized) World War II soldiers returning from the battlefields of Europe and North Africa![1] Modern invasive medical procedures are still one of the more commonly overlooked sources of trauma.

As modern medicine becomes more sophisticated with sonograms, brain scans, and other devices, there are more opportunities for stressful procedures that some consider routine. Children need to be prepared and supported before undergoing tests and treatment so that the advances in technology can do more good than harm.

MEDICAL AND SURGICAL PROCEDURES

- Surgery and medical procedures (stitches, needles, IVs, exploratory exams)
- Dental procedures
- Life-threatening illnesses and high fevers
- Prolonged immobilization (casting, splinting, traction)
- Poisoning
- Fetal distress and birth complications (cord around neck, anesthesia, drugs and alcohol, etc.)

Violent Acts/Attacks

Physical and sexual abuse, as well as the effects of war, have been given more attention by professionals and the press since the women's movement of the 1970s and the return of veterans after the Viet Nam War. However, many parents are still unaware of the prevalence of attacks on their own children, often in their very homes and neighborhoods. This book aims to show you how to identify symptoms in children, as well as how to talk to children in a way that can minimize the chances of victimization.

A frequently overlooked subcategory of violent acts is witnessing. Our children are now part of "Generation M" (electronic "M"edia). Like it or not, they are bombarded with violent images from video games, TV, computers, and music. When multi-tasking, they may be receiving multiple images from different source simultaneously. The "M" word for parents is "Monitor" what your child sees and hears. Of course, when they grow older this becomes practically impossible. However, keeping open dialogue regarding the impact of violent images with your pre-teens and adolescents is a must.

VIOLENT ACTS/ATTACKS

- Bullying (school, neighborhood, siblings)
- Animal attacks (dog, snakebite)
- Family violence
- Witnessing violence (live and vicariously through video games and TV)
- Physical and sexual abuse and neglect
- War, displacement, and its intergenerational effects
- Threat of terrorist attack
- Kidnapping

Loss

No child escapes childhood without loss. Death of a family member or pet is inevitable. Divorce affects approximately half of all families in the United States. Yet, you can do so much to help children cope. This book discusses the important differences between shock and grief and how to help youngsters through both stages.

LOSS

- Divorce
- Death of loved one or pet
- Separation
- Being lost (at the mall or in a strange neighborhood)
- Possessions (home and other belongings following a disaster or theft)

Environmental Stressors

After the Indian Ocean tsunami and Hurricanes Katrina and Rita, the devastating impact of natural disasters became obvious to us all. Other environmental stresses, such as loud noise and extremes of temperature that may be tolerated (even though not appreciated) by older children and adults, can create traumatic symptoms in babies and small children who do not yet have the ability to self-regulate or move out of harm's way. A hot car or a freezing cold room can be experienced by an infant as a near-death experience.

ENVIRONMENTAL STRESSORS

- Exposure to extremes of temperature
- Natural disasters (fires, earthquakes, floods, tornadoes, hurricanes, volcanoes, and tsunamis)
- Sudden loud noises for babies and young children (arguments, violence, thunder—especially if left alone)

It is important to understand that if any of these things have happened to your child or one you know, it does not necessarily mean that he will be traumatized. A few minutes spent with your child using the first aid outlined in Part II can help minimize the chance of lasting effects. Trauma first aid can also make your child more resilient to inevitable stress, kind of like a "stress inoculation" for life.

Curtis, whom we met earlier as a witness to a drive-by shooting, is a great example of how a little adult support can go a long way in relieving acute distress. After receiving trauma first aid, his lingering symptoms resolved overnight. Luckily, an astute school counselor noticed Curtis' increasing irritability and how he, uncharacteristically, "looked like he wanted to pick a fight." After one session that moved his body out of shock and restored his confidence in his weakened defenses, Curtis' distress disappeared. In a follow-up several months later, he continued to be symptom-free. In Chapter Twelve, which provides activities and examples to help traumatized students after a crisis, we take a closer look at how Curtis was supported to completely discharge the irritating "fight" energy that had been stored in his body when he was an innocent witness to a violent attack.

Obvious Sources of Childhood Trauma

Unfortunately the obvious and appalling sources of trauma cannot be said to happen much less frequently than the more "common" garden-variety spills, injuries, separations, and illnesses that are a part of growing up. Violence in the form of physical, sexual, and emotional abuse is prevalent. The most widespread and devastating sources of trauma tend to be found within families and with other familiar adults. When a child suffers from physical or sexual abuse at the hand of someone they trusted to protect them, such as a family member, neighbor, teacher, or religious leader, the complexity of betrayal, secrecy, and additional shame is in itself overwhelming. Because of this complexity, it is of utmost importance to seek professional help for the children in your care. This book is intended to aid you in increasing your awareness of how and why your child is suffering from trauma and how to support her or his recovery. However, this is not a substitute for the help of a qualified child therapist who specializes in treating victims of abuse.

The Shocking Prevalence of Family and Community Violence

Sadly, millions of children are victims of, or witness to, violence in the home, community, or school, according to the investigations of Dr. Bruce Perry and others.[2] It's been said that the home is the most violent place in America.[3] In 1995, the FBI reported that 27% of all violent crime involved family-on-family violence, and 48%

involved acquaintances, with the violence occurring inside the home.[4] If not the direct victims of violent crime, children are often the witnesses.

It is estimated that less than 5% of domestic violence is reported. Yet familial abuse happening at home—that is, spousal and child abuse—accounts for the majority of physical and emotional violence suffered by youngsters. Sometimes children are directly attacked by a parent or parent's boyfriend/girlfriend. Physical, emotional, and sexual abuse by a step-parent is especially common. Often children are humiliated, treated as "property," or threatened with abandonment. Witnessing violence can be equally damaging. A child who with wide-eyed terror hears and/or sees her parent, sibling, or grandparent brutalized often fares worse than the one attacked. Frozen and helpless, perhaps hiding under a table or plastered flat against a wall, the child attempts to become "invisible." Countless adults have had a life-long fear of "being seen" as a result. To survive the turmoil within their homes, the need to stay small, silent, and still was essential.

Violence from older siblings, such as Carlos experienced at the hands of his older, mentally disturbed step-brother, is another source of abuse that children endure more frequently than caregivers realize. Straus and Gelles have estimated that more than 29 million children in the U.S. are assaulted by their own siblings each year.[5] Parents frequently punish both children or dismiss the child who was hit as a "tattle-tale." Sibling rivalry and conflict is inevitable, but when one child holds the power to hurt and humiliate a younger or weaker brother or sister as a steady diet, it is a set-up for grim consequences. Furthermore, there are reasons why kids bully other children; it is important to look for causes in the family and environment.

In addition, school violence has increased dramatically in the form of intimidation, threats, and outright assaults. In the U.S. alone, it has been estimated that more than 250,000 students are attacked in school each month.[6] While the most heinous form of violence, school shooting, has garnered massive publicity, the pervasive bullying that puts fear into the hearts of our children is often overlooked, denied altogether, or goes unreported to harried school officials.

Yet bullying exists in both Western and Eastern cultures from Finland and Australia to Japan and China. In an article entitled "Kids Hurting Kids" in a 2001 issue of *Mothering* magazine, we learn that three million bullying incidents are reported each year in the U.S. alone, and at least 160,000 children miss school each day for fear of being bullied.[7] In Japan, such bullying is so prevalent that it has been given a name—*ijime*. In 1993 there were more than 21,500 reported incidents of schoolyard bullying in Japan, with three that resulted in suicide, pushing *ijime* into the headlines.[8] Meanwhile, in Toronto, Canada, Debra Pepler of York University recorded 52 hours of videotape using remote microphones at a schoolyard. What she discovered is astonishing: more than 400 episodes of bullying were documented. Yet teachers noticed and intervened in only one out of 25 episodes! It is estimated that in a mid-sized school bullying happens once every 7 minutes.[9]

To add to the problem, many parents think that bullying is a normal part of growing up, and especially for boys, standing up to bullies by fighting is a rite of passage. While conflicts and aggression are a normal part of life, bullying should not be tolerated among siblings or on the schoolyard. Bullies are a different breed. Their intent is to hurt, humiliate, socially isolate and/or extort from their victims. It is not a fair match. One child always holds more power due to size, strength, age, or some other factor, as in the case of Carlos and his emotionally disturbed brother. Long-term studies have shown that both bullies and the children they torment suffer well into their adulthood. While the scapegoats (victims of bullying) tend to be depressed and anxious later in life, the bullying behavior appears to develop into job and relationship havoc, with higher rates of court appearances, alcoholism, criminal activity, and personality disorders. Frequently the bullies themselves are suffering from very early trauma.

When children are asked to "turn the other cheek," "put on a happy face," or "strike back" in situations where they are experiencing daily terror, they do not learn character. On the contrary, they lose self-confidence and a sense of safety necessary to succeed. It's not surprising that so many children suffer from depression, anxiety, learning difficulties, and hyperactivity. Alarming statistics show increasing rates of suicide among children who were bullied, reported it to a dismissive adult, and then suffered in silence until they exploded, sometimes taking others with them, as in the increasingly shocking high school shootings.

In Part II, you will learn what parents and the school community can do to help both the bullies and the bullied. Neither of these youngsters will fare well without adult intervention. It is our responsibility to build a culture of safety and alternatives to violence in our neighborhoods and schoolyards. One of the best ways to protect children from victimization is to cultivate their confidence. Teaching children how to recover from any traumatic incident, restore their sense of self, and regain their ground can prevent them from being singled out by an aggressor.

Vicarious Violence: Media's Shadow

Violent images are everywhere. Even in non-violent homes, children are being bombarded, fascinated, frightened, and captivated by these images. Like it or not, another potential factor that was nonexistent a few short decades ago is the result of the rapidly growing technological revolution. It is estimated in the U.S. that the average child spends more than three hours a day watching television. Dr. Bruce Perry cites 1992 research by Huston and colleagues estimating that the average eighteen-year-old will have viewed 200,000 acts of violence on TV.[10] While a raging debate continues regarding the influence of violence in the media as a cause of violent behavior in children, there is a majority of evidence linking media violence with increased aggression and anti-social behavior, desensitization to future violence, and contributing to a sense that the world is more dangerous than it is—paradoxically perpetuating more violence!

While television, music, and movies have become increasingly more violent, video games seem to be leading the market on vicarious aggression.[11] Viewed in the privacy of kids' bedrooms on laptops, these video and computer games are even less likely to be subject to parental monitoring than the family viewing venues of movies and TV. *Psychological Science* and *Contemporary Pediatrics* published overviews of studies conducted during the last two decades. The authors of the *Psychological Science* article analyzed more than 30 reports and concluded that the data "clearly support the hypothesis that exposure to violent video games poses a public-health threat to children and youths."[12] In 1997, *The Canadian Journal of Psychiatry*'s authors summarized the meta-analysis of the *Contemporary Pediatrics* study as follows: "The majority of studies show that children do become more aggressive after either playing or watching a violent video game."[13]

On an empirical level, several teens referred for aggressive "acting out" behavior demonstrated rage reactions towards parents and teachers when game-playing privileges were suspended after the violent content was discovered by the adults who "caught" them. The adolescents openly admitted that they had become addicted to the thrill of the violence and "needed" the games to feel OK. These individual clinical cases demonstrate the contribution violent media can make in shaping the nervous systems and psyches of our youth.

What can you do? The most obvious action one can take, of course, is to pay attention to what your child watches at home and elsewhere. Watch together and hold family discussions. Limit exposure with older children and teens, and protect younger children from access. Do not leave the TV on constantly. Use parental controls on computers. Allow video games that are appropriate for family viewing and need not be watched secretly behind closed doors. Make sure that you scrutinize what your children are watching. They will most likely protest if not throw full-scale tantrums (particularly if they are already addicted); however, several studies have substantiated that our kids need and want our guidance.[14] Talk to your children's friends' parents. Have community meetings to address the issues through education and establishing a "culture of non-violence" in your own neighborhood. If you know or suspect that your children have been exposed to violent media, pay attention to their body language and changes in their behavior or attitudes. Address them right away. Chronic exposure of children to witnessing violence is another worrisome source of trauma that can be kept to a minimum by prudent parents.

The Perils and Prevalence of Sexual Molestation

Unfortunately, even by conservative estimates, one in every four persons worldwide has been sexually abused in one way or another. For girls and women, the likelihood is considerably higher. Exact statistics are not as important as knowing that *millions* of children are living with the torment of sexual predation, mostly by people who are supposed to love and protect them! The list of abusers is not limited to parents or aberrant neighbors. It includes clergy, coaches, grandparents, and scout leaders. Marilyn Van Derbur, esteemed lecturer and author of *Miss America By Day* (2003), summarized the startling facts regarding the numbers of children that have been violated by siblings and babysitters.[15] In fact, "The estimates are that incest between siblings may be *five times* more common than paternal incest."[16]

What makes sexual abuse so devastating is that it violates the deepest core of the child's formative sense of self. It is fraught with so much secrecy that the child is forced to live in silence with unbearable shame and guilt. Their most personal boundaries are "ruptured" in such a way that self-perceptions become distorted. Children are unaware that something bad is happening to them; instead they often think that *they* are bad.

A host of symptoms erupts from sexual abuse; these symptoms are discussed in more detail in Chapter Nine. Suffice it to say at this point that a hallmark symptom of sexual violation is a kind of body-override that psychologists call dissociation. This shows up as anything from distractibility and forgetfulness to numbness in parts of the body and amnesia for parts of childhood. Often children live in a dream-like state with a sense of not feeling "real."

While helping children to distance themselves from unbearable pain, dissociation interferes with the ability to be in one's body, as well as interferes with the ability to learn and to form close friendships with others. It has been well documented that children who have been sexually violated feel *so* different from others that they become isolated. The lack of social engagement with classmates in elementary school continues on into high school and beyond. This creates impaired development that affects later sexual intimacy and relationships in general. And children who have been abused are vastly more likely to abuse drugs and engage in promiscuous sex.

Part of Chapter Nine is dedicated to providing guidance on what signs to look for, what questions to ask your child, and what you can do to protect youngsters from being vulnerable to sexual assault. You will also learn how to help a child who has already fallen prey to an attack. Once again, however, it is important for you to understand that in cases of sexual abuse nothing can replace the expertise of a professional therapist who specializes in childhood abuse recovery. Enlisting the aid of a professional may prevent more serious symptoms common to molestation that develop during the teen years, such as eating disorders and self-injurious behavior.

A Word about Prenates, Infants, and Toddlers

So often people remark, "But she was only an infant when it happened" or "Good thing the car crash happened before he was born," implying that this diminished or eliminated any impact. Such statements reveal a widespread misunderstanding about the nature of trauma. What happens from the fetal period until two years of age creates the blueprint that influences every system in the body from immunity to the expression and regulation of emotion, to nervous system resilience, communication, intelligence, and self-regulatory mechanisms for such basics as body temperature and hormone production.

Knowing that the standard response to threat is "fight or flight," it makes sense that an infant, with neither option available, will have a different response. Unable to flee the chaos, from conflict and loud quarreling to outright violence, many adaptations take place. The little body may squirm, its muscles stiffen, its digestive organs contract, its back may arch, etc. Finally it just collapses in apathetic resignation. Even more disturbing, the growing brain organizes itself to be more reactive to survival functioning at the expense of development in the limbic and cortical areas responsible for the modulation of impulse and emotion. The infant brain becomes hyper-alert to the perceived danger. In other words, the brain becomes programmed in such a way that feelings of terror and helplessness become a "normal" state of being.

This early molding has vast repercussions for the child's emotional and behavioral development, as well as for its hormonal and immune systems. Prolonged exposure to a stressful environment leads to numbing and shutdown as the fear and pain become increasingly unbearable. This eventually develops into lifelong patterns that are commonly (mis-)diagnosed years later (usually when the child begins school) as Anxiety Disorder, Attention Deficit Disorder, Hyperactivity, Dissociative Disorder, Conduct Disorder and/or

Depression. According to research conducted by Dr. Bruce Perry, when infants and young children experience threats of violence that are chronic and occur early enough, the stage is set for a host of learning and behavioral problems.[17]

In *Ghosts from the Nursery: Tracing the Roots of Violence*, authors Robin Karr-Morse and Meredith S. Wiley present compelling research meant to be a wake-up call alerting all of us to the vulnerabilities of the first 33 months of life (fetal period to 24 months). They have outlined factors ranging from prenatal drug, nicotine, and alcohol exposure and other prenatal distress to infant head injury, physical abuse, and emotional neglect that bring the child into the world with an already overwhelmed nervous system. Such children are predisposed to impulsive, violent behavior and/or mental disorders (such as depression and anxiety) due to the interactive experiences that shaped the brain during the critical period. It is important to remember that "the first environment actively shaping the human brain is the womb. Even before first smiles or tantrums, the womb is host to an interactive biological and neurobiological dance between the mother and the fetus. For more than half a century we have known that what affects mothers emotionally also affects babies. In 1934, Drs. Sontag and Wallace, using very primitive measures of heart and respiratory activity of the mother and fetus, found that when a pregnant patient was pursued by a psychotic husband, the baby was alarmed along with the mother."[18]

Now, more than seventy years later, sophisticated research techniques measuring cortisol and ACTH levels in fetal monkeys are coming to the same conclusions. The fetuses whose mothers were stressed during pregnancy reflected their mother's emotional states. The lesson from this is a simple one: if you are pregnant or a new mom you need to be wise. Namely, refrain from stressful careers and lifestyles during this crucial period, and surround yourself with calming, nurturing people and activities that bring your own life into a healthy balance. Monitor your own stress levels by checking in with yourself regularly and taking the time to notice your body's responses as you go about your day and through your pregnancy. If you're feeling uptight, pause. Take a walk, lie down and put your feet up, meditate, get a gentle massage, read a book, take a bath, or call a friend for lunch. Or, you can do something we call "tracking sensations" (see exercise in Part II) until you notice your bodily tensions release and you begin to feel your breath flow harmoniously and spontaneously from head to toe.

Another critical developmental stage during infancy occurs between six and eight months. This is the typical period in which a baby begins to connect sensations, such as discomfort or hunger, and his/her own actions to regulate those feelings, such as crying or fussing directed at a caregiver. Through eye contact and vocalization in relationship to responses from the caregiver, self-regulatory modulation is being mapped in the frontal lobes of the young brain. The successful establishment of effective self-soothing processes is dependent on the quality of the face-to-face responsiveness of an emotionally present adult. Without the playful interactions of an unstressed, mentally attuned, and emotionally stable caregiver, healthy attachment simply does not occur.

Fortunately, due to the persistence of researchers in the field of attachment such as John Bowlby, Mary Main, and Mary Ainsworth (with a legacy that dates back to the extensive studies by Margaret Mahler in the 1950s),[19] together with the last decade of neurobiological research that chronicles early brain development, preventive efforts, backed by community and government grants are beginning. Although not the primary focus of this book (many splendid books have been written on this topic), simple tips are given in Part II to guide parents of infants, toddlers, and preschoolers in forming secure attachments with their little ones.

When the Source of Trauma
Remains a Mystery

Ideally this chapter has sensitized you to the scope and prevalence of trauma from a variety of sources. Because trauma is a root of health problems and so much psychological and societal distress, our children are often suffering silently. They may be living a life filled with daily terror. Or, even worse, they can become progressively numb and unresponsive to all that life has to offer.

If any perceived or real threat has the potential to cause shock, how can you tell if your child has experienced trauma? The next chapter explores the range of symptoms that traumatized children exhibit and discusses how to pay attention to these symptoms. There are times when the source of distress is not immediately apparent or cannot be traced even after close examination. What's important to remember is that anything that overwhelms the ability of the child to cope, process strong emotions, and to defend herself has the potential to create symptoms. The younger the child, the more vulnerable he is by nature of limited resources to protect himself. Remember, trauma is defined by its effect on a particular individual's nervous system, not on the intensity of the circumstance itself.

Fortunately, our approach to the prevention and treatment of trauma, called Somatic Experiencing®, is based on biology, *not* on biography, so the method of working to alleviate suffering does not rely on knowing the story. Although it can be useful to know the source, it is an unnecessary part of helping. Often, however, because the body *holds* the story, as children are supported through their distress, the source is often revealed. Most importantly, the body holds the solution as you will soon discover.

CHAPTER THREE

Signs and Symptoms
of Trauma in Children

She was holding her son again, but in many ways
she was holding a different boy. He felt to her (his mother)
like the shell of an egg, something brittle and hard.

– excerpt from a story about a boy who
was kidnapped in Colombia in 2003
(Los Angeles Times, *December 31, 2003)*

A dramatic event such as a kidnapping brings symptoms that are expected and varied. The mother quoted above continues her story about how her four-year-old son Oscar had nightmares in which men were slitting his stomach and choking him. His mother poignantly noted:

His face is a stage on which heartbreaking emotions play out. Sometimes he looks lost, a boy alone. Other moments he seems sad, his gaze downcast. Other times, terror bolts across his face, like a child who wakes from a bad dream confused by what he has seen. He has not spoken much of his time alone.

How does trauma express itself in our children? What does it look like and feel like? Can frightening events that are more "ordinary" than the kidnapping described above also leave residual traumatic effects? If your youngster "misbehaves," how can you tell if it is trauma-related "acting out" or ordinary naughtiness? In this chapter we explore these issues and use case examples to assist in answering these questions. You will learn the core symptoms that define trauma and the symptoms that often develop when "first aid" to prevent further distress is not forthcoming.

You will also learn why some children are left with lasting intrusive symptoms such as bad memories, dreams, and bursts of anger that affect their social relationships, academic competence, and health, while other children appear to be relatively unscathed.

Universal Symptoms of Trauma

Whether it was an adult *or* a child that was dealt a blow greater than could be tolerated, distinguishing signs appear soon after the event. They are: 1) hyperarousal, 2) constriction, 3) dissociation, and 4) feelings of numbness and shutdown (or "freeze"), resulting in a sense of helplessness and hopelessness. These reactions represent universal symptoms. Together they characterize the essence of the mind and body's response; they are the telltale trademark of trauma.

All children, but especially infants and the very young, show symptoms that are distinctively different from those of adults. This is due to a combination of factors including brain development, level of reasoning and perceptual development, incomplete personality formation and dependency, as well as attachment to their adult caregivers. Together with restricted motor and language skills, children have limited capacities to respond or cope. In addition to having a grown-up brain, adults have the freedom to access resources that reduce stress and anxiety. An adult, for example, can choose to take a nature hike, meet with friends, work out at the gym, write in a journal, go to therapy, or take a class (like yoga, aikido, or tai chi) as healthy options to help "manage" their feelings and symptoms.

Children, on the other hand, are totally dependent on their grown-ups to "read" and meet their needs for safety, support, nurturance, self-regulation, and reassurance. When adults haven't developed their own wholesome resources and do not have a support system to reach out to, they may act out by abusing substances and their families, exhibiting explosive tempers at the workplace, or exposing themselves to dangerous situations. Our children act out, too! Sometimes it is the only way they have of signaling us for HELP. When children do not "act out," they often "act in," giving adults subtler clues that something is wrong. The signs and symptoms of both externalized and internalized emotion and behavior, and their importance in helping children heal, are described and illustrated in these pages through real-life examples.

Before delving into the specifics of how children let us know they are hurting, it is important to remember that some trauma symptoms are *normal* responses to overwhelming circumstances. The heightened arousal energy together with shutting down (when there is no escape) are biologically hard-wired survival mechanisms. *However,* this protective system is meant to be time-limited; our bodies were designed to return to a normal rhythm soon after the danger ends.

But when the intense survival energy that was summoned to defend us during a perceived threat does not get "used up," we continue to experience life as if the threat is still present. Because infants and children are less able to defend themselves, they are more vulnerable than adults to retaining an excess of this highly charged arousal energy. Without specific and directed help from caring adults to aid children, the unresolved energy eventually finds expression in a wide array of behaviors and symptoms. Remember that children have a very limited behavioral repertoire to deal with life's stresses and difficulties.

To give an example, three-year-old Jared witnessed a frightening car crash during the day and awoke at 2 a.m. with night terrors. This sleep disturbance—characterized by his inconsolable crying, agitated motor movements (thrashing and kicking), and autonomic responses of rapid breathing, a racing pulse, and sweating—is a prime illustration of the expression of hyperarousal in a child. In reality the accident is over, the cars have been towed away, and no one was injured. Jared's reality, however, is very different; the activation that began earlier showed up that night (but could have shown up even later) with a fury as the arousal continued. Jared awoke in panic as if the screech of brakes, the clash of metal, the smell of burned rubber, and the sight of shattered glass were still happening!

The initial universal reactions to shock are often obvious. Other times they are more subtle, especially when you don't know what to look for. Parents are often simultaneously filled with fear for the worst and with hope that their child will experience the best outcome. Because both adults and children can have intense emotions, important clues can easily be overlooked in the "heat of the moment." Interestingly, universal metaphors perfectly reflect many of the clues we need to know about the bodily experience. Expressions such as "scared stiff," "speechless," "collapsed in sorrow," "pale as a sheet," and "white as a ghost" abound in any language. They literally reflect physiological responses that take place in the brain and body.

The following pages illustrate each of the initial trauma symptoms as a child might experience them. Although they are described separately for clarity, the core signs of a traumatic reaction are often experienced together. Due to variation in children's temperament, age, pre-existing vulnerabilities, and the nature of the actual incident, it may be easier for you to detect a predominance of symptoms from one category over another.

Depending on age and the level of cognitive, social, and emotional maturity, children's symptoms manifest differently from adults and differently from each other at various stages of development. With this in mind, symptoms are described in three stages: 1) Infants to Preschool, 2) School-Age, and 3) Adolescence. Bear in mind that these are broad stages with a great deal of overlap and variation depending on temperament, maturity, and other individual differences. Note that there are some similarities between childhood and adult symptoms, especially with adolescents. Research studies have also found some differences between boys and girls, and these will be included when relevant.

Recognizing Symptoms in the Very Young: Infants to Preschool-Age Children

Infants and young children have limited motor and expressive language skills. They cannot narrate what happened to them, and they cannot protect themselves with the facility of the older child or adult. Young children, therefore, are more likely to develop new fears and avoidance behaviors or to experience irritability, withdrawal/shutdown, and impulsive behavior. Because infant and toddler growth happens at a rapid rate, when trauma symptoms persist, normal developmental milestones may even be delayed. Symptoms of traumatic stress can show up after a single event, a series of events, or with ongoing stress.

Young children often tell us that they are traumatized through their play, sleep patterns, altered activity levels, exaggerated emotional responses (fear and anger), and somatic complaints such as tummy or head aches and regression to an earlier developmental level that may feel safer. For example, a child who had formerly been confident when left with a babysitter may instead anxiously cling to his parents when they are about to leave. A child may literally attach himself to dad's leg with the tenacity of an octopus rather than cooperate and separate after experiencing something traumatic.

Even if your child has sufficient language skills to talk in complete sentences, it is highly unlikely that she would be able to indicate her distress with words. The examples below will help you to recognize how children go about the business of showing adults what hurts.

Infants and Children "Shut Down" When Overwhelmed

When babies and young children become overwhelmed, they may exhibit frantic distress reactions such as wailing, gasping, and flailing about. However, quite frequently they instead shut down, constrict, and "go away." Infants especially have few options other than to go numb. This is not something they choose; it is an automatic response when their distress is no longer tolerable. They simply detach or withdraw (the infant version of dissociation).

What appears insignificant to an adult can readily overwhelm an infant. This is especially true for babies who came into the world more vulnerable from the start due to fetal distress, a long, difficult or complicated birth process, and/or an immature nervous system. By the nature of being babies—which implies total dependency—all infants are defenseless.

When babies are overstimulated by too much activity or intensity, and when their needs are not attended to in a timely manner, they deal with it by "zoning out." Since they cannot walk or talk, their choices are limited to fussing, crying, and protesting. When these options have been tried in vain and exhausted, the baby will go numb. This shutdown must be distinguished from a "good-natured" placid temperament!

Caregivers need to be alert for the vacant look in the baby's eyes, lack of facial expression, and no affect. When an infant's eyes look glazed over, it means that he can no longer manage his internal signals and requires an adult who can recognize that he needs to be provided with comfort and relief. "Reading" your baby's expression and saying something fitting in a soothing voice can help the baby to reconnect when he's ready. For example, if loud sounds are startling, you could say, "All that noise was too much, wasn't it? It really must have frightened you. Let's find a nice quiet place and I'll rock you gently if you'd like." Whether or not you believe that your baby can understand your words is less important than the tone with which you say them.

Because an infant's nervous system is immature, it cannot yet self-regulate. Therefore, it depends on its parents for everything from temperature regulation to emotional regulation. If an older child has to wait too long for lunch, he may get impatient and cranky. However, he knows from prior experience that he will be fed. An infant does not know this. Being made to wait too long for sustenance can be *perceived* as a matter of life or death. If parents take the time to notice what their baby needs to feel safe, comfortable, and nurtured *and* they meet those needs most of the time, a bond of trust and basic "goodness" is likely to develop. A secure attachment can then be formed that sets in motion healthy relationship patterns for life.

Providing Safety and Nurturance

Safety and nurturance take the form of warmth, cuddling, food, comfortable positioning, face-to-face playful interactions, rocking and holding, protection from the elements, and a balance between quiet rest and stimulation. But nurturance is also more nuanced than that. It means noticing your baby squirm or stiffen when a visiting aunt or uncle is smothering your newborn with unwanted "cheek-pinching" or kisses, and then gently removing your baby from the discomfort. This shows your baby that you will protect her *and* that she never has to be touched by someone or in some way that doesn't feel right to her. As far-fetched as this may sound, your actions send a message to your infant's developing brain that might be instrumental in preventing sexual or other violations later in life. Children whose needs and boundaries are honored will develop a "sixth sense" when an approach from an adult is, somehow, not right.

It is in this crucial period of development (from newborn to toddler) that the ability is formed to trust that basic needs can be met, personal boundaries can be honored and wholesome relationships can be rewarding. The quality of this fine attunement to needs in the relationship between caregiver and baby lays down neural pathways and patterns in the brain that will last a lifetime.

How Babies Show Us They Are Stressed

Signs of excessive stress with toddlers and preschoolers might take the form of "hyperactivity" or numbing and shutdown, including withdrawal from play or from people, lethargy, and/or excessive shyness. This may alternate with bouts of inconsolable crying or tantrums. Traumatic stress might also show up as regressive behaviors to an earlier stage of development. Behaviors such as thumb-sucking, bed-wetting and soiling, wanting to nurse (or asking for a bottle) after being weaned, and talking "baby-talk" are common symptoms of distress.

These signs of a traumatic reaction give a clear signal that your child needs more time, reassurance, and assistance from you to help him regain confidence. It is equally important that you understand these are normal reactions to stressful events. Each child has a different temperament, personality, and vulnerabilities. What may cause a regressive reaction in one child may not affect a sibling or neighbor's child the same way. This is a time when it is especially important not to shame a child even though you may find these regressive behaviors to be a nuisance. Compassion and patience will hasten the healing process. And, if you find yourself more stressed and short-tempered during this period, remember to refrain from judging and shaming yourself! If you practice loving kindness to yourself when facing your own shortcomings, both you and your child will automatically gain. And of course if the child's symptoms persist, it is advisable to seek competent professional help.

How Toddlers and Young Children Show Us Symptoms of Traumatic "Re-Experiencing" through Play

While infants may alternate between protesting and numbing, toddlers and preschoolers have a wider variety of coping mechanisms.

Children often experience the trauma as if it is still happening and show you through their actions. To help you tune in to how your child is being affected, be alert to how your child expresses herself during playtime at home or preschool.

An overwhelmed youngster may funnel an energy overload (hyperarousal) into repetitive play that portrays some aspect of the traumatic event. This type of play lacks imagination and variety. An astute adult can then become sensitive to the parts of the event that are still plaguing their child. For example, you may notice your child repeating, or re-enacting, one or more scenes or themes. This type of play appears to be driven almost out of desperation and does not seem to bring any satisfaction or relief. Examples would be smashing two toy cars together over and over again following an auto accident, or repeatedly pushing a doll's face down under the water after a near-drowning.

It is not uncommon for children who have been the victims of harsh physical punishment, or witnessed a sibling being abused, to re-enact the scene with dolls or toy figures such as soldiers and warriors. Play may alternate between perpetrator and victim roles. For example, a doll may at first be scolded harshly and spanked by the child. Afterward the child switches positions and consoles the doll with soothing pats and simple words, such as "It's alright, baby."

Kevin's Play Tells His Story

Sometimes the connection between what left a disturbing imprint on the child and the constricted play is not so obvious. This is especially true when the precipitating event was not considered to be traumatic. For example, do you remember the earlier reference to three-year-old Kevin (in Chapter Two) whose parents were bewildered by his "autistic-like" play? He repeatedly got on the floor, stiffened his body, and pretended that he was dying and slowly coming back to life, saying, "Save me ... save me!" No one considered that a prior surgical procedure that had gone "remarkably well" held such a powerful grip on Kevin. Because his surgeries during infancy had saved his life, the traumatic aftershocks were never associated with his peculiar repetitious play. Until Kevin was given the active support to move the story forward during play, there was a dampening of both his creativity and his capacity to experience joy. His social development was also delayed. Kevin, at three and a half years of age, had still been playing *next to* other children (parallel play typical of two-year-olds) rather than *with* them.

In order to help Kevin, he was presented with an assortment of little toy figures. He quickly selected and lined up the knights with shields and swords to wipe out the "bad guys" (plastic soldiers). He aggressively "smashed" every last one of the "soldiers." When Kevin was asked who the "bad guys" were that the knights had just destroyed, he sternly replied, "doctors," much to his mother's surprise. The link between his aggressive play and his medical trauma became clear.

After continued support, Kevin started varying his play, moving him nearer to a creative resolution, which eventually led him to thank his doctors! This satisfying ending came spontaneously only after he had expressed both anger and fear, through his play, about his hospital experience.

Other Ways Young Children Show that They Are Still Re-Experiencing the Event

In addition to play, young children also let us know that they are re-experiencing a traumatic episode through repeated nightmares, distress at reminders of what happened, and/or preoccupation or fascination with some aspect of the event (such as wanting to watch forest fire videos over and over again after witnessing a house fire or wildfire). Young children often attribute magical qualities to these reminders, giving them added power to frighten them. For instance, if the house that burned down was an old wooden one that had just been painted yellow, they may think all buildings that are old, wooden, and yellow are dangerous. Or they might worry that painting a house might cause it to burn.

Reminders can be unconscious (or dissociated from the child's experience) but nevertheless cause fidgeting or cranky behavior with no obvious connection to the trigger. An example of this would be if you noticed a change in your child's mood or behavior when she hears an airplane fly overhead after witnessing the terrorist attack of 9/11 on television. Another example would be clinginess after seeing or hearing a train following the Madrid bombings in 2004.

How Young Children Show Trauma Symptoms through Hyperarousal

If you have ever been subjected to unwelcome tickling or watched someone getting tickled, it is easy to understand the concept of hyperarousal. The metaphor "tickled to death" is an apt description of the experience. The child may be laughing, but when playful tickling turns intolerable, it is not funny. Instead it can turn to torture. The youngster's heart is pounding as the whole body is involved in the struggle to make it stop. Rapid breathing may turn to gasps for air as the child suffers from the intensity of the experience, including the fear of suffocation.

When children are in a state of hyperarousal they are in a "revved up" internal state even though no tickling or other outside stimulation is present. The stimulation is coming from within the child—from a nervous system that they cannot turn down. When the child is scared or highly stressed, whether the danger is real or perceived, increased heart rate and breathing make it possible for their internal "engines" to go from idle to high speed within seconds even though the child may appear calm. They can get "all wound up" very easily and not be able to come back down. This stirred-up state may keep them awake at night and/or nervous during the day. Deep relaxation becomes impossible until the excess energy is released.

You have probably witnessed what happens to children who are already overtired and then allowed to "rough-house" right before bedtime. This excess energy in an overtaxed body can play havoc with a youngster's sleep. So too can the excess energy from the stress of unresolved trauma, but the difference is that the sleep and other problems persist. The earlier illustration of Jared's night terrors is a good example of a symptom of hyperarousal. Other difficulties include falling and staying asleep, hypervigilance, and an exaggerated startle response. When hyperarousal symptoms become chronic they can begin to resemble Attention Deficit Disorder with Hyperactivity (ADHD). Unfortunately, far too often traumatized children are misdiagnosed with this disorder and medicated (inappropriately). The symptoms of hyperarousal may be the easiest for parents and teachers to observe because the behavior is hard to miss! At times the youngster's energy is wild and unmanageable, which can be very trying for the adults who care for them.

How Young Children Show Us Their Sense of Helplessness through Intense Emotion

The distressing excess energy that is pent up after situational or ongoing overwhelming events may be expressed through intense emotional outbursts that can be perplexing for parents. Often worry and anxiety as well as anger and aggression emerge. New fears are common, especially when separating from an adult, when meeting strangers, and meeting new challenges. Both clinginess and tantrums are typical symptoms that can be particularly annoying to adults who do not understand their origin or what to do when these new symptoms arise. Toddlers may express fearfulness by insisting on being carried or held constantly in an attempt to feel adult protection, for example. Preschoolers may become afraid of the dark, fearing "monsters" and "ghosts" in the closet or under their beds.

A sign of emotional turmoil that a parent might not only notice, but get annoyed by, is their child's response to what were once normal outings or routines. The child may express exaggerated protests or an endless barrage of questions. Your child is really not trying to drive you crazy. He is managing anxiety in the best way he knows how. The relentless questioning, such as: "Who will be there?" "And who else?" and "How long will we be there?" may be an attempt to maintain a sense of safety and control.

The symptom of aggressiveness frequently develops in conjunction with too many stressors and overwhelming circumstances. Common signs that young children have more feelings inside than they are able to manage are: temper outbursts, tantrums, throwing toys, hitting or bullying siblings and playmates, biting, grabbing, and kicking. Parents may wonder if this is just the predictable stage of the "terrible twos" (or fours). One way to differentiate is to notice the timing of the onset of the new aggressive behavior. If the emergence of out-of-the-ordinary conduct coincides with the list of potentially traumatizing events and stressors outlined in Chapter Two, be suspect that it is trauma-related.

How Young Children Show Us Traumatic Constriction and Shutdown through Physical Symptoms (somatic complaints and a dampening of pleasurable feelings)

Once the body's nervous system has been hyperaroused, adrenaline is released into the blood stream to prepare the large motor muscles for movement. Certain muscles, by their nature, must tense or constrict in order to perform. But with trauma, the whole body braces. This includes a tightening of the muscles, joints, and internal organs. Additionally, the sensory and respiratory systems are tense and constricted. In this stage the primary symptom is "shutdown." You might notice that your child has withdrawn, become excessively shy and more dependent on you than before the event. Rather than overly energetic behavior, you may notice lethargy and fatigue.

Other symptoms of constriction that you might observe in your child are: a stiff or awkward appearance, rigid gait with poor coordination, or tense neck and shoulder muscles. His insides may feel tight, and the ability to see, hear, smell, feel, and taste may become dampened so that food just isn't interesting. Your child's focus may then become narrowed towards sources of possible danger even though there are none. This constricted awareness serves to reduce anxious feelings. This can prevent your child from literally feeling like he is falling apart. However, over time, this tension can re-create the very feelings the child is trying to avoid. (The same is true for adults as well!)

Unfortunately, in this state, without the guidance and safety provided by an adult, it's unlikely that a child can relax enough to notice what's around—even if what's around them could be rewarding. Relaxing would mean letting down the guard of "protection." This shutting down was meant to be temporary. When it is not (like in the example of Sandra below) constriction can lead to both physical pain and the loss of fun and excitement in exploring and enjoying simple pleasure. Because the world is now perceived as a dangerous place, healthy risk-taking—as in exuberant play—is, sadly, avoided.

Your child may be incapable of expressing somatic complaints. Infants and toddlers may simply get fussy or cranky just like they do when teething because they can't tell you what hurts. Physical symptoms are characteristic of trauma at any age. Young children are particularly vulnerable, however, to "sensitive digestion," diarrhea, and constipation, with frequent tummy and headaches. Another sign of distress, although somewhat less common, is the appearance of fevers not due to an infection or other known medical reason. Shallow breathing, or on the other hand, hyper-ventilation can be symptoms of traumatic stress. Both can limit oxygen flow to the brain and body, causing fatigue and lethargic behavior sometimes mistaken for "laziness."

Serious feeding or eating difficulties may follow an acute trauma. However, even a sudden separation such as a move or a parent going back to work can create havoc with a child's normal eating routine. An example of this can be seen in the following story about Sandra.

The Little Girl Who Couldn't Eat

Let's look at what happened to bright and curious Sandra when she was just barely four years old. Sandra had been living with her extended family at her grandparents' house since she was born. Although close to her mom and dad, Sandra was quite attached to her grandma, who provided additional safety, shelter, and nur-turance. Sandra's dad, Ricardo, worked very hard so that he could purchase a home for his growing family. Everyone was very excited when the day finally came, except Sandra. When she moved into her brand-new house, the separation from both her grandmother and her old room proved more than she could bear.

Rather than noticing her colorful new room and big backyard, her focus narrowed to just one thing—going back to grandma. Sandra's body became so tense that she was unable to eat anything or fall asleep without difficulty. Sandra's parents called me with grave concerns. Not only wasn't she eating, but she wasn't acting like herself. The pediatrician's only recommendation was to put Sandra on Pedi-Assure (liquid nutrition) so that she wouldn't starve to death! Her mom, Stephanie, had tried all kinds of tricks to entice Sandra to eat solids, but Sandra hadn't eaten anything in *over three months*—she wouldn't even take one bite of her favorite food!

When Sandra entered my office, she was not the least bit

interested in meeting me, exploring the toys and puppets, or touching the art materials. She appeared frightened, sad, and shut down—definitely not the exuberant child she had been a few months before. Her eyes never searched the room. Instead she held tight to her familiar teddy bear. Sandra didn't want to talk about her new house or grandma. She did shake her head up and down to acknowledge that she was very sad, but no tears came ... at first. Her emotions were constricted too.

I brought out a drawing pad and crayons, and with a little help, Sandra drew a simple house. Drawing helped her to loosen up just a little, especially when she saw that I wasn't going to ask her any more questions. Then together we examined "Teddy's" sad heart and his tummy that couldn't eat. Soon, Sandra pointed to the place in her tummy where the food wouldn't go down. I had her place her hand on this "stuck" spot, first on her teddy bear and then on herself. With her permission I gently placed my hand over hers as she sat next to her father. I wasn't at all surprised at the tightness in her tummy. It was as if her body's organs were holding on for dear life. Sandra wasn't on a hunger strike. Constriction is involuntary. It's not that Sandra wouldn't eat; Sandra *couldn't* eat!

It took only two sessions with Sandra and her parents to demonstrate how to give the gentle touch with patience and time for her tummy to let go of its grip. She drew all the "ghosts" that were in her new house and began to vent her feelings, setting her tears free. Stephanie called to tell me that little by little Sandra started eating again. She couldn't get enough of her favorite food—her grandmother's *sopitas* (a Mexican sweet bread). Within a very short time, Sandra was eating full meals. But that's not all. Ricardo described his daughter's remarkable change with these words: "She is like a flower that bloomed in the middle of the night."

Recognizing Symptoms
in School-Aged Children

School-aged children, like preschoolers and teens, exhibit variations of the common symptoms of trauma that were described at length earlier in this chapter: hyperarousal, dissociation, constriction, and shutdown (or freeze), accompanied by feelings of helplessness. This age group (roughly from five to eleven years old) likewise is susceptible to re-living the event, having sleep disturbances, suffering from somatic complaints, and exhibiting inconsistent behavior punctuated with new fears and aggression. They are particularly susceptible to worry, with graphic "worst-case scenario" thinking that is far more imaginative than plausible. It is this age group that comes up with superstitious rhymes and jump-rope verses, such as "Step on a crack, break your mother's back!"

This older group has more resources available, including more highly developed language and reasoning skills, as well as more advanced moral consciousness and altruism. Additionally, because the children are of school age, they have more demands and responsibilities placed upon them to concentrate and learn. Because of these factors, for many children who have experienced trauma, the signs and symptoms may surface (or become more pronounced) at school due to the additional pressures of academic achievement and socialization.

Many times teachers are the first to notice trauma symptoms as they manifest in the classroom and on the playground. This is sometimes diagnosed as "school phobia," ADHD, depression, and/or conduct disorder. Chapters Eleven and Twelve in Part IV are written especially for teachers, school counselors and psychologists, administrators, and others who wish to gain a better understanding of how to help students in the school setting. In the climate of escalating school violence and school shootings, it is more important than ever for educators to be equipped to spot symptoms of students with failure to cope, as well as to have the tools to intervene, *before* a major melt-down or violent acting-out occurs.

Like very young children, older children often re-enact the details of a traumatic event during their play. Because they have more developed language skills, they also re-enact by telling the story of what happened over and over again. Fear and helplessness often show up as disorganized or agitated behavior. Although they may recount the event, children usually are not able to put their feelings into words or even to understand exactly what it is they are feeling other than "mixed up," "upset," or "all shook up."

These youngsters may be concerned with more than just the details of the event itself. Their preoccupation may center on a recounting of their own actions or inability to act during the incident. They may feel responsible and be plagued with feelings of self-blame or shame that they keep as a deep dark secret, frequently alienating them from family and friends. They think that if they had done something differently, the "terrible thing" would never have happened. This is particularly true with issues of separation, such as death and divorce.

Lenore Terr, MD, a psychiatrist, renowned trauma researcher, and author of *Too Scared To Cry,* reported that school-aged children tend to have less avoiding and numbing symptoms. Besides finding that they are more likely to communicate through story and play, she noted an increase in "omen formation," or believing that certain signs were warnings of the traumatic event that occurred and will reoccur.[1] This is connected to the magical thinking of younger school-aged children.

Surprising New Emotions

Because of more sophisticated moral development, school-aged children think of others as well as themselves. They may worry about what has happened to the other victims of the tragedy and their families. If one parent got hurt, they may fear that the other parent might get hurt, too. They anxiously monitor parental responses. Because they have a more developed sense of the future, they may have fears for the first time about safety, fearing their future has been ruined, that they may no longer have anything to look forward to, or that they may not even have a future! Children in this age group are sometimes frightened by their own feelings of grief, which most probably are being experienced for the very first time.

Another surprising new feeling may be a desire to seek revenge. Recall Curtis, the middle-school boy mentioned in Chapter Two who wanted to "kick someone—anyone" after witnessing violence at the bus stop. These new emotions can be painfully confusing to children at a time when personalities are still taking shape. They will need your support in sorting out all the sensations, emotions, thoughts, and images that occupy them day and night.

Symptoms at School

Symptoms may get stimulated more easily when a child is around others, such as in the classroom or on the playground. Signs of trauma may manifest as a lack of ability to concentrate, finish a task, or process new information in an efficient manner, thus impairing learning. This may happen to such an extent that learning disabilities develop.

Chronic hyperarousal can quickly become hypervigilance. In school, signs of this might show up as fidgeting, a quick startle reflex, and fearful darting eyes that notice the most minute noise or motion on the other side of the room. Teachers may report that your child is a compulsive talker, unable to stay seated at his desk (fearful of those around him). Or they might describe your child as having "restless leg," being easily distracted, or as a bully who is "always looking for a fight"—or a "bite" in the case of kindergarteners!

Shutdown and dissociation might be observed as inattentiveness, fatigue, and "daydreaming." It can also be observed in social interactions as extreme shyness, withdrawal, and even isolation from peers. It is not unusual, for example, for sexually abused children to be the loners on the playground.

Research has indicated gender differences in symptom formation in school-aged children. Boys have a predilection for externalized symptoms while girls tend to internalize their symptoms. What this means is that boys may act out their anger by hitting, bullying, and teasing. They may try to mask their fears by engaging in dangerous "daredevil" activities. Girls, on the other hand, turn their anger inward, causing more of a depressed affect, somatic symptoms, anxiety, and self-denigration.

Symptoms of Immobility/Freeze/Dissociation and Helplessness in Children

Directly after a frightening event, whether catastrophic (such as an explosion) or ordinary (such as a bicycle accident), a child experiencing freeze will often be spared the initial impact of the incident through the mechanism of physiological shock and dissociation. This temporary numbing (actually mediated by the internal secretion of opiates—the endorphins) serves to tamp down the horrible physical and emotional pain of the event. Let's take a look at what happened to Suzie.

Suzie's Shock

Seven-year-old Suzie exemplifies the feelings of freeze that accompany the shock of an impact. Suzie rode her bike down a very steep hill for the first time. It felt so exhilarating that she decided to do it again! The second time the pedals started moving much faster than her feet and soon the bike was out of control. This runaway bike finally hit a sharp bump in the sidewalk, which stopped it abruptly while Suzie was catapulted over the handlebars face down into the hard concrete!

This stunned little girl was left frozen and immobile after this accident that abraded the skin from her beautiful face as it grazed the sidewalk, leaving her scraped and bleeding. She was dazed but did not feel anything. A neighbor lifted her from the sidewalk and carried her up the steep hill to her home. Suzie was in shock. All her tears were somewhere inside, solidly frozen. They had not yet been able to form.

When Suzie's mother saw that no bones were broken and Suzie could stand up, she praised her daughter by saying, "What a good girl—you're not even crying!" Mother, too, was stunned by her daughter's bloody face. Relieved that Suzie was not more "seriously" injured but still in shock herself, Mom did not notice the pallor, weakness, and terror written all over Suzie's face and in her body language. Suzie was limp, and there were plenty of tears congealed deep inside, but due to her frozen, dissociated state, they did not appear. Her body was too numb to feel her emotions or the pain of injury due to the release of endorphins and epinephrine, which, thankfully, temporarily anesthetized what would have been a very painful abrasion. Given support, time, and permission, Suzie's tears would have eventually spilled from her eyes (probably within five to thirty minutes), rather than decades later as they finally did. Suzie rode her bike again, but she was tight and less free, holding onto the handlebars stiffly "for dear life."

As an adult, Suzie shared that after that bike accident when she was seven years old, she had felt awkward and clumsy into adulthood. She stopped taking dance classes and lost confidence in her physical agility. As an adult, she continued to bicycle for many years but described herself as "always on guard" and "unable to keep up with her friends." She had several bad spills and, finally, put her bike away after the last tumble left her with a shoulder injury.

Suzie recently worked through the shock that was still lodged in her body from so many years before. As the tears spilled down her face, she mentioned that she felt some mild stinging—the sting from the abrasion that she had never felt before. As these sensations subsided, her face gently softened. Gradually, Suzie gained confidence in herself. One day with a big smile, she reported that she bought a brand-new bike and starting riding with a new sense of freedom and ease!

The "freeze response" is a vital survival mechanism. In Part II you will learn what to say and do to help gently guide any child who shows signs of immobility. Using animal imagery (like "playing possum") can help ease children into feeling that this is a natural stage of the healing process. This can help them understand and feel better about themselves when they are in a most vulnerable and helpless state. It is also reassuring to know that with just a little time and patience those feelings can give way to a "letting go" that may feel shaky at first but soon ends with a smile—as in the story of Suzie, but without having to wait twenty years!

Symptoms of Trauma During Adolescence

Shocking numbers of adults have suffered through symptoms and/or sought out treatment (medical or psychological) after having been victimized. Most of the traumatic events that preceded the troublesome complaints occurred not in adulthood, but as children and teens. Dean Kilpatrick, PhD, reported that he and his colleagues conducted telephone surveys of 4,023 boys and girls (twelve to seventeen years old), asking them carefully worded questions about the major traumatic experiences in their lives to uncover incidents of sexual assault and physical assault, as well as personal experiences of witnessing violence (not in the movies or on TV). This study revealed that "A high percentage of teens—*nearly one-half*—had experienced some traumatic event in their adolescent years." Forty percent of them had witnessed violence in person.[2]

Of significance, those teens who had witnessed violence were three times more likely to be involved in substance abuse. Some gender differences have been reported. Girls who showed internal trauma symptoms (withdrawal, depression, somatic disturbances) or external trauma symptoms (irritability, defiance, acting-out) had a higher incidence of substance abuse than girls who showed no symptoms; while for boys, only externalizing behaviors correlated with substance abuse.

Those who themselves had been physically assaulted were twice as likely to suffer clinical depression; while sexual assault victims were 80% more likely to suffer from post-traumatic stress syndrome than other teens. It is estimated that nearly one-fifth of the teens in the U.S. are suffering from emotional disorders. Sad but true.

Adolescence is not an easy time under the best of circumstances. All of the jokes about the "terrible twos" can be repeated again for the "terrible teens," compounded by hormonal chaos in large bodies that will soon, if not already, be dating and driving cars! Normal teen development can be chaotic and confusing for the youngsters inhabiting those new bodies *and* for their parents. In addition to the academic pressures of school-aged children, they have the additional tasks of individuation, planning their future and sexual development. They are also subjected to intense peer-group pressure that is bound to collide with family ideals.

Given all of the above, adolescent symptoms still resemble those of adults. They tend to re-experience the events through flashbacks and make every effort to avoid activities, thoughts, and feelings that trigger recollection of the distressing events. If they do not dissociate the unpleasant memories, they will go to any length to numb out. For this reason it is common for traumatized teens to turn to drugs, alcohol, nicotine, sex and dangerous thrill-seeking behavior as avoidance mechanisms to self-medicate and cope. They also tend to suffer more sleeplessness, irritability, depression, anxiety, and inattentiveness than their younger siblings. All of this can lead to truancy, poor grades, and defiant behavior that can be mistaken for "oppositional behavior." Depression and anxiety in teens are often symptomatic of traumatic stress. Unfortunately, like hyperactivity in younger children, these conditions are treated with medication rather than by treating the unresolved issues underlying their symptoms.

Hyperarousal and Dissociation in Teens

I have a little brain that's tucked safely
in my head . . . and another one that's in the air instead!
That one follows me and plays with me in bed.
The other one confuses me . . . the one that's in my head.
– *anonymous thirteen-year-old Ugandan girl*

As mentioned earlier, teens will go to great lengths, many times getting themselves into unsavory situations, attempting to avoid (or alternatively to recreate) thoughts, feelings, and situations that trigger recollection of the troublesome event. Testing and pushing the limits is part of adolescent behavior. However, in trauma re-enactment it takes a further escalation. And when the arousal energy slides out of the "zone of toleration," often youngsters will seek out ways to numb themselves through food, drugs, sex and music. Some adolescents, however, do not need to "self-medicate" through the use of illegal substances and dangerous activity (although they often do). Especially in the case of sexual and physical abuse, the body's own chemical numbing mechanisms kick in to help alleviate the pain and, temporarily, eradicate the horrible memories. Or alternatively, some kids may cut or otherwise injure themselves as a way to diminish their pain and, paradoxically, to get some control over their feelings. Cutting is thought by many professionals in residential treatment settings to increase the levels of the neurotransmitter dopamine. Research conducted by Gerald Huether in Germany indicates that cutting may be a maladaptive attempt at hormonal and nervous system regulation.[3]

When arousal energy, in the form of anxiety or nervousness for example, builds to an unbearable level, dissociation is the body's fail-safe mechanism that prevents a youngster from feeling like she is going crazy. It allows the compartmentalization of terrifying experiences from everyday reality. It's like a circuit breaker that keeps the electrical output of a building from exceeding its capacity to prevent a devastating fire (or like a submarine sealing the compartmental doors when hit by a torpedo to prevent flooding of the whole sub and sinking). The mind and body separate in such a way that part or all of the memories of the unpleasant experience are disconnected. In this way, when painful reminders enter consciousness they can instantly be avoided—as though they don't exist. This is not something the teen wills to happen; it is involuntary and serves to prevent overwhelm and possibly a "nervous breakdown."

Dissociation can be as minor as a momentary lapse of attention, daydreaming, or "spaciness." At its most serious, although rare, dissociation can result in long periods of amnesia or the assuming of various "sub-personalities." For example, different parts of the psyche can act out repetitiously, shifting back and forth between hitting and being hit. The victim and aggressor do not recognize each other. More often, dissociation is felt as being somewhere other than in one's body. It has been described by teens as "feeling like I am on the ceiling looking down at myself" or "part of me is on the other side of the room" or "I just don't feel like I'm all here." Sometimes the teen will not know how she got to a place or even where she is. These are called "fugue states." Often dissociation occurs following a flashback or the beginning of a terrifying thought, image, or feeling, like in the following example of a bright high school student named Gloria.

Gloria

An eleventh-grader named Gloria described the world she had inhabited ever since her father committed suicide when she was two years old. (He shot himself in an adjacent room.) "I cannot control leaving my body," she said. "I can't go to sleep and I see pictures in my mind, and when it becomes too much, I sort of drift away." She was living the nightmare over and over again. Gloria's sense of security had been shattered early in life. This memory, etched into her very being, caused her to be suspended in time as if it were still happening. Unable to live in the present moment, Gloria felt increasingly isolated and different from her classmates. Her private suffering did not come to the attention of her teachers or counselors until Gloria, a gifted teenager, became chronically truant, causing a decline in her grades.

Denial is a mild form of dissociation. It is a trickster that leads both children and adults to exclaim, "I'm fine" or "Nothing's wrong" when queried about their feelings. Even examining physicians and psychologists will often echo the refrain, "Nothing's wrong; she'll be just fine."

Woody Allen said it this way: "I'm not afraid of dying; I just don't want to be there when it happens." Beware! Underlying all the protection that dissociation and denial afford is a highly traumatized child. Although the youngster is masked in a calm exterior, it is important to remember that she could actually be in a highly aroused state that is under the surface of conscious awareness. All it takes is a simple reminder, such as a sound, smell, or even the season of the event, to blow the fragile cover and let loose the dam of sensations, thoughts, and feelings in a deluge—as in the following example of Elizabeth.

Elizabeth

In 2002, a fifteen-year-old honor student named Elizabeth was kidnapped from her Salt Lake City home. She was sexually assaulted and systematically tortured by her deranged abductor and his unkempt wife. When she was found and returned to her parents, everyone who participated in her recovery was amazed at how "strong" and "well" she was. By now you probably realize that this is denial and dissociation at work!

Insensitive to Elizabeth's deep wounds, investigators requested that she go with them to visit the remote spot where her harrowing experience began. This, of course, brought her hidden horror to the surface. One newspaper reported that she is now "suffering from insomnia, terrifying flashbacks and guilt over not trying to escape." The article went on to say that Elizabeth "is fine one minute, laughing with friends or her siblings. Then she'll seem to drift off, and her eyes glaze over."

It was immobility that prevented Elizabeth from trying to escape her captors. She reported feeling guilty about her failure to try to run away. The guilt is partly because she doesn't understand that she didn't have a choice.

Immobility, freeze, helplessness, and dissociation are involuntary psycho-physiological reactions to overwhelm. They are meant to be time-limited. It is the defensive response of the opossum (a small, slow, rather unprotected little creature) that cannot outrun his predators, or the mouse that looks dead when caught by the cat. When the danger is over, the opossum shuffles off and the mouse scurries home through the hole in the wall. Humans share the same capacity with other mammals but *do not know it!* When the tremendous "fight/flight" energy that was frozen begins to release, it can feel terrifying without the gentle voice of an adult to help the youngster feel safe. This can be accomplished by explaining that the strong sensations that are surfacing are normal, and by helping them to feel confident enough to accept these involuntary reactions.

It is understandable why Elizabeth felt mystified or embarrassed about not attempting to escape. As her immobility lessened, she was, possibly, able to experience the impulses to flee *now* that she couldn't feel *then* while still frozen. The symptoms of shame and guilt arise as a normal part of coming out of the freeze. The body was helpless but, unlike other mammals, the human mind passes judgment anyway. These intense feelings of helplessness and vulnerability can be extremely painful, especially for adolescents whose identity and reputation are at stake. In Part II, you will learn the important role that adults can play in helping youngsters through this crucial phase of recovery.

When freeze, immobility, and the accompanying feelings of helplessness do not resolve they can manifest as a cascade of physical and emotional symptoms. Symptoms can be observed behaviorally in both teens and school-aged children. Children "stuck" in helplessness typically do not initiate activities, try new things, or demonstrate creativity. Other predictable signs are irritability, clinginess, aloofness, and depression. At school, teachers might notice a lack of motivation, failure to complete work, and difficulty transitioning to new tasks. Physically, you may notice signs of listlessness, such as collapsed posture (draping one's body across the desk like a rag doll) or complaints of ongoing fatigue. Your child may also have difficulty persisting with difficult tasks and give up easily, perhaps being mislabeled as a "quitter" or "just plain lazy."

Adolescence: A Critical Developmental Stage

Although symptoms in teens may be similar to adults in many ways, the long-term effects are different due to the impact on the sense of self. The teenage years are the juncture for completing the task of autonomy that began at two years of age and ends with differentiation by the end of adolescence. During this critical period, morality, relationship skills, and personality are in the process of forming. Resources such as competence, humor, relatedness, and intelligence (all characteristics of personality) provide a protective barrier to ameliorate some of the effects of trauma. Overwhelming stress during this vulnerable period can influence the shape of personality and derail healthy development. Slipping into dissociation on a regular basis during the teen years can lead to disorders of identity. This is especially true when the abuse has been long-term and from trusted adults who have betrayed them.

Because of this vulnerable phase of life, adolescent symptoms include a caricatured self-consciousness laden with fears, shame, and guilt. A light-hearted adolescence may be usurped by a premature and grim entrance into adulthood. The following is a checklist of troublesome behavioral signs of trauma.

TEEN TRAUMA SYMPTOM CHECKLIST

✓ Abrupt changes in relationships like sudden disinterest in favorite people

✓ Becoming detached and withdrawn

✓ Radical changes in grades, life attitudes, and/or appearance

✓ Sudden changes in behavior like life-threatening re-enactment or other acting-out

✓ Sudden changes in mood, especially anxiety, depression, and thoughts of suicide

✓ Dependency on alcohol and drugs

✓ Sudden disinterest in favorite hobbies or sports

✓ Irritability, anger, and the desire to take revenge

✓ Sexual promiscuity

Delayed Traumatic Reactions

When adults are prepared to spot the four initial symptoms of hyperarousal, constriction, dissociation, and freeze, it is relatively easy to lead a child through the steps necessary to restore his or her nervous system to balance. Without this awareness, the child may be left in a partial state of shock, only to develop "secondary" symptoms weeks, months, or even years later. In fact, as unbeliev-able as it may seem, symptoms can be delayed for decades, as we shall see in the next story.

The Story of Johnny

Johnny, age five, proudly riding his first bicycle, hits loose gravel and careens into a tree. He is momentarily knocked unconscious. Getting up amid a flow of tears, he feels disoriented and somehow different. His parents hug him, console him, and put him back on the bike, all the while praising his courage. They do not realize how stunned and frightened he is.

Decades after the soon-forgotten incident, John, driving with his wife and children, swerves to avoid an oncoming car. He freezes in the midst of the turn. Fortunately, the other driver is able to maneuver successfully and avoid catastrophe.

One morning several days later, John begins to feel restless while driving to work. His heart starts racing and pounding; his hands become cold and sweaty. Feeling threatened and trapped, he has a sudden impulse to jump out of the car and run. He real-izes the "craziness" of his feelings, and gradually the symptoms subside. A vague and nagging apprehension, however, persists throughout most of his day at work. Returning home that evening without incident, he feels relieved.

The next morning, John leaves early to avoid traffic and stays late, discussing business with some colleagues. When he arrives home he is irritable and edgy. He argues with his wife and barks at the children. He goes to bed early, yet wakes covered with sweat in the middle of the night and faintly recalls a dream in which his car is sliding out of control. More fretful nights follow.

John is experiencing a delayed reaction to the bike accident he had as a child. Incredible as it may seem, delayed post-traumatic reactions of this type are common. After working for more than thirty-five years with people suffering from trauma, we can safely say that at least 75% of our clients have traumatic symptoms that remain dormant for a significant period of time before surfacing. For most people, the interval between the event and the onset of symptoms is six to eighteen months; for others, the latency period lasts for years or even decades. In many instances, the reactions are often triggered by seemingly insignificant events.

Of course, not every childhood accident produces a delayed traumatic reaction. Some have no residual effect at all. Others, including those viewed as "minor" and forgotten incidents in childhood, can have significant after-effects, particularly if they are compounded with other traumatic events. A fall, a seemingly benign surgical operation, the loss of a parent through death or divorce, severe illness (particularly when accompanied by high fever or poisoning), even circumcision and other routine medical procedures can all cause traumatic reactions later in life, depending on how the child experiences them at the time they occurred.

One thing is certain. Secondary symptoms of trauma develop over time. Just as it takes time and exposure for a Polaroid photo to fully develop, childhood traumatic symptoms can continue to show up in the months, years, and sometimes decades after the incident. The sooner the child is given first aid by a familiar adult or treated by a professional when indicated, the less likely it is that secondary symptoms will develop. Another certainty is that lasting symptoms tend to be pervasive: they affect the child's physical, emotional, spiritual, cognitive, and behavioral development. You might want to begin writing symptoms down to see if a pattern is developing. See the appendix for a sample ("Worksheet: Observing and Noting Symptoms").

Sexual Trauma Symptoms

The sexual molestation and assault of children has the added shroud of secrecy and shame. In addition, less than 10% of predation is perpetrated by a stranger. Because children are usually violated by someone they *know and trust,* the symptoms are layered with the complexity of the repercussions of betrayal. They are often asked to keep the activity secret—or worse, threatened with physical harm if they tell.

Most often children will not tell us with words. If their assailant is an authority figure, such as a parent, coach, teacher, or clergy, children blame themselves. They carry the shame that rightly belongs to the molester. Frequently they are afraid to tell because they fear punishment or that no one will believe them. Sadly, this is all too often the case.

How then do our children tell us? What symptoms should we be suspicious of? Use the following as a guide:

1. Look for sexualized behavior that is not age-appropriate. Examples would be French kissing, touching an adult's genitals, simulating intercourse, using seductive or sensual gestures with an adult, or masturbating in public.

2. Pay attention to sudden refusal, reluctance, or fear at being left alone, with a certain person or in a particular place that they once enjoyed.

3. Notice if a child withdraws from other children, or has difficulty making friendships with a tendency to cling to a safe person, such as a teacher, counselor, or mom.

4. Take particular note of pain, burning, itching, or bruising in the genital and/or anal areas.

5. Have your child examined for an unusual discharge or signs of a sexually transmitted disease.

6. Listen to what your child says to other children or to you. Often they tell you indirectly. Examples are: "I don't want to be an altar boy anymore." "Angelina's daddy wears underpants with teddy bears on it." "What does it mean when ... a man puts his penis in somebody's mouth?"

7. Watch for general symptoms already mentioned such as bedwetting, returning to earlier behaviors like thumb-sucking, difficulty sleeping and eating. Inability to concentrate, dreaminess, living in a fantasy world, and other variations of dissociation are especially common.

8. Be suspicious of personality changes such as chronic irritability, sudden mood shifts, excessive shyness and postures that reveal a sense of shame, guilt, or secrecy.

9. *Do* ask questions. In Chapter Nine, you will learn what questions to ask and how to approach children so that they will trust you to protect them and will tell you what you need to know.

As cautioned earlier, it is important to remember that physical or sexual abuse almost always requires the additional support of a professional trauma therapist. But whether a particular child needs a therapist or not, there is a lot that you as parents, educators, and medical professionals can do to prevent and heal trauma. Part II gives the specifics on how to guide children through trauma. Please read on!

Understanding Why Some Children Have Trauma Symptoms and Others Do Not

You may wonder why one child suffers trauma symptoms and another does not. A number of factors affect whether or not a child or adult will remain traumatized. The discussion in Chapter Two explained that trauma is in the nervous system rather than the event itself. You may remember by definition that trauma symptoms develop when the physiological mechanisms for self-protection, set into motion for escape, are thwarted (prevented for any number of reasons, either physical or through conflicts). In other words, the child or adult did not get to accomplish the full cycle of: 1) utilizing the chemical and hormonal program, 2) energizing the sensory-motor activities of protection, orientation, and defense, then 3) discharging the excess activation, and finally, 4) returning to a relaxed alertness or physiological homeostasis.

Some of the factors that affect the ability of a child to respond appropriately, complete the cycle outlined above, and emerge victorious include: the child's physical characteristics, the child's external resources, their skills and capabilities, and the event itself. For example, the child's developmental level and stage of dependency are critical. Being left alone in a cold room can be totally overwhelming to an infant, frightening to a toddler, distressing to a ten-year-old, and only mildly uncomfortable to an adolescent or an adult. Not only can teens tolerate extremes of temperature better physically, they have choices to do something to change the circumstances. They can put on more clothing, change the setting on the thermostat, move to a different spot, rub their arms, or do jumping jacks.

The child's physical characteristics include age, strength, agility, speed, and overall fitness. It also includes constitution, which is a combination of genetics, temperament, and early environment. Stress and trauma incurred during the period from fetus to three years old, with no corrective experience, predisposes the young child to vulnerability later in life. This is due to the likelihood of a less resilient nervous system because it is during infancy that the myelinated parasympathetic branch of the autonomic nervous system is fully developing within the context of attachment. This is the branch that de-activates arousal and is responsible for returning the child to a state of well-being.

The child's external resources include supportive and loving family, teachers, and friends. It also includes healthy outlets for stress that bring pleasure to the child. Examples are sports (that the child chooses and which are not overly competitive), cooperative games, hobbies, the performing arts, music, pets, the martial arts, play, drawing and painting. Participation with others in organized groups and clubs that foster a sense of belonging and connection with a peer community can also bring a stronger sense of self. For teens, groups that encourage volunteer activism (such as community beautification projects, visiting the elderly, or peer tutoring) can also bring a deepened sense of belonging and competence that serves to lessen the impact of a traumatic event.

Other factors in determining symptom development have to do with the intensity of the event, whether there were multiple events, and if the traumatic stress was prolonged, as in the case of childhood abuse, family chaos including alcoholism, physical and emotional abuse, and of course war. Finally, a large factor that can prevent or exacerbate symptoms is the quality of the care the child receives immediately after the frightening incident, including the first aid detailed in Part II of this book. When a child has the ability to move out of freeze into a state of flow, resources build within the child's own body that promote confidence, fortitude, and self-esteem.

When Symptoms Persist: How Trauma Affects a Child's Brain

To help you better comprehend why symptoms persist and affect children's behavior let's examine how a traumatized brain behaves. This may help you to understand what makes a child behave the way they do after the danger is over.

When overwhelming events have been exceptionally intense, prolonged, and/or repeated, there is a change in the function of the brain that elevates vigilance to a high priority. Much like the color-coded warnings of an impending terrorist attack, the brain has switched from a watchful yellow state to the red of high alert.

Because the functioning has changed, a child's sense of safety becomes highly distorted, causing a perception of danger when there is none. This is because heightened activity continues in the deeper structures of the reptilian brain and limbic system, especially with simple reminders of the frightening event, even though the actual danger is over. The "rug that was pulled out from under your child" continues to leave him suspended in time and space due to the physiological changes in the way the brain works after it has become traumatized.

MRI scans clearly show how the electrical activity routes messages from the amygdala's early warning center directly to the "fight/flight/freeze" survival mechanisms, leaving the (frontal) neocortical (thinking, planning, and reasoning) brain high and dry. Broca's area, responsible for language, is dampened, with little activity. No wonder children and adults are left "speechless" and cannot describe with words their horrible experience. Normally, with a brain that is not traumatized, when the amygdala sends warning messages to the higher centers of the brain, the neocortical ("higher") brain assesses the novelty and decides whether a real danger exists. If none exists, the activity of the amygdala subsides and all is well. Unfortunately, when a child is suffering from trauma the brain behaves differently. It may register any novelty or excitement as potentially harmful. This sends a cascade of unneeded chemicals, marching like soldiers to the battleground (to the most primitive parts of the brain), to fight a war that doesn't exist. It is this continuing pattern of excess energy that creates trauma's symptoms.

Clusters of Secondary
Trauma Symptoms: A Summary

In our earlier discussion of trauma, we explained how symptoms arise when there isn't enough time, strength, speed, or size to overpower the forces against us. Physiologically, whatever our age, size, or shape, we are programmed to produce the hormones and chemicals that spark the energy and muscular activity we need to protect and defend ourselves and our loved ones. This chapter addressed the initial symptoms of trauma: hyperarousal, constriction, dissociation/shutdown, and immobility with freeze/ helplessness. We also described extensively how these symptoms manifest in infants, children, and adolescents, with case examples to illustrate each age group.

When these core symptoms remain unresolved, over time new symptoms emerge. In addition, as children move from one stage of healing to another, different symptoms may emerge that were not present before. For example, if a child moves out of freeze too quickly, constriction may be replaced by anxiety. If traumatic symptoms continue, dominant patterns tend to form. Patterns or "symptom clusters" are grouped in the following charts for simplicity.

When Hyperarousal Predominates

In general, the following symptomatic behaviors may be observed in children with a pattern of continuing hyperarousal:

WHEN HYPERAROUSAL PREDOMINATES
THESE SYMPTOMS MAY APPEAR OVER TIME:

- panic attacks, anxiety and phobias
- flashbacks
- exaggerated startle response
- extreme sensitivity to light and sound
- hyperactivity, restlessness
- exaggerated emotional response
- nightmares and night terrors
- avoidance behavior, clinging
- attraction to dangerous situations
- frequent crying and irritability
- abrupt mood swings, e.g. rage reactions
- temper tantrums
- regressive behaviors, such as wanting a bottle, thumb sucking, bed-wetting, using fewer words
- increased "risk-taking" behavior

This category of heightened vigilance leads to an exaggerated and quick response that escalates out of control like the acceleration of a turbo-charged race car. These symptoms are the result of super-charged energy stored in the body's sensory-motor memory cells. Hypervigilance and hyperactivity are symptoms that can predominate no matter what the event. The following is the story of an active child who, due to circumstances, was restrained during a period that thwarted her natural motor development. When the restraint is long-lasting, these symptoms may alternate with those of depression and resignation.

Kara's Leg Braces

Kara is a good example of how symptoms can escalate. At ten months old when this curious little girl normally would have been exploring the world by cruising the furniture, she was stuck in metal leg braces to correct a congenital hip abnormality. She was in leg braces on and off until she was thirteen years old. Later in life, she was a bundle of energy that overwhelmed her parents, to use their own words, "on a daily basis!"

In school Kara was labeled hyperactive. She had also experienced dental trauma, including orthodontia. This led to avoidance of the dentist as an adult due to feelings ranging from dread to terror. As a teenager, Kara compensated for her heightened arousal by devoting herself to professional and competitive ice-skating. However, she was plagued with panicky feelings when off the rink, had difficulty with relationships, and suffered with chronic restlessness. She was not happy unless she was engaged in movement.

After Kara discharged much of this excess energy during her Somatic Experiencing® sessions, her chronic high arousal was reduced to a pleasant level of manageable energy. As she was able to "settle down" in her body, her life settled down as well. Agitation was replaced by contentment in her everyday life and relationships.

When Dissociation/Shutdown Predominates

While some youngsters live in an agitated, restless state, others may live in a fog. Often, children with unresolved physical and/or sexual abuse, victims of high-impact head injuries, and children unprepared for intrusive medical procedures and anesthesia typically manifest secondary symptoms that develop from the core symptom of dissociation.

WHEN DISSOCIATION PREDOMINATES,
THESE SYMPTOMS MAY EMERGE OVER TIME:

- distractibility and inattentiveness
- amnesia and forgetfulness
- reduced ability to organize and plan
- feelings of isolation and detachment
- muted or diminished emotional responses, making it difficult to bond with others
- easily and frequently stressed out
- frequent daydreaming and fear of going crazy
- low energy and easily fatigued
- excessive shyness with time spent in an imaginary world or with imaginary friends

---

In Marilyn Van Derbur's eye-opening book about incest, *Miss America By Day,* she shares her harrowing experience (and that of others) as her entrenched pattern of dissociation—which initially served as a vehicle for her survival—began to erode. All through her childhood, Ms. Van Derbur assumed two separate identities. Her "day child" and her "night child" lived totally different realities.[4] This ability to dissociate is not willed. It is a phenomenon that allows a child to cope and survive through adaptive mechanisms that temporarily block out the pain. At home or at school, when dissociation is prevalent your child may appear to be daydreaming, stare blankly, be inattentive, or look as if she has her "head in the clouds." What she says may not be congruent with what you see due to a defensive denial of reality. It is more difficult for the child to connect with other children, and parents may comment, "He's in his own little world." Such a traumatized child may miss the instructions at school, be labeled "attention-deficit disordered," or frequently be known to ask, "What did you say?" as they float in and out of present-time awareness.

Constriction/Freeze/Immobility Cluster

Constriction, freeze, and immobility are so closely related that they are grouped together for simplicity. When constriction, freeze, and immobility continue for prolonged periods, a parent may notice (or a child may complain of) the symptoms listed in the box below. These may be in addition to, instead of, or alternating with the symptoms of dissociation and hyperarousal.

WHEN CONSTRICTION, FREEZE, AND IMMOBILITY PREDOMINATE, THESE SYMPTOMS MAY EMERGE:

- headaches and stomachaches
- spastic colon, asthma, digestive problems
- feelings and behaviors of helplessness
- bed-wetting and soiling
- feelings of shame and guilt
- avoidance behavior
- repetitive play
- diminished curiosity
- diminished capacity for pleasure
- postural and coordination problems
- low energy/fatigues easily
- clinginess/ regression to younger behaviors

When somatic complaints predominate they can be very frustrating to both parents and medical personnel. It becomes easy for a circular quandary to develop in an attempt to resolve the health issue. Melissa's experience, described below, serves to illustrate this all-too-common dilemma.

Sweet Nine-Year-Old Melissa

This sweet, brown-eyed, nine-year-old girl was molested by her adolescent step-brother. Her brother, because he was nineteen years old, was arrested and jailed. Understandably, Melissa began having a variety of symptoms, including social withdrawal from other children and clinging to her school counselor and teachers. Her chief distress, however, was a chronic stomachache that kept her on familiar terms with the school nurse.

Melissa's mom took her to a psychotherapist at the local hospital clinic in the hopes that her daughter's symptoms would be alleviated. What happened instead was quite the opposite! The therapist wanted to rule out digestive disease or blockage and referred her for medical testing. Melissa was traumatized yet again—this time by the intrusive procedures. When the doctor couldn't figure out what was wrong, exploratory surgery was suggested. Melissa refused to go back to the hospital. Fortunately, her mother called the school for help, and the principal referred her to me [co-author Maggie Kline].

What Melissa needed most was support to release the constriction in her belly from the shock of the sexual abuse. In two 45-minute sessions her tummy aches disappeared. *After* her digestion returned to normal, she was able to put her experience into words and express her conflicting emotions to me, her mother, and her therapist—which was exactly the support she needed to get through her trauma.

Conclusion

Ideally, you now have a greater understanding of what trauma is, the wide range of potential trauma triggers for children, recognizable symptoms and behaviors in various age groups, and how unresolved trauma affects the developing brain. In Part II you will be given a step-by-step working guide to help you avoid the pitfalls that lead to trauma in the aftermath of overwhelming circumstances. With this practical information you will have the skills and confidence to prevent and heal trauma in your own children and those children entrusted to your care. And again, when there is any question concerning the severity or intractability of a behavior or other symptom, the guidance from a trained professional can help remove the "log-jam" and assist in your child's recovery and your peace of mind.

GENERAL GUIDE FOR PREVENTING CHILDHOOD TRAUMA

Emotional First Aid or
How to Be a "Good Band-Aid"

You can discover more about a person
in an hour of play than in a year of conversation.

– Plato

Understanding atomic physics is child's play
compared to understanding child's play.

– Neils Bohr

I n Part I you learned valuable information about what trauma
is, what can cause it, and how to recognize its symptoms. In
Part II you will learn practical tools to help minimize or prevent traumatic symptoms from developing after stressful events.
Chapter Four provides a variety of exercises designed to help adults
and children discover the rich landscape of sensations that exist
within the body. Suggestions will help you acquire a new vocabulary for this language of sensation—the language spoken in the
deep recesses of the reptilian ("instinctual") brain. You will become
adept at working cooperatively with these voluntary and involuntary internal signals in order to heal the rift between conscious
and unconscious bodily processes, just as our wild mammalian
friends are able to do naturally. This experiential knowledge will
not only give you the tools to assist your traumatized child; it will
help to keep *you* from becoming overwhelmed as well.

Chapter Four also discusses how to attune to a child's needs
and rhythms, with a guide to hone your observation skills through
looking, listening, and resonating with the child. This chapter

includes the story of Sammy, a case study that illustrates how to engage your own child through play to relieve stress after a mishap, whether or not he has already developed symptoms. All children use play as a vehicle to regain their balance and resilience. You will learn how to recognize the difference between the type of play that moves children forward through the healing process versus play that is merely a re-enactment of their trauma You will learn the basic principles that guide play towards the completion of the energy bound up in distress—or, later, in symptoms.

Giving Appropriate Support to an Overwhelmed Child

In order to prevent or minimize trauma, it is important to make sure that *you're* not overwrought by your child's mishap. It goes without saying that this is not always easy! It may reduce your anxiety to know that children are both resilient and malleable. When supported appropriately, they are usually able to rebound from stressful events. In fact, as they begin to triumph over life's shocks and losses, they grow into more competent, resilient, and vibrant beings. Because the capacity to heal is innate, your role as an adult is simple: it is to help the little ones access this capacity. Your task is similar in many ways to the function of a band-aid or a splint. The band-aid or splint doesn't heal the wound, but protects and supports the body as it restores itself. The suggestions, exercises, and step-by-step guidelines provided throughout Chapter Four are meant to enable you to be a good "band-aid" for the child.

The importance of the adult's calmness cannot be overemphasized. Your calmness is essential! When a child has been hurt or frightened, it is normal for the adult to feel somewhat shocked or scared, too. Because of your own fears and protective instincts, it is not uncommon to respond initially with anger, which can further frighten the child. The goal is to minimize—not compound—

feelings of fright, shame, embarrassment, and guilt the child is likely to be experiencing already. The best antidote is to tend to your own reactions first. Allow time for your own bodily responses to settle rather than scolding or running anxiously towards your child. Experiences with our adult clients in therapy confirm that often the most frightening part of an incident experienced as a child was their parents' reaction! The younger the child, the more he or she "reads" the facial expression of their caregivers as a barometer of how serious the danger or injury is.

What Goes Up ... Must Come Down

The way to develop a calm adult presence is through experiential exercises that increase your ability to restore equilibrium, quickly and naturally, so you are more likely to experience grace under pressure. Once *your* body learns that "what goes up (charge/excitation) must come down (discharge/relaxation)," you are on the way to a more resilient nervous system that can weather the ups and downs of life. You will become more like the tall bamboo or wispy willow that bends, sometimes to the ground, but does not break even during a monsoon! When your nervous system "gets it," you become contagious—but in a *good* way. Through the mechanism of body language, facial expression, and tone of voice, your own nervous system communicates *directly* with the child's nervous system. This is how we connect with our children without words. But before we attune to children's sensations, rhythms, and emotions, we must learn to attune to our own.

The first step in this attunement process is to understand the importance of experiencing both comfortable and uncomfortable sensations, incrementally tolerating and "tracking" them as they progress through a natural cycle towards more comfort and completion. After you understand *why* this is important, the second step is to expand awareness of *your* sensations, thereby teaching your children to be more "at home" with *their* sensations.

A simple explanation of our exquisite three-in-one triune brain will make it clear why the essence of change lies in awakening the consciousness of the inner landscape of sensations. This deeper experience of ourselves, often neglected, shapes our core being. It is from our own breath and belly that we form our core sense of self. It is from this place that we know precisely *what* we are feeling moment by moment and *how* we know *that* we know *what* we know![1]

Developing a Calming Presence

Now that you have reflected on the importance of being a calm, centered adult presence, you may be wondering: "How in the world can I *achieve* this aspiration?" Given the modern stresses of juggling family and career responsibilities—not to mention personal problems and any of your own unresolved traumas—how on earth is a parent or other care-giver supposed to be calm and resilient? This is especially true in the case of emergencies, such as watching a toddler's first acrobatic plunge that, for a split second, looks like it could cost life or limb!

The answer is not very complicated once you get the basic feel for it. In order for adults to become more resilient and effective—not only in handling emergencies, but with parenting in general—it's imperative that they gain an *experiential* sense of how their instincts operate when in danger or under stress. Clearly, before we can communicate we must learn the language it speaks.

The Triune Brain Simplified

Humans have a triune brain (three brains functioning together as one mind). Simply put, this means that there are three integral parts that, ideally, work in harmony. The neocortical ("new") part of the brain is responsible for inhibition of inappropriate actions, perception, problem-solving, planning, and other complex rational thinking skills. The mammalian (midbrain), also referred to as the limbic system or "emotional brain,"[2] processes memory and emotion. The reptilian ("lower" or "primitive") brain is responsible for survival and the myriad functions that accompany the regulatory mechanisms of basic existence. Each region has very specialized functions, and each speaks its own language. The thinking brain speaks with words, while the emotional brain uses the language of feelings, such as joy and sorrow. (For young children it's easy to label the emotions: mad, sad, glad, and afraid.) Unlike the "newer" thinking and feeling brain segments, the primitive reptilian brain speaks the unfamiliar but vastly important language of *sensation*.

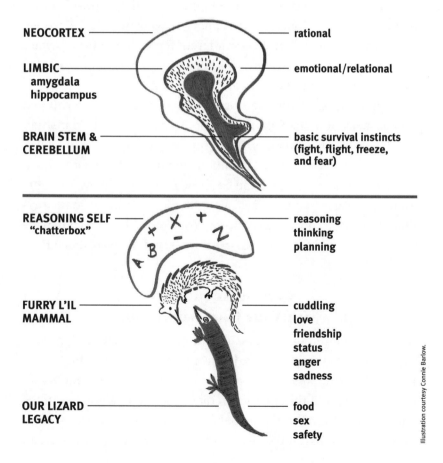

NEOCORTEX ———— rational

LIMBIC——
amygdala
hippocampus
———— emotional/relational

BRAIN STEM & ———— basic survival instincts
CEREBELLUM (fight, flight, freeze, and fear)

REASONING SELF ———— reasoning
"chatterbox" thinking
planning

FURRY L'IL ———— cuddling
MAMMAL love
friendship
status
anger
sadness

OUR LIZARD ———— food
LEGACY sex
safety

Illustration courtesy Connie Barlow.

The language of sensation is, to many, a foreign language. There is a world of sensation and sensation-based feeling inside you that exists whether or not you are aware of it. Fortunately, it is a language that is easy to learn, and it's as essential to be familiar with when traveling the "road to recovery" as learning basic survival phrases when traveling abroad. In order to help a child, it only makes sense to get acquainted first with *your* own inner landscape. All it takes is some unhurried time, set aside without distractions, to pay attention to *how* your *body* feels. Sensations can range from pressure or temperature changes on the skin to vibrations, "butterflies," muscular tension, constriction or spaciousness, trembling or tingling, and heat. *This* is the language of the primitive brain that acts on our behalf when in danger or when we meet a change in the environment. It is a very different focus than most of us are accustomed to. It is within neither the realm of language nor thought—nor, even, the territory of emotion.

Because it is the reptilian brain that ensures our survival and homeostasis, it is the wise adult who befriends this deep instinctual layer of consciousness. No equipment or costs are involved. All that is necessary is time, attention, and intent. With some quiet, focused time this language can easily be mastered. Below are some exercises to give you the "feel" for it. Remember: because the reptilian brain does not register words, you cannot learn its language merely by reading about it. ***Sensations must be experienced!***

Getting Acquainted with Your Own Sensations

Although children may not be able to verbalize what they are feeling because they are too scared and/or too young to talk, they know how a shocking upset feels and so do you! It is the undeniable dread in the pit of the stomach, a racing heart, the tightness in the chest, or the "lump in the throat." Turn on the news after a natural disaster or listen to a bystander who has just witnessed an accident and hear what the people interviewed have to say about their experience. "I don't have words for it." "It's such a cold feeling." "It was like getting the wind knocked out of me." "I just feel numb." "My heart wouldn't stop racing, but I couldn't move."

Think about your own experiences when something upsetting happened out of the blue.

What were some of the sensations you felt? Did your heart pound rapidly? Did you get dizzy? Did your throat or stomach tighten in a knot? And when the danger was over, how did the sensations gradually shift or change? Perhaps you noticed that you could breathe easier or felt some tingling or vibration as your muscles began to relax.

NOTICING SENSATIONS

Let's try this brief experiment to get you started on deepening your awareness.

Find a comfortable place to sit. Take some time to notice how you are feeling physically. Pay attention to your breathing. Are you comfortable or uncomfortable? Where in your body do you register your comfort level? What do you notice? Are you aware of your heart beating or your breathing? Perhaps you're more aware of muscle tension or relaxation or the temperature of your skin, perhaps sensations like "tingly." When you feel settled enough to go on, try the simple exercise below.

Imagine it's a pleasant day and you're driving down to the beach with your favorite music playing. You're not in a rush because it's your day off. Take a minute to notice how you are feeling before you read the next paragraph. Note the sensations in various parts of your body, such as your belly, limbs, breath, muscles, and skin.

Suddenly, from out of nowhere, a hot-rod motorist cuts in front of you, nearly causing a disastrous collision. Furthermore, he is rude and shouts profanities at you as if you had done something to cause the mishap. What are you noticing in your body right now?

How were you feeling when you started the exercise? Pay attention to changes. What feels different? Where does it feel different? Are you warm, hot, or chilled? Do you feel tension or constriction anywhere? Notice changes in heart rate and respiration. When you check your body to feel your reactions and sensations in the present moment, you have entered the realm of the reptilian brain.

Now take a little time to let any activation settle. Look around the room, being aware that you are safe and that the visualization was only an exercise. Place both feet on the floor and direct your attention to something in the room that brings comfort, such as a flower, photo, or a favorite possession. Notice how you are feeling in your body at this moment.

This brief exercise was intended to help you see that the language of sensation isn't really so foreign, even though your family members probably don't use sensation words to describe their day while seated around the dinner table! Although, perhaps they describe a full stomach or one that feels warm and cozy after sipping hot chocolate.... When children do tell adults how they feel, it is typically expressed as a mood or emotion, such as happy, cranky, mad, excited, or sad. Noticing sensations may not have been among your "hobbies," but the more you learn about your own body consciousness, the more intuitive, instinctual, and confident you will become. You may not know this, but your sense of a harmonious self is based on your body's ability to self-regulate—rather than to escalate out of control. And this capacity for self-regulation is enhanced through sensate experience.

Building a New Vocabulary Together with Your Child

When learning skills with any new language, it helps to develop and practice vocabulary. The box below will get you started. To create a balance, be sure to include sensations that are pleasurable or neutral, as well as those that may be somewhat uncomfortable at first. Your child and you can have fun adding to the list and watching it grow as you get acquainted with this strange and wonderful world inside of you!

SENSATION VOCABULARY BOX

- cold/warm/hot/chilly
- twitchy/butterflies
- sharp/dull/itchy
- shaky/trembly/tingly
- hard/soft/stuck
- jittery/icy/weak
- relaxed/calm/peaceful
- empty/full
- flowing/spreading
- strong/tight/tense
- dizzy/fuzzy/blurry
- numb/prickly/jumpy
- owie/tearful/goose-bumpy
- light/heavy/open
- tickly/cool/silky
- still/clammy/loose

*Note that sensations are different than emotions. They describe the *physical* way the body feels. Non-verbal children can be invited to point to where in their bodies it might feel shaky, numb, or calm, or where the owie is, etc.

MAKING A SENSATION TREASURE CHEST

Sensory awareness is a very important part of early childhood develop-ment. It not only promotes cognitive growth and self-awareness, it is fun for children to explore taste, smell, sight, sound, and touch. The two easy activities below can get you started. You'll need paper and pen for many of these activities if you want to take notes about the sensations. Space prohibits us from providing a workbook format in this volume.

Activity 1

1. Find an empty box, can, or bag in which to hide about 10–12 objects.

2. Select items that have distinctly different textures such as: a feather, a piece of sandpaper, a variety of rocks of different shapes, sizes, and textures, a cotton ball, a slimy toy, a piece of satin or silk fabric, steel wool, etc., and hide them in the box.

3. Have your child close his eyes (or use a blindfold), pick an object, and try to guess what it is by the way it feels.

4. Once all objects have been identified, have your child touch each object, then tell how it feels on his skin (tickly, prickly, cool, heavy, etc.).

5. Next, have your child compare the rocks of different weights by holding them in his hands and noticing how his muscles feel when a rock is very light, light, medium heavy, heavy, and very heavy.

6. Ask him to notice the difference he feels it in his body when he touches something slimy as compared to something soft, etc. Have him point to the place in his body where he notices the difference. Is it in his arms, in his tummy, or on his skin, or in his throat?

7. Have your child make up some questions for you, and take turns continuing to compare and contrast sensations.

8. Make a list of the sensations that were discovered.

Activity 2

1. Now try the above game using a "tasting tray" instead of a box. Fill tiny cups with a variety of edibles with different tastes and textures such as: sweet, salty, bitter, spicy, tart, crunchy, soft, etc.

2. Using a blindfold to avoid visual clues, have your child identify the various foods. You can give a cracker between each taste test to clear the palate.

3. As your child tastes each sample, have him tell you how the texture feels (creamy, hard, slippery, gooey, etc.) and then how it tastes.

4. Now ask how each sample makes her tongue feel (tingly, prickly, cold, slippery, dry, relaxed, curled, numb, hot, etc.).

5. Repeat steps 6, 7, and 8 from Activity I, contrasting sensations caused by taste rather than touch.

Before an emergency occurs, it's a good idea to become acquainted with your own sensations in a *variety* of situations and to help children to become aware of theirs. Together you can create and add to your family's vocabulary. It's easy to do. But like any new skill, training yourself to become more observant and notice how you feel as you regain your equilibrium after an upset takes a bit of practice. And with this practice of deepening awareness, you will be ready to assist a child under almost any circumstance!

"Pendulating" Between Pleasant and Unpleasant Sensations, Emotions, and Images

In Somatic Experiencing®, the term "pendulation" refers to a natural rhythm (of contraction and expansion) inherent within us that guides us back and forth between uncomfortable sensations, emotions, and images to more comfortable ones, allowing for new experiences and meanings to emerge. The uncomfortable feelings are usually associated with stress or trauma when we were lacking the resources to avoid defeat. Of course, with trauma, the present is colored by the past, which overlays both our sense of self and our world view. When this natural process has been shut down, it must be restored. Pendulation is what keeps the momentum of change happening over time. With this rhythm restored there is, at least, a tolerable balance between the pleasant and unpleasant. And no matter how bad a particular feeling may be, we know that it will soon change.

The next exercise was chosen to further deepen your awareness of sensations, as well as to give you a sense of your natural rhythm of pendulation. This time you might find it helpful to pair up with a partner. Having a witness can help you to stay focused. When a trusted friend "stands guard," as many animals in nature do, it can create a deeper sense of safety. With an attitude of curiosity, use the exercise below to explore your changing, pendulating, inner landscape of sensation.

EXPLORING SENSATION AND PENDULATION

Note: You may wish to have your partner read this to you in a slow voice with plenty of pauses to give you a chance to develop more refined awareness. Another option is to record the exercise in your own voice to listen to with or without someone else.

Take time to get comfortable in your chair. Notice where your body is touching the seat; notice how the chair supports your body. Settle into the chair. Notice your breathing and how you are feeling and your overall sensations. As you slowly follow the story below, take the time to notice the sensations, thoughts, and images that come up. Some will be subtle and others obvious. The more attention and time you take, the more your awareness will grow.

Now, imagine that today's your birthday. Even though it's a special day you feel lonely. You don't want to be alone so you decide to go see a movie. You start to get ready. As you reach for your wallet you have a dreadful feeling as you notice it is missing. What are you feeling? Take some time to notice feelings, sensations, and thoughts in your body and your mind.

If you feel dread, what does it feel like? Where do you feel it in your body? Common places to experience sensations are: solar plexus, chest, and throat. Do you feel a tightening or a sinking sensation—perhaps queasiness? Do you notice any temperature changes in your hands? Do they feel sweaty, hot, or cold? Is there any place you feel unsteady or wobbly? And notice how these sensations change over time as you attend to them. Does the intensity increase or decrease; does the tightening loosen or change to something else?

As you settle, the thought comes to you that: "Oh, perhaps I left my wallet in the other room." Imagine that you go and look there. You check out other places you might have left it. You can't find it and you begin to get a bit frantic. Again, focus your attention inward and take time to notice your bodily sensations, your feelings, and your thoughts.

Now, you slow down a bit and your thoughts become a little clearer. You begin to hunt for the wallet more methodically. Is it in the drawer? Maybe when I came in I left it over there on the table ... but then I went to the bathroom ... you think ... could I have left it in the bathroom? (Pause here to notice sensations.) However, while you're looking, you are interrupted by the ring of the telephone. You pick up the phone. It's your friend and she tells you that you left your wallet at her house. You take a big sigh of relief! Feel that and notice how you smile as you think about your previous frantic state of mind.

Your friend tells you that she's leaving shortly, but she'll wait if you come right now. So you walk briskly to her house. Feel the strength in your legs as you walk briskly. You knock on the door and there's no answer. You knock a second time and there's still no answer. You begin to think that you must have missed her. You begin to feel a bit irritated. After all, she said she would wait and you came as quickly as you could. Where do you feel the sensation of irritability? What does it feel like? Take your time and notice the range of sensations just as you did before. How do you experience the irritability? Where do you feel it? What does it feel like?

From the back of the house, you hear your friend's muffled voice. She's telling you to come in. You open the door and it's really dark. You slowly find your way in the dark. You begin to make your way down the hallway. Notice how your body feels as you fumble through the darkness trying to get to the back of the house. You call again to your friend, but you're interrupted by a chorus of voices yelling, "Surprise!"

What are you feeling in your body now, in this moment, as you realize it's a surprise birthday party for you?!

This exercise was intended to acquaint you with a variety of sensations that occur in different situations such as frustration, expectancy, relief, conflict, and surprise. If you noticed different feeling states and were able to move smoothly from the pleasant to the unpleasant and back again, you now have an idea of what it feels like to pendulate.

The twists and turns of the visualization above were filled with many surprises. Surprise (novelty) activates the nervous system. In the case of a good surprise, something gets stored in the body that makes you feel better about your sense of self. On the other hand, in the case of a horrifying surprise, distressing sensations can become stuck, resulting in a diminished sense of self and feelings of helplessness. When you're in touch with sensations, you can begin to move with fluidity out of one state and into another.

Remember, anything that feels bad is never the final step. It is this movement from fixity to flow that frees us from the grips of trauma.

Ideally, you were able to feel this fluidity within yourself. If you did, you are well on your way to learning the skills to help a child fluidly glide through sensations. If, in any way, you felt "stuck" or frozen on an unpleasant sensation, emotion, or image while practicing, take the time now to look around, get up, move, and take notice of an object, movement, thought, person, pet, or natural feature that makes you feel comfortable. Then return to the place in your body where you were stuck and see what happens now!

Attuning to Your Child's Rhythms, Sensations, and Emotions

So how can adults give appropriate support? First of all, it is important to let your child know that any powerful emotions that she/he may be having (e.g. sadness, anger, rage, fear, and pain) are OK. (We will see later that there may be exceptions when you would distract a child from those feelings, such as when needing to calm her in preparation for a medical procedure.) Children are comforted and empowered by the knowledge that their pain is time-limited—that it *won't* last forever and that *whatever they are feeling now* is accepted. Paradoxically, children tend to move through their feelings rather quickly when they are not hurried by an adult's time schedule or emotional agenda.

Having the patience to attune your pace to your child's rhythm gives him/her permission to be authentic. The importance of this acceptance and respect is not to be underestimated. Just like the splint sets a broken arm properly, your undivided attention and soothing, non-judgmental language set the conditions for the child, in his or her own time, to rebound to a healthy sense of well-being.

Children are astute readers of facial, postural, and vocal cues from parents. Often children react the way they think the adults expect them to because of a desire to please, avoid criticism, or do the "right" thing. They will act "strong" and "brave," overriding their own feelings only to end up with trauma symptoms that could have been averted. Countless adults in therapy have reported stifling their feelings as children to protect their parents from feeling bad. Other times, their restrained demeanor appeared to be more of a reflexive mechanism serving to reduce the anxiety of a bewildered parent.

How to Avoid the Pitfall of Overriding Your Child's Needs

The first step is to be alert to the possibility of your own feelings of terror or vulnerability when something unexpected happens. The next step is to connect with your body. When you are momentarily "beside yourself" you literally need to get back inside yourself. Feel how your feet contact the floor. As you ground yourself by checking your sensations, you may be surprised to experience a spontaneous breath and a feeling of being back on center. It is amazing how these two simple steps can make you feel empowered and fully present to be with your child. It's the same idea as with the announcement made by the flight attendant to bring the oxygen mask to your nose and mouth first and then help the child sitting next to you.

By tending to yourself, paradoxically, you are in a better position to tend to your child. When you can feel your center, can notice that your breath slows down, and you experience the fluidity of changing sensations, you have moved out of a momentary "freeze." Your energy is now available to pay close attention to your child's needs and expression. In this way, you will naturally circumvent complicating your child's reactions with your own.

Guidelines to Assess if a Child is in a State of Overwhelm

The next step is to assess if a child has been overwhelmed and is in shock. Use the following guidelines: Carefully observe the child. Notice changes in skin color, muscle tone, and temperature. Is the complexion pale, are the palms cold and sweaty, are the muscles (posture) rigid or collapsed?

1. Check facial expression, particularly the eyes and mouth. Are the eyes and/or mouth wide-open in an expression of startle? Do the eyes appear glazed or vacant? Are the pupils dilated?

2. Pay attention to breathing and heartbeat. Is the breath rapid and/or shallow? Is the heart pounding fast or unusually slow?

3. Watch for any cognitive or emotional reactions (or absence of).

4. Does your child appear dazed and confused?

5. Is she talking as if she were somewhere else?

6. Does he have a vacant look on his face?

7. Is she overly emotional? Hysterically crying? Screaming in terror?

8. Is he overly tranquil, showing a blank expression as if nothing has happened?

Answering "yes" to one or more of the descriptions in the checklist above indicates that your child needs your attention. She may be experiencing anything from chronic stress to acute shock. If she is experiencing a medical emergency, use common sense to determine whether to administer medical first aid, call the paramedics, or both. But even a moment or two of attention first can be very beneficial. (Refer to Part III, Chapter Six, "First Aid for Accidents and Falls," where you will find an eight-step guide for ordinary mishaps.)

How to Attend to an Overwhelmed Child

When there is shock, it is common not to feel much at first because the chemicals released for "fight" or "flight" and "freeze" also serve as a kind of natural analgesia. For example, if your child is cut, she may not notice it until she actually sees the blood. The pain may be delayed until the shock begins to wear off. Your child may seem dazed and pale but act as if nothing much happened. (Remember Suzie's bike accident?) On the other hand, he may be crying hysterically. Validate your child's emotional and physical reactions in a calm voice, assuring him that you ...

1. understand what he must be going through by letting him know that his feelings are OK;

2. know what to do to help him, conveying that you, the adult, are in charge;

3. will protect and take care of him as a top priority;

4. are confident that the worst is over (if it is) and things will soon be better;

5. will stay with him until he begins to feels better.

"Staying with" him or her is meant to be taken both literally and figuratively. Literally, your physical presence is essential. Figuratively, it means developing an ability to be emotionally available in a way that your child is able to feel your undivided attention to the assessment and needs of the situation moment by moment. What you are doing is setting the conditions of safety for the healing to take place. Being available is an important message to the unconscious mind: "Now you are safe; I will take care of your needs."

Once the message is received, the body can relax, give up control, and surrender to the involuntary sensations (shakiness, tears, trembling, shivering, heat, etc.) that discharge the excess mobilized energy and release the high activation. Saying "just relax" or "stop crying and we'll get an ice cream cone" doesn't work to achieve relief. In fact, it can strengthen a child's defensiveness. What it may convey is impatience, misunderstanding, or that the adult wants me to "keep a stiff upper lip." This is not the way to prevent traumatic symptoms from happening—it is a way to promote body armor!

Instead, when your tone, demeanor, and carefully chosen words convey safety, your child can return from an "out-of-body" altered state amazingly quickly. The following example illustrates what we mean.

> A teenager on a motorcycle had been knocked off his bike on the city street. He hit his head, but luckily he was wearing a helmet. His arms and legs were scraped badly. Most obvious was his pale skin, wide eyes, and altered state. The teen crawled to the curb where I had been standing and, as you can imagine, he was in shock.
>
> Quickly, I asked a passerby to call an ambulance and then sat down next to the young man and simply said, "There's an ambulance on its way." Then, with a voice of authority and confidence (because I know the importance of emotional first aid and what needs to be done to start the healing process), I said, "You're in shock. I'll stay here with you until the ambulance comes." As soon as I finished my sentence, the teen began shaking. I put my hand on the outside of his upper arm (deltoid) and encouraged his involuntary sensations: "That's right . . . just let it all go . . . let the shaking happen . . . you're doing good . . . you're going to be fine." Three minutes later the color returned to his face. Soon, his shaking changed to gentle trembling and he released a few tears. A spontaneous breath came all of a sudden and he looked around as if to see what had just happened. He was returning to his senses, to himself!

The critical idea here is that when we are vulnerable, we benefit most from the sense that there is a calm, centered human in charge who is accepting, confident of what to do, and is able to convey a sense of safety sufficient to contain the enormous amount of "shock energy" as it's being released. This happens by setting the necessary priority of time and quiet space. As the highly-charged trauma physiology returns to normal, the spirit and body reconnect in *present* time. The cycle is complete when a sense of curiosity and interest in what's happening in the outside world seems to arise naturally, as it did when the teenager who had the motorcycle accident began to look around to check things out.

Helping a stunned child (whether your own, a neighbor's, a student, patient, or a total stranger) to discharge traumatic energy in order to leave the scary past behind is the most efficient trauma prevention that we know. It works to dissolve the root cause of later symptoms by deactivating the "fight or flee" energy *before* it has the chance to become traumatic memory and bind into traumatic symptoms. Now that you have become familiar with the language of sensation and understand that it is indispensable in the de-activation process, how do you use it to prevent trauma? The step-by-step guide below outlines a plan to do just that.

First Aid for Trauma Prevention: A Step-By-Step Guide

1. Check your own body's response first.

Take time to notice your own level of fear or concern. Next, take a full deep breath, and as you exhale s-l-o-w-l-y feel the sensations in your own body. If you still feel upset, repeat until you feel settled. Feel your feet, ankles, and legs, noticing how they make contact with the ground. Remind yourself that you know what to do and any excess energy will help you meet the challenge. The time it takes to establish a sense of calm is time well spent. It will increase your capacity to attend fully to your child. If you take the time to gather yourself, your own acceptance of whatever has happened will help you to focus on the child's needs. Your composure will greatly reduce the likelihood of frightening or confusing the child further. Remember, children are very sensitive to the emotional states of adults, particularly their parents.

2. Assess the situation.

If the child shows signs of shock (glazed eyes, pale skin, rapid or shallow pulse and breathing, disorientation, overly emotional or overly tranquil affect, or acting like nothing has happened), do not allow her to jump up and return to play. You might say something like, "We're going to sit (or lie) still together for a while and wait until the shock wears off." Remember, a calm, confident voice communicates to the child that you know what's best.

3. As the shock wears off, guide your child's attention to his sensations.

Softly ask your child how he feels "in his body." Repeat his answer as a question—"You feel okay in your body?"—and wait for a nod or other response. Be more specific with the next question: "How do you feel in your tummy (head, arm, leg, etc.)?" If he mentions a distinct sensation, gently ask about its location, size, shape, color, or weight (e.g. heavy or light). Keep guiding your child to stay with the present moment with questions such as, "How does the rock (sharpness, lump, "owie," sting) feel now?" If she is too young or too startled to talk, have her point to where it hurts. (Remember that children tend to describe sensations with metaphors such as "hard as a rock.")

4. Slow down and follow your child's pace by careful observation of change.

Timing is everything! This may be the hardest part for the adult; but it's the most important part for the child. Allowing a minute or two of silence between questions allows deeply restorative physiological cycles to engage. Too many questions asked too quickly disrupt the natural course. Your calm presence and patience are sufficient to facilitate the movement and release of excess energy. This process cannot be rushed. Be alert for cues that let you know a cycle has finished. If uncertain whether a cycle has been completed, wait and watch for your child to give you clues. Examples of clues include a deep, relaxed, spontaneous breath, the cessation of crying or trembling, a stretch, a yawn, a smile, or the making or breaking of eye contact. The completion of this cycle may not mean that the recovery process is over. Another cycle may follow. Keep your child focused on sensations for a few more minutes just to make sure the process is complete. Wait to see if another cycle begins or if there is a sense of enough for now. If your child shows signs of fatigue, stop. There will be other opportunities to complete the process.

5. Keep validating your child's physical responses.

Resist the impulse to stop your child's tears or trembling, while reminding him that whatever has happened is over and that he will be OK. Your child's reactions need to continue until they stop on their own. This part of the natural cycle usually takes from one to several minutes. Studies have shown that children who are able to cry and tremble after an accident have fewer problems recovering from it over the long term.[3] Your task is to convey to your child through word and touch that crying and trembling are normal, healthy reactions! A reassuring hand on the back, shoulder, or arm, along with a few gently spoken words as simple as "That's OK" or "That's right, just let the scary stuff shake right out of you" will help immensely.

6. Trust in your child's innate ability to heal.

As you become increasingly comfortable with your own sensations, it will be easier to relax and follow your child's lead. Your primary function, once the process has begun, is to not disrupt it! Trust your child's innate ability to heal. Trust your own ability to allow this to happen. If it helps you in letting go, take a moment to reflect on and feel the presence of a higher power, or the remarkable perfection of nature guiding you in the ordinary miracle of healing. Your job is to "stay with" your child, creating a safe container. Use a calm voice and reassuring hand to let your child know that he is on the right track. To avoid unintentional disruption of the process, don't shift the child's position, distract her attention, hold him too tightly, or position yourself too close or too far away for comfort. Notice when your child begins to re-orient to the environment. Orientation is a sign of completion.

7. Encourage your child to rest even if she doesn't want to.

Deep discharges generally continue during rest and sleep. Do not stir up discussion about the mishap by asking questions. Later, the child may want to tell a story about it, draw a picture, or play it through. If a lot of energy was mobilized, the release will continue. The next cycle may be too subtle for you to notice, but the rest promotes a fuller recovery, allowing the body to gently vibrate, give off heat, go through skin color changes, etc., as the nervous system returns to relaxation and equilibrium. In addition, dream activity can help move the body through the necessary physiological changes. These changes happen naturally. All you have to do is provide a calm, quiet environment. (Caution: Of course, if your child possibly has had a head injury, you want her to rest but not sleep until your doctor declares it safe.)

8. The final step is to attend to your child's emotional responses.

Later, when your child is rested and calm—even the next day—set aside some time for her to talk about her feelings and what she experienced. Begin by asking the child to tell you what happened. Children often feel anger, fear, sadness, worry, embarrassment, shame, or guilt. Help your child to know that those feelings are good and that you understand. Tell the child about a time when you or someone you know had a similar experience and/or felt the same way. This will help "normalize" and encourage expression of what the child is feeling. Let the youngster know that whatever she is feeling is OK and worthy of your time and attention. Set aside some time for storytelling or for relating the details of the incident to assess if there are any residual feelings. Drawing, painting, and working with clay can be very helpful in releasing strong emotions. Play, as you will learn in the story of Sammy, works especially well with the pre-verbal or less verbal child. Additionally, silly verses that you and your child can make up with (or without) accompanying illustrations can be a fun way to promote further healing from the myriad emotional wounds children suffer (see Chapter Five).

Now that you know *what to do,* the next step is to increase your skill in *how to do* what you need to do. Although few words are used in the process of de-activating the "trauma charge," the ones that you select carry weight. Just as important as your language, the pace and tone of your voice have the power either to instill confidence that all is well *or* to instill instead unnecessary fright. What do you need to know to avoid the latter and comfortably engage the instinctual brain to set this healing process in motion?

Courting the Reptilian Brain: Language Skills

Since words powerfully influence our capacity to either impede or facilitate healing, the *words* we choose, the *tone* with which we use them, and prudent *pacing* are essential elements of ministering to an overwhelmed child. Because sensation accesses a wordless felt sense awareness of life energy, it has the capability of moving time forward from a "stuck trauma-fixed" past into the fluidity of the present. Therefore, it is extremely important to be skillful in choosing words that engage the instinctual brain, *not* the thinking brain, which can cleverly put up a maze of defenses.

The trick is to awaken the sleeping primitive brain while tiptoeing around the neocortical "higher" brain to avoid stimulating its favorite pre-occupations: rationalization, denial, judgment, and blame. How do we engage this smaller, deeper, ancient, wiser brain without disturbing the giant? Healing instincts can easily be enticed either through play or a sense of playful curiosity.

For tips on honing your skill, first *read* the general guidelines listed below in the *Love Your Lizard Tip Box.* After reading these tips, *practice* the exercise that follows. You might want to pair with a friend, neighbor, spouse, or other family member. You might even invite older children to practice with each other.

LOVE YOUR LIZARD TIP BOX

In order to lure your "inner lizard" during the practice of these exercises, strive to:

- Watch with a sense of playful curiosity as you wait for sensations to develop.
  (It may help to imagine a Polaroid photo as it develops over time: first you see nothing and slowly a few hazy blotches appear until eventually the outlines become crisp and clear and the colorful details materialize.)
- Use neutrality. Refrain from judging what you notice as right/wrong or good/bad.
- Notice and stay present with a sensation until it changes.
- Develop a focused awareness and tolerance for experiencing difficult sensations.
- If practicing with a partner, when he describes sensation, reinforce that he is on the right track. (Example: "That's right ... and as you feel that, what else do you notice?")
- Allow plenty of time. Reptiles are slow, routine, and methodical! Use a slow and gentle voice to encourage an unusually leisurely pace.

- If sensations are too unpleasant or difficult, establish a "safety zone" that can include looking at or connecting with something that brings a sense of comfort. This may include:
  – a place in the body, such as feet, or hands or heart;
  – an object such as a photo, rock, feather, toy, stuffed animal, blanket, or souvenir;
  – something living such as a pet, flower, tree, friend, or grandma;
  – something in the room, such as artwork, a soft pillow, colors or design of fabric;
  – a fantasy place made up in the imagination.

TRACKING SENSATION WITH A PARTNER

Often it is easier to concentrate on internal sensations when you have a partner to help you focus. Choose someone you feel comfortable with and sit across from each other. The object of this exercise is to "track" sensations, with your partner being the safe container. Simply put, "tracking" means developing an awareness of your present state with a focus on noticing how sensations change moment by moment. As images, thoughts, and feelings come and go, make note of them and what impact they have on your sensations. Your partner follows your lead and helps you to expand the details of your sensations and keep you moving forward through time by a few gentle invitational words keeping pace with your rhythm—just like you are learning to do with your child. Then switch places. Your partner will practice tracking sensations and you will practice creating safety, expanded awareness, and movement towards increased fluidity and flexibility. Allow 10–15 minutes each and discuss what you discovered afterwards.

Note: Read the "Language of Sensation" Idea Box below with your partner before getting started. This box serves as a model to ask questions that "turn on" the reptilian brain, rather than the analytical thinking brain. Refrain from asking "Why?" questions.

LANGUAGE OF SENSATION IDEA BOX

Open-Ended

- What do you notice in your body? *rather than* Are you feeling tense?
- Where in your body do you feel that? *rather than* Do you feel it in your chest?
- What are you experiencing now? *rather than* Do you still feel shaky?

Invitational

- What else are you noticing about your eyes? *rather than* Notice your eyes twitching.
- Would you be willing to explore how your foot wants to move? *rather than* It looks like your foot wants to move, or Try moving your foot.
- Would you be willing to stay with that feeling and see what happens next? *rather than* Stay with that feeling.

Explore Sensation With Details

- What are the qualities of that sensation?
- Does it have a size? Shape? Color? Weight?
- Does it spread? Notice the direction as it moves.
- Does the (pressure, pain, warmth, etc.) go from inward to outward or vice versa?
- Do you notice a center point? An edge? (or where the sensation begins and ends?)

Broaden Awareness of Sensation

- When you feel _____ what happens in the rest of your body?
- When you feel that _____ in your _____ how does it affect your _____ now?

Move Through Time

- What happens next? (even if the person reports feeling "stuck")
- As you follow that sensation, where does it go? How does it change?
- Where does it move to (or want to move to if it could)?

> *Savoring and Deepening Sensations*
> - Allow yourself to enjoy that (warm, expansive, tingly, etc.) sensation as long as you'd like.

It Doesn't Have to Hurt Forever

By now, if you have practiced the exercises, you realize that with time, intention, safety, and awareness, unpleasant sensations do and will change. Trauma cannot always be prevented; bad things will happen. That *is* a fact of life. However, trauma can be transformed; it does not have to be a life sentence. The physiological "chain of events" within the body only becomes traumatic because of an interrupted process. Remember that this process is naturally inclined to complete itself whenever possible. The sensation activities and ideas that you have experienced were designed to help you create the opportunity for children to complete the momentum of this process in order to avoid the debilitating effects of trauma.

Creating an opportunity for healing is similar to learning the customs of a new country. It is not difficult—just different. It requires you and your child to shift from the realm of thought or emotion to the much more basic realm of physical sensation. Once again, the primary task is to pay attention to how things feel and how the body is responding. In short, opportunity revolves around sensation.

The youngster who is in touch with internal sensations is likely to notice subtle changes and responses, all of which are designed to help discharge excess energy and to complete feelings and responses that were previously blocked. Noticing these changes and responses enhances them.

Changes in sensation can be extremely subtle: something that feels internally like a rock, for example, may suddenly seem to melt into a warm liquid. These changes have their most beneficial effect when they are simply observed and experienced—*not* interrupted or interpreted. Attaching meaning to them or telling a story about them too early may shift the child's perceptions into a more evolved portion of the brain, which can easily disrupt the direct instinctual connection. It is important, therefore, not to stir up discussion about the incident until *after* the cycles of all biological processes are finished.

Bodily responses that emerge along with sensations typically include involuntary trembling, shaking, and crying. The body may want, slowly, to move in a particular way such as a turning of the head. A kind of "sign language" in the form of gestures or postures may emerge. For example, a leg may be poised as if to run, or an arm might lift to protect the face, or the neck may retract as if to duck.

● Another feature of the level of experience generated by the instinctual brain is the importance of rhythm and timing. Think about it—everything in the wild is dictated by cycles. The seasons turn, the moon waxes and wanes, tides ebb and flow, the sun rises and sets. Animals follow the rhythms of nature. This is evident in their mating, birthing, feeding, hunting, sleeping, and hibernating rituals, which are in direct response to nature's pendulum. This is also true of responses that bring traumatic reactions to their natural resolution.

For human beings, these rhythms pose a two-fold challenge. First, they move at a much slower pace than we are accustomed to. Secondly, they are entirely beyond our control. Healing cycles require an open receptivity as they are observed and respected; they cannot be evaluated, manipulated, hurried, or changed. When given the time and attention needed, children are able to complete the healing cycle.

Resolving a stress reaction does much more than eliminate the likelihood of developing trauma later in life. It also fosters an ability to move through any threatening situation with greater ease and flexibility. It creates, in essence, a natural resilience to stress. A nervous system accustomed to experiencing and releasing stress is healthier than a nervous system burdened with an ongoing, if not accumulating, level of stress. Children who are encouraged to attend to their instinctual responses are rewarded with a lifelong legacy of health and vigor!

After using the eight-step first-aid trauma prevention guide outlined above, you may be wondering if following the process once is adequate. In many cases, it may very well be. With *minor* accidents, falls, and other ordinary happenings, once is generally enough. On the other hand, it is possible that further working through is necessary. Certain behaviors soon after the incident should be suspect.

To find out whether an uncustomary behavior is indeed a traumatic reaction, try mentioning the frightening episode and observe the responses. A traumatized child may not want to be reminded of the predisposing event, or conversely, once reminded, may become excited or fearful and unable to stop talking about it.

Reminders are revealing retrospectively as well. Children who have "outgrown" unusual behavior patterns have not necessarily discharged the energy that gave rise to them. The reason traumatic reactions can hide for years is that the maturing nervous system is able to control the excess energy. By reminding your child of a frightening incident that precipitated altered behaviors in years past, you may well stir up signs of traumatic residue. Remember that a reaction which does not readily disperse may well indicate the need for help from a competent professional experienced in working with children.

Reactivating a traumatic symptom need not necessarily be cause for concern. Rather, it is an opportunity to discharge any residual traumatic energy and complete the process. The physiological sequences involved, primitive as they may be, respond well to interventions that both engage and allow them to follow the natural course of healing. Children are wonderfully receptive to experiencing the healing side of a traumatic reaction. While applying these first-aid measures, trust yourself. Don't think too much about whether you're "doing it right." Your job is simply to provide the opportunities and conditions for the transformation to occur. One way that you learned to provide these healing opportunities was through the vehicle of moving stuck sensations forward in time.

Another way to set the conditions for healing is to help your child "feel and deal" with difficult emotions. After you have helped your child to recover from the initial shock of an accident or event through the vehicle of sensations, next the emotions need tending. Emotions, unlike sensations, are probably more familiar to you. Children can be taught to name and express them in healthy ways from a very tender age. For young children it's easy to label them: mad, sad, glad, and scared. Disgust is another strong emotion that we see expressed by children scrunching their faces, twisting their lips, and sticking out their tongues as if to rid themselves of the awfulness of the situation. Emotions are difficult to hide (as much as we wish we could), as they are revealed by our facial expressions and in our posture and body language. Darwin taught us that primary emotions provide instant communication among all mammals arising from our physiology—yet another survival mechanism!

Sensations and Emotions Are Not the Same!

Although both sensations and emotions are referred to as "feelings," sensations are best described as the sense of the physiological happenings inside us. Developing an awareness of them and purposefully attending to their details helps sensations to change and move out of a fixed state so that we can feel more alive and alert. Sensations simply describe the physical way the body feels (its ins and outs), free of interpretations and judgments. A few examples of sensations are: warmth, numbness, cold, open, shaky, calm, "like Jell-O," stiff, jittery, tense, pressure, "butterflies," and vibration. As emphasized earlier, this is *the only* language the reptilian brain speaks and understands. The capacity to navigate sensations is largely responsible for the internal shifts that lead to transformation. Remember, trauma resides in our biology, not primarily in our psychology. These internal shifts do not originate with our thoughts and emotions, even though the latter are far more familiar to most of us. Because the core symptoms of trauma are physiological, they must be released through the body.

Emotions, like sensations, are physiologically based, and as such hold an energetic charge as well. That is why when a person pays attention to the bodily signals that register anger, for instance, she can pinpoint its origins. It may be experienced as a feeling of "blood boiling," a tightening of the shoulders, or hands fisted in preparation to fight.

Emotional difficulties generally begin as a *combination of thoughts and sensations*. A simple example that could apply to both adults and children might be the following scenario:

> As the teacher announces a surprise test (event), I'm aware of the "butterflies" in my stomach (sensation) and have the idea that if I fail this test, I will fail the course (thought), which then turns to fear (emotion). The idea of failure (thought) can then lead to a racing heart (sensation), shallow breathing (sensation), and heaviness in the pit of the stomach (sensation), which can result in a panic attack.

In the above scene, imagine that you are "practiced" in noticing the first sign of concern (the sensation of butterflies in the stomach) and you befriend these sensations long enough for them to change. In such a case your sensations, which may have been bothersome at first, are more than likely to either settle down or else energize you to act quickly—perhaps to do a very focused five-minute review of notes. You might still have the troubling thought of failure, but now imagine that you skillfully put any such thoughts aside for the moment and return to experience pure sensation with patient watchfulness and curiosity as you wait for a shift to occur. In all probability the sensations will be reduced to a more comfortable level of "relaxed alertness," or the energy of the "nervous butterflies" will be used productively to perform. In either case the outcome would most probably be favorable as the emotion of fear ebbs rather than accelerates, thereby avoiding your worst nightmare—panicking and going blank during the test!

When the sensations underlying emotions are not felt, "tracked," and modulated (or this ability is impaired), feelings can escalate out of control. Rage, hysteria, and terror are examples of emotions run amok. The body simply cannot *contain* the energy and—like a rainstorm breaching the banks of a river, or a bathtub tap that's been turned on and left unattended—an emotional flood spills its contents outside the container of the body. Those unable to modulate affect, whether it's a two-year-old's tantrum or an adult's rage, are literally "beside themselves" rather than "inside themselves."

Parents who practice sensing their physical responses and model "embodied" emotions will be likely to have children whose behavior is not out of control. In our experience with adults who were raised by raging parents, it appears they have difficulty feeling nuances of affect and modulating emotion. Rather than shades of emotion, life is experienced as black or white. Imagine a child or young teen being trapped in the presence of an adult family member on an "emotional binge."

If the parent's nervous system cannot contain its own escalating emotions, what do you think happens to a child's fragile nervous system when it's exposed to rage or hysteria? It is important to remember that children's brain development and their well-being are at stake. Neurons that fire together wire together! The ability to self-regulate affective states is shaped by the interactions a child has with each of its caregivers. The last decade of neuroscience has taught us that a child's brain and nervous system do *not* develop in isolation but as an interactive dynamic with the various external relationships.

Children may deny their emotions. It is not uncommon for children, especially teens, to be disconnected from their feelings or confused about their "mixed emotions." If a child is in shock, particularly after a loss, he may be spared temporarily from his pain and grief through dissociation that (as you learned in Part I) goes part-and-parcel with traumatic reactions. At other times, children hide what they feel. They often fear the repercussions of sharing their emotions with adults. Adults can make it safe for children to open up by showing warmth, a non-judgmental attitude, and by modeling their own openness to expressing authentic feelings.

Whether your child is numb to her feelings due to a grief or shock reaction, has "buried" them, or is purposely concealing them, you can check her facial and postural expressions. Like the old Chinese saying—"a picture is worth one thousand words"—visual and behavioral clues such as glazed eyes, slumped posture, easy startle, or clinginess tell the story. Children may try to mask how they feel with words that are not congruent with what you observe. Trust your own eyes and what the child's *bodily expressions* reveal. The body doesn't lie!

So how *do* you help your youngster with her buried emotions? Now that you have some tools to help a child with stuck emotions or uncomfortable *sensations*, you will better appreciate the subtle differences in helping children complete stunned, frozen, or hysterical *emotional responses*.

Tending to Emotional Needs by Following the Children's Lead

The best way to assist children is, once again, to respectfully follow their lead. If you have practiced the exercises to help build an awareness of and containment for your own experience of sensation, it will be relatively easy to connect with the child on an emotional level. An effective way to begin is to observe—with your eyes, ears, and "felt" sense—what *they need* moment by moment. There is no "one size fits all" recipe. It is an improvisational dance between you and the child. Although there is no rigid formula for learning this dance, the following illustrative examples will assist you in learning how to combine tending to children's sensations *and* emotions.

TALKING THE LANGUAGE OF SENSATIONS AND EMOTIONS

If your young child has been threatened by another child and you notice signs of a freeze response, state what you observe:

"You're shivering and look pretty shaken up. That big bully must have really scared you!" (emotion)

"Thank goodness he's gone and can't hurt you now."

"Grab mommy's hands and feel how warm they are."

"As you feel my hands, notice what happens to *your* hands!" (sensation) (Allow time for *any* change to occur as the child becomes more aware of their body in the present moment, such as warmth, color, shaking, relaxation and/or tears.)

"That's right . . . just let those teardrops fall like soft raindrops. Your body knows exactly what to do to help you feel better."

(After child is obviously relieved and back to looking and feeling like herself) "How wise you were to yell for help!"

"Let's make a plan for what you can do if you ever see him near our house (school, neighborhood, church, park) again."

If your teen's reptilian brain is in "fight" mode after his parents separate:

"I know you told me that you're not mad, but you look tense and your hands are balled up into fists as if you're ready to punch someone!"

Watch for your teen's reactions. Be empathetic rather than combative!

One of two types of responses is fairly predictable:

"Duh! My whole life has been ruined! What did you expect?"

A simple scowl or "Why can't you just leave me alone?"

"Following their lead" would obviously require very different responses from the adult.

In teen response #1, although your teen is very angry, she is still willing to interact even though in "fight" mode. In order to help her to access the more cooperative social engagement system which is the higher "thinking" brain that is able to problem-solve, you must first empathetically join her churned-up lower "feeling" brain to help tune it down a few notches. Start by validating her feelings:

"You're right, sweetheart, your life is different now. You have every right to be angry. It's not your fault."

Again, wait for her lead. When you become deeply attentive and attuned, putting your agenda aside (perhaps of wanting her to feel differently than she does), she will more likely give you the details of what is hurting her. It may surprise you!

*Refrain from ending by making it about *your* feelings. Many parents start out great with wonderful intentions, but then bring up their *own* feelings while the child is still hurting, canceling out the initial progress.

In teen response #2, your teen is beyond upset, and both his thinking and feeling brains are tuned down. The distress is closer to a "freeze" or shocked state, and he is probably shutting down more involuntarily than voluntarily due to overwhelm. He literally feels trapped and hopeless. "Following his lead," in this case, means giving him a way out. It also means showing him that *you* have not given up on him, even though *he* may have given up. To make progress show him that he is not alone! Again, start by validating and mirroring his state:

"It's obvious that you don't want to talk. I just want you to know that I know you're deeply upset . . . and I'm here for you whenever you're ready."

If you're toddler's reptilian brain is in "flight" after witnessing something gory:

"Following her lead" when she's agitated and running around frantically in circles may sound and look something like this:

"Nick's dad got a really messy 'owie' on his leg, huh?"

"Your legs are big and strong! You can run almost as fast as mommy right now! [mom joins her by running next to her and making a game of it.] Feel your legs run! Run, run away . . . you made it! You're safe!" Watch to see if the child looks shocked or engages fluidly in play.

If the child is in shock, shift the game so that your toddler runs to you each time and rests safely in your arms. Notice the eyes. Are they wide-open in surprise? Do her hands cover her eyes so she doesn't have to "see" the nasty mishap? Watch neck movements. Is she able to look all around and change directions as she runs? Does she seem playful and fluid in her movements, or does she run like she's scared stiff and too frozen to have fun?

Continue to follow her lead, while moving time along by noticing what she needs next. If her eyes show a shock reaction, you might make up a "peek-a-boo" type game where she gets to alternate between "looking" and "not looking" at her own pace. Gradually help her to alternate between active "chase" type play and more restful contact with you. The safer she feels with you as she senses your calmness, tone, and proximity, the more she will be able to slow down.

As her "big" energy settles down, you may notice a discharge of the stress energy through a sigh, slight trembling, shaking, or tears. Once the color is back in her face and she seems to be moving out of shock, you can tend the emotions by saying something like:

"Nick's dad's 'owie' scared you so much you had to cover your eyes!" Notice the child's response and what she needs next. Ask yourself:

1. Does my child need to feel safe?

2. Does she need to feel assured that Nick's dad is safe?

3. Does she need to move from the stuck picture of the bloody cut to the next "frame" of the story?

4. Does she need to discharge the emotion through tears or anger?

If your child is still "seeing" the horrible image, you can continue with the "peeking" game and add a stuffed animal or action figure (pretending it's Nick's dad). Empower your child to look at the toy soldier, superhero, or teddy bear's leg a little bit at a time in a playful way. For example, you can model covering your own eyes and then peeking through a small opening in your fingers with just one eye and looking away. Take small incremental steps, "following your child's lead" for pacing until she can examine the toy without distress.

*If your toddler has previously experienced a nasty cut herself, she may be working through her own earlier injury that was re-stimulated. You can make up a little story about it, emphasizing any parts that you know felt comforting to your child—perhaps the hot chocolate she got to make with grandpa when the trip to the hospital was over. Or, the bubbles she got to blow as the stitches came out and the "owie" was all better. When a child feels the safety of the comforting parts of the experience, they are more likely to tolerate the uncomfortable "trauma" parts with more confidence so that rather than going numb this time, they can discharge the excess stress energy. The tears or fears or angry feelings are finally set free with the adult as her witness and her anchor.

The younger the child, the more susceptible she or he is to imagining the worst-case scenario. In the example above, after moving through the initial reaction, you could explain how blood washes "owies" clean and then role-play first aid. The last step would be to check her reaction if you suggest visiting Nick's dad to see how he is doing now that he's had an opportunity to heal. This is the real test of whether or not your child has moved forward in time or is still stuck in the past. If she is stuck, again follow her lead as to what she needs next. You can ask what she thinks Nick's dad's "owie" looks like now. If she is too young to talk, you can ask her if she is still scared and have her nod "yes" or "no" and continue playing "fix the cut" until any residue of shock and fear is gone.

Helping Your Traumatized Child Through Play

If the first-aid guidelines minimized the traumatic effect but did not prevent it altogether, or if your child has been suffering from symptoms caused by an earlier event, you can still help him to complete the energetic cycle. Children show adults what parts of the overwhelming experience are unresolved through their drawings and play.

Parents and others who work with children, such as teachers and medical personnel, are routinely confronted with re-enactments of traumatic events. These situations often surface during playtime. The question is, what can be done to help resolve the feelings of shame, injustice, and betrayal that usually underlie the compulsion to re-enact an experience? Let's take a look at the story of Sammy to see how setting up a play scenario, with the appropriate guidance, can lead to a reparative experience with an empowering outcome. The following is an example of what can happen when a relatively common incident goes awry and is later transformed into success.

The Story of Sammy

Sammy has been spending the weekend with his grandparents, where I am their guest. He is being an impossible tyrant, aggressively and relentlessly trying to control his new environment. Nothing pleases him; he displays a foul temper every waking moment. When he is asleep, he tosses and turns as if wrestling with his bedclothes. This behavior is not entirely unexpected from a two-and-a-half-year-old whose parents have gone away for the weekend—children with separation anxiety often act it out. Sammy, however, has always enjoyed visiting his grandparents, and this behavior seems extreme to them.

They confide to me that six months earlier, Sammy fell off his high chair and split his chin open. Bleeding heavily, he was taken to the local emergency room. When the nurse came to take his temperature and blood pressure, he was so frightened that she was unable to record his vital signs. The two-year-old child was then strapped down in a "pediatric papoose" (a board with flaps and Velcro straps). With his torso and legs immobilized, the only part of his body he could move was his head and neck—which, naturally, he did, as energetically as he could. The doctors responded by tightening the restraint and immobilizing his head with their hands in order to suture his chin.

After this upsetting experience, mom and dad took Sammy out for a hamburger and then to the playground. His mother was very attentive and carefully validated his experience of being scared and hurt. Soon, all seemed forgotten. However, the boy's overbearing attitude began shortly after this event. Could Sammy's tantrums and controlling behavior be related to his perceived helplessness from this trauma?

I discovered that Sammy had been to the emergency room several times with various injuries, though he had never displayed this degree of terror and panic. When his parents returned, we agreed to explore whether there might be a traumatic charge still associated with this recent experience.

We all gathered in the cabin where I was staying. With parents, grandparents, and Sammy watching, I placed his stuffed Pooh Bear on the edge of a chair in such a way that it immediately fell to the floor. We decided that it was hurt and had to be taken to the hospital. Sammy shrieked, bolted for the door, and ran across a footbridge and down a narrow path to the creek. Our suspicions were confirmed. His most recent visit to the hospital was neither harmless nor forgotten. Sammy's behavior told us that this game was potentially overwhelming for him.

Sammy's parents brought him back from the creek. He clung frantically to his mother as we prepared for another game. We reassured him that we would all be there to help protect Pooh Bear. Again he ran—but this time only into the next room. We followed him in there and waited to see what would happen next. Sammy ran to the bed and hit it with both arms while looking at me expectantly.

"Mad, huh?" I said. He gave me a look that confirmed my question. Interpreting his expression as a go-ahead sign, I put Pooh Bear under a blanket and placed Sammy on the bed next to him.

"Sammy, let's all help Pooh Bear."

I held Pooh Bear under the blanket and asked everyone to help. Sammy watched with interest but soon got up and ran to his mother. With his arms held tightly around her legs, he said, "Mommy, I'm scared."

Without pressuring him, we waited until Sammy was ready and willing to play the game again. The next time grandma and Pooh Bear were held down together, and Sammy actively participated in their rescue. When Pooh Bear was freed, Sammy ran to his mother, clinging even more tightly than before. He began to tremble and shake in fear, and then his chest opened up in a growing sense of excitement, triumph, and pride. The next time he held on to mommy, there was less clinging and more excited jumping. We waited until Sammy was ready to play again. Everyone except Sammy took a turn being rescued with Pooh. Each time, Sammy became more vigorous as he pulled off the blanket and escaped into the safety of his mother's arms.

When it was Sammy's turn to be held under the blanket with Pooh Bear, he became quite agitated and fearful. He ran back to his mother's arms several times before he was able to accept the ultimate challenge. Bravely, he climbed under the blankets with Pooh while I held the blanket gently down. I watched his eyes grow wide with fear, but only for a moment. Then he grabbed Pooh Bear, shoved the blanket away, and flung himself into his mother's arms. Sobbing and trembling, he screamed, "Mommy, get me out of here! Mommy, get this thing off of me!" His startled father told me that these were the same words Sammy screamed while imprisoned in the papoose at the hospital. He remembered this clearly because he had been quite surprised by his son's ability to make such a direct, well-spoken demand at two-plus years of age.

We went through the escape several more times. Each time, Sammy exhibited more power and more triumph. Instead of running fearfully to his mother, he jumped excitedly up and down. With every successful escape, we all clapped and danced together, cheering, "Yeah for Sammy, yeah yeah! Sammy saved Pooh Bear!" Two-and-a-half-year-old Sammy had achieved mastery over the experience that had shattered him a few months earlier.

Discussion: *What Might Happen to Children Who Don't Receive Help?*

If Sammy hadn't received help, might he have become more anxious, hyperactive, clinging, and controlling? Or would his trauma possibly have resulted in bed-wetting or in avoidant behaviors later? Might he have violently re-enacted the event as a teenager or young adult? Or would he have developed physical symptoms like tummy aches, migraines, and anxiety attacks without knowing why? All of these scenarios are possible, and equally impossible to pin down. We cannot know how, when, or even whether a child's traumatic experience will invade his or her life in another form. However, we can help protect our children from these possibilities through prevention. This "ounce of prevention" will help them develop into more confident and spontaneous adults.

Children like Sammy rarely get the help they need immediately following an incident such as this one. Yet youngsters can easily be supported at this critical time while they literally shake and tremble while working through the immobility, shame, loss, and rage. Through guided play, children can safely discharge the intense energy mobilized in a failed attempt to defend themselves against a frightening and painful experience. But they must do this in the context of support and protection from you. If this discharge doesn't happen, later therapeutic interventions that focus on the "story" of what happened will be limited and may cause further distress.

Discussion: *What's the Difference between Traumatic Re-Enactment and Therapeutic Play?*

It is important to appreciate the differences between traumatic play, traumatic re-enactment, and the re-working of trauma that we saw with Sammy. Traumatized adults often re-enact an event that in some way represents, at least to their unconscious, the original trauma. For example, a victim of childhood sexual abuse might become promiscuous, a sex offender, or else avoid the possibility of sex altogether.

Similarly, children re-create traumatic events through their play. While they may not be aware of the significance behind their behaviors, they are deeply driven by the feelings associated with the original trauma. Even if they won't talk about the trauma, traumatic play is one way a child will tell his or her story of the event. It is a *sure* clue that your child is still troubled.

In *Too Scared To Cry*, Lenore Terr describes the responses of three-and-a-half-year-old Lauren as she plays with toy cars. "The cars are going on the people," Lauren says as she zooms two racing cars towards some finger puppets. "They're pointing their pointy parts into the people. The people are scared. A pointy part will come on their tummies, and in their mouths, and on their . . . [she points to her skirt]. My tummy hurts. I don't want to play anymore."[4]

Lauren stops herself as her bodily sensation of fear abruptly surfaces. This is a typical reaction. She may return over and over to the same play, each time stopping when the fearful sensations in her tummy become uncomfortable. Some psychologists would say that Lauren is using her play as an attempt to gain some control over the situation that traumatized her. Her play does resemble "exposure" treatments used routinely to help adults overcome phobias. But Terr cautions that such play ordinarily doesn't yield much success. Even if it does serve to reduce a child's distress, this process is quite slow in producing results. Most often, the play is compulsively repeated without resolution. Unresolved, repetitious, traumatic play can reinforce the traumatic impact in the same way that re-enactment and cathartic reliving of traumatic experiences can reinforce trauma in adults.

The re-working or renegotiation of a traumatic experience, as we saw with Sammy, represents a process that is fundamentally different from traumatic play or re-enactment. Left to their own devices, most children will attempt to avoid the traumatic feelings that their play evokes. With guidance, Sammy was able to "live his feelings through" by gradually and sequentially mastering his fear. Using this stepwise renegotiation of the traumatic event and Pooh Bear's support, Sammy was able to emerge as the victor and hero.

A sense of triumph and heroism almost always signals the successful conclusion of a renegotiated traumatic event. By following Sammy's lead after setting up a potentially activating scenario, joining in his play, and making the game up as we went along, Sammy got to let go of his fear. It took minimal adult direction and support to achieve the unspoken goal of aiding him to experience a different outcome.

Five Principles to Guide Children's Play Towards Resolution

This analysis of Sammy's play experience is designed to help you understand and apply the following principles when working with your own children.

1. Let the child control the pace of the game.

Earlier in this chapter, you learned the importance of attuning to your child's needs. Healing takes place in a moment-by-moment slowing down of time. That is true for everyone! Your child's pace may be very different from yours. In order to help your child feel safe, follow her pace and rhythm; don't subject her to yours. If you put yourself in your child's "shoes" through careful observation of her behavior, you will learn quickly how to resonate with her. Let's look at Sammy's behavior.

What Sammy "Told" Us

By running out of the room when Pooh Bear fell off the chair, Sammy told us quite clearly that he was not ready to engage in this new activating "game."

What We Did to Help Sammy Feel Safe

Sammy had to be "rescued" by his parents, comforted, and brought back to the scene before continuing. We all had to assure Sammy that we would be there to help protect Pooh Bear. By offering this support and reassurance, we helped Sammy move closer to playing the game.

What Sammy "Told" Us

When Sammy ran into the bedroom instead of out the door, he was telling us that he felt less threatened and more confident of our support. Children may not state verbally whether they want to continue, so take cues from their behavior and responses. Respect their wishes, as well as the mode in which they choose to communicate. Children should never be forced to do more than they are willing and able to do.

What You Can Do to Help Your Child

Slow down the process if you notice signs of fear, constricted breathing, stiffening, or a dazed (dissociated) demeanor. These reactions will dissipate if you simply wait quietly and patiently while reassuring your child that you are still by their side and on their side. Usually, your youngster's eyes and breathing will tell you when it's time to continue.

EXERCISE

Read Sammy's story again and pay particular attention to the places that indicate his decision to continue the game. There are three explicit examples in addition to the one cited above.

2. Distinguish between fear, terror, and excitement.

Experiencing fear or terror for more than a brief moment during traumatic play will not help the child move through the trauma. Most children will take action to avoid it. Let them! At the same time, be certain that you can discern whether it is avoidance or escape. The following is a clear-cut example to help you develop the skill of "reading" when a break is needed and when it's time to guide the momentum forward.

What Sammy "Told" Us

When Sammy ran down to the creek, he was demonstrating avoidance behavior. In order to resolve his traumatic reaction, Sammy had to feel that he was in control of his actions rather than driven to act by his emotions.

How to "Read" Your Child's Experience

Avoidance behavior occurs when fear and terror threaten to overwhelm your child. This behavior is usually accompanied by some sign of emotional distress (crying, frightened eyes, screaming). Active escape, on the other hand, is exhilarating. Children become excited by their small triumphs and often show pleasure by glowing with smiles, clapping their hands, or laughing heartily. Overall, the response is much different from avoidance behavior. Excitement is evidence of the child's successful discharge of emotions that accompanied the original experience. This is positive, desirable, and necessary.

Trauma is transformed by changing intolerable feelings and sensations into palatable ones. This can only happen at a level of activation that is similar to the activation that led to the traumatic reaction.

How to Support Your Child

If your child appears excited, it is OK to offer encouragement, and continue as we did when we clapped and danced with Sammy.

However, if your child appears frightened or cowed, give reassurance but don't encourage any further movement at this time. Be present with your full attention and support; wait patiently while the fear subsides. If your child shows signs of fatigue, take a rest break.

3. Take one small step at a time.

You can never move too slowly in renegotiating a traumatic event. Traumatic play is repetitious almost by definition. Make use of this cyclical characteristic. The key difference between renegotiation and traumatic play is that in renegotiation there are small incremental differences in the child's responses and behaviors.

What Sammy "Told" Us

When Sammy ran into the bedroom instead of out the door, he was responding with a different behavior indicative that progress had been made.

Monitoring Your Child's Progress

No matter how many repetitions it takes, if your child is responding differently—such as with a slight increase in excitement, with more speech, or with more spontaneous movements—he is moving through the trauma. If the child's responses appear to be moving in the direction of constriction or repetition instead of expansion and variety, you may be attempting to renegotiate the event with scenarios that involve too much arousal for your child to make progress.

How to Help Your Child Take One Small Step at a Time

Ground yourself and pay attention to your sensations until your own breathing brings a sense of calm and confidence in your spontaneity.

Slow down the rate of change by breaking the play into smaller increments. This may seem contradictory to what was stated earlier about following your child's pace. However, attuning to your child's needs as a wise adult presence means preventing your child from getting overwhelmed. In order to do this, you may need to slow down the pace of the game.

If your child appears wound up, it's OK to invite some healing steps. For example, when re-negotiating a medical trauma, you might say, "Let's see, I wonder what we can do so (Pooh Bear, Dolly, etc.) doesn't get so scared before you (the doctor/nurse) give him the shot?" Often children will come up with creative solutions that demonstrate what was missing from their experience.

Don't be concerned about how many times you have to go through what seems to be the same old thing. (We engaged Sammy in playing the game with Pooh Bear at least ten times. Sammy was able to renegotiate his traumatic responses fairly quickly. Your child might require more time.) You don't need to do it all in one day! Resting and time help your child to internally reorganize his experience at subtle levels.

If these suggestions don't seem to help, re-read this chapter and look more closely at the role you are playing and observe more carefully how your child is responding. Perhaps there are some signals you are missing. Once your child begins responding, forget your concerns and enjoy the game!

4. Become a Safe Container.

Remember that nature is on your side. For the adult, perhaps the most difficult and important aspect of renegotiating a traumatic event with a child is maintaining your own belief that things will turn out OK. This feeling comes from inside you and is projected out to the child. It becomes a container that surrounds the child with a feeling of confidence. This may be particularly difficult if your child resists your attempts to renegotiate the trauma.

If your child resists, be patient and reassuring. The instinctive part of your child wants to re-work this experience. All you have to do is wait for that part to feel confident and safe enough to assert itself. If you are excessively worried about whether the child's traumatic reaction can be transformed, you may inadvertently send a conflicting message to your child. Adults with their own unresolved trauma may be particularly susceptible to falling into this trap.

Don't let your child suffer as a result of your own unresolved experiences. Ask someone else to help your child and don't procrastinate in seeking help for yourself!

5. *Stop if you feel that your child is genuinely not benefiting from the play.*

Sammy was able to renegotiate his experience in one session, but not all children will. Some children may take a few sessions. If, after repeated attempts, your child remains constricted and does not move toward triumph and joy, **DO NOT** force the issue. Consult qualified professional help. Healing trauma in children is an immensely important task and, at times, can be complex. This is especially true when there were multiple events, the stressor was prolonged, and/or the youngster was unsupported due to the circumstances. As mentioned, trauma becomes increasingly complicated if the child was betrayed by a trusted adult.

Conclusion

The idea of developing a sensation vocabulary was probably an unfamiliar concept to you. Unless you have studied "Focusing" (a therapeutic "felt-sense" method developed by Eugene Gendlin, PhD)[5] or have practiced certain forms of meditation designed to bring about a deeper awareness of bodily responses (such as Vipassana), this may have seemed rather strange. After all, the language of sensation is not taught in the school curriculum, although we would like it to be! (See Chapters Eleven and Twelve for suggestions and activities that educators and school-based mental health professionals can use to help traumatized students.) If this novel bodily approach seems alien to you, we sincerely hope that you will, at your own pace, use as much as feels comfortable, little by little.

As we conclude Chapter Four, we cannot stress enough the importance of becoming comfortable and fluent by completing and repeating, if necessary, the exercises designed to help you and your family. By noticing your own changing sensations in everyday situations, you will be able to alleviate your own stress. You will also increase your ability to feel centered more often than not and to return to a sense of calm more quickly and automatically. Remember that the language of sensation is the only language that our "old" brain understands. Since the energy of trauma is the energy of survival regulated by the deep structures within the brain, we *must* speak its language in order to heal and prevent the wounds of trauma in ourselves and our children. In Chapter Five you will learn how to make up simple verses and use artwork to help rebuild "resources," empowerment, and joy after your child has weathered an overwhelming situation.

Sensations, Images, and Feelings: Using Animal Imagery and Rhymes to "Resource," Empower, and Transform Trauma Symptoms

C hapter Five shows how to help children become aware of and strengthen resources already within them. The creative use of animal imagery and rhymes goes a long way with children. Use our suggestions as models to make up your own verses to help your child. Children can illustrate the verses with colored pencils, markers, or paint. If they are old enough, they can make up their own verses and stories, or you can make them up together.

What Are "Resources" and Where Do They Come From?

Everybody has resources. It can also be said that every *body* has resources. The *Oxford Thesaurus* offers no fewer than twenty-five synonyms for "resource." Among those listed are: initiative, ingenuity, talent, imagination, cleverness, aptitude, qualifications, and strength. Also listed under Colloquial British usage is "gumption," and the slang for resource is "guts." In addition to personal qualities, including "intestinal fortitude," assets such as wealth, property, and possessions are included.

Our definition of resources includes all of the above and more. Resources are whatever support and assist physical, emotional, mental, and spiritual well-being. They can be obvious or hidden.

They can be active or forgotten. They can be external, internal, or both. Children are born with internal resources but are dependent on adults (an external resource) to mirror and nurture them so the resources will become tangible. In this way, a child can call upon her own reserves, as needed, from an accessible reservoir.

Examples of a child's **external resources** might be:

- Loving caregivers who can be depended upon to meet development needs

- Other nurturing family members, friends, and pets

- Access to the natural environment (grassy meadows, parks, sandy beaches, mountains, forests, the ocean, etc.)

- Objects and other things that stimulate and/or comfort the senses, such as color, light, space, soft blankets and cloth, music, textural variety, cuddly stuffed animals and other huggable toys

- Access to an enriched environment with developmentally appropriate toys, music, construction and art materials, books, etc.

- A caring community that aids the child's development such as cultural, social, athletic, and/or religious organizations that mirror the child in healthy ways. These might include scouting, team sports, boys' and girls' clubs, children's activity groups at places of worship, and such things as hobby groups and theater troupes. For young children, it could be playgroup or preschool; and for the teen it can include volunteer service groups to improve the environment or bring cheer to the infirm and elderly, as well as clubs based on common interests ranging from intercultural exchange to political activism.

Examples of a child's **internal resources** might be:

- Natural gifts and talents such as a special propensity for science, music, art, movement, math, athletics, crafts, academics, animal husbandry, leadership, construction, linguistic fluency, gymnastics, overall intelligence, etc.

- Energetic and kinesthetic qualities such as large and/or small muscular agility, healthy constitution, energy, sense of humor, charisma in making friends, and a sense of balance, etc.

- Personality characteristics such as wit and wisdom, initiative, ingenuity, dependability, integrity, generosity and thoughtfulness, etc.

- An internal spiritual center that brings a sense of wholeness and peace through connection to something greater than oneself.

The division between internal and external resources is somewhat artificial. Music that is sung or played to a child is only a resource if it is perceived as pleasurable. Once sound enters the child's body through vibration in the ears, bones, and elsewhere, it then registers as an internal resource. On the other hand, if the sound is disturbing it is not a resource.

This rule holds true of anything that we as adults might conceive of to support and nurture our children. If it doesn't register in the body as something healing, comforting, or pleasurable, it is not a resource for them no matter how good our intentions.

The feelings of confidence, physical well-being, and/or team spirit that one child may get from the opportunity to participate in sports may feel aversive to her sibling. While grandpa may bring joyful laughter to little Billy, grandpa's presence may be barely tolerated by his older brother.

In other words, resources are uniquely personal. To be considered a resource, the "support" must be perceived internally as creating pleasure and healthy development. When it is registered in the bodily memory as resource, the "imprint" or impression of the sensation can be called upon to help relieve pain in times of emotional upheaval, stress, and overwhelm. For example, years after Billy's favorite grandpa has died, an object or photograph reminding him of their deep connection may bring up warm and moving sensations around Billy's heart that sustain him during turbulent times. That's a resource!

EXTERNAL RESOURCES/INTERNAL RESOURCES

(You will need two pieces of paper and a pen or pencil.)

1. Take one of the pieces of paper and fold it in half vertically. On one side of the fold, begin to make a list of your external resources; on the other side of the fold, list your internal resources. If you're not sure where to put it, place it on both sides.

2. As you glance at your list, notice which resources "jump out" as the strongest supports for you in times of stress. Take some time to focus on each, one at a time, waiting to feel what *sensations* and *emotions* emerge, and where in your body you feel them. Notice if they register as muscular strength, warmth around the heart, power in the belly, "grounding" in the lower body or pelvis, etc. List them or journal about them to emblazon them in your sensory memory.

3. Notice if there are categories of missing or weak resources, such as few satisfying relationships or lack of a spiritual center. Make a list of ways to begin to enrich your life by adding resources to close the gap. For example, if you feel inadequate physically and have little companionship, you might join a Tai Chi group or ask an acquaintance to become a "walking buddy." If these activities prove to be a source of more connection to yourself and others, add them to your list.

4. Using the other piece of paper, make a list of *your child's* external and internal resources, or help an older child to create his or her own lists following Steps 1–3. Put an * next to the resources that bring the most comfort during stress. Help your child to deepen their awareness of the sensations that accompany resources. Be careful not to impose *your* ideas on your child, but instead to be open and receptive to their ideas and needs.

The Body as Deepest Resource

If you have taken the time to feel the sensations accompanying one or more of the resources on your list, you probably have already discovered that the best resource of all is the ability of your body's sensations to change. For example, if you are feeling tension in your shoulders and place your awareness there long enough, they might just relax on their own. Or, you might notice that your arms are also tense and that your hands are fisted and ready to fight. Next, you may notice the emotion of anger emerge from sensations that are coupled with an image from something that happened long ago. As you sit with these sensations, noting *that in this moment* these feelings are coming from *inside* you, it is likely that next you notice a shifting in your musculature from rigidity to flow. An idea may emerge regarding reasonable steps to complete any unfinished business; or, it could be that as the sensations shift, the issue becomes a *non-issue* and gently releases.

Other examples of shifting sensations would be if you are feeling upset and notice trembling in your knees and legs. Or perhaps you are having difficulty falling asleep and are plagued with "restless leg" and feel like running. Again, as you take time to notice these sensations and imagine your legs, knees, ankles, and feet running to a favorite place (perhaps a meadow, a park, or to a favorite friend or relative's house), you may feel a shift from feelings of vulnerability to feelings of strength in your limbs. If you are feeling jittery before a party, exam, or public speaking engagement, take the time to ground by feeling how your feet contact the floor and notice your breath. Then, surrender to the "jitters" while orienting to the room (rather than blocking the jitters), and you may soon experience a change from nervousness to excitement.

It is this ability to move or "pendulate" between bodily sensations of helplessness and sensations of empowerment that builds resourcefulness. This pleasurable rhythm of expansion and contraction instead of shutdown and overwhelm is our birthright.

When your child is encouraged to experience and "track" his sensations, this innate rhythm, which may have been lost in trauma, can be restored. Adeptness at returning to a sense of fortitude and competence after feeling vulnerable creates a sense of confidence that is the foundation of healthy self-esteem. It builds inner stability because it is not based on the "ups and downs" of life (external events); rather it is based on a resilient nervous system in action (internal events). This ability of the body to shift out of a state of shutdown, anxiety, aggression, helplessness, or feelings of estrangement into a sense of vitality, joy, hope, initiative, and connection is the **best resource** of all!

Different Sensations That Can Help Your Child Heal

Children need their caregivers to make ample time for them to experience, through bodily sensations, specific elements that relate to their recovery from things that have overwhelmed them. These include sensations related to empowerment, such as strength, grounding, and centering. Strength is most easily experienced by children in the muscles, in the bones, and in the stomach and belly (intestinal fortitude). When they run, hop, jump, skip, dance, and perform somersaults and other gymnastic feats, they experience their strength and agility. Strength can be experienced as the ability of a child to defend himself and feel the energy of his natural aggression when presented with a threat. This can be observed as a lengthening of the spine to appear taller, the flexing of muscles in the arms to push away, and a flow of strength in the legs to kick.

Grounding is a feeling of a solid connection to the earth that enables a child to be directly connected to his or her body's sensation. This is in contrast to feeling "flighty," "spaced out," disconnected, or out of the body altogether. Centering is a feeling of connection to oneself in a balanced relationship to gravity. It is the feeling that no one can distract you, literally or figuratively. You feel solid enough in your body that you cannot be pushed off balance, and if you are, you bounce back. Generally, the center is in the belly below the navel.

Using Rhymes and Stories
to Prevent and Heal Trauma

The nature and animal rhymes, stories, and illustrations in the following section were created for use with children from approximately three to eleven years of age. They may, however, appeal to youngsters slightly older or younger and can be adapted in any way that suits your child. Different verses are crafted for different reasons. A rationale for each set is presented before the actual verses. After the verses, look for suggestions on how to get the most out of them. Enjoy!

How to Use the Verses That Follow

1. Read the verses silently first.

2. Read the notes that follow with ideas about how to use the verses interactively with your child to get optimum results.

3. Read the verses to your child slowly, observing any responses.

4. Taking cues from your child, try the exercise suggested. Take time to help them process any sensations or to discuss their responses and questions, whichever seems the most appropriate.

5. Do not rush! You might only read one paragraph per day. The important thing is to use the verses as a starting point, utilizing only what is relevant for your child's age, stage of development, and situation.

The nature-based rhymes and images that follow are accompanied by drawings from Juliana DoValle, then age eleven. They were designed specifically to help children build empowering resources. The first verse, "The Magic in Me," will help your child connect with his own body through the grounding and centering exercise that follows. (These rhymes are read aloud in *It Won't Hurt Forever: Guiding Your Children Through Trauma*. This CD audio series by Sounds True is a recommended companion to this book).[1]

THE MAGIC IN ME

We're going to play, but before we begin,
I want you to find your own magic within.
Just take some time to feel and to see
All the great things that your body can be.

Pretend you're a tree with your branches so high
That you can reach up and tickle the sky.
What's it like to be strong like a big old oak tree?
With roots in your feet and your leaves waving free?

Suggestion: After reading the above verses to a child, ask them to stand up and pretend that they are the "big old oak tree" or their favorite tree, if they have one. Give them the time to stomp and explore their connection with the ground. They can pretend that they have long roots growing out the bottom of their feet deep into Mother Earth. Ask them to tell you how it feels to have roots that go deep into the ground.

The verses continue:

Or you can be like a river that flows clean and free ...
From high in the mountains right down to the sea.
Your breath can flow through you, just like a river
From your head to your toes, feel yourself quiver!

Now you're connected to the earth and the sky
It may make you laugh, it may make you cry.
It doesn't matter when you go with the flow ...
Your branches up high, and your roots way down low.
Hear the breath in your body, if you listen it sings
Now you are ready for whatever life brings!

Suggestion: After the child (or children) explore their connection to the ground, alone or in a group, have them pretend that the wind is blowing through their leaves and branches. Encourage them to hold their arms up high, sway to and fro to find their center, and move their arms, feeling their resilience. You might have them bend their "branches" from side to side, noticing how close to the ground they can get before they lose their balance. Have them find their center again and again. You might play music of various speeds. They can experience different paces and rhythms, imagining gentle breezes and tropical storms. After modeling a few possibilities, encourage them to create their own movements.

Animal Poems

The next set of verses uses animal imagery to provide children with the resources of power and strength. Children need this to transform trauma into a positive experience. For example, when children pretend to chase away the scary saber-tooth tiger with their spears, they feel the strength in their bodies to defend themselves against threat.

SCARY THINGS HAIRY

A long time ago, before there were cars
Before we had TV, people watched stars.
We huddled together inside of a cave
It was cold, it was dark, and we had to be **BRAVE**.
   [deep voice]

We had to stay hidden, outside it was scary,
With saber-tooth tigers and other things hairy.

They tracked us down when out we'd go
'Cause they could run fast, and we ran too slow.
Sometimes that hairy, giant-toothed bunch
Pounced down upon us and had us for lunch. (Ugh)

We found fire and then we had heat
But still it was hard to get something to eat.
So we invented weapons and tools
Then **we** *could start making some of the rules.*

With weapons and tools we went out in the sun
We hunted and gathered and even had fun!
And when the saber-tooth tiger came near
We chased him away by throwing our spears.

Now it's time for you to pretend
That you live in the wild with family and friends!
Feel the **strength** in your legs and the spear in your hand
As you chase the saber-tooth over the land.

Can you feel it right now, that spear in your hand?
What's it like when you throw it, where does it land?
Throw it right now *with all* that you've got
Feel the **power** in your ARM, like a giant slingshot.

Feel the **power** in your LEGS; it grows as you run.
Your legs are strong and jumping is fun.
Do you get the feeling your legs are like springs
When you chase a tiger, or other big things?

What does it feel like inside when you're **BIG** and
    you're **STRONG**?
When you can chase animals all the day long?
It's lots more fun than when they're chasing you
Or maybe you think that might be fun too!

Suggestion: Stop at any verse to play "pretend" along with your child or group of children. Be sure to allow plenty of time for experiencing the powerful feelings in their arms and legs as they pretend to chase the tiger. You might have them jump or run in place, imagining a time when they felt their body's strength and power. Ask the child to describe these feelings. The idea here is not merely for your child to run or visualize running, but rather to take sufficient time to notice the sensations in their muscles, heart, lungs, and so on. Children love to flex their arm muscles to "show off." Give them a chance to exaggerate their strength and tell you about a time they felt victorious.

The next set of verses about Rapid T. Rabbit will help children engage their innate "flight" resources, which will enable them to feel the power, exhilaration, and the crucial energy discharge of a successful escape from danger.

HOW FAST CAN YOU RUN?

Charlie Coyote is ready for lunch
Being quite clever, he follows a hunch
He crouches down quietly in the tall grass
Then patiently waits for a rabbit to pass.

Rapid T. Rabbit bounds down the trail
She stops to eat clover, then washes her tail
Up jumps coyote, he makes a great leap
Hoping to catch Rapid Rabbit asleep.

Rapid moves quickly, with a jig and a jog
With a zig and a zag, then she hides in a log.
Coyote is clever, Coyote is tough
Coyote is fast, but not fast enough.

Have YOU ever had to run fast and escape?
Can you feel your LEGS, their **strength** and their
   shape?
You have a body that's healthy and strong.
You can jump high and you can jump long.

Feel the **power** in your arms, they swing as you run
Feel the **b·e·a·t** of your HEART and the **warmth** of
   the sun.
Feel the **b r e e z e** on your face; does it tickle your hair?
Feel your HANDS and your KNEES as you fly through
   the air.

Now you have come to a **safe** hiding place
Take a **deep breath** because you won the race!
How does it feel in your TUMMY and CHEST
Now that you've found a safe place to rest?

Pay attention to all the movement within
How does it feel right after you win?
Be aware of your breath, it comes in then goes out,
When you feel great, you might even shout!

Suggestion: The verses above can be used to deepen awareness of two important elements to overcome trauma—the bodily sensations of escape and safety. In the first part of this rhyme, allow time for children to deepen the sense of power as they feel the instinctual forces of running and jumping (and any others that emerge, such as ducking, twisting, kicking, "zigging" and "zagging" etc.). When children associate movement with strength and the power to avoid threat, they develop self-esteem that comes from their core. This builds into the kind of confidence that remains even when children are under stress because it has become an automatic "motor memory," like riding a bicycle. In the second part of this rhyme, children get the chance to pause to experience what it feels like to be safe inside their body.

This rhyme continues with a further exploration of the location of sensations of safety:

> *Do you feel the tingling and the warm energy?*
> *Where do you feel it ... can you show it to me?*
> *When you feel glad, you're full of happiness*
> *Can you tell me, inside you, where your*
>   *happiness is?*
>
> *When you get scared what does that feel like inside?*
> *Where is the feeling that makes you want to hide?*
> *Does your throat get tight, is breathing a strain?*
> *How about your tummy, do you feel any pain?*

Suggestion: Pause to take time to explore body sensations and have children point to and/or name the different parts of the body where they feel safety and where they feel fear. If old enough to draw, they can make a "gingerbread person" outline of a body on a big sheet of paper. Have the child choose different-color markers to make squiggles and shapes in various parts of the body to indicate feelings of safety and feelings of fear. See the image near the end of Chapter Eight for a sample drawing and color chart (under the subheading "Giving Emotional Support ...").

If the fear takes more room than the safety, find ways to help the child feel safer and spend time developing "islands of safety" inside. This can be done by reminding her of a time she felt safe, showing a photo of a favorite family member she feels safe with, giving her a favorite toy or stuffed animal, holding, rocking and hugging or any safe touch that the child responds positively to, etc. You can also have her "build" her own hiding place with pillows and sheets or cardboard boxes and play hiding games.

The last part of this rhyme helps move sensations "stuck" in discomfort. These verses give specific suggestions for what a child can do if this happens:

If you pay attention to the places you point to and name
Does it change how they feel, or do they stay the same?
If they stay they same, here's what **you** *can* **do**
To help the stuck feelings **move** *right out of you.*

[You might even close your eyes for a minute or two]

See if there's a color *or* shape *you can name,*
As you watch it closely, it becomes like a game.
Your feelings may move from place to place.
Watch *the fear go without leaving a trace.*

Imagine that you're at your favorite place,
It's quiet *and* safe *in your own* special space.
Who would you like to be there with you?
Your mother, your father, or Winnie the Pooh?

Your brother, your sister, your dog, or your cat?
Or perhaps Dr. Seuss, with his cat in the hat.
Would you like to be held by someone, just right?
You can R E L A X *and* breathe easy *as they hold*
   you tight!

Or, would you like to have someone close by
Just in case you get **MAD***; or you need a* good cry*.*
Sometimes crying can make you feel better,
It's just like laughing, only it's wetter!

Suggestion: To help children release uncomfortable feelings that seem to stay stuck, such as a pain in the tummy or a feeling of heaviness in the chest, use the verses (along with the following suggestions) for releasing the sensations. With eyes open or closed, have the child focus on the sensations for a minute or two. Gently ask if the "knot," "owie," "pain," "rock," or whatever they are experiencing has a size, shape, color, or weight. Allow sufficient time between questions for the child to quietly feel and process images and sensations. Next, guide her to the present moment by asking how the "owie" feels NOW. Continue, proceeding slowly, until you notice the "stuck energy" beginning to open up by closely observing the child's body language for subtle shifts (especially more relaxed breathing and posture), as well as listening to their words.

Towards the end of this section of verses, where the rhyme asks children who or what they want with them, take the answers seriously. Take some time to validate their wishes and explore their emotions. Allow time to assess and support any needs that come up, especially to help reinforce a sense of safety and security by being a good container for any tears, anger, sadness, or fears that may arise. This simply means calmly listening and acknowledging that you are present for whatever they are feeling. Your job is not to "fix" the child's feelings but to give your undivided attention so that they can feel what's real for them, and process feelings so the sensations and emotions can move forward on their own as nature intended.

In the next set of verses, Oscar Opossum demonstrates that the "freezing response" (or "playing possum") is a very important survival mechanism. When children can't fight or run, this response protects them. This instinctive behavior is, unfortunately, often judged by humans to be cowardly or weak. The Oscar Opossum rhymes have the purpose of letting your child know that their "freeze" behavior is not only normal, but smart.

When youngsters listen to the story of how Oscar outwits Charlie Coyote by pretending to be dead, two things will be accomplished. First, the "freezing response" will be seen as positive and empowering; second, the identification with the opossum's ability to come out of his frozen state without fear of his own bodily reactions can help children move through their own frozen states without fear or shame. This understanding can lead to better feelings about themselves when they've experienced these helpless and troubling involuntary states of being. It is also reassuring that with a little time and patience those feelings give way to a "letting go" that may be shaky at first but soon leads to relief and, perhaps, even a smile!

In the rhyme below, Oscar Opossum shows children how he temporarily freezes to protect himself. When the "coast is clear," Oscar easily comes out of this natural protective state by simply shaking and trembling away all the "boiling energy" he was holding inside.

OSCAR OPOSSUM

Oscar Opossum is **slow as molasses**
He plods right along, while everyone passes
When he sees coyote, he **can't run***, so instead*
He rolls up in a ball and **pretends that he's dead!**

Oscar **escapes***, you see, by* **lying quite still**
Not *like the rabbit who* **runs** *up the hill!*
Oscar has all his energy **BOILING** *inside*
From holding his breath to pretend that he died.

Can you **pretend** *that you're Oscar rolled up in a ball?*
You're **barely breathing***, and you* **feel very small.**
It's cold and it's lonely as you hold on tight
Hoping coyote will not take a bite!

Suggestion: Pretend with the child that you are both being chased by something bigger and faster than you. Ask the child what he wants to "chase" him. It might be a tiger, bear, other beast or monster. Stop running and, instead, roll up in a tight ball holding as still and quiet as possible to "trick" the beast into passing you by because you are so well hidden or look like you've died! Take time to explore sensations without talking and hold still for as long as you can so that there is a sense of release and relief when you finally let go, get your breath back, and let all your muscles relax.

The verses continue with questions to help explore normal emotional responses that may arise before and after coming out of the "freeze response."

> *Do you remember ever feeling this way?*
> *You wanted to run, but you had to stay.*
> *Were you SCARED, were you **sad**, did it make you*
> **MAD***?*
> *Can you tell what you felt to your mom or your dad?*

Suggestion: Children may "open up" with their true feelings and thoughts after you read the above verse. Allow sufficient time for them to share. Pause, observe, and listen to the child carefully, validating any and all emotional expressions that may emerge. After acknowledging their feelings, making it safe for them by refraining from judging or fixing, you might help the child explore more deeply. Ask open-ended questions, such as "What else do you feel?" or use statements such as "Tell daddy what else about that scared you." Or simply, "Tell mommy more."

The Charlie Coyote and Oscar Opossum verses continue:

YOU DON'T HAVE TO BE AFRAID

Oscar Opossum has to lie low
But inside *his body, he's ready to blow.*
When Charlie Coyote finally takes off
Oscar Opossum gets up *and* shakes off.

See Oscar tremble, *see Oscar* shake
Just like the ground in a little earthquake.
After he trembles and shakes for a while
He feels good as new, *and walks off with a* SMILE!

Coyote has gone, now get up *and run [whisper]*
But first *you might* tremble *and* shake *in the sun.*
Before long you can jump, you can skip, you can stomp
Or play in the meadow and have a good romp.

Feel *the* blood flow *through your* HEART *and*
  your CHEST
Now you are safe *and now you can* rest!

Suggestion: Have the children pretend to shake and tremble, first exaggerating the movements by dramatizing them. After some fun active movement, have them lie down and rest, noticing the energy and flow inside their body. This will help them to feel more subtle sensations that will most likely be pleasant and warm.

The next set of verses, "Bowl of Jell-O," is silly and intended to playfully expand children's awareness of their inner landscape of sensations.

BOWL OF JELL-O

*Can **you pretend** you're a big bowl of Jell-O?*
Red, purple, green, or even bright yellow?
Now make-believe someone gives you a jiggle
*And you start to **shake** and **tremble** and wiggle!*

As your fingers tremble, feel your heart pound,
Now feel the shaking go down to the ground,
*Feel the **trembling** in your arms, the **warmth***
  in your chest,
Don't try too hard; you're doing your best.

*In your belly and legs, feel the **vibration**,*
Let it flow like a river, it's a pleasant sensation!
*Feel the energy **move** from your head to your toes,*
Feel the strength in your body, as the good feeling
  grows.

Suggestion: Continue by making up your own verses (together with the child if she is old enough), appropriate to her situation and needs. Verses like the ones above can help children experience bodily sensations without becoming unduly frightened. Through this heightened body awareness, the discharge of energy necessary to return to a normal state can occur safely and playfully.

In this last section, there are six couplets listing common events that can significantly frighten children. It is important to monitor the child's reaction and pause if she reacts strongly through agitation, distracting behavior, or silent withdrawal. Take all the time they may need to talk, to feel, to draw pictures, to be held or rocked, move freely, or to play.

THINGS THAT CAN SCARE YOU

What is it like when things happen so quick
That there's no time to run, to hide or to kick?

And you have to tense up and freeze just like ice—
Maybe that's happened to you once or twice.
What kinds of things can make you feel frozen?
Here is a list of at least a half dozen:

1. *Did you ever get lost at the mall*
   When you were little, and lonely and small?

2. *Maybe you went for a car ride and out of the blue*
   Another car crashed right into you!

3. *Could be you were sick then along came a nurse,*
   When you saw the needle it made you feel worse!

4. *Maybe one day you were playing around,*
   When a big earthquake came and shook up the ground.

5. *Or during recess, the game was a blast,*
   Then the school bully shook his fist as he passed!

6. *They stitched up your knee so you'd be good as new,*
   It hurt a lot, and the needle scared you!

In the last set of rhymes, "Things That Can Scare You," you may have been surprised by how seemingly minor some of the scenes described in the couplet verses appear to you as an adult. If you had this reaction, before passing the lines off as petty, read the paragraphs below about worry to help you see what it's like to experience the world through the eyes of an anxious child, or sense what it's like to "walk in their shoes" when they are alone with their fears.

Why Children Worry

Children have magical imaginations. When something bad happens, this quality puts them at a disadvantage. Not having the same resources as adults to gather the facts needed to make a realistic assessment, their imaginations *run wild*. Often youngsters picture a variety of worst-case scenarios. Bessel van der Kolk identified children's worry about the safety of a family member or friend following an incident as one of six factors involved in the complexity of their reaction to trauma.[2] They worry about the pain and hurt of others, especially when there has been an accident or illness. Children also worry about their own safety and that the bad experience will happen again, even if highly unlikely. They may develop false beliefs that interfere with their sense of safety. One child, for example, revealed the mistaken belief that cancer is contagious.

Because worry runs rampant with children, it is important for adults to find out exactly what they are worried about. Whether you are preparing your child for an imminent surgical procedure or a long separation, it is a sure bet that your child has worries that need to be addressed. Some may be reality-based, while others may be fantasy. Adults are usually surprised to learn that children's worries can be allayed rather easily because so often they are far-fetched. For example, one little boy thought that because his parents were getting divorced, *he* would be homeless. Once his mom and dad explained that instead of being homeless, he would actually have *two* houses, worry evaporated instantaneously. If you don't ask your child about his/her worries, you will never know the hidden burden your child may be carrying unnecessarily.

Conclusion

Chapters Four and Five offer the essential tools to gently guide children through their overwhelming sensations and emotions. This is the best prevention and treatment of trauma that we know because it works with the root of the problem—bringing a child out of shock and back to feeling alive, empowered, and in tune with herself.

What you have learned is applicable to any circumstance involving overwhelm. It integrates animal imagery and other rhymes and verses to teach parents and children how to develop and expand external resources. Even more importantly, the animal tales were designed to help children access and deepen the internal resources within their own bodies. The poems are meant to be used interactively and to be a source of adventure, fun, and connection between adults and children.

Part III expands on this foundational knowledge by analyzing *specific* commonly occurring situations that almost all children face, at some time or another, as they grow up. The chapters in Part III each deal with different categories of potentially traumatic events and are complete guides by themselves. They can be read out of sequence. It is suggested, therefore, that you glance through the topics in Part III and read the chapters in the order most relevant for your family or situation.

WORKBOOK FOR COMMONLY OCCURRING SITUATIONS

Now that Part II has guided you through the basics, such as being a good "band-aid," learning the language of sensation, and empowering children through the use of animal imagery and other resources, you are ready for Part III, which gives step-by-step de-activation procedures for specific potentially traumatic situations. Since not every circumstance can be covered within the scope of this guide, we have chosen to include the types of common events that are encountered by just about everyone at some time.

Chapter Six covers specific first aid for accidents and falls, which are an inevitable part of childhood. Chapter Seven is a guide for parents and medical personnel, filled with tools to prepare children for medical and surgical procedures, with the goal of preventing or reducing traumatic reactions. It is hoped that medical staff and parents can work together as a team in the best interest of children. Chapter Eight aims to assist parents and counselors as they help children face the painful experience of separation and loss through divorce, death, and abandonment. Chapter Nine will help you recognize if a child has been sexually frightened or traumatized in order to help him or her begin the healing process sooner rather than later. You will also learn ways to communicate with children in order to decrease their likelihood of becoming vulnerable to assault.

CHAPTER SIX

First Aid
for Accidents and Falls

A ccidents and falls are probably the most commonplace source of potential trauma. They are a natural part of growing up. In fact, as infants turn into toddlers, they *must* fall in order to learn to walk. It is actually the sense of moving from equilibrium to disequilibrium and back to equilibrium that spurs growth. Although falling and accidents are unavoidable nuisances, living with trauma symptoms afterwards can easily be avoided. Remember, too, that what may appear insignificant to an adult can be shocking to a child even though there is no physical injury. Also, traumatic impacts can be easily hidden by a child who believes that "not being hurt" or "being a big girl or big boy" who doesn't cry will keep parents happy.

Of course, not all falls are overwhelming. Nevertheless, even in a minor fall, extra energy is aroused just before "the point of no return" in an attempt to right oneself before it's too late. When the body first senses that it is off-balance, it tends to do a bit of acrobatics to prevent what could be a painful landing. Especially when there is no injury or scare, minor mishaps are a gift in that they provide the opportunity for any child to enhance her sensory awareness and practice "first aid" as she builds resiliency as a kind of "emergency preparedness" for whatever life brings.

In any case, the "First Aid for Accidents and Falls" guide listed below will appear somewhat familiar, as it overlaps with the basics that you learned in Chapter Four. The "old" material will serve as a review of the "nuts and bolts" of trauma prevention, no matter what the event; while the new material pertains specifically to accidents and falls. The following guidelines can be used whatever your perception of the severity of the mishap. Beyond a doubt, an ounce of prevention is worth a pound of cure.

First Aid for Accidents and Falls: Basic Guidelines

1. Attend to your responses first. (This step, as outlined in Chapter Four, cannot be overemphasized!)
Take time to notice your own level of fear or concern. Next, take a full deep breath, and as you exhale slowly sense the feelings in your own body until you are settled enough to respond calmly. An overly emotional or smothering adult may frighten the child as much, or more, as the fall or accident itself. Remember the analogy of "putting your own oxygen mask on first" when sitting next to a child on the plane.

2. Keep the child still and quiet.
If safety concerns or the nature of the injuries require that the child be picked up or moved, make sure that he is supported properly. Carry the child—do not allow him to move on his own, even though he may be able to. Remember that he is probably in shock and does not realize the extent of the injury. Because the child's body is likely to be surging with adrenaline, this might be difficult. Use a firm, confident voice with a ring of authority that conveys in a loving manner that you are in charge of protecting him and know exactly what to do. Keep the child comfortably warm by draping a sweater or blanket over his shoulders and torso. If there appears to be a head injury, do not allow the child to sleep until your doctor gives the "OK."

3. Encourage plenty of time for safety and rest.

This is particularly true if the child shows signs of shock (glazed eyes, pale skin, rapid or shallow breathing, disorientation, overly emotional or overly tranquil affect or acting like nothing has happened). Do not allow him to jump up and return to play. Help the child know what to do by modeling a relaxed, quiet, and still demeanor. You might say something like, "After a fall, it's important to sit (or lie) still for a while and wait until the shock wears off. Mommy's not leaving your side until that happens." A calm confident voice communicates to the child that you know what's best.

4. Hold your child.

If the child is an infant or very young, you will probably be holding him. Be sure to do so in a gentle, non-restrictive way. Avoid clutching tightly, as well as excessive patting or rocking, as it might interrupt the recovery process by interfering with natural bodily responses. To communicate support and reassurance to an older child without disturbing the process, it is suggested that you place your hand in the center of her back, behind her heart, or on the side of her upper arm near the shoulder. Healing touch can transmit "groundedness" as *your* calmness is directly communicated in a tactile way to the child.

5. As the shock wears off, guide the child's attention to her sensations.

(Steps 5 and 6 serve as a review from Chapter Four and are at the heart of preventing and healing trauma.)

The language of recovery is the language of the reptilian brain— which is the language of sensations, of time, and patience. Softly ask the child how he feels "in his body." Repeat his answer as a question—"You feel okay in your body?"—and wait for a nod or other response. Be more specific with the next question: "How do you feel in your tummy (head, arm, leg, etc.)?" If he mentions a distinct sensation, gently ask about its location, size, shape, color, or weight. Keep guiding your child to stay with the present moment with questions such as "How does the rock (sharpness, lump, "owie," sting) feel now?" If they are too young or too startled to talk, have them point to where it hurts.

6. Allow a minute or two of silence between questions.

This may be the hardest part for the adult, but it's the most important part for the child. This allows any cycle that may be moving through to release the excess energy to completion. Be alert for cues that let you know a cycle has finished. These cues include a deep, relaxed spontaneous breath, the cessation of crying or trembling, a stretch, a yawn, a smile, or the making or breaking of eye contact. Wait to see if another cycle begins or if there is a sense of enough for now.

7. Do not stir up discussion about the accident or fall during initial first aid.

Do not stir up discussion about the mishap by asking questions to alleviate your own curiosity, anxiety, or "need to know." The reason for this is that the "story" can disrupt the rest needed for discharging the excess energy through involuntary sensations. Later on the child may want to tell a story about it, draw a picture, or play it through. If a lot of energy was mobilized, the release will continue. The next cycle may be too subtle for you to notice, but rest (rather than talk or play) promotes a fuller recovery, allowing the body to gently vibrate, give off heat, exhibit skin color changes, etc., as the nervous system returns to relaxation.

These changes happen naturally. All you have to do is provide the calm, quiet environment. This can be challenging when family members gather around asking, "What happened?" In response, you might simply and politely say, "Not now ... we'll talk about it later after your sister rests a while." Talking about the details of the accident to your child (or in front of your child) can aggravate an already activated nervous system, adding an additional layer of unnecessary fear. This can abort the healing process! If siblings want to express their care, they can follow your lead by saying something calming, such as "Stay real still so you can be good as new soon" or "It's okay to cry, little brother. It can make you feel better." Refrain from shaming statements, such as "I told you that you'd get hurt playing on those stairs!" Also, refrain from judgmental statements, such as "You are such a clumsy kid!"

8. Continue to validate the child's physical responses.

Resist the impulse to stop the child's tears or trembling. But keep contact with her, reminding her that whatever has happened is over. In order to return to equilibrium, the child's distress needs to continue until it stops on its own. This part usually takes from one to several minutes. Studies have shown that children who are able to cry and tremble after an accident have fewer problems recovering from it.[1] Your job is to use a calm voice and reassuring hand to let the child know that "It's good to let the scary stuff shake right out of you." The key is to avoid interrupting or distracting your child, holding her too tightly or moving too far away.

How Long Does It Take?

With minor tumbles and accidents, the steps outlined above may be all that is needed. This relatively easy first-aid protocol can be followed right on the spot where the calamity occurred. For example, if your child has twisted an ankle while skating on the front sidewalk, grab some ice and a blanket and minister to him at the site of the fall (if safe).

It can take anywhere from five to twenty minutes for all the physiological cycles to complete. It's not unusual for the trembling to start *after* the blanket and ice are applied as the child feels tended and safe. Teeth may begin to chatter after a few minutes of rest, and/or tears of release may begin to roll down the cheeks before a sigh of relief completes a cycle.

When the fall or accident creates a medical emergency, the protocol can be used by the parent while in the car or ambulance on the way to the medical facility or hospital. Once your child discharges the energy, you can prepare him for what to expect at the doctor's office.

Choose your words wisely when preparing for the medical procedure. Use simplicity and honesty framed in a way that will benefit your child. You can do this by using therapeutic suggestion. For example, if your child needs stitches, let him know that they will make the "owie" heal faster and better. Discuss and practice what you will do to focus attention away from the pain. For example, have your child squeeze your arm and imagine that with every squeeze special "numbing cream" makes the pain float away like a balloon. See "The Power of Language to Soothe and Heal" in this chapter for more on timing and choosing words wisely.

The Purpose of Touch When Helping a Child in Shock

While paying close attention to a child's bodily responses, you will be most effective in supporting each reaction as it emerges by taking special care to not interrupt the natural cycle for coming out of shock. If you are caring for an infant or young child, hold him safely on your lap. If it's an older child, you can place one hand on her shoulder, arm, or middle of the back. Physical proximity of a caring adult can help a child to feel more secure. Be careful, however, not to hold the child too tightly or in such a way as to stop the natural discharge that will follow. The focus of intention when touching a child is to convey:

- Safety and warmth so the child knows she is not alone;

- Connection to your grounded and centered adult presence;

- Confidence that you have the ability to help the child surrender to his sensations, emotions, and involuntary reactions as he moves towards release and relief by not interrupting his process due to your own fears;

- Trust in your child's innate wisdom that allows her body to release as she moves towards resolution and recovery as her own person at her own pace.*

Your body language is important. Because we are social animals, we read each other's clues to assess the gravity of a situation, especially in an emergency. Your children not only read your expression but rely on it for their sense of safety. Translated into practical terms, this means that the look on the adult's face can foster either safety or terror.

In order to minimize unnecessary upset with your own wide-eyed expression (when what you really want is to be a steady anchor), familiarize yourself with what to expect. Become mindful of your own involuntary responses. Practice brings poise. Opportunities in modern life abound to practice first aid on your own self. For example, after a near collision in your car, pull over to a safe place and track your sensations until you feel a sense of relief and completion. This can also be done after witnessing violence in the media, or experiencing a fall, injury, or shocking news or other stressful event. You can even practice during a scary movie.

The Power of Language to Soothe and Heal

When something dramatic happens out of the blue, it can put a person in an altered state in which they are particularly susceptible to therapeutic suggestion. Toddlers, preschoolers, and primary-school youth tend to be in an altered state simply by the nature of

---

* Remember, no matter the age of the child, she has the advantage of millions of years of evolution on her side. The survival mechanisms of her reptilian brain are at work; they do not require words, thoughts, or preparation. These mechanisms simply require an adult who understands the language of this ancient wisdom to support, rather than interrupt, the process as the sensations change through time and the nervous system returns to a healthy state.

early childhood. And, of course, with medical procedures that require anesthesia they are in an induced altered state. Skillfully selected words and the timing and tone of voice with which you use them have the power to speed recovery or further complicate and compromise the healing process. This is true whatever the nature of the frightening event.

In *The Worst Is Over: What to Say When Every Moment Counts* by Acosta and Prager, the authors cite numerous examples of verbal first aid that salvaged seemingly hopeless situations, stopped serious bleeding, and even prevented scar tissue from forming in burn victims![2] We know how easy it is for words to either put us at ease or make us tense. Words can turn an ordinary experience into a romantic one, raise or lower blood pressure, and bring either laughter or tears.

There is a useful framework for choosing words wisely. When an accident happens, first say what you see in simple, honest language that the child will understand and which acknowledges that *you understand* what it must be like to be in his shoes.

Then say something that will help to accomplish the following:

- Establish rapport by acknowledging what happened with compassion.

- Ensure that the child feels safe and connected rather than alone.

- Reassure them that whatever happened is over (if it is!)

- Help "move time ahead" from the past to the present by guiding them to notice sensations until there is a discharge and shift.

- Remind them of their resources.

For example, after a fall resulting in a small cut with heavy bleeding, you might simply say something like this: "That fall really took you by surprise, huh? That tiny cut sure is bleeding! Let's clean it up good and I'll hold a cool cloth on it to stop the bleeding and make it feel better. Then you can pick your favorite colored band-aid. I know just what to do so you'll be good as new."

Then, after the immediacy of the injury has been tended, look for bodily clues such as pale skin, cold sweaty palms, shallow breathing, and wide eyes. The child is probably still somewhat stunned and should be sitting or lying down. You might say, "The hard part's over; your cut is healing already! But, honey, you're still a bit shook up ... Daddy will stay right here with you until the [shaky or numb, etc.] feeling wears off. You might get a little shivery or jittery or wiggly ... or maybe even a little giggly. It could be that some more tears will come. I'll stay with you (or you can sit on my lap) until the very last tear (or jitter or shiver) is gone. Then we can make up a silly story (or draw a picture if your child enjoys this more) about what happened to share with Mommy."

EXPERIENCING THE POWER OF WORDS TO HEAL

Not only are words powerful at the time they are spoken, in times of openness and vulnerability they become etched in our memory. Take a moment now to recall words that have shaped the peaks and valleys of your life, and you will have an experiential understanding of just how penetrating they are and how they have textured your existence.

Part A

1. Write a paragraph or two, using all of your senses to describe everything you can remember about a kind person who used words, touch, gestures, and/or actions to comfort and soothe you after something terrible happened. Recall in as much detail as possible what it was that made you feel better and heal faster.

2. Find a comfortable place to rest. Recalling what you just wrote, notice how you are feeling in your body. Take some time to focus on sensations, emotions, thoughts, and images. Notice what happens to your body's expression and posture as you sink into the experience. Note what sensations let you know that this memory was a pleasurable one!

   It's possible that when you did this exercise, an unpleasant experience surfaced also. That's because the amygdala, the part of the brain that imprints these memories, is an "equal opportunity employer." Intense emotional experiences are registered, whether they are pleasant or unpleasant. It may be that you recalled insensitive treatment when you required nurturing. This can be especially hurtful when it was a parent or other close family member who didn't understand your needs.

If this is the case, you can do the following exercise to have a restorative experience. As you heal your own wounds, you are less likely to react to your child blindly by repeating the family pattern. Perhaps that is exactly why you are reading this book!

Part B

1. Write a paragraph or two, using all of your senses to describe everything you can remember about an insensitive person who used words, touch, gestures, and/or actions that made things worse instead of soothing you after something terrible happened.

2. Without giving any more thought to what you described, allow an opposite image to erase the image, words, sensations, feelings, etc. Don't censure what pops up. Allow the new scene to provide as many healing details as possible. Let yourself hear the words now and see the actions that you needed then—do it in this moment, just as you would do for your child. What words, touch, gestures, and actions are bringing you relief? What in particular is comforting you, making you feel better and soothing any wounds from the past?

3. Find a comfortable place to rest. Recalling your restorative image, notice how you are feeling in your body. Take some time to focus on sensations, emotions, thoughts, and images. Notice what happens to your body's expression and posture as you sink into the experience. Note what sensations let you know that this new memory, using your adult resources, is a pleasurable one!

Addressing the Emotions
Through Listening and Storytelling

In more serious or complex situations, your child may have lingering emotional responses that need tending. Children and adults alike often feel embarrassed or awkward about falling, especially if it was in front of peers. They may feel shame or guilt, especially if the accident caused damage to property, clothing, or special possessions. They may have these same feelings due to medical or other expenses that were incurred.

After you have completed giving emotional first aid and the child is rested and calm, set aside some time to discuss feelings about what she experienced. This can be done later that day, the next day, or whenever new emotions emerge. In addition to shame and guilt, children often feel anger, sadness, and fear. Help the child to know that those feelings are normal. Listen carefully and reflect back what was said so that the child knows that you heard and understood. Refrain from trying to fix or change their feelings. Trust that feelings change by themselves when parents or other supportive adults can "hang out" with a child. This is what makes discomfort more tolerable.

Once you have connected with the child such that you are certain that she feels understood, she will most likely be more receptive to your inspiration and guidance. It is at this point that sharing a similar experience that you or someone you know has had might be helpful. Another idea is to make up stories and verses like the ones provided in this book. For example, "The Story of Dory," below, is about a girl who had a bad fall from her bicycle and became overwhelmed. One way to use this story is as a starting point or model for you and the child to make up one of your own. Customize verses to your particular child's age, needs, and situation.

Another way to use the story below (and others like it) is as an "assessment" tool. Parents, teachers, and therapists can use stories and drawings to assess whether a particular situation has left lingering distress. Read "The Story of Dory" aloud slowly while carefully watching your child's reactions, as well as noticing what he has to say. Do his eyes widen like saucers? Does his body stiffen? Does he say, "I don't like this story" and try to slam the book closed? Or, does he get "squirrely" and agitated? If your child identifies with some of Dory's reactions to the fall, the likelihood is that he has had a similar experience and relates to her feelings. When you observe a reaction, stop the story and help your child experience the sensations and emotions that he is struggling with by being present as a calm, non-judgmental witness until the uncomfortable emotional expression begins to change to relief.

After reading the story, you can have your child illustrate it and make up a picture story of his or her own (as a young friend of ours did for this book). If children are too young to draw a picture, have them scribble to indicate how they feel. Provide an assortment of colored crayons or markers and model for them how to make different lines, such as squiggles, circles, jagged, wavy, and straight. They will automatically draw in a way that reflects their feelings.

"THE STORY OF DORY"

Sit back, relax, and I'll tell you a story.
The hero, my friend, is a girl named Dory.
She plays first base on her Little League team,
To have a new bike was her favorite dream.

On her last birthday, this girl's dream came true.
She got a new bike that was bright shiny blue.
She jumped on the bike and rode down the block,
Faster and faster, then the bike hit a rock.

She felt the wheels skid, and she flew off the seat,
And then she landed real hard on the street.
She hit the pavement with a big thud,
Then she saw that her knees were covered with blood.

She started to cry, but the sound wouldn't come,
She couldn't breathe, and her body went numb.
When she noticed the blood on her knees,
Like Oscar Opossum, she started to freeze.

Later that day Dory felt bad.
She also felt sad, and then very mad.
On her new bike things had happened so fast
That she could do nothing at all, except crash.

It wasn't her fault, but she took the blame,
When she thought of her bike, Dory felt shame.
If something like this ever happens to you,
Can you tell mom and dad what you might do?

Suggestion: Take time to discuss with your child how she might deal with a similar situation. Remind her of the lessons learned earlier from our animal friends, Charlie Coyote and Oscar

Opossum, and the importance of letting the sensations and feelings move freely through the body.

After you shake, you can jump, you can run,
You can hide like a rabbit or play in the sun.
You can kick, you can cry, you can laugh, you can feel,
You can dance, you can sing, or do a cartwheel!

Help with Constructing the Story

Earlier in this chapter, you were given step-by-step guidance to help prevent traumatic symptoms immediately after an event. Frequently this is all that is needed. However, when the event was particularly threatening to your child, symptoms may still develop despite your best efforts. Stories and drawings are especially useful when a child's upset continues after you have given "trauma first aid."

When using stories, generally the adult needs to tell the story of what happened (from the adult's perspective). The next step is to invite the child to add to this story or tell his version. A child who at first is reluctant to talk will usually be glad to chime in to "correct" the adult with his version by saying, "No, that's not what happened; here's what really happened!" Be sure to look for certain universal elements that need to be addressed whenever a child is overwhelmed. You can find those crucial elements in the example of Dory above. They include:

- The excitement before the accident
  (Verses: "On her last birthday, this girl's dream came true" and "She jumped on the bike and rode down the block.")

- The scary parts before the actual impact (where energy is mobilized)
  (Verses: "Faster and faster," "hit a rock," "wheels skid," and "flew off the seat.")

- The actual impact of the accident
  (Verses: "landed real hard" and "hit the pavement with a thud.")

- The resulting physical injury (if there is one) and horror
  (Verses: "her knees were covered with blood.")

- The freeze response
  (Verses: "the sound wouldn't come," "she couldn't breathe," "her body went numb," and "like Oscar Opossum, she started to freeze.")

- The emergence of mixed emotions
  (Verses: "Dory felt bad. She also felt sad, and then very mad.")

- The emergence of inevitable guilt and shame
  (Verses: "she took the blame" and "Dory felt shame.")

- The discharge of activation from overwhelming
  sensations and emotions
  (Verses: "you can shake, you can jump, you can run, you
  can kick, you can cry, you can laugh, you can feel.")
- The resolution of traumatic activation with a successful
  outcome
  (Verses: "You can dance, you can sing, or do a
  cartwheel!")

Adults are frequently puzzled by intense reactions that appear disproportionate to the nature of the event. It is important for you to take your child's reactions seriously. Sometimes children are communicating lingering upset from an earlier unresolved incident that was provoked. Take the opportunity to work it through. This is more likely when the recent event stirs up reminders of an earlier situation in which the child was more vulnerable due to age. The body records and remembers everything from infancy and toddlerhood. Conscious memory may be lacking since preverbal experiences have no narrative. You may be surprised at what concerns, guilt, or shame emerge from constructing these informal stories and from your child's artwork.

More on Working with Stories

Sometimes, especially with very young children, it is best to use a make-believe child, animal, or doll as a substitute for them in the story. This may initially help to give needed distance from the event to make it less frightening. In the story be sure to include some of the scary stuff *one element at a time.* For example, if your child fell down the stairs, if it's not too disturbing, add in the part about the stairs if your child leaves it out. Observe your child closely to see if he identifies with the reactions and feelings that the make-believe character in the story has. Stop the story to help your child process any sensations and emotions that get triggered. If she gets anxious, follow the same steps as recommended for first aid. For example, have her point to where she feels the scary feelings and ask her to tell what color, size, or shape they are. Remind your child that you will stay with him as his sensations change their shape and size and finally disappear! Insert any of the elements listed above that are missing and seem to be essential for resolution of the trauma.

Working with Accidents and Falls
When Symptoms Are Present

When working with falls, big soft pillows can be helpful in giving a child the opportunity to practice falling safely. With your hands to support the child securely, gently guide a slow fall, pausing if she seems to stiffen or startle. It's often best to start with the child sitting and gently rock him from side to side and then forward and backward. Then he can "fall," a little at a time, into your supporting arms and onto the pillows.

This type of "play," which involves a guided fall with a safe landing, helps to develop good protective reflexes and restores confidence. Recovering from a fall involves re-establishing equilibrium responses. A child-size fitness ball can be used for practicing going from balance to off-balance and returning to balance. Again, use soft pillows on the floor around the ball so there is a safe landing. Have the child start with eyes open and feet spread apart to form a solid base. Gently rock the child from side to side and see what emerges. If more challenge is needed, have her close her eyes the next time. Once there is a sense of falling, all parts of the body engage to prevent the fall. When prevention is not possible the arms, elbows, wrists, hands, knees, legs, ankles, and feet end up in all types of configurations in an attempt to buffer the impact. Don't be surprised if you see the whole "ballet" sequence performed through this type of "pillow play" as you catch your child from a free fall.

If the child needs more distance from the fall because the fear is too intense, you can begin by using a doll or favorite stuffed animal to create a scenario similar to the child's real-life experience. An example would be: Babar the elephant falls backwards out of the high chair. Refer back to the story of Sammy in Chapter Four to assist you in setting up the scene. As the child role-plays, be sure to watch his responses closely. Always leave him with a sense that he can succeed, giving him only as much support as is needed. Gradually introduce the idea of the child taking turns with the stuffed animal and/or with you or her siblings.

Tips for Working with Automobile Accidents

When a child has been involved in any kind of accident, you may eventually need to reintroduce (and "desensitize") her to the ordinary objects and experiences that remain "charged." The child's behavior when the offending object or experience is seen or mentioned will let you know which elements of the accident bring up painful or overwhelming reminders. Sometimes the connection is obvious; at other times it is not. Sometimes the "charge" doesn't develop into full-blown symptoms until the period of shock and denial has worn off. The main idea is to introduce the "activators" slowly so as not to overwhelm the child further. The following example of working with an automobile accident can be adapted for a variety of ages and situations.

After an automobile accident, the infant's or toddler's car seat could be brought into the living room. Holding the infant in your arms, or gently walking with the toddler, gradually move towards it together and eventually place the child in the seat. The key here is to take baby steps, watching and waiting for responses such as stiffening, turning away, holding the breath, or heart rate changes. With each gentle approach towards the avoided or fear-provoking encounter, the same step-by-step procedure outlined in steps 4 through 8 at the beginning of this chapter can be used as a guide. The idea is to make sure that your pacing is in tune with the child's needs so that not too much energy or emotion is released at once. You can tell if the latter is occurring if the child seems to be getting more "wound up." If this happens, calm them by offering gentle reassurance, touching, holding, or rocking. Stop if the child shows signs of fatigue. The whole sequence does not need to be done at once!

More Tips: Using Toys, Art, and Crafts

If a child is in preschool or school-aged, he can make a drawing or play with toys, showing, for example, how the cars crashed together. For some children the feel of modeling clay helps them to be in touch with their aggression and with their bodies in general as they take control of and mold this soft material. (There are all kinds of non-toxic, easy clean-up, modern-day clay substitutes, such as Model Magic by Crayola.) A younger child may be more likely to express her feelings in colors or crude shapes and "blobs" rather than in specific pictures or objects.

You might remember the story in Chapter Three of Sandra, the girl who couldn't eat after she moved away from Grandma's into a brand-new house. She wasn't yet able to draw a square. Instead, Sandra made a plain line to show her new house. With hand-over-hand help, the other lines were slowly added. Next, she pointed to her tummy to show me where she hurts when she's in her new house. Sandra was given paper for "homework" to draw pictures when she felt scared. She ended up drawing wavy figures that she called "ghosts." Her mother then placed a soft hand on Sandra's tummy and comforted her with soothing words until her tummy ache went away, as was modeled the week before during an office visit. With only two office calls and mother doing follow-up with her at home, Sandra regained her appetite and started eating solids again in no time at all! The trick was to work back and forth, shifting focus between her drawings and her inner sensations, until her terror subsided.

Whether art materials or toys are used, it is important to monitor and help minimize repetitive behaviors because repetition can reinforce, rather than resolve, feelings and symptoms. If a child seems "stuck" and perseverates (such as crashing the cars wildly into each other over and over again), have him pause after a moment or two and check in to find out what he is experiencing in his bodily sensations and feelings.

The idea is to gradually allow the energy from these feelings to release, guiding the child to a more successful outcome. For example, together with the child, slow the cars down. Perhaps you can say, "Show daddy which way the cars should go if they went slow enough so that they didn't have the crash" or "Be the driver and show me how to steer fast so the cars won't crash." Use creativity and watch the child's creativity blossom as she resolves any incomplete responses. You might use cardboard boxes that the child can actually sit in rather than using little toy cars. Decorate the boxes and use them to play "Bumper Cars," with the object being to steer away in order to avoid the "crash." The important thing is to have fun as your joint imaginations run wild.

These same techniques can be used with artwork by asking the child to describe the sensations he feels as he shares his drawings or sculptures with you. The purpose is not primarily to elicit the story, but to have the child sense and discharge any residual trauma energy or express any troubling emotions that spontaneously emerge from their artwork. Frequently, children (or adults) don't know why they feel the way they do until the worry, anger, or sadness shows up in their art. Because play, crafts, drawing, and painting are activities that use the "other side of the brain" instead of the thinking, calculating, "rational" side, images that champion the healing process surface from the unconscious—just like what happens during dreamtime.

Puppets, dolls, or miniature toy figures can also be useful in assessing if any trauma indications exist, and helping a child move through them. For example, after a child's physical injuries have healed following a surgery, a miniature bed, surgical mask, medical instruments, gauze, band-aids, cotton balls, etc., can be provided for play. Be sure to include play figures that represent a child, parents, doctors, and nurses. As your child role-plays with you, watch his reactions closely. With the suggestions you have learned thus far, gently guide the child to sense his body's reactions and to release pent-up energy through movement or discharge. If the child was pinned down, have her notice the way her body wanted to move but couldn't. Let her show you how to make that movement now that it's safe to do so!

Using Music to Heal Trauma

Music is a wonderful healer. You can purchase music that creates different effects and moods, from soothing lullabies to energizing rhythms. If you choose music to stimulate and excite, be sure to follow it with music that helps to relax, rest, and settle the nervous system. Alternating or "pendulating" between a state of heightened activity and calm trains children's nervous systems to de-activate and self-regulate over time.

Children are natural music makers. In addition to listening to music, they can make their own. Homemade shakers can be fashioned with empty soda cans or cardboard tubes from empty toilet paper rolls filled with lentils or beans and then sealing them with tape. Drums can be made from old oatmeal boxes or coffee cans. Remo, Inc.,* a music company, makes drum sets called "Sound Shapes" that are round, flat, and lightweight. They take up very little space, making them easy to transport. The set includes

---

* (Contact www.remo.com. Remo, Inc., is located in the U.S., and Remo Europe is in London.)

a variety pack of six sizes and colors ranging from 6 to 18 inches in diameter. You can also purchase several smaller Sound Shapes separately for your youngest music-makers. Making music is especially fun in groups. As children dance, shake, march, or drum, they are beginning to find their own rhythm, pace, expressive movements, and grounding.

Art and music are well suited to teens. Collages made from magazines they like can be especially revealing for them as they create an identity through this medium. They can take music they like and change the lyrics to fit their own life situation. They can rap and write poetry with or without illustrations. A parent, teacher, or school counselor can gently guide them towards creating solutions. If every line is repetitiously "dark," hopeless, and stays stuck in that mode, ask the teen to tell you about what images, activities, or thoughts lift them out of the darkness. Encourage them to integrate resources into their writing so that it becomes more balanced between despair and new possibilities.

Poetry, song-writing, and creative story-writing come naturally to many adolescents. Diaries and journals can be provided to encourage daily entries as expressive outlets.

Summary

At the end of this book (in the appendix) you will find a "Quick Reference Guide" to copy (or cut out) and place in a convenient location, such as on the refrigerator or on the first-aid cabinet door. This brief eight-step guide is to be used as emotional first aid for accidents and falls, *after* the child has been moved to safety and medical needs are attended to (if these extra steps are called for). In most cases, these simple tools will prevent unnecessary symptoms from developing. If minor symptoms develop anyway, the same steps can be used to help a traumatized child simply by adding the elements of play, drawing, crafts, puppetry, role-play, and/or music.

If, however, serious or complex symptoms arise or minor symptoms persist, it is strongly recommended that you seek help from a competent child therapist who specializes in treating trauma. You cannot make a better investment in your child's well-being!

———————————— 🍃 ————————————

CHAPTER SEVEN

Prevention Tools for Parents and Health Professionals

The Importance of Preparation When Medical Procedures Are Necessary

One common and frequently overlooked source of trauma in children is routine and emergency medical procedures. Armed with the knowledge you will acquire in this chapter, parents can work together as a team with clinic and hospital personnel to reduce unnecessary overwhelm from invasive medical and surgical procedures. But before the strategies, first a story that may surprise you.

Teddy

"Daddy, daddy, let it go, let it go! Please don't kill it! Let it go!"

These are the terrified screams uttered by ten-year-old Teddy as he bolts from the room like a frightened jackrabbit. Puzzled, his father holds a motionless tree shrew in the palm of his hand, one that he found in the back yard and brought to his son. He thought it an excellent and scientific way to teach Teddy how animals "play possum" in order to survive. Startled by the boy's reaction to his seemingly harmless gesture, Teddy's father is unaware of the connection that his son has just made to a long-forgotten event. It was an "ordinary" event, similar to one that millions of us have experienced.

On Teddy's fifth birthday the family pediatrician and lifelong friend came for a visit. The whole clan gathered around the doctor as he proudly showed them a photograph he had taken at the local hospital of baby Teddy at age nine months. The boy took a brief look at the picture and then ran wildly from the room, screaming in rage and terror. How many parents, teachers, baby-sitters, and health care providers have witnessed similar mysterious reactions in children?

At nine months of age, Teddy developed a severe rash that covered his whole body. He was taken to the local hospital and strapped down to a pediatric examination table. While being poked and prodded by a team of specialists, the immobilized child screamed in terror under the glaring lights. Following the examination he was placed in isolation for seven days. When his mother, who had not been allowed to see him for over a week, arrived at the hospital to bring him home, Teddy did not recognize her. She claims that the boy never again connected with her or any other family member. He did not bond with other children, grew increasingly isolated, and began living in a world of his own. Though by no means the only factor, the hospital trauma experienced by nine-month-old Teddy was an important, possibly critical, component in the shaping of Theodore Kaczynski, the convicted "Unabomber," who sent letter bombs to various people involved in technology and wielding corporate power—arguably, his revenge against the same dehumanizing forces that overwhelmed and broke him as an infant.

The Hospital Experience as a Possible Source of Trauma

Without appropriate support, children do not have the inner resources to comprehend the blinding lights, physical restraints, surgical instruments, masked monsters speaking in garbled language, and drug-induced altered states of consciousness. Nor are they able to make sense of waking up alone in a recovery room to the eerie tones of electronic monitoring equipment, the random visitations of strangers, and possibly moans of pain coming from a bed across the room. For infants and young children, events such as these can be as terrifying and traumatizing as being abducted and tortured by revolting alien giants. Ted Kaczynski's "crusade" (though utterly misguided) against dehumanization by technology begins to make sense when we learn about his traumatic hospital ordeal as an infant. This systematic and sociopathic murderer thought deeply about the ideology behind targeting corporate offenders (and left reams of writing behind in his wilderness shack), yet his unsuspecting letter-bomb victims were mere cogs in the same dehumanizing machine. It was a futile, and randomly harmful, gesture of impotent rage. It is the type of tortured adult behavior now being statistically correlated with childhood trauma.

Unfortunately, this story is not an isolated incident. All too many parents have witnessed the disconnection, isolation, despair, and bizarre behavior of their children following hospitalization and surgery. The evidence suggests that these long-term behavioral changes are connected to traumatic reactions to "routine" medical procedures. But, is this possible? The answer is yes.

Does this theory imply that if your child has been traumatized by a medical procedure, he will become a serial killer? Not likely. Most traumatized children do not become criminally insane. Instead, events like these become internalized in a process we call "acting in," which may later show up as anxiety, inability to concentrate, or aches and pains. Or they may be "acted out" as hyperactivity or aggressiveness. Let's look at a more "ordinary" story from the pages of the American magazine *Reader's Digest,* entitled "Everything is Not Okay," where a father describes his son Robbie's "minor" knee surgery:

> The doctor tells me that everything is okay. The knee is fine, but everything is not okay for the boy waking up in a drug-induced nightmare, thrashing around on his hospital bed— a sweet boy who never hurt anybody, staring out from his

anesthetic haze with the eyes of a wild animal, striking the nurse, screaming, "Am I alive?" and forcing me to grab his arms. . . . Staring right into my eyes and not knowing who I am.

Stories like this are commonplace, often leading to the formation of tragic psychic scars. In 1944, Dr. David Levy presented extensive evidence that children in hospitals for routine reasons often experience the same "nightmarish" symptoms as "shell-shocked" soldiers.[1] Fifty years later, our medical establishment is just beginning to recognize and acknowledge this vital information. What can be done to reverse the tide of unnecessary medical trauma that harms millions of children annually?

What You Can Do Now: Reducing the Risk of Medical Trauma

Fortunately you do not have to wait for our medical care system to change. If the above-mentioned frustrated father had been trained in a few easily learned procedures, he could have helped his son overcome the terror brought about by the surgery. Traumatized children can become fearful, hyperactive, clinging, withdrawn, bed-wetters, or impulsively aggressive or even violent bullies in the aftermath of medical procedures handled insensitively. When concern for children's emotional safety is minimized (or worse, ignored altogether), there is a huge price to pay. Often they later have nightmares, headaches, upset tummies, and so on.

As parents and involved adults, you can become proactive. If you select a doctor and hospital wisely, you've won half the battle. Medical personnel frequently don't want parents to be partners on the team—for good reason. An emotional, demanding parent would interfere with safety and efficiency, to say nothing about upsetting the child. If you remain calm with a helpful presence, the staff is more likely to allow you to push the limits a bit in terms of how much you can be with your child. It is important to *educate* not dictate!

Guidelines When Preparing a Child for Surgery or Other Medical Procedures

All kids want a parent to be with them during treatment. According to a *U.S. News and World Report* cover story in June 2000, that is one point on which all experts can agree. Yet there is a good deal of apprehension among these same experts regarding the efficacy of having parents present. In this magazine article, Leora Kuttner, a psychologist who studies pain in children at British Columbia's Children's Hospital in Vancouver, tells of working tirelessly with a youngster about to receive a spinal tap, but she was unable to distract him from his fear of pain. Knowing how important it was for him to relax in order to prevent a terrible treatment, she continued to try. After exhausting every technique without success, she glanced around, only to discover the sideshow that was happening behind her! This is what the psychologist reported: "Behind my back was Mom, sobbing, sabotaging everything, sending the message, 'My darling, what are they doing to you?' Her fear got in the way, and she undermined what help could be given to her child."[2]

Your presence can be helpful if you are not visibly anxious yourself! During the procedure the parent needs to reassure and comfort—at times, even distract—the child. Don't make the situation worse. If you feel like you are going to break down in tears, you may instill fear and tears in your child. However, *during* the procedure this is *not* what is needed. (Although, as we have seen, right after the child is injured and before medical procedures are begun, crying can allow the child to discharge fear and shock.)

For medical personnel, the idea of having a parent in the room may be new, may go against typical medical school training, and at first glance may appear counter-productive. However, if knowledgeable medical workers take the time to educate the willing parent or other adult with what they know to be helpful, or if the parent is informed and can teach something to the clinic or hospital worker, the pay-off to children undergoing various procedures will be enormous. In addition, the reputation of the clinic, office, or hospital will grow when the statistics begin to show improved recovery time and consumer satisfaction. A shortened hospital stay and speedy recuperation cut costs for the health care and insurance companies. It's a win-win situation for all the parties involved.

Since it is common for children to be traumatized by surgeries and other medical interventions, concrete recommendations for parents and medical personnel are outlined here in hopes that their wide adoption will ameliorate this potentially devastating situation. Two procedures that can be particularly terrifying to a child are: 1) being strapped down to an examining table, and 2) being put under anesthesia without being properly prepared. You can assist children to feel more comfortable and thereby reduce the inclination to panic.

The steps listed below are intended to support parents and other adults in becoming proactive, and to educate medical personnel who have not given sufficient thought to this topic. The recommendations are organized into activities one can do before, during, and after the impending procedure, whether you are a parent or a health care professional.

Before the Day of Surgery

1. If you are a doctor or other professional who works with children, be sensitive to the children's needs. If they are being resistant or fussy, it is for good reason. Do all you can by your words and actions to validate their worry, and through kindness, playfulness, distraction, and honesty work with them, not against them.

   If you are a parent, choose a doctor and hospital that are sensitive to children's needs. Not all facilities are created equal! Take the time to "shop around." Some hospitals even have social workers with specially designed programs using story and role-play with children to

prepare them for what to expect. In some of these programs even the youngest children get to meet the surgeon or anesthesiologist in the role-play room. *Sometimes
doctors aren't aware of these programs, so investigate on
your own and find a user-friendly team that will listen to
what you have to say and adopt a patient-centered
approach.* Remember, you are the consumer!

2. Prepare the child for what will happen. Tell them the
truth without unnecessary details.

   Children do better when they know what to expect;
   they do not like medical surprises. If you tell them it won't
   hurt when it will hurt, you have betrayed their trust. They
   will come to fear the worst when they cannot rely on you
   to be honest with them. Children and teens undergoing
   surgeries have been observed to be remarkably less frightened at hospitals with a staff that orients them to each
   and every step.

3. Staff and parents can arrange a time beforehand so the
   child can meet with the doctors (especially the surgeon
   and anesthesiologist) in their ordinary doctor attire
   before they are dressed in surgical garb and mask. It is
   important for your child to see that the doctor is a
   human being who will be helping her, not some
   monster. Perhaps your youngster can put on a doctor's
   costume too! If that's not possible, he can put a dispos-
   able surgical mask on himself, a doll, or favorite
   stuffed animal.

4. If the hospital does not have a program to prepare
   children, or even if it does, you can have your child
   dress up in a gown to play "hospital." Children can
   dress puppets, dolls, or stuffed animals in medical
   attire and play "operation" at home, going through all
   the steps in advance. These include riding on a gurney,

getting injections, and preparing for anesthesia. Have
a dress rehearsal. Most toy stores have play figurines
and "medical kits" for children.

5. Prepare the child for entering (and coming out of) an
altered state by telling (or making up together) a
fantasy story. An example would go something like
this: "Hibernating Bear" goes to sleep very, very
quickly but wakes up very, very slowly and when he
does, he looks for Mamma (Daddy) Bear (or Nurse
Nancy Bear) and something good to eat! (Obviously
the parents have to make sure that they will be there if
this is how the story goes.) Or you could use favorite
characters from fiction, such as Harry Potter gets the
magic-potion injection that puts him to sleep so he
recovers with speed from a terrible whopping by the
Smitherins. Or you can use fairytale characters such as
Sleeping Beauty. Make sure that the child relates to the
character and that you have fun together with the
fantasy. Explain that the potion or pill may make them
feel like they are floating or spinning. Children can
practice this feeling by pretending that they are on a
cloud or in a pool. They can also spin gently and then
rest, noticing the different sensations. The idea here is
to help children become familiar with what they might
experience so that they are not frightened by the
unexpected.

6. Multiple studies have shown that healing from a
surgical wound is more rapid, involving far less
complications, when a local anesthesia has been
administered along the line of the actual incision (as
opposed to only a general anesthesia that makes one
fully unconscious).[3] Unfortunately, this relatively easy-
to-do procedure is still not routine, and general

anesthesia given without benefit of a local is far more common, even for simple surgeries. If a general anesthesia must be administered for a particular procedure, it is still important that a local be given as well. Doctors and parents together can advocate for medical facilities to adopt such policies. By all means discuss the types and methods with which anesthesia will be given well in advance of the operation date. Of course, if a local anesthetic can be used alone, and the child can be kept from being terrified, then that is generally best. One of the graduates from our program carried out a small pilot study at the University of California–San Franciso Medical Center. Her outpatient pediatric rheumatology patients had to undergo an extremely distressing (and repeated) procedure for which they were frequently "put under" because of their terror at having the procedure. Using techniques like the ones just described, she found a dramatic improvement in the children's capacity to undergo the procedure without general anesthesia; and in many cases without much fuss. (See Chapter Thirteen for more details regarding the work at UCSFMC).

On the Day of Surgery

1. Parents and medical personnel need to work out an arrangement whereby parents can remain with their child as much as possible before and after the operation. Children do better when a calm parent can be with them during administration of pre-operative drugs. It is also best if they can get permission to stay until the child transitions from waking consciousness to a "twilight" state.

2. A child should ***never*** be strapped down to an examining table or put under anesthesia in a terrified state. This leaves an imprint deep in their psyche and nervous system. The child should be soothed until calmed. Ask the doctor if you can hold him or her. If the child must be strapped down, explain this to the child and remain with her/him until comforted and supported enough to go on. Fear coupled with the inability to move puts a child in a terrified shock reaction—a recipe for trauma!

3. Medical staff and parents need to know that, ideally, parents should be in the post-operative room when their child is waking up. The child should ***never*** awaken in the "recovery" room alone. Without a familiar adult to comfort them, many youngsters wake up disoriented and panicked. The state is so altered that they may believe they have died or that something horrific has happened to them. It is important that parents and hospital personnel decide together who will guide the child as she comes to—and be sure to let her know in advance who it will be. If parents are absolutely not allowed, request strongly that there be a nurse or someone else there (whom the child has already met) to make soothing contact when the child awakens. To awake alone in the post-operative room can be terrifying—even to an adult.

After the Surgery is Over

1. Rest speeds recovery. All of the child's energy needs to be directed towards healing physically. This conservation of energy is important, but children may not understand this. If they want to play, it needs to be quiet play with lots of encouragement to rest.

2. If your child is in pain, have him or her describe the pain and then find a part of the body that is pain-free, or at least less painful. As you sit with your child, encourage the alternation of awareness between the part that hurts and the part that doesn't hurt so much; this can often alleviate the pain. You can also distract your child a little through the tough spots by humming with them or having them clap or tap a part of their body. Suggesting that they imagine a variety of colored balloons holding the pain and taking it way up into the sky as they float away can be useful.

3. If the child appears fearful, assist him by using storytelling. Use another child's name or make a story up about their favorite stuffed animal. Begin it with "I know a little child named Jake who. . . ." Watch the child's body language. Slow down and work with the parts that seem to be stuck by using the tools listed under "First Aid" in Chapter Six. The main idea is to help your child through any "frozen" or shocked states, into the shaking and trembling of discharge, and finally to calming and resolution.

Note, especially for parents: Remember to monitor your own level of calmness, as you learned in the beginning of this book. Fear is contagious and so are calmness and confidence!

When the Medical Procedure is an Emergency

1. Once the imminent danger is over—and, for example, you are riding with your child in the ambulance—take the time to observe and assess your own reactions. Allow time to reflect and remind yourself that you now have tools to help; allow time to settle your own shakiness, and wait for your own breath to come

before proceeding. A sense of relative calm should be your first task.

2. Reassure the child that everything will be OK, that the doctor knows how to make them better, help them stop bleeding, fix the broken arm, stop the pain, etc.

3. Distracting the child right before the medical procedure can be helpful. Retell their favorite story, bring out their favorite toy, or talk about their favorite place, like the park—making plans, perhaps, to go there when they are better. If the child is in pain, you can have him clap, sing, or tap himself to lessen the pain. Or you can ask him to tell you a place in his body that feels OK or has less pain, and direct him to focus on that body part. Let him know that it's OK to cry.

4. If children are old enough to understand, tell them what will happen at the hospital or doctor's office. For example: "The doctor will sew up the cut so it will stop bleeding." Or: "The nurse will give you either a pill or a needle with medicine to stop the pain, and that will make you feel better," etc.

A Word about Emergency Rooms

More horror stories have been uncovered from the emergency room experience than from any other area in the hospital. By its nature, there is a frenetic atmosphere. It has been reported to us that although the hospital procedure itself went well, the emergency room was outright frightening and left unforgettable images. Some hospitals have recognized the detrimental nature of exposing children to critically injured adults in the waiting room and treatment area. Families are encouraged to visit their local hospitals (urban areas usually have several) before an emergency arises. You may be astonished at the variation in quality of care and nurturance among them. In doing research for this book, I visited three local hospitals, all within twenty minutes of each other. One was so chaotic, with many being treated for domestic violence and gunshot wounds, I left immediately. Another was more or less ordinary, with a pleasant waiting room and the typical long line of patients. The third hospital, much to my surprise, was as conscientious about protecting children's psyches as they were about healing their bodies. To shield the children from the adults, both the waiting and treatment rooms were clearly divided. The children's waiting room had colorful child-pleasing murals on the walls, a big fish tank, and *no* injured adults. Unlike the ward-like atmosphere of the adult treatment room, the children's side had individual rooms to safeguard them from exposure to the frightening sights and sounds of injuries and procedures of their peers. This was not done out of economic motivation; rather, it was done because individual staff members recognized the importance of sheltering children from unnecessary misery. Unless twenty minutes made a life-or-death difference, which hospital would you take your child to if you knew what was available in your community? Unless your child is delivered in an ambulance, chances are the waiting room time will far exceed the few extra minutes' driving time.

Elective Surgeries

Unnecessary surgeries could easily be the topic of another entire book. Without going into depth, suffice it to say that there are two procedures that are administered routinely due to their purported health benefits that you would be wise to question. These are circumcision and cesarean surgery. Weigh the advantages and disadvantages by reading as much as you can and talking to professionals on both sides: those who advocate and those who discourage the procedure.

Of course, in the case of cesarean births, they are often performed as an emergency procedure to save lives. But if your cesarean is an elective one that was suggested by your doctor for convenience, take some time to explore the options. You can also check the hospital's records to see if cesarean births are almost a standard operating procedure. It is better for infants whenever possible (when safety is not an issue) to work their way into the world fully engaged in the process of their own birth. (Refer to Chapter Ten for more details regarding birthing and babies.)

If you choose to circumcise for religious or other reasons, at least make sure that a local anesthetic is given and that your baby is calmed. Do not allow your infant to cry and scream until exhausted. And many operations that were once considered "routine," such as tonsillectomies and operations for "lazy eyes," have now come into question. Always seek second and third opinions to assess if a surgery is really necessary.

Sensitivity to Children's Pain

As mentioned earlier, remember that all doctors and medical facilities are not created equal. Many pediatricians are so focused on saving lives or on the accuracy of the procedure itself that they lose sight of the vulnerability of the little human being they are treating. The "get-it-over-quick" attitude devoid of sensitive care to the terror and pain that a child is going through must not prevail. Much of this attitude comes out of two common but mistaken beliefs that seem astonishing upon even cursory examination. One is that infants and young children don't feel or remember pain, and the other belief is that even if they do feel pain, there will be no long-term consequences! For those skeptics, let's take a look at the long-term effects of the surgery experienced by a boy named Jeff.

Jeff

As an adolescent, Jeff gathered dead animals struck by pickup trucks and cars. He brought these animals home, cut open their bellies with a knife, and removed their intestines.

At four years of age, Jeff had been hospitalized for a hernia operation. When it was time to put the anesthesia mask on his face, the terrified child fought so hard that the doctors had to strap him to the operating table. Following the surgery, the boy seemed to "snap." He withdrew from family and friends and became awkward, secretive, and depressed.

Do you remember the story of Teddy at the beginning of this chapter? Just as his hospital trauma was more than likely a critical factor in the shaping of Theodore Kaczynski, the alleged "Unabomber," it is likely that the terrifying hernia operation described above figured significantly in the formative process of Jeffrey Dahmer, the serial killer who tortured, raped, dismembered, and ate his victims.

The parents of both these men have spent many anguished hours trying to understand the actions of their sons. They had witnessed the disconnection, isolation, despair, and bizarre behavior of their children following hospitalization and surgery.[4] The evidence pointed to the possibility that these permanent behavioral changes were connected to traumatic reactions to "routine" medical procedures.

Fortunately a growing number of doctors, nurses, and medical centers understand the importance of easing pain at both ends of the age spectrum. Palliative care for our elderly is now being practiced by some. It is the rare pediatrician who would intentionally abuse a child. Yet, the change in mind-set regarding the reality of pain in children was only "discovered" by researchers a little over a decade ago! Doctors actually believed that newborn infants were prevented from feeling pain because of an immature nervous system. It was also thought that young children in general did not remember pain. As a result, babies as old as 18 months underwent invasive procedures including surgery without anesthesia. Doctors also hesitated to use narcotics on children because they feared the drugs would cause respiratory problems and addiction.[5] Little did they understand that addiction is more likely to come from the disconnection caused by the trauma of cruel treatment.

What many sensitive parents and professionals may have suspected has now, auspiciously, been given credibility by discoveries in developmental science. A *U.S. News & World Report* article in the year 2000 stated:

> Babies probably get the worst of two worlds: a mature nervous system able to feel pain coupled with an immature ability to produce neurochemicals that can inhibit pain. And even when children cannot remember the actual experience of pain, it seems to get permanently recorded at a biological level. Children who received painful bone marrow aspiration treatments without pain medication, for example, suffered more during later procedures even when those were done with painkillers, according to a 1998 study in the *Archives of Pediatrics & Adolescent Medicine*. "If [pain] is not dealt with early, it's worse later," says Charles Berde, a pediatric anesthesiologist who directs the pain treatment service at Children's Hospital in Boston.[6]

In other words, the initial "pain experience" leaves a deep (traumatic) imprint on the nervous system which is then re-activated during later procedures.

After reading the first section of this book on the biological nature of trauma, you probably understand better why children are the most vulnerable to overwhelm due to their inability to fight or flee. As if that were not enough, medical/surgical procedures are by their very nature the most potentially traumatizing to people of *all* ages due to the feelings of helplessness that come from being held down, at the mercy of strangers, and in a sterile room when you are in unprecedented pain! Having to remain still while you are hurting and being hurt is the epitome of the terror of immobility! It is the prescription for trauma!

Simple Things You Can Do to Ease a Child's Pain

- Be sure to ask for a local anesthetic along the line of incision for surgeries. Some facilities even go so far as to use a spray (Elemax) to numb the site of IV insertion for children. Ask your doctor what will be done to ease your child's pain and request localized relief.

- Use stuffed animals and dolls as props for playing doctor and nurse to help make the sick "puppy" or "baby" or "bear" all better. This is a great way for children to get involved in a distraction from their own pain. It gives them a chance to role-play what will happen to them, and gives the adults a chance to assess the youngster's level of worry in order to give adequate reassurance.

- Older children can be taught relaxation techniques. Audio cassettes in the health section of bookstores and in teacher supply stores have guided instructions to release tension from head to toe. Some use visual imagery as well, such as *Quiet Moments with Greg and Steve* (Los Angeles: Youngheart Records, 1983—www.edact.com), while other recordings use affirmations of well-being during surgery on one side of the tape or CD, with subliminal messages hidden in music on the other. Still others work specifically with breathing techniques combined with systematic tensing and releasing of various muscle groups throughout the body.

- Involve the child's mind in fantasy games and voyages, like taking a magic carpet ride and visualizing leaving the pain behind. This can work wonders. Have the child keep adding details to the mental picture to absorb them.

- Distractions for the younger child such as blowing bubbles or squeezing a "koosh" ball can alleviate pain.

- Biofeedback is offered in some medical centers. No equipment is necessary if temperature-sensitive "sticky dots" are purchased that change color when skin warms or cools to give a remarkably simple reinforcement for deepening relaxation.

Hooray for Teens with Attitude

A terrific find for teens is a video series produced by the Starbright Foundation that prepares them for what to expect from their hospital experience and how to get the most out of it. This company has even produced a video about the often painful process of re-entry to the trials and tribulations of social and academic life (if the teen's treatment required a prolonged stay, such as with burn victims and children with cystic fibrosis, organ transplants, or cancer). This candid, cool, uplifting, and empowering series is called *Videos with Attitude* and can be found at www.starbright.org. *"What am I, Chopped Liver?"* (Starbright 1998) exposes teens to the incivilities of hospital life and lays out their rights and how to communicate with their doctor rather than feeling, as one teen expressed it, "so helpless." Below is a useful summary about the rights of teens. These rights include:

- To be talked to directly by the doctor

- To talk *privately* with the doctor (yes, this means without parents)

- To be told the truth without "sugar-coating"

- To decide what you want to hear and don't want to hear

- To be treated as a person, not an object

- To speak your mind

- To ask any and all questions—medical, social, physical

- To question the doctor if he/she's doing something you don't think is right

- To be informed about procedures and what will happen

- To ask questions (and get answers) about side effects of medications, such as if your appearance or ability to participate in sports will change, etc.

- To write a note or have your parents ask the doctor questions if you are too shy

- To let someone know if you are in pain

- To share your fears, hopes, and other emotions (don't keep things bottled up inside)

- To share your needs and personality so that the doctor knows you as a person

- To change your doctor

One common complaint is that the doctor often treats the teen as an object or "case" and fails to introduce himself to the patient, speaking instead to the parents as if the teen weren't even in the room! One girl in the video expressed how much trust she had in the second doctor who "walked past my parents, shook *my* hand and said, 'OK, I'm gonna get you through this.'"

In *Plastic Eggs or Something? Cracking Hospital Life* (Starbright 1998), teens get to see and hear other teens' impressions of the harsh reality of the glaring lights, hospital attire, and other things not-so-fun, such as the food. One teen described hospital life as "a cross between a battlefield and a prison." This hilarious journey through hospital halls prepares teens for what to expect and how to roll with the punches of the unavoidable atrocities. What was the best advice from these adolescents? Make sure to bring a CD player, headphones, and plenty of your favorite music; bring your own sheets, pillows, and clothing if you will be there long term; keep a notepad for questions for the doctor; and "Don't think you're just the receiver at the end. It's YOUR life—be part of the whole process."

CHAPTER EIGHT

Divorce, Death, and Separation— Helping Children Grieve Their Losses

T he spotlight in this book thus far has been mostly on situations that happened accidentally, suddenly, and "out of the blue." In this chapter, the focus is on how to help a child with the grief that accompanies loss, whether sudden or not. Sometimes the loss from separation is temporary and intentional, such as when a parent travels long distances for work or is in the military. Frequently the event may have been in the making for several years, as in the case of a divorce or the death of an elderly or ill member of the family. At other times, loss is unexpected and sudden, like in the case of Jessica, whose mother drowned in a riptide on a family vacation. Another example, as hard as it is to fathom, is when a parent walks out of a child's life never to return. In these examples, both shock and loss are inextricably woven together. This chapter was designed to assist in guiding a child through the painful terrain of both.

Distinguishing Emotions

Symptoms of Grief versus Trauma

Whenever there is trauma, there is also grief. Grief is the emotion that accompanies loss. Whether the trauma is from a disaster, such as a fire or flood, or from a betrayal, such as molestation or abandonment by a trusted adult, something of value has been lost. Whether it is material, such as the family's house and personal possessions, or something less tangible, such as the loss of innocence, the sense of the world as a safe place seems to be gone forever. It is possible to have grief without trauma; it is not possible to have trauma without grief.

The symptoms of grief and trauma are different. For example, when a child experiences grief, such as the death of a very old family pet that had been ill, it is usually easier to talk about what happened; with trauma, often there are no words. If, in its prime, that same pet had been struck by a car in front of the child, the grief becomes complicated by trauma. Because the death was sudden, unexpected, and graphic, it is too difficult to assimilate the feelings and images all at once. The horror itself needs to be worked through so that the shock of it can be released. Without this the grief is more likely to be disowned.

In contrast to the day-to-day reality of caring for an ailing pet through its final days, the tragic death of an active dog or cat seems unreal. While grief feels *real*, shock seems *surreal*. This is one major difference between trauma and grief, despite the fact that in both cases, the loss of a pet is a painful experience.

In 2001 social researchers William Steele and Melvyn Raider compiled a chart illustrating significant ways in which trauma reactions differ from grief reactions.[1] Our adapted comparison, more suited to body-based treatment, is listed in the box below:

GRIEF	TRAUMA
Generalized reaction is SADNESS	Generalized reaction is TERROR
Grief reactions stand alone	Trauma generally includes grief reactions
Grief reactions are known to most professionals and some laypeople	Trauma reactions, especially in children, are unknown to the public and many professionals

GRIEF *(continued)*	TRAUMA *(continued)*
In grief, talking can be a relief	In trauma, talking can be difficult or impossible
In grief, pain is the acknowledgment of loss	In trauma, pain triggers terror, a sense of loss, of overwhelming helplessness, and loss of safety
In grief, anger is generally non-violent	In trauma, anger often becomes violent to others or self (substance, spousal & child abuse)
In grief, guilt says, "I wish I would/would not have ... "	Trauma guilt says, "It was my fault. I could have prevented it" and/or "It should have been me instead"
Grief generally does not attack nor "disfigure"our self-image and confidence	Trauma generally attacks, distorts, and "disfigures" our self-image and confidence
In grief, dreams tend to be of the deceased	In trauma, dreams are about self as potential victim with nightmarish images
Grief generally does not involve trauma	Trauma involves grief reactions in addition to specific reactions like flashbacks, startle, hypervigilance, numbing, etc.
Grief is healed through emotional release	Trauma is released through discharge and self-regulation
Grief reactions diminish naturally over time	Trauma symptoms may worsen over time and develop into PTSD and/or health problems

Why the Distinction Between Trauma and Grief Is Important

You may be wondering why the distinction between trauma and grief is so important. There are several reasons. First of all, the physiological after-effects on a child whose nervous system has been jolted into shock typically either go undetected or are misdiagnosed as something else, such as depression or behavioral problems. When parents, educators, and medical personnel are savvy enough to make this distinction, children benefit by being less likely to suffer from misunderstanding and mistreatment.

Another reason it is essential to know the difference between grief and trauma is that it enables you to guide a child through the initial traumatic (shock) reaction caused by the suddenness and horror first; then the grieving process can freely move through its normal course. When this shock state is ignored, grief remains unresolved. Additionally, a prolonged state of shock leaves the child with a lingering sense of powerlessness that heightens vulnerability to post-traumatic stress disorder—a diagnosis given when symptoms either continue or develop one month or more after the event.

When trauma *is* resolved, children can get on both with the business of grieving *and* living. When it is not, they so easily get stuck in the fantasy of *how it was then*—before the "terrible thing" happened—rather than *how it is now*. The result is a failure to develop emotionally. In this way there is a literal disruption of the child's life, as if frozen in time. As remarkable as it may seem, I have witnessed teenagers of divorce draw family portraits of their biological parents still together as living "happily ever after"; while their step-parents and step-siblings are conspicuously missing! And this may be ten years after one or both parents have remarried!

Unfortunately, the above example of denial and lack of acceptance of the loss and accompanying lifestyle changes is more the rule than the exception. The grieving process itself is impeded by the traumatic reaction to the divorce, death, or separation. This is why it is so important for parents to understand the similarities and differences between shock and grief. Although the pain of death, separation, and divorce cannot be avoided, it can be alleviated. Helping children untangle shock from grief and navigate the turbulent waters of divorce and death will be the main thrust of the rest of this chapter.

Two Views of Divorce: Rosy or Dark?

I did it for you, and the boys,
because love should teach you joy,
and not the imitation that your
momma and daddy tried to show you.
I did it for you, and for me,
and because I still believe there's only
one thing you can never give up,
or ever compromise on . . .
and that's the real thing you need in love.

*– Kenny Loggins ("The Real Thing"
from his album* Leap of Faith*)*

Tammy Wynette, a famous American country-western singer, croons a tune about divorce in which she calls it "a dirty little word"; while pop singer Kenny Loggins writes a poignant song for his daughter Amanda called "The Real Thing," hopeful that she will forgive him for leaving her mother. He sings that he doesn't want her to mistake marital discord for "the real thing." He is fearful that his little girl will confuse the stressful dynamics between her mother and himself for love.

We all know that there is no escaping the painful journey that begins when a family is in the process of breaking up. Experts have published conflicting research on the long-term effects of divorce on adult children in terms of happiness and success in marriage, career, and life in general.

Currently two extreme views exist: 1) Parents **should** stay together "for the sake of the children" because divorce leaves permanent scars that will follow them into their adult relationships; and 2) Parents **shouldn't** stay together just for the children because, as Kenny Loggins sings, an unhappy marriage is a poor model for relationships, and the kids will be adversely affected by the sham. Worse still, it is presumed that they will repeat the pattern when they get married, being almost hypnotically attracted to what feels, sounds, and looks "familiar." In the article *"Two Portraits of Children of Divorce: Rosy and Dark"* by Mary Duenwald (*New York Times*, March 26, 2002), the findings in both camps regarding the adult prognosis for children of divorce are examined, with interesting theories on both sides.

The Unexpected Legacy of Divorce: A 25-Year Landmark Study, co-authored by Dr. Julia M. Lewis and Sandra Blakeslee, presents the research of Dr. Judith Wallerstein. Her findings show that children of divorce typically end up ill-prepared to form their own intimate relationships. "I'm not saying these young people don't recover," Dr. Wallerstein said. "I'm saying they come to adulthood burdened, frightened, and worried about failure."[2]

On this note, some couples in their twenties have started a new trend in an attempt to protect their future offspring from the pain they experienced as a result of their parents' divorce. To formalize this sense of protection, many are opting for "commitment agreements" when they marry. In *addition* to their marriage vows, they sign a couple-made contract *before* they enlarge their family by having children. Basically, the agreement "guarantees" that the couple vows to hammer out their problems and remain together (even if unhappy) until their children are grown and have left home!

On the more optimistic side, Dr. Mavis Hetherington's studies— published in her book, *For Better or Worse: Divorce Reconsidered*— showed that although divorce is always traumatic for children, resulting in deep sorrow and pain, by the third year there is generally a fairly good adjustment.[3] Also, although 20 to 25% of children from divorced families show psychological and academic difficulties, so too do 10% of children from non-divorced (intact) families. In cases of domestic violence and child abuse, divorce was always the best choice.

Even more important, Dr. Hetherington found that the single best predictor of children doing well is the presence of an involved, competent, caring adult who has high standards for behavior. On the other hand, when children were caught in the middle—in the crossfire between parents—they had the worst possible prognosis for later success. Girls from this group frequently were depressed and anxious; whereas boys in this group were more aggressive and displayed anti-social behavior. When one parent demeans the other parent, and the conflict is sustained after the divorce, it causes extreme distress.

Regardless of disparate views, both sides agree unequivocally on this truth: divorce hurts! Whether it is hostile or mutual, the child's relationships, living arrangements, financial circumstances, and family life are changed forever. The adults suffer; but the children suffer more. Simple as that sounds, it is not so well understood. Because of both their dependency status and their developmental needs, children are the most vulnerable, and their emotional needs *must* take priority even as one or both parents may be dealing with their own devastating grief. Children experience the family coming apart as "their divorce." They will ask revealing questions, such as "Do *we* have to get divorced?" as if the child were divorcing the parents! Whatever the adults are going through you can be sure, whether obvious or hidden, the children suffer more.

Surviving Divorce: A Guide to Preserving Your Child's Wholeness

Fortunately, we don't believe you have to make a choice between two extreme outcomes. Between the "black and white" conclusions from research studies, there are a lot of "gray" areas that encompass factors within *your* control. Although some studies included children who had received grief counseling to support them in making adjustments to a new family structure, *none* included helping children work through the shock-trauma in their physical body. In other words, most professional counselors haven't yet been trained to disengage traumatic shock patterns. Perhaps this is because parents are typically only offered cognitive-behavioral or emotional counseling for themselves and their suffering children. The good news is that alternative or complementary solutions exist: first, *you* can substantially help your child reduce the level of shock by thoughtful preparation. Next, you can help them move through the traumatic reactions you observe because you now know the differences between shock and grief.

Although none of the counseling support mentioned in the research included working with the body, there is no lack of understanding about what the pain of those going through a divorce feels like. In her article "Divorce: 10 Things I Learned," freelance author Vicki Lansky wrote the following about her own experience:

> Going through divorce is a *physical experience.* This one took me by surprise. My body seemed to experience a death-defying whirlpool. I hate speed, roller coasters and the feeling of one's stomach dropping when on a turbulent airplane ride. But I can remember having all those feelings ... simultaneously ... while just sitting in a chair after we separated. Yuck! Fortunately this usually passes in three to nine months.*[4]

---

* From our clinical experience, these physical symptoms—though mutated or "adjusted to"—may linger for a *much* longer time. This is especially true for children who have no control over any of their changing circumstances and are powerless in the matter of divorce.

If the above passage is an adult sharing her personal story, can you even begin to imagine what *physical experiences* children go through who have no control over what their parents do and what happens to them as a consequence? We believe that when parents divorce in such a way as to focus on becoming conscious co-parents, helping their children through the physiological *and* emotional reactions of shock and grief, the devastating effects of divorce can be significantly minimized. Despite the family's distress, when parents provide the continuity of safety and security to their children by recognizing and honoring their needs, everyone fares better in the long run.

Buffering the shock: what do you say to your children?

Whether you fought in front of the kids, discreetly hid your problems, or "swept difficulties under the carpet" while your marriage died a silent death, divorce to a child is shocking and undermining. Although you cannot avoid it altogether, you can certainly buffer this shock by preparing your children as co-parents, talking to them truthfully and consciously framing what you say to reduce the impact. Children need guidance throughout the process. But be aware that there are predictable times when they are the most vulnerable:

Eight vulnerable moments for children when parents divorce

1. When the divorce is first announced
2. When told that one parent will move out (or has left)
3. When custody arrangements are being determined
4. When the marriage settlement/financial agreement is being hammered out
5. When they begin living in a split world: Mom's house/Dad's house
6. When one or both parents start dating

7. When one parent decides to move away

8. When parents decide to re-marry and a step-family is created

Sweet Heartbroken Jacob

Jacob's parents' marriage had been falling apart for some time. They were both very busy with careers and graduate school. They spent little time together and seldom argued. They both cherished their son; whenever the couple was together the activities revolved around the three of them. Jacob's parents rarely spent time alone. As their professional lives were peaking, their marriage was silently dying. Because they were happy with their individual lives, friendships, and financial success, no one expected a sudden break-up! After fifteen years of marriage, Jacob's family was the envy of their friends.

Jacob's father had an affair. His mother detected it immediately. She confronted him. Anger and grief filled the household. Jacob didn't know why. His mother "protected" him, not wanting to say anything bad about his father. Although she went to counseling, she couldn't contain her hysterical outbreaks.

Her husband stopped the affair one month after it began. Jacob's mother had forgiven her husband in her heart, even though he only gave lip service to saving the marriage. He promised to make room for "couple time," and they agreed to do something special together once a month. Jacob was almost thirteen years old and involved in scouting outings and sleepovers with friends, so this agreement appeared to be a way to rebuild their marriage. This raised hope for Jacob's mother. The couple had one promising weekend. But one week later Jacob's dad announced that he wanted to cancel their next "date" and wasn't interested in spending time alone with his wife.

Jacob's mother realized that without couples counseling, this marriage was over. She loved her husband and was hopeful once again when he agreed to therapy. The counselor asked Jacob's dad if he loved his wife and was committed to the marriage. He answered, "I don't know." The therapist then looked at Jacob's mom and said, "How much time are you willing to give him to make up his mind?" A light went off. Jacob's mom recalled painful memories of her husband never being able to say, "I love you." He told her that was just "Hollywood crap she picked up from the movies." At times throughout the marriage whenever she asked him how he felt, his answer was standard: "I don't know." Jacob's mom gave up hope. After only a moment's reflection, she looked at her watch to see how much time was left in the session, and much to everyone's surprise, including herself, she replied, "I will give him fifty minutes!"

By the end of the session, Jacob's father still didn't know how he felt. Reluctantly, his mother knew she had to let go. She knew how important it was to keep their son's established routines, disrupting his life as little as possible. Since Jacob's dad did not want physical custody of Jacob, she suggested that her husband pack up his belongings and leave. He agreed so that Jacob could remain in the same house and school and still have his friends. Having an amicable arrangement, they *never* discussed another issue again! They had the illusion that this was sufficient to protect their son from the impact of divorce.

Without speaking or making a plan about how they would tell Jacob, they drove home in an awkward silence. When Jacob was getting ready for bed, they both looked at each other and decided to "get it over with." They went into his room and, without beating around the bush, told Jacob that they were getting divorced and his father would be moving out within two weeks.

Of course, Jacob went into shock. He didn't cry. He lay on his bed frozen with overwhelm at the sudden news. Both parents, in shock themselves, held him in their arms. Mom and dad wept together. Young Jacob lay silent in bed with his soft brown eyes wide open as if he had just seen a ghost. His skin was pale. His mother tried to console him and let him know that whatever feelings he was having were okay. But Jacob wasn't feeling his emotions. He was paralyzed by the physiological shock reaction, which his parents had no understanding or awareness of, and thus they were helpless to help Jacob or themselves.

Within five to ten minutes after he was told that his father was leaving, Jacob said that he had a sharp pain in his chest. He asked his parents to call an ambulance because he was "having a heart attack." He *insisted* it had nothing to do with the news of the divorce. He kept repeating, "You don't understand.... I'm physically sick.... This is a different thing."

Unfortunately, they *didn't understand* that Jacob was in a state of shock. Nor did they understand what shock was or how to deal with it. Had he been able to cry in his parents' arms and begin the grieving process, his suffering might not have lasted for more than a decade, stunting his adolescent social and emotional development.

Discussion: *A happier scenario for Jacob*

Jacob's initial reactions of shock and denial covered over his deep grief. He felt misunderstood by his parents—and he was! He went to counseling twice before refusing and felt misunderstood again—and he was! What Jacob needed was for someone to understand his physical responses *before* his emotional responses could be addressed. He could have then been guided to release the deep constrictions he felt that manifested as sharp chest pain, and later, headache and nausea. These sensations would have, no doubt, changed from frozen terrified shock into a softening in his chest that might have allowed the tightly locked tears to flow sooner—as he was held in his parents' arms—rather than (much) later.

If you refer back to the "Grief vs. Trauma" comparison box earlier in this chapter, you will notice that Jacob's symptoms are immediately characterized as trauma by the first five items on the checklist: 1) His initial response was terror, rather than sadness; 2) His grief was covered by his traumatic shock; 3) Neither parents nor the professionals he saw understood the trauma reaction; 4) Jacob did not want to talk about it—divorce was not a topic he had words for or cared to discuss; 5) He had an immediate terror reaction accompanied by a sense of powerlessness and loss of safety. Trauma symptoms from the rest of the list appeared one by one over the course of many years. And this young man did not begin to really express his grief until his mid-twenties.

Fortunately, you can help to avoid the above scenario with your children if a divorce or separation is imminent. Grief is *unavoidable;* but trauma is preventable! Tips on guiding children through the grieving process are in the next section. But before the grief, at the very least, two things could easily have been done for Jacob to soften the blow:

First: Remember that "when the divorce is first announced" is number one on the list of the eight most predictable high-impact traumatic moments children experience in a family break-up. Jacob was stunned by the sudden, devastating announcement of the abrupt divorce and the impending separation from his father. What his parents could have done instead of announcing the divorce while *they* were still in shock (and right before bedtime) was to work through their own shock first, process some of their emotions, and then prepare Jacob. After having a day or two to recover, his parents could have brainstormed a plan focused on Jacob's needs for stability and continuity. An example would have been having dad find an apartment while continuing to spend some time at home with Jacob for a month or two to get him accustomed to the change. Details of visits with dad, including how often and how long, would have been worked out so that Jacob's close relationship with his father would be preserved. Later, Jacob could be involved in making some choices about the arrangement so that he would know he was important, instead of feeling powerless to affect, at least in some ways, circumstances that were forced upon him and for which he bore no responsibility.

Parents can buffer much of the shock at this *very* vulnerable time by paying *very* careful attention to **how** their children are told. Children need to know the specifics of how they will be affected right away. They worry, "Who will take me to soccer or scouts?" "Will I be able to still see my friends?" "Will I be able to get to school on time; who will pick me up?" "Who will Spot, the family dog, go with?"

Simple things like keeping a color-coded calendar for tracking which parent the child will be with on each day and who will transport her to various functions can help your child to feel more secure, knowing that both parents will continue caring for him or her. It also gives the child something to anticipate that's based on reality rather than wishful thinking.

Second: The news, no matter how delicately handled, will still be fraught with some shock reaction. And *you* already know what to do! Using the same principles learned earlier regarding tracking sensations, images, and feelings, you would gently guide your child through any frozen or difficult places. You can even use the handy "first aid" list covered in Chapter Six on accidents and falls as a "cheat sheet" because the principles are essentially the same. Initial shock organization in the body is similar no matter what caused it.

Earlier, you also learned to assess the physical expressions of shock in your child through quick observation. It is the details that arise later in grief responses that differ. In the case of Jacob, his pale skin, wide eyes, shallow breath, and severely constricted chest (that kept his heart protected from feeling overwhelming grief) were dead giveaways of his trauma. Gently placing a warm, secure, and reassuring hand over Jacob's heart, exactly on the spot he said he hurt, might have softened the blow. Being as fully *present* as possible and assisting your child with this kind of touch can bring needed relief to your child that Jacob did not receive.

It was many years before Jacob actually proceeded through his grief: from denial to a mixture of intense anger, sadness, and finally, an acceptance of his parents' divorce while coming to grips with its impact on his life. You can see by Jacob's example that although the emotions that accompany divorce cannot be avoided, the complications that result from traumatic shock can be. The sensitivity illustrated in the discussion above can easily be applied to each item on the "Eight Most Vulnerable Moments" list for children when parents divorce.

Divorce and Children's Development

It is of primary importance that decisions made regarding child custody arrangements when parents separate or divorce be based on the developmental and temperamental needs of the child and not based on what's convenient for the parents. Children need close contact with both parents. Recent research shows that this is even truer for infants and toddlers.[5] Security issues are paramount with babies and very young children. They need to feel safe in order to form healthy attachments. Their task is to trust that the world is a good place and that they are welcomed.

Consistency of routines, sensitive transitions, and regular exposure to *all* attachment figures (including extended family) is best. Babies feel safety through their senses. When they are held, rocked, fed, smiled at, and otherwise nurtured by *both* parents on a daily basis, they will know they are loved by both. You cannot *explain* with words to a baby that dad will be back next week. The baby needs the comfort of dad's *physical presence* to know that dad still exists!

As children grow older and begin to separate from their parents, their unique identity is formed through the mirroring given by both parents. When they lose contact with one parent, it is as if a part of themselves is bad, has died, or both. Be cautious not to diminish the other parent, as it has the predictable effect of diminishing the self-worth of the child as well. Since *both* parents live inside the child, whether or not you wish that were so, it *is* the way that it is.

Because infants and toddlers have not yet developed the concept of object constancy (that whatever is unseen still exists), there is evidence that they need to have the absent parent visit daily in order to form a secure bond. On the other hand, teenagers do just fine with less frequent visits, yet they are still in need of strong parental figures who can set firm rules as teens venture forth into the world, becoming more and more independent. Just like toddlers, who want the stability of a parent nearby in case they're needed, teens find that without a firm home base, divorce can be quite disorienting for them as they hazard into differing value systems among their peer group. Step-parenting can be particularly awkward with teens as they mature physically. Step-daughter and step-father can feel uneasy in the expression of affection. In addition, there is a higher prevalence of sexual molestation between step-dads and step-daughters; and often the step-dads are "fighting" their sexual impulses towards their step-daughters. (Of course, this can hold true even with biological dads.) Research data reveal that children ten to fifteen years of age are the least likely to accept a step-parent.[6]

All children need to know that they can remain children even when their family has been permanently restructured. Often what happens, especially in single-parent families, is that children are forced to grow up too soon. If they take on adult responsibilities and emotional burdens, it compromises the development of their own unique identity and sense of self.

Luckily, this distortion of self can be avoided by providing the safety and security of routines, avoiding discord in front of the children (especially when it's about financial or custodial arrangements for them), and not obscuring their childhood needs due to the adult's own pain and inability to cope. If the divorce has been unbearably painful for you, the best way you can help your child is to get professional help for *yourself*. It can also be helpful for your child to join a "divorce support group" if one is available in your local community or at school.

Almost all children hold two fantasies: one is that their parents will one day reunite, and the other is that they (the children) are, at least in part, to blame for the divorce. This is called "magical thinking," especially common in children between the ages of four and eleven. If they believe they had something to do with the break-up, then they believe they can fix it. This magical thinking must be dispelled. If a parent continues to hold on to false hope of re-marrying the spouse who has left, it becomes an almost impossible task for the children to grow and move on.

Another universal belief of children—one that leaves them frightened and shaken—is the fear that since one parent left, the other parent is likely to leave them, too. This is especially true of school-age children, who are sure that their behavior had something to do with their mother or father leaving. This age group is also more vulnerable to a variety of fears because they have the capacity for vivid imagination. The best antidote is to make it convenient—yes, even if you despise your ex-spouse—for the children to see the non-custodial parent as much as possible. Children often worry, "Who will take care of me?" and "Where do I belong?" If in both mom's house *and* dad's house kids have a special place of their own that is comfortable, with toys, clothes, books, CDs, stuffed animals or other favorite possessions that stay at each house, it can help a child substantially in knowing they have a firm place in each parent's heart. It's important for them to know that they *live* at both houses—not live at one and "visit" the other as if a stranger in a strange land. This holds true even though the children may, in fact, spend less time with one parent than the other. And, most of all, *reassure, reassure, reassure* them that parents don't divorce children. Adults divorce adults.

Even in the best-case scenario, when a mutual decision is reached by two mature adults who acknowledge that they are no longer a good fit and each would benefit considerably by parting, divorce is not pretty for children. Knowing that their parents no longer love each other is both painful and inexplicable. It may even leave questions about the foundation of their existence. In addition, explaining to teachers, neighbors, and playmates that they live in two places and have two families can be embarrassing and confusing.

It is beyond the scope of this book to discuss the nitty-gritty of differing needs of children during different ages and stages when going through a divorce. The above information has summarized the most critical points for you to be aware of if you plan to, or have already, divorced your partner. There are dozens of excellent divorce books on the market to help adults make decisions that will help kids. The following three are highly recommended: *Mom's House Dad's House, Co-Parenting Through Divorce,* and *Good Parenting Through Your Divorce* (based on the Kid's Turn Workshop Program). There are also many beautiful children's books readily available, such as *Dinosaurs Divorce, The Boys and Girls Book About Divorce, Parents Are Forever,* and *It's Not Your Fault, Koko Bear.*

Conclusion

In summary, you now have a working guide to enable you to discern the difference between traumatic shock and grief in order to help your child survive and thrive through the pain of both experiences. In addition, it's important for you to realize that children's reactions vary depending on developmental stage, temperament, and attachment to their parents. More important, though, is the active cooperation of all the adults involved to assist children through the various stages of vulnerability. Even when mom and dad are with new partners, they need to remain sensitive, responsible co-parents. This caring and planning makes the difference in how well children adjust.

Now that we have addressed how to minimize the traumatic aspects of divorce, we will address your child's grief. There is much you can do to help children cope with painful emotions, whether due to divorce, death, or some other loss. When children go through unwanted change and disruption in their lives, they may experience many confusing and conflicting feelings. For example, they may feel anger, hurt, and fear while they are also feeling a sense of relief. Other emotions that may be expressed (or repressed) include emptiness, rage, disappointment, loneliness, sadness, and guilt. Learning how to support children through the grieving process is one of the most important ways we can help them to deal with the unsavory twists and turns that are an inevitable part of growing up—and living life in general. Children transform into mature adults not by protection from frustration and pain but by having skillful parents who, through example, gentleness, compassion, and support, help their children to face frustration head-on as they move through their uncomfortable emotions at their own pace and in their own unique way.

Helping Your Child Grieve

Grief is not something that happens only when a person dies. Grief is a sense of loss and sorrow when someone or something we cherished is gone forever. John W. James and Russell Friedman, from The Grief Recovery Institute (based in Sherman Oaks, California, and Ontario, Canada), give the following definition that encompasses all loss experiences: "Grief is the conflicting feelings caused by a change or an end in a familiar pattern of behavior."[7]

Grief is a part of life. Joy and grief go hand in hand. We can't have one without the other. For children, the most common times of grief are divorce, death of a grandparent, parent, or other relative, the loss of friends due to moving out of the neighborhood, the loss of special possessions, and the loss of a pet.

The grieving process is not linear. Nevertheless, the wisdom of the stages of grief that Elizabeth Kübler-Ross delineated many decades ago in her classic book *On Death and Dying* is still a good guide.[8] These stages will be passed through, visited, and revisited by your child at various times. Just when you think a child is no longer sad, the feelings pop up again. This can be particularly true on anniversaries, holidays, and other circumstances that serve as reminders of their loss.

The first stage of grief is denial or disbelief. As we learned in the section on divorce, however, a deeper shock reaction frequently occurs at this first stage. If this is the case, you will need to assist your child to move out of this frozen state by helping her identify and feel sensations until they shift and change. This is important so that she does not stay stuck in the fantasy that the death did not happen or that her parents will remarry.

The next two stages deal directly with emotional states. In stage two, sadness and grief will emerge. Stage three involves feeling anger and resentment. These two stages, in particular, tend to alternate for a while. They also include more nuanced emotions, such as irritability, frustration, emptiness, disappointment, and worry. There is nothing more difficult than being separated from someone you love. Being upset is a normal part of the grieving process. When your child is able to express feelings, it is a good sign that he is moving out of immobility, helplessness, and fantasy. Your job is to help make a safe "container" to hold your child's heartbreak and anger.

Bargaining is the fourth stage of grieving. At this stage it is important to help children keep a strong sense of self—a sense of confidence that they can handle the pain in the here and now, instead of making a futile attempt to change the circumstances through mental manipulations to bring the past back. This is the stage of pining in which we hear: "If only I had ..." or "If I woulda, coulda, or shoulda, maybe this 'bad' thing would never have happened." It may also involve making deals in a futile attempt to change circumstance: "If I pray harder, please make him come back." This stage is similar to the first stage—denial. It is denial with a little more thinking, blaming, and guilt tossed in. Again, at this stage it is important for the child to receive help with the *sensations* that accompany these thoughts in order to not stay stuck in shame and guilt. Instead, the child can be encouraged to express genuine remorse for what they wish they had or hadn't done before the person died or left, and then let it go. Later in this chapter you will learn other ways to help them experience "emotional completion" as a prelude to saying good-bye to a person, pet, traditional family structure, or favorite possession.

The final stage of grieving is acceptance of the reality of what happened and the willingness to go on with life to the fullest extent possible—sometimes with even greater vitality and purpose. This is fundamentally different from an attitude of "just get over it" or "it's time to move on" or "burying feelings." It doesn't mean that the child will never feel sad again about his loss. It does mean that energy that was bound up in a combination of shock and grief reactions has been freed so that there is an authentic sense of completion. The child's energy can then be used for the business of childhood as she meets the challenges of the various developmental tasks along the road to mature young adulthood.

Dealing with the Death of a Pet

For many children the loss of a beloved pet is actually their first experience of profound grief. It is also an opportunity to learn about unconditional love. As mentioned before, grief is not linear. Although there are various stages, children grieve in their own unique way. Some of their behavior may seem illogical to adults.

Most young children who are old enough to talk and express feelings will need only that you follow their lead, give compassionate support according to their cues, and do your best to give them the space and time they require.

The following story about a little girl's grieving process after the loss of her pet is written as a letter by her parents to her in order to document their deep respect and awe at their daughter Rachel's unusual grieving process. It includes how Rachel dealt with the stages of sadness and shock as her parents supported her process without interrupting, followed by lots of hugs.

For Rachel

On November 15, 2003, your cat, Briar Rose, was killed by neighbor dogs. How you handled this experience at not quite 6 1/2 years old was quite amazing to Rob and me, so I jotted it down for you to read when you are older.

We had just come home from a soccer game. Rob [Rachel's dad] was home first. When we drove up he whispered to me that something had happened to Briar. You and I went in the house and played. When your dad came back he came to you, kneeled down, and said he had bad news. "Briar is dead." You wailed for a long time in his arms. Ryan [Rachel's brother] and I were right beside you. You suddenly stopped crying and asked if Rob had Briar. He said he would bring her inside.

We all sat by the front door. You held Briar in your lap. She was still warm. As you stroked her, you said many things about her— what a great kitty she was, how she was too young to die, how much you loved her, etc. You also had questions about how she died. Her tongue was hanging out; her eyes wouldn't close. Why not? Are you sure she isn't just asleep? There was no obvious wound, but a bit of blood by her nose. What happened to her? We answered your questions as best we knew, but most importantly, we all supported you, and each other, in letting the sadness out.

Rob had wiped away blood from her mouth. All of us were tearful. Then suddenly you said you were finished holding her and that Rob could take her back outside till we could bury her in the morning.

You were not hungry for dinner, but you sat with us. During our meal you said your head was really hot and you wanted to cool it with water. I suggested a bath ... "no" ... a shower ... "no." You replied instead, "I want to fill up the kitchen sink with cool water and put my head in." You pulled up a chair to the sink, filled it, took off your shirt, and dunked your head. You lifted your head from the water and wanted me to time you holding your breath under water—which I did. You had some fun doing that. Then you wanted to call some of your friends. So we dried your hair and you phoned two friends and one adult. You had to leave two messages: "Hi, this is Rachel. I'm calling to tell you I am heartbroken because my cat died tonight."

Next, you said you needed to do something to make you laugh. You explained by saying, "When Daddy told me Briar had died, I had just been playing. All that sadness came into me and pushed all my laughter into my feet and now they don't feel good, so I have to do something that will make me laugh." I said I would try to think of something.

Moments later, Rachel said everyone was going into the hot tub. I said I'd be there in a few minutes. When I got in, she said, "Mommy, the laughter got out of my feet!" I asked how, and you said, "Ryan tickled my feet!" I asked where the sadness was now and you said, "All that's left now is love." In the hot tub, you alternately wanted to be held or played with in the water, splashing, sinking, and floating.

At bedtime, our usual routine of lullaby/chant singing, hand massage, and snuggling just seemed to make you sad about Briar. "Mommy, I can't talk about it anymore. I just want my relaxation CD." So, you put on your headphones and within minutes were asleep.

In the morning, you told me about a dream you had. "I dreamed that there were two Briars—a good Briar and a bad one. The bad cat wanted to eat us up, but the good Briar said she would help us. I held her paw and you, Daddy, and Ryan held her other paw and each other's hands and Briar flew us up into the sky with her wings. It was really Briar. Her body came back to me and she saved us."

Later in the morning, you wanted to participate in every aspect of Briar's burial. You picked the spot, helped dig the soil. When Rob brought Briar's body out, you were very surprised to notice that she was cold and stiff. We talked about the fact that her spirit and life force weren't in her body anymore. You picked out several crystals that Granddaddy Pete had given to you before he died. You put them in the pillowcase with Briar and said that she wouldn't be alone, that Granddaddy Pete would show her spirit around in heaven. Cloudy, Briar's brother, sniffed at her body quite a bit, and since her death has been more affectionate with us. He seems to realize that she is gone.

When the hole was ready, you helped Rob lower her body and put the first dirt on her. We all shared something about her; we were all crying. You wanted to pray and kneeled down just like the pictures of little children—hands folded, head bowed. You weren't quite sure what to say. You helped Ryan shovel, filling the hole with dirt. After that you wanted to sing "Home, Home on the Range," which we did. In the afternoon, Rob helped you make a cross to put on her grave. You wrote "Briar Rose, Rachel's cat, I love you so" with lots of hearts.

Since then you have had many moments of tears and sadness over Briar. You will see a cat or hear something that reminds you of her and then have to process your sadness. It also triggers your sadness "for all my ancestors that I never got to meet." You seem to bring up death more as you hear about it: Jesus dying on the cross, children dying from the flu, etc. We just listen to what you have to say and hold you if you want that.

It is a long process to come to grips with death, but you are doing such a marvelous job of it so far. What impressed us so much on that first day was how you knew *exactly* what you needed to do to help yourself—crazy things like dunking your head and having your feet tickled. We just supported you in your process and you took care of yourself in a most exquisite way. We love you so much, Rachel!

One Year Later

I checked with Rachel's mom a few months after Briar's death, and she said that Rachel still missed her cat but seemed to be moving through her grief nicely. As the one-year anniversary of Briar's death approached, I checked with Rachel to see how she was doing. Without my mentioning a word about the anniversary, this seven-year-old told me that she still missed Briar and that it was "getting harder" because it was getting close to the date she died; also she feels "uncomfortable" watching Ryan (her brother) play with Cloudy (Briar's brother). I found out that Rachel had requested and gotten a new cat named Misty. But Misty was not like Briar.

Replacing the loss of Briar, of course, did not do the trick to complete the grieving process. No two pets or people are alike. Children usually adjust to a new pet, friend, step-parent, etc., more easily when they have completed the grieving process, organically coming to an acceptance of their loss. That is because *prematurely* "replacing" the loss of an animal or person with which a child has formed a deep bond is usually nothing more than a vain attempt to reduce the hurt accompanying the loss. It seemed to me that clever Rachel had done much to resolve her grief. She had even "pendulated" between pain and pleasure by alternating between crying and playing. However, she was still in quite a bit of emotional pain. Wondering what might be causing this, I recalled that an obvious piece was missing from her grief process. Nothing was mentioned regarding regrets or remorse. And there is nothing that brings regret, with guilt as its companion, more easily than death. Guilt and regret can occupy a lot of a child's mental and physical energy!

Debunking Common Myths
(The Continuing Story of Rachel and Briar)

Attempting to "replace" the loss of a loved one quickly as a method of resolving grief is a common myth believed by grown-ups. Another common myth in our culture is that time, by itself, will heal all wounds. This simply is not so. Of course, time and distance can "take the edge off" the pain; but they also can bury the pain more deeply. This is another myth that adults seem to be adept at believing. Burying the pain is not an efficient method of coping with grief because of several reasons: a) It can come back to haunt you unexpectedly; b) It can create difficulties with bonding and intimacy due to fear of pain; c) It takes a "truckload" of energy to keep the buried feelings entombed. In other words, it resolves nothing and teaches people to avoid suffering at all costs.

As all spiritual practices and religious philosophies teach, pain is part of life on this Earth plane. When children learn to tolerate emotional pain in small doses, and realize that if they do, it won't last forever, they have learned one of life's most valuable lessons. They can enter adulthood with solid emotional and physical health.

Time did not heal Rachel's sadness. Anniversary dates offer another opportunity to finish "unfinished" business because they bring the suppressed emotional energy quickly to the surface. With the knowledge that Rachel had not "bargained" (stage three) or shown remorse for anything she had done or neglected to do prior to Briar's death, I asked her, "Did you take care of Briar?" She explained that she touched her, played with her, fed her, and gave her water. Next I asked, "Is there anything you wish you had done differently?" Unhesitatingly, Rachel replied, "One thing—I wanted her to feel like she was in a good home." She then went on to explain that she wasn't sure if Briar felt good in her home because she held her kitten too much when Briar clearly didn't like to be held down. This information poured out of her. Rachel sounded relieved just to let that "cat out of the bag" with her mother and me there to listen as she confessed what she had been holding inside. I have a feeling that after Rachel's planned anniversary ceremony for Briar that she will now be able to move into the final stage of grieving: acceptance.

By the way, another myth about grieving in modern culture— unlike both traditional and primitive cultures—is that you're supposed to keep your feelings to yourself. In other words, the myth is that, at least after the funeral is over, if you're not over it, *you should grieve alone.* In fact the opposite is true. This is why grief groups are so important in helping both adults and children come together to witness each other's grief as a shared human experience. Coming together communally can move the process along so that grievers can avoid prolonged suffering that interferes with other developmental tasks. More information on "steps to resolving grief" will be given later in this chapter.

When grief is accompanied by shock, it is more complex. With Rachel, two clues indicated that she had experienced shock: 1) the suddenness of her kitten's death, and 2) her unusual "head-dunking" behavior that followed. For this reason, when I interviewed Rachel I told her that I was curious about why she wanted to dunk her head in water and how this may have helped. Rachel again responded without hesitation: "There was a blood stain on my pants from holding Briar. When I saw it, I was upset and wanted to barf [vomit]. My head was hot. Dunking my head made me feel less upset, not as tense, and I wouldn't have to throw up."

Traumatic shock often creates nausea. Seeing blood can be horrible for anyone, but especially for young children. It's obvious that Rachel's blood-stained pants triggered another shock reaction. Placing her head in water appeared to have the effect of soothing her nerves, which settled her tummy. This may not make sense to you, but it makes perfect sense from a scientific standpoint.

Without getting too technical, it may be helpful for you to know that the vagus nerve, the longest nerve in the body, travels all the way down to the gut where it provokes nausea and also reduces blood pressure (producing feelings of faintness). Remember that Rachel *saw* Briar's blood; next, she felt like vomiting. The stimulus of the cold water on her face helped to counter this reaction. Placing a hand on your child's tummy until it begins to settle can also help break up this feedback loop, preventing unnecessary discomfort. Little Rachel intuitively used the cool water to self-soothe as her compassionate parents stood by her, letting Rachel lead the way.

Steps That Help Children Resolve Their Grief

Besides moving through sensations of shock and the emotions of grief, there are a few tasks to be completed by the child before saying "good-bye" to his or her loved one. Recall how Rachel needed to "get off her chest" (tell someone) that she felt sorry she had held Briar even when the kitten clearly didn't like it *and* that she feared the cat might not have felt she was in a "good home" because of her actions. Stating what you wish you had done differently is part of releasing yourself from a loved one. Whether it's a pet or a person, the process is the same.

────────────────── 🌿 ──────────────────

GRIEF RECOVERY

This five-part exercise helps a child make all the completions that are a prelude to letting go. It is modeled after the Grief Recovery Institute's Program that was founded by John W. James and Russell Friedman in Sherman Oaks, California, and can be found in their book, When Children Grieve *(see bibliography).*

Part A

1. Make a timeline starting from the time you first met that person or pet until their death. The example below was made by a high school student:

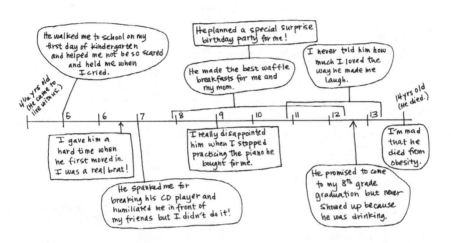

TIME LINE FOR MY STEP-DAD

He walked me to school on my first day of kindergarten and helped me not be so scared and held me when I cried.

He planned a special surprise birthday party for me!

He made the best waffle breakfasts for me and my mom.

I never told him how much I loved the way he made me laugh.

4½ yrs old (He came to live with us.)

14 yrs old (He died.)

5 6 7 8 9 10 11 12 13

I gave him a hard time when he first moved in. I was a real brat!

I really disappointed him when I stopped practicing the piano he bought for me.

He spanked me for breaking his CD player and humiliated me in front of my friends but I didn't do it!

He promised to come to my 8th grade graduation but never showed up because he was drinking.

I'm mad that he died from obesity.

2. Write several happy memories that stand out as highlights of your relationship above the line in chronological order.

3. Add a few things above the line that you appreciated the most and wish you had expressed while your loved one was still alive.

4. Write several things that your loved one did that upset you below the line.

5. Add several regrets below the line for things you did that upset your loved one.

Part B

List the memories you wrote under the following headings:

- things I miss about my loved one
- things that hurt me that I'd like to forgive now
- things I feel guilty about that I'd like to be forgiven for
- things that I appreciated and never said aloud

Part C
SHARING YOUR THOUGHTS, MEMORIES, AND FEELINGS

Share the lists you made with someone who loves you and will understand. Ask this person or group of people to help you by listening to any feelings that may surface as you complete this set of exercises.

Part D
SAYING GOOD-BYE

When you feel ready, compose a special letter for your loved one. Use the memories you listed to express anything you would like. Don't hold back. Be sure to balance your letter with things that helped you and things that hurt you. Express gratitude for experiences, and feelings that you never said "thank you" for before or wish to repeat again now. Admit your short-comings and forgive anything that you feel you want to forgive. Be honest. Don't force yourself to forgive certain things that you don't want to, but be sure to take this opportunity to forgive the things you do. Most of all, forgive yourself. Ask your loved one to forgive you for anything you feel ashamed of and wish you didn't do. Now is the time to come clean so that you can say good-bye without anything holding you back.

This letter can be very hard to write. Have someone you love help you if you cannot do it yourself. But be sure they are your thoughts and feelings, *not* someone else's. If you are too young to write all those big words, you can have an older person write your words for you. If you can do it all by yourself, you might want a friend or relative in the same room with you just to keep you company if you have strong feelings that come up. You might want a hug, or someone to hold you if you cry, or someone to share your memories and feelings with. In the final line of your letter you tell your loved one "good-bye."

Part E
SHARING YOUR LETTER

When you feel ready, read your good-bye letter to your loved one aloud in front of someone you can trust with your private thoughts and feelings. Then you might want to have a ceremony and bury or burn your letter. Or you might have some very creative ideas of your own to complete the process of grieving.

Giving Emotional Support through the Tears, Fears, Outbursts, and Confusion of Grief

Whether children are grieving a death, divorce, separation, or loss of some other kind, you can be assured that they will be experiencing a range of different emotions. Young children may not have labels for their feelings. Older children and adolescents may not want to talk about them for many reasons. Following are suggestions to help you help children of various ages. See also "Tending to Emotional Needs by Following the Children's Lead" in Chapter Four to review the information on helping your child with unpleasant feelings.

For young children who do not have a feeling vocabulary but are old enough to at least scribble with crayons or markers, it can be useful to have them indicate the colors of their feelings. Or you can have them make shapes to show their feelings, or point to the place in their body where they have "bad" feelings. Another useful activity for any age is to draw a large outline of a "gingerbread" person on drawing paper. Together with the child make a "color key," with each color representing a different feeling. (Older children need very little or no guidance with this.) Typical colors children choose are:

- blue = sad
- red = mad
- yellow = scared
- green = glad
- purple = calm
- black = depressed

After the outline and color code are finished, the child simply fills in the outline with the various colors to show how they feel in different parts of their body. For example, they might color the

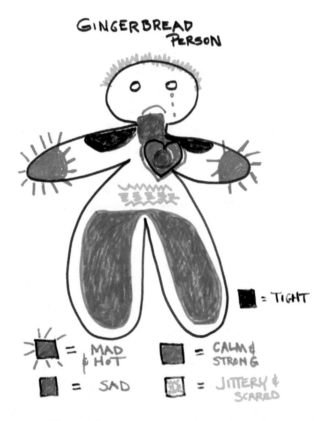

entire person blue if they are extremely sad; or they might color the heart area blue, the feet and hands red, and the tummy yellow. Drawings like this help in two ways: 1) The sensory-motor act of drawing helps to relieve the feelings through artistic expression as it engages the intuitive right side of the brain; and 2) The process gives you, the adult, valuable information about what's troubling the child and what feelings still need to be expressed and listened to with compassion.

Sometimes children will draw their difficult emotions first. As they start feeling better, they may shift and draw pleasant feelings that indicate their natural resilience and resourcefulness. Feelings can be worked through using clay and paints as well. Clay or Play-Dough is especially good for expressing anger, since it can be pounded on, rolled, and reshaped any way the child wishes.

Feelings Are a Natural Part of Grieving

Often children (and adults!) are embarrassed about their feelings. They might also hide them because they do not want to cause their parents additional pain. This is especially true in the case of divorce or when a sibling, spouse, or grandparent dies. As is often the case, the parent(s) may be going though their own unbearable emotions. It's OK for adults to cry together with their children. In fact, it's important to tell your children that tears, fears, and anger are a normal part of the grieving process. Modeling your own healthy emotions without embarrassment can help. Crying tears can release a great deal of pain and stress.

It is critical, however, that you not burden your children with your ongoing suffering or overwhelming feelings of anxiety, depression, rage, or hysterical sobbing (these extremes do not bring relief). Get help from friends and/or counselors if your own grief is not resolving. Refrain from judging or making disparaging remarks about the person who has left in front of your child. It will confuse your child about his or her own loving feelings for that person.

It is important to ask your child often how she feels and what she thinks. Children may have very different feelings than adults. They need to be able to express authentic emotions without having to filter them through an adult lens. They also need to feel safe to ask questions about their feelings on *their* own timetable. Often children aren't ready to talk about their emotions. Try again later, giving them many opportunities to share with you and unload their burdens.

Many adults find it easy to hug and comfort a sad child, but find it difficult to deal with a mad child. It is normal to get mad when someone you love leaves. It's important to let children know that mad feelings are normal, too. They may need to talk about it, stomp their feet, draw or write about it, tear up some paper, or take a walk. Some children may want to be left alone for a while to work through their feelings on their own or talk with peers. This is especially true for teens. Just let them know that you are available to them when *they are ready*.

Children become afraid when they don't know what's going to happen next. Whether a child is about to go to the dentist or his parents are about to divorce, he needs to know how he will be affected. You can avoid a lot of catastrophic worry by providing the details of how your child can continue contact by phone, mail, and visits with the relatives that are still in their lives. In the case of divorce, it helps children to know where they will live, what life circumstances will change, and which ones will remain the same. Providing telephone numbers, addresses, stamps, and stationery to encourage connections can help your child feel more relaxed (even when you would rather not—such as in the case of an ex-in-law you despise). Remember, this is your child's grandfather! Encouraging calls to grandparents, aunts, uncles, cousins, etc., on both sides of the family is important. Keeping a connection with extended families often gives children a sense of continuity and security that helps them cope better.

Life *Will* Get Better!

When children's lives go through upheaval, they may ask hundreds of questions in hundreds of ways. "Why can't dad live with us?" "Why did grandma have to die?" "Why did mom leave?" "Will she come back?" "Why can't things be different?" You may not be able to answer these questions. But letting the child know that you are aware that they are feeling sad, frustrated, hurt, mad (or whatever you notice they are feeling), and that you are right there with them to listen, hold them, tell them a story, or plan ways to make their new life as comfortable as possible can help children begin the process of completion and acceptance of the unavoidable changes in their lives.

When children are dealing with difficult life transitions, they need to know that life *will* get better with time. It's a delicate balance between supporting your child to express difficult emotions while also conveying the sense that "it won't hurt forever." It is important for them to know that transitions are difficult at first but that over time, things shift and get easier. One thing you can do is a regular "feelings check-in" as a daily or weekly ritual to see how emotions begin to change over time. Another thing you can do is hold regular family meetings to share new feelings that come up and how each family member is coping. The emphasis can be on listening compassionately to each other's feelings and problem-solving ways to manage. Suggestions for family fun-time can also be made together. It's important for children to have a balance between the business of grieving and the business of growing up, which means plenty of time for fun, frolic, and other pleasurable experiences.

Asking often for their input to make them feel more at ease can empower children when they feel powerless due to circumstances beyond their control. Often tiny adjustments can be made to improve the child's life that you would never have dreamed of. Children can be very creative in coming up with solutions to their own problems!

CHAPTER NINE

*Preventing and Healing
the Sacred Wound
of Sexual Molestation*

God, please give me patience. But hurry.

– *Marilyn Van Derbur, author of*
Miss America By Day: Lessons
Learned from Ultimate Betrayals
and Unconditional Love[1]

And then the day came when the risk
to remain tight in a bud was more painful
than the risk it took to blossom.

– *Anaïs Nin*[2]

Unless you have personally experienced the deep wound of sexual trauma, it may be difficult to imagine how complex, confusing, and varied the long-term effects can be. This is especially true when the molestation was perpetrated by someone the child trusted or even loved. When a child's innocence is stolen, it affects self-worth, personality development, socialization, achievement, and later, intimacy in adolescent and adult relationships. In addition, these children are prone to somatic symptoms from physical rigidity or excessive weight gain/loss, born of a conscious or unconscious attempt to "lock out" others and to not be in the body. Also common is the tendency to live in a fantasy world, have problems with attention, space out, daydream, and dissociate in order to compartmentalize their awful experience.

If you are reading this chapter because you suspect that your child may have been victimized, you may want to review the extensive list of indicators of sexual trauma in Chapter Three before continuing. While the specific symptoms of sexual trauma were delineated earlier, this chapter focuses on awareness, prevention, and how to approach children in a way that will earn their trust in your ability to protect them so they can tell you what you need to know. Children do not tell that they have been molested unless they understand that they have a right to their own body, are confident that they will be believed (not blamed), feel secure that their feelings will be understood (not overlooked), and trust that they will be spared from further harm. They also need to know that it is *never ever* their fault.

Safeguarding Children Against the Wound of Sexual Trauma

Sexual trauma varies widely from overt sexual assault to covert desires that frighten and confuse a child by invading his or her delicate boundaries with un-bounded adult sexual energies. When parents have had unresolved sexual violations themselves or were lacking models for healthy adult sexuality in their families of origin, it may be difficult to protect children without conveying a sense of fear and rigidity around issues of touch, affection, boundaries, and sensuality. Or, conversely, parents might avoid offering either discussion or protection due to their own lack of experience in sensing, within themselves, the difference between potentially safe or dangerous situations and people.

This chapter is a guide to help you recognize what sexual trauma is, assist you in protecting children without frightening them, illustrate ways to help them develop healthy boundaries, and support you in creating an atmosphere of healthy sexuality within your current family. It is far less likely that children will be victimized if they have parents who listen for opportunities to discuss topics of touch and sex. In addition, they need parents who foster strong body awareness and can be counted on to believe and protect them.

No child, even with solid parental support, is immune to the risk of molestation. In fact, conservative reports estimate that one out of every four individuals worldwide has suffered sexual violations—many of these as children under the age of thirteen. With females, the risk is even higher.[3] If your child suffers from sexual trauma, by all means seek the help of a therapist. It is best to find a professional who is experienced in working with sexually traumatized children.

Are Some Children More Vulnerable Than Others?

The majority of parents, communities, and school programs warn children to avoid "dangerous strangers." Sadly, strangers are seldom the problem. Other myths persist, such as the one that only girls are vulnerable, and that most assaults happen at or after puberty. Although statistics vary, the numbers of preschoolers and school-age children reporting sexual assault are astonishing. Approximately 10% of sexual violations happen to children *less than five years old*[4]; more children between eight and twelve report molestation than teenagers; and 30 to 46% of all children are sexually violated in some way before they reach the age of eighteen.[5] Sexual trauma is pervasive—it prevails no matter the culture, socioeconomic status, or religion. It is not uncommon within the "perfect" family. In other words, *all* children are vulnerable; and *most* sex offenders are "nice" people that you already know! If you have been putting off talking with your children about sexual molestation until they are older or because you are uncomfortable with the topic, we hope that what you learn here will bolster your confidence to begin these discussions sooner rather than later.

The Twin Dilemma of Secrecy and Shame

The sexual molestation of children has the added shroud of secrecy. Since 85 to 90% of sexual violations and inappropriate "boundary crossings" are by someone they know and trust, the symptoms are layered with the complexity of the repercussions of betrayal.[6] Even if not admonished (or threatened) to keep the assault secret, children often do not tell due to embarrassment, shame, and guilt. In their naiveté they mistakenly assume that *they* are "bad." They carry the shame that belongs to the molester. In addition, children fear punishment and reprisal. They frequently anguish over "betraying" someone who is part of their family or social circle and fantasize what might happen to their perpetrator. This is especially true if it is a family member they are dependent on.

If not a family member, the violator is usually someone well known. Neighbors, older children, babysitters, a parent's boyfriend, and other friends of the family or step-family are frequently the offenders. Or it may be someone who has prestige and social status, or serves as a mentor, such as a religious leader, teacher, or athletic coach. For example, the BBC News reported in February 2004 that 11,000 cases went on record of American youths sexually abused by priests over the last half century. How can children know—unless you teach them—that they are not to blame when the perpetrator is usually not only someone known, but someone who may be revered? Parents can pave the way to safety for their children by teaching them to trust and act on their own instincts versus submitting to an older child or adult who is using their status for their own gratification.

What Is Sexual Violation?

If sexual violation isn't typically a "dirty old man" luring a child with candy into his car, what is it? Simply put, it is *any* time that *anyone* takes advantage of their position of trust, age, or status to lead a child into a situation of real or perceived powerlessness around issues of sex and humiliation. In other words, when children must passively submit to the will of another rather than having the choice to defend themselves or tell someone, whether or not they are "forced," it constitutes sexual violation or assault. This can range from being shown pornography by a teenaged babysitter, to an insensitive medical examination of a child's private parts, to being forced to have sexual intercourse with a parent or other adult. While actual rape by a parent or step-parent is less common, exposure to pornographic material or being asked to strip, look at, or handle exposed genitals, as well as rough handling during medical procedures, is far too common.

Steps Caregivers Can Take to Decrease Children's Susceptibility

1. **Model Healthy Boundaries:** No one gets to touch, handle, or look at me in a way that feels uncomfortable.

2. **Help Children Develop Good Sensory Awareness:** Teach children to trust the felt sense of "Uh-oh" they may feel as dread in the gut or rapid heartbeat, which lets them know something is wrong and they need to leave and get help.

3. **Teach Children What Sexual Violation Is, Who Might Approach Them, and How to Avoid Being Lured:** Teach children how to use their "sense detectors" as an early warning sign.

4. **Offer Opportunities for Children to Practice their Right to Say "No."**

5. **Teach Children What to Say and Do:** Also, let them know that they should always tell you so that you can keep them safe and help them with their feelings.

Let's take a more detailed look at these steps:

1. Model Healthy Boundaries

There is a delightful children's picture book by James Marshall about two hippopotami that are good friends. One's name is George, the other Martha. They visit and play together and have dinner at each other's house. One day Martha is soaking in her bathtub and is shocked to see George peeking through the window looking right at her! George was surprised at her outrage and his feelings got hurt. He thought that this meant Martha didn't like him anymore. Martha reassured George that she was very fond of him. She explained in a kind manner, "Just because we are good friends, George, doesn't mean that I don't need privacy when I'm in the bathroom!" George understood.

This little *George and Martha* story models making boundaries, communicating them clearly, and honoring the boundaries of others. Parents need to show good boundaries themselves, respect children's need for privacy (especially beginning between the ages of five to seven), and support them when they are in situations that are unappealing and are defenseless to help themselves. This begins in infancy. The following illustration will help you understand how to offer this protection:

Little baby Arthur fussed and arched his back each time Auntie Jane tried to hold him. His mother, not wanting to offend her sister, said, "Now, now, Arthur, it's OK, this is your Auntie Jane. She's not going to hurt you!"

Ask yourself what message this gives to Arthur? He is already learning that his feelings aren't important and that adult needs take precedence over a dependent's needs. Babies show us their feelings by vocal protests and body language. They are exquisitely attuned to the vocalizations and facial expressions of their parents. The brain circuits are being formed by these very interactions that are specifically about respect for feelings and boundaries around touch. For whatever reasons, Arthur did not feel safe or comfortable in Aunt Jane's arms. Had his "right of refusal" been respected, he would have learned that his feelings *do* make a difference, that he *does* have choices, and that there *are* adults (in this case his mother) who will protect him from other adults whose touch he does not want. A few tactful words to Jane, such as "Maybe later, Jane—Arthur's not ready for you to hold him yet," would leave an imprint impacting the baby's newly developing sense of self. And if his mother's appropriate protection continues, Arthur's brain is more likely to forge pathways that promote self-protective responses that may safeguard him from an intrusion and assault later in his life. Although not in his conscious awareness, these unconscious body boundaries formed in the tender years of infancy will serve him well.

Trauma is a breach of energetic and personal boundaries. Sexual trauma, however, is a sacred wound—an intrusion into our deepest, most delicate and private parts. Children, therefore, need to be protected by honoring their right to personal space, privacy, and to be in charge of their own body. As different situations develop at various ages and stages, children need to know that they do not have to subject themselves to "sloppy kisses," lap sitting, and other forms of unwanted attention to please the adults in their lives.

Other Areas Where Children Need Respect and Protection of Boundaries

Children instinctively imitate their parents. Adults can capitalize on this favorable attribute when it comes to toileting behavior. A lot of power struggles and unpleasantness for toddlers and parents alike can be avoided altogether. By respecting your child's timetable, she will joyfully model mom's behavior and toilet-"train" herself. Take the "train" out of toileting and your little boy will proudly do it like "daddy does" at his own pace. Prevent unnecessary trauma in this major developmental area by following your child's lead rather than listening to the "experts" who believe in timetables. Forcing a child who is not ready to use the toilet disrespects his right to control his own bodily functions and sets a life-long pattern that being dominated by someone else is to be expected. By encouraging rather than pushing, you will be assisting your children to develop healthy self-regulatory habits and a natural curiosity about their own body. In some cases, you may even be preventing eating disorders, digestive problems, constipation, and related difficulties—and as a side effect, producing happy, spontaneous children.

Another area that is often overlooked in protecting children's boundaries has to do with medical procedures. Many adult therapy clients report a vague sense of sexual trauma without clear memories. Rather, they suffer with symptoms such as depression and anxiety accompanied by images and body sensations of being violated. Often, when these bodily sensations are processed in a therapeutic session, the adult discovers feelings of suffocation directly related to an early surgery, such as a tonsillectomy, eye surgery, or intubation. Sometimes the "sensation" of sodomy with no known history relates back to roughly administered enemas instead.

Parents need to act as advocates on their children's behalf. Pelvic exams, needles, disrobing, and insertion of instruments into the mouth, anus, or vagina should be done with preparation, care, and gentleness. In addition, listening to and helping children with their feelings before, during, and after any necessary "boundary crossings" can prevent the incidents from becoming traumatic boundary violations.

2. Help Children Develop Good Sensory Awareness

You already have a good start on step number two if your family has been practicing awareness of sensations. Part II of this book emphasizes teaching you and your children how to locate and name bodily sensations, then focus attention on them long enough for them to change. Protecting children from sexual abuse can begin by talking about different kinds of touch, checking in with various sensations that touch can provoke, and teaching them to trust their instincts when the touch feels uncomfortable, unsafe, frightening, or painful, or makes them feel "dirty," or secretive, or ill-at-ease.

A pilot project used in schools called "Child Sexual Abuse Prevention Project, Minneapolis, Minnesota" explains touch in a simple manner on a continuum from "good touch" to "confusing touch" to "bad touch." It describes good touch as feeling like something has been given. Children, when asked what types of touch feel good, will usually mention a hug, petting an animal, playing games, a soft blanket wrapped around them, cuddling, back rubs with mommy and daddy, etc. Examples of bad touch include hitting, pushing, hair-pulling, spanking, aggressive tickling, and touching genitals or breasts—in short, *any* touch that is not wanted.

In addition to touch that clearly feels "good" or "bad," there is a touch that is confusing to a child. *Something about it just doesn't feel right.* It may frighten or overwhelm them, but they tolerate it because it comes from an older person they love. Or it may be confusing because it feels pleasurable to receive the special attention and "private time," but fear surrounds the secrecy. Sometimes the touch itself may feel both pleasurable and sickening at the same time, compounding the confusion.

Teaching children to be savvy by trusting their felt sense, intuition, and confusion as a red-alert to danger can go a long way in preventing sexual abuse. They may feel a sensation of dread in the pit of their stomach or a rapid heartbeat and sweaty palms that let them know something is very wrong with what they are seeing, hearing, or being asked to do, and that they need to get help from someone they trust. Sometimes children will know something isn't right because they feel numb, helpless, paralyzed, or frightened. Other times, their gut registers a vague "Uh-oh" type of early warning signal. Or children may feel a sense of shame, embarrassment, or guilt without understanding why. They may feel outright disgust that literally makes them feel sick to their stomach.

In any case, you can train your children to: 1) recognize and trust their inner sensations; 2) ask for help immediately (from you or someone nearby they feel safe with) if they experience any bad, uncomfortable, or confusing feelings; and 3) be assured that you will believe and protect them no matter who the person is or what that person told them or threatened would happen if the "secret" is revealed.

3. Teach Children What Sexual Violation Is, Who Might Approach Them, and How to Avoid Being Lured

In addition to being trained how to trust their "sense detectors" as an early warning sign, children also need to be taught what traps to avoid. Again, if they know in advance that a few older children and adults have problems and may try to take advantage of them, they are less likely to blame themselves if approached. They are also less likely to "take the bait."

In *No More Secrets* by Caren Adams and Jennifer Fay, the authors suggest that if a request . . .

- feels funny
- seems like it would separate her/him from other children
- goes against family rules
- involves a secret
- seems like an unearned "special" favor

. . . children should refuse the request, report it, and expect our support in backing them up *no matter who the authority figure is or how convincing she might appear.*[7]

Depending on the age of the child, it is important to give direct information. You might define sexual molestation by describing it as: someone touching you, looking at you, or asking you to touch them or look at them in a way that gives you a confusing, uncomfortable feeling. But it is also useful to name specific body parts and possible situations rather than to be vague. For example, you might say to a teenage girl, "Someone may brush up against your breasts and pretend it was accidental." To a school-aged child, you might say, "An older child, teacher, or other grown-up may want to touch your penis (vagina, anus) in the washroom." Give a variety of different examples relevant to your child's age, understanding, and situation. To a preschool child, you might explain, "Someone may want to hold you too close, rub against you, or put his hands in your pants."

Children Need to Know Who the "Someone" Might Be

Children, of course, need to be warned about taking rides, candy, gifts, etc., from strangers. They also need to be told that it may be a next-door neighbor, a relative, a babysitter, their teacher, coach, scout leader, recreation director, older sibling, or religious leader. They need to know that people can be nice and still have problems that cause them to do mean things sometimes. They also need to know that other children (almost always abused themselves) may be sexual abusers.

In doing research for this chapter, one of the most startling statistics uncovered was the large percentage of children molested by older brothers and teenage babysitters. "The estimates are that incest between siblings may be ***five times*** more common than paternal incest."[8] Two other statistics from this source are: the average age a sibling is violated is 8.2 years, and the most frequently reported age when abuse begins is 5 years old! This is a special age when kids are spontaneous and naturally loving. Dispelling the "dirty *old* man" myth, both the *Child Adolescent Psychiatry Journal* (1996) and the Criminal Justice Source Statistics (2000) report that the average age of most offenders is 14, and these 14-year-olds also comprise the ***largest number of sex offenders*** in any age group.[9] "Fifty-nine percent of child molesters developed deviant sexual interest during adolescence."[10] Adolescent hormones are raging, and teens are often troubled by their newly emerging sexual impulses and drives. Additionally, young teens do not comprehend the long-term damage that is done to vulnerable children and need the guidance of parents to teach them these things.

To prevent children from becoming either victim or victimizer, it is important to tell them in *simple language* what is and what is not appropriate touch and behavior between siblings. Sexual activity among siblings is not OK! It is also important to talk to *all* babysitters. According to an article in the *Journal of the American Medical Association*, "Although most perpetrators are boys or men, up to half of female perpetrators are teenage babysitters."[11] Talk to your children about what is and *is not* appropriate when they are in someone else's care. Make it clear to the sitter that your children have been taught to tell and *will tell* if they are touched, handled, or treated in any way that makes them uncomfortable or goes against the family rules. This can be done in a way that is firm but not heavy-handed.

Although babies and toddlers can't say when they have been sexually violated, *their bodies* encode the memories. They may have emotions and behaviors with no conscious memories to help them or their parents understand why they are anxious, withdrawn, or preoccupied with their private parts. These "body memories" may resurface at later developmental stages and throughout adulthood. They may cause inexplicable stomachaches, painful intercourse and other sexual dysfunctions, somatic illnesses in the pelvic area, and difficulties with sexuality. Preverbal children can't tell. This knowledge may help you to choose babysitters very carefully and perhaps avoid hiring younger teens who may be easily aroused and eager for sexual experimentation. They may be too young to understand that manipulation and stimulation of the baby's genitals causes distress and overwhelming physiological sensations. In fact, "early sexual stimulation causes a release of certain hormones and may activate the sexual organs to prematurely develop."[12]

Children also need to be taught that someone trying to abuse them may use force, but more often they will use trickery by promising something special. Again, give concrete examples, such as: a babysitter or older child who knows how much you love cats may say, "I'll let you have one of my kittens (or pet my cat), if you will sit on my lap and watch this video." Or the priest from your parish might offer, "You can be an altar boy, but first let's take off your clothes and try these vestments on to see if you're big enough yet." Children also need to know that they may be warned not to tell. If there are threats to keep secrets, your children need to know that is because the person who asked them has done something wrong, and that they must tell you so you can protect them from harm.

4. Offer Opportunities for Children to Practice Their Right to Say "No"

In order for children to develop the capacity to stop someone from improper, hurtful, uncomfortable, or confusing touch, they must have practice and experience with the right of refusal in other areas of their life. In this way it becomes a natural part of their self-confidence and becomes imprinted in their developing brain.

This organic process happens when parents respect children's likes and dislikes and allow them to make age-appropriate choices whenever possible. Examples of this are choices in food, clothing, and play activities. Parents show disrespect by forcing a child to wear something she dislikes or eat something distasteful, "just because I'm your mother (or dad) and I say so!" Or, if they chronically disregard a child's feelings, tastes, opinions, and sensibilities by overriding them with their own, it leaves an indelible mark in a child's consciousness, communicating that "father" *always* knows best and that authority should *never* be questioned. It also teaches kids not to trust their own instincts. Adults foster these impressions by saying things such as "How can you be cold when it's so warm outside?" or "Don't color those flowers blue—they're supposed to be orange!" or "You get to choose when you're a grown-up."

When children grow up in this type of authoritarian climate, they cannot be expected to have the wits about them to suddenly say "no" to an adult (especially one who taught them to put their own feelings aside for the sake of the grown-up) when they are under stress and are confused or frightened. These children, then, are the most vulnerable to blaming themselves and feeling chronically ashamed, guilty, and separate if they are lured into a sexual assault.

Children who grow up knowing that their choices are valued and their grown-ups will protect them from intrusive, rough, or otherwise unpleasant handling by another are more likely to assert their right to say "No!" when they sense that they are about to be trapped in a dangerous situation.

This begins by parents attending to a baby who is fussing because he has been picked up by someone he doesn't feel safe with. It is important for parents to stop older siblings or classmates from bullying, tickling beyond toleration, punching, biting, and kicking. If children do not want to be hugged or cuddled for whatever reason, they should not be forced or made to feel bad about themselves. If we ignore or ridicule children's right to set up protective boundaries (to control touch), how will they be able to protect themselves later in life? Instead we must honor each child's non-verbal "no" and give him lots of practice in saying "No," "Stop," or "Don't." This can then be applied when he does not like the way a certain touch makes him feel.

Children have an instinctive sense about which adults and older children are safe and which are unsafe. We need to trust this sense and foster its continuing development rather than try to change a child's mind. Since the molester is most often a family friend or relative, it is common for the assault to happen in stages over time, starting with lewd thoughts long before an actual assault takes place. The following story illustrates just how important it is to listen to your children.

Jenny and Uncle Sherman

When Jenny was eight years old, she began to get a "funny feeling" around her Uncle Sherman, but could not understand why. She loved to play with her cousins but was more relaxed when they visited her house. Now, at twelve, she figured out why she was so guarded. Jenny came back from an overnight quite upset. The next day, she told her mother that when her uncle played the "wrestle game" with the kids, Sherman pinned her down and intentionally rubbed his body on hers, gently brushing up against her newly developing breasts.

Jenny's mother dismissed this "red flag" and protected her brother's reputation rather than protecting Jenny! She told her daughter that Uncle Sherman "would never do anything like that, was a nice man, and probably touched her by accident in play." Her mother missed a clear opportunity to reinforce Jenny's gut feelings and protect her from future attacks by having a frank talk with Uncle Sherman about what happened and how it affected her daughter so that he never treats Jenny or any other child that way. And that he will not be allowed to be alone with her. She also missed an opportunity to help her daughter process her feelings, and to know what to do or say if anything similar happened again.

Instead, Jenny had to deal with her feelings alone. She felt uncomfortable with her budding sexuality because of what happened with Uncle Sherman and became ashamed of her body. She also thought, like most children who aren't informed, that something was wrong with her or this would never have happened. When Jenny was sixteen her mother asked Uncle Sherman to pick his niece up from school and bring her home while her car was being repaired. Jenny was shocked when Uncle Sherman began to drive towards the mountains rather than towards her house. He said he was going to take his favorite niece for a hamburger. After eating, they continued towards the mountains. When they arrived in an isolated wooded area, he told her how much he had always "loved" her, yearned for her, and asked if she would remove her bra so that he could make her feel "really good." Not having a clue what to do, Jenny sat in her uncle's truck motionless while he continued his assault by undoing the clasps himself.

Remember how Jenny distrusted Uncle Sherman as early as age eight! Perhaps she felt those "icky" sensations because of the lewd way he looked at her, or maybe she sensed a strong sexual-energy directed at her that made her feel uncomfortable. If Jenny's mother had taught her that even family members sometimes do hurtful things, taken her daughter's instinctual feelings seriously, validated her discomfort, and taken action to further protect Jenny, the later sexual assaults could have been avoided and Jenny most likely wouldn't be struggling with painful feelings now, as an adult, whenever her loving husband desires to admire or touch her breasts.

5. Teach Children What to Say and Do

Just as naturally as you teach children about other safety issues, such as crossing the street, wearing seat belts, and water safety, you can teach them the difference between "good" touch and "secret" (confusing or bad) touch. Often, however, parents assume that children understand what this is and how to respond when actually they do not! One way to test their comprehension after a "talk" is to ask them to use their own words to tell you what they think you mean. Another way is to role-play possible scenarios, tailoring them to your child's vulnerabilities and age. Children learn best through games and guided practice.

In *No More Secrets,* the authors offer four different games that provide enjoyable rehearsals.[13] These are paraphrased from that book and described below:

─────────────── ✐ ───────────────

GAMES

WHAT IF . . .

This is a good game to play to check understanding and to practice plans for a variety of situations. The whole family gets to ask questions and create different answers. Sample questions to stimulate children's thinking are:

- What if your bicycle got a flat tire and someone offered to give you a lift home?
- What if a bully took your ball and told you to follow him to his garage to get it?
- What if the new neighbor down the street asks if you can keep a secret?

STORYTELLING

This is a way to provide positive, concrete examples of children acting on their own behalf and being successful. A story might go like this:

There was a little boy who had an older brother who always bought him whatever he wanted. But the brother would scare him by hiding and jumping out at him in the dark. The little boy didn't like to be scared, but he didn't know what to do. One day he asked his father if he was ever scared. His dad said, "Sometimes." The little boy asked him how he got unafraid. Dad asked him if something was frightening him, so the little boy told about his big brother. His dad helped him figure out that he could tell his brother not to do that anymore and could come to him if he still didn't stop.

FACE-OFF OR "SPACE INVADERS"

This game helps children understand their own body space and boundary needs.

Two children stand face to face, back up from each other, and then walk towards each other until one of them becomes uncomfortable with the closeness. They can then point to or name the place in their body that feels uncomfortable and describe what the sensation feels like. They can then be encouraged to make a movement and sound or word that lets the other child know they do not have permission to come closer. Have them continue until their body language clearly shows that they really mean it.

Children may goof off at first and bump into each other, but they can tell the point where they are too close as a sign to protect their "space." Have them try the same game side by side and back to back or approach each other from different angles. After children explore body space boundaries with each other, they can practice with an appropriate adult if they wish. The adult might play different roles, first pretending to be a stranger, then an acquaintance, and then someone well-known, like a parent or neighbor.

The game can help children identify quickly when someone is invading their space. This reinforces refinement of (and trust in) their own body clues and instinctive signals that we talked about earlier. This alerts them to when they need to go to an adult for help.

"NO!"

This game increases the likelihood that children will say "No" to an exploitative approach.

1. Brainstorm rules that seem to encourage children to do things they might not want to do. Examples:
   - Be nice to people.
   - Don't hurt people's feelings.
   - Don't be rude. If someone speaks to you, answer.
   - You are responsible for taking care of other people.
   - Think of others' needs before your own.
   - Don't question adult authority.
   - Obey the babysitter.

   Rules like these, named, discussed, and acknowledged, lose power and everybody can make choices about when it might be good to follow those rules and when it's better to say "No!"

2. Practice saying, "No!" Start by having two children or one child and one adult take turns asking pretend favors. Start with a simple "No!" answer that the partner must accept. Adapt the difficulty level as children become more skilled by saying things like "What's the matter, don't you like me anymore?" and then see where it leads. Be sure to give the children chances to say "No!" to adults.

   You may be surprised at how easily children (especially girls) "cave in" to adult requests because they think they are being mean, disobedient, or disrespectful to do otherwise. This game can help you assess how your children might behave in an assault situation and give you a chance to help them practice being strong and assertive in saying, "No!"

Help your children to counter learned physical helplessness around people who are bigger, stronger, or have authority over them. In addition to the games above, organized sports, martial arts, fitness exercises, running games, arm wrestling, and other activities like a special kids' "model mugging" class can promote a sense of physical competence as an antidote to a sense of helplessness. Children must receive clear messages from adults that it is permissible and expected for them to protect and defend themselves whenever possible and to get help from an adult when they cannot.

The Little-Discussed Emotion of Disgust

Although the symptoms of trauma—how children show rather than tell us that they have been sexually violated—were thoroughly covered in Chapter Three, it would be remiss to not mention the common symptom of disgust that is so pervasive with sexual trauma. In her 2004 book *Disgust: The Gatekeeper Emotion*, Susan B. Miller describes "the self's need to safeguard itself against noxious intrusions from without and simultaneously to nourish itself through contact with 'otherness'."[14] The emotion of disgust works in unison with the body's digestive tract, forming these natural boundaries between us and disgusting smells, tastes, experiences, and images. When working with both children and adults who have experienced sexual trauma (and invasive medical trauma), we find that it is not unusual for them to show symptoms of nausea, feeling "sick to their stomach," "like they could vomit," or being left with "a bad taste in the mouth." Noses, mouths, and tongues will scrunch up often as a prelude to a memory. It is crucial to accept these signs and symptoms as a desire for the body to complete its defensive "disgust responses" by exploring them with curiosity until they subside on their own.

Because sexual molestation is such an unsavory experience,

clinical evidence indicates that when this "distasteful" emotion appears symptomatically, it often leads to the origin of just such abuse. Let's look at how Amy's mother began to suspect that her daughter was suffering from sexual trauma.

Amy's First Date

Fifteen-year-old Amy was excited that Erik, the boy she had a serious crush on, asked her to go to the movies. He was cute, thoughtful, smart, and made Amy laugh. Her parents gave her permission if she promised to be home by 10:30 p.m. Surprisingly, Amy ended up at home long before curfew.

What went wrong? Amy had been so happy until Erik reached over to innocently hold her hand. Both of them were surprised at her reaction. Amy felt sick to her stomach, excused herself at the theatre, and with profound embarrassment made her way to the ladies' room as quickly as her legs could carry her. There she vomited. She felt humiliated by her puzzling experience.

The following week, the same thing happened when Erik walked Amy home from school and, this time, asked to hold her hand. Just the thought of holding hands provoked disgust, although she knew it was not towards Erik, whose company she thoroughly enjoyed. Amy's mother made an appointment for her to work through these deeply ingrained feelings of disgust of unknown origin at the thought of normal physical contact with a boy.

As Amy focused on the sensations of nausea when she remembered Erik reaching for her hand at the movies, she had an image of a fifteen-year-old male who lived next door when she was about four or five years old. He had come into her back yard where she was gleefully playing alone, took her roughly by the hand, and touched her on her crotch, which sent waves of terror through her little preschool body.

Amy quickly made the connection of the association of terror of what might happen next with the thought of a teenage boy grabbing her hand. The disgust, nausea, and vomiting she experienced was a way for her body to make a boundary to safeguard itself against noxious intrusions, since her body memory had in the past "tagged" hand-holding with an adolescent boy as "dangerous." Fortunately, within two sessions of working to uncouple her sensations and images, Amy was symptom-free and able to enjoy hand-holding with her first love.

The Frequently Overlooked Repercussions of Sexual Abuse before Puberty

Although any trauma can cause havoc in the developing core self of a child, sexual trauma is second only to neglect in its damaging long-term effects. At a time when youngsters need to be open to making friends and experiencing new things, the intense fear of their shameful secret being exposed causes children who bear the scar of this sacred violation to hide from their peers. Over the years this lack of socialization and the failure to create a network of close friendships causes difficulties and loneliness that, without intervention, follow children into adulthood.

A childhood featuring sexual abuse compounded with absence of social support has been shown by researchers to be the early origins that are clearly linked to later self-destructive behaviors, including suicide attempts, cutting, eating disorders, and dangerous risk-taking behaviors, such as substance abuse and promiscuity.[15] The research goes on to explain that sexually abused girls typically cannot tolerate friendships. They cope by becoming too aggressive or too shy. Their hormone levels are significantly different from girls who were not abused. Without friendships to help them develop, these girls grow up with a poor sense of self, few negotiation skills, and a lack of healthy communication skills, boundaries, and pleasure. Loneliness coupled with high levels of testosterone substantially increases their risk of sexually provocative behavior, sexually transmitted disease, and teen pregnancy.

Parents and school personnel can intervene when they understand the importance of helping school-age girls (and boys, too) develop friendships. Between second and fourth grade, girls determine a "pecking order" in the classroom and on the playground. They scapegoat children who act "different" or "strange." Girls, especially, can be extremely cruel to other girls by laughing, teasing, gossiping, exclusion, and other acts of betrayal. When the family is stable and girls are able to get help after being abused, they are able to have girlfriend relationships and are far less likely to engage in "voluntary" premature sexual experiences.

Juanita's Social Isolation

While I was working as an elementary school psychologist, a sweet, shy, fourth-grader named Juanita was referred to me by her teacher and the school principal. She had been molested by a family member, but that was not the primary reason I was asked to meet with her. Although totally comfortable around adults, Juanita had *zero* friends her own age. She occasionally played "mother" to a few second-grade children by protecting them on the playground. Mostly, Juanita learned quickly that if she offered to help the teacher at recess and hang out around my office before and after school "to help out" she could successfully avoid relating to peers. If forced to go out to recess, Juanita followed the school principal around the playground making small talk. By the end of the first school month, her clinginess was beginning to get on everyone's nerves.

Fortunately, Juanita was able to process her sexual molestation in weekly one-to-one counseling sessions. Understanding her need to learn friendship-making skills, I urged Juanita to join a newly forming friendship group for third- and fourth-graders. She was timid at first with the girls her own age and bossy with the younger girls. It took some time, but she finally made at least one tentative new friend by the end of the first semester.

When I was transferred to a high school, I was struck by the number of teenage girls who complained that they had no friends, seemed oblivious to their own aggressive behavior, and literally hung their identity on whether or not they had a boyfriend. *These girls were the most vulnerable to suicide, cutting, dropping out of high school, and pregnancy.* As I got to know them and they trusted me with their secrets, I learned that ***every one of them had a history of sexual assault.*** Parents and teachers need to make sure that girls who isolate themselves from others or become highly aggressive in elementary school are given the support they need to make friends and to process any known sexual trauma as soon as possible. When no sexual trauma has been reported, but no friendships are forthcoming, parents and/or counselors need to ask the sensitive question that every parent should ask from time to time: "Has anyone ever touched you in a way that made you feel uncomfortable?" Early intervention is the ounce of prevention worth the pound of cure.

Why Most Children Don't Tell, and How to Make It Safe for Them to Tell You

In *Miss America By Day,* Marilyn Van Derbur poses the question: "Is it safe for children to tell?" She answers that rhetorical question: "Only if you and I make it safe."[16] What does she mean by this? Research she cites goes on to explain that the average age of first-time violation is five to six years old. Those who told a parent before age eighteen encountered the following negative parental reactions (some experienced multiple responses):

- Anger with them (the child) (42%)
- Blamed them (49%)
- Ignored the disclosure (50%)
- Became hysterical (30%)

Although it may seem unbelievable, the average child *never tells!* As a school psychologist, I can attest to this by the fact that countless children told me that I was the first one they ever confided their secret to! Children typically fear blame and punishment. Common responses I have heard are "She would kill me if she knew!" "My mother/father would just call me a liar." "She wouldn't do anything anyway because she wouldn't want to upset him." "He'll say it was all my fault."

The good news is that you can cultivate a climate of safety in your household. And it will pay big dividends for your youngsters. Another study attests to the benefits: "Those who told immediately or very shortly after the abuse *and were believed and supported* showed relatively few long-term traumatic symptoms. Those who either did not tell (typically due to fear or shame) or who told and then encountered a negative, blaming, disbelieving, or ridiculing response were classified as extremely traumatized."[17] Ms. Van Derbur wrote that when she first started advocating on behalf of children, she had bumper stickers made and placed on hundreds of cars that read BELIEVE THE CHILDREN.

To increase the odds that your child will tell you: 1) Teach them about inappropriate touching as early as preschool; 2) Let them know it is *never* their fault; 3) Teach and role-play when and how to tell you or another safe adult; 4) Let them know in advance that you will believe and protect them; 5) Let them know that you will never reject or punish them. In other words, *make it easy for your child to tell!*

Date Rape and Other Teen Issues

Teens who have had early unresolved sexual wounds or who have grown up without healthy role models in the areas of personal privacy, boundaries, and sexuality may find it difficult to even be aware of personal safety (let alone practice it) on-the-spot when they begin dating. If their feelings, opinions, and rights were disregarded or minimized by parents, grandparents, or older siblings, these teens—who may never have practiced saying "no" (and have it respected) at home—are headed for trouble when they find themselves on a date, alone with a boy, in a car on a dark night, or even on a high school campus in broad daylight!

Unfortunately, date rape in high school and college happens far too often. One landmark study in the U.S. reported that one in four college women was the victim of rape or attempted rape.[18] Parents need to establish ongoing conversations with pre-teens and teens. Find out what your son's and daughter's concepts are regarding acceptable and unacceptable behavior under various circumstances. Don't assume that adolescents can make clear judgments when their hormones are raging, or that they don't need your guidance because they suddenly are in adult bodies. Teens often need more guidance at this important juncture than ever before.

According to the American Medical Association, a survey of 1,700 eleven- to fourteen-year-old boys and girls revealed that 51% of boys and girls said that forced sex was acceptable if the boy spent a lot of money on the girl; 65% of boys and 47% of girls said it was acceptable for a boy to rape a girl if they had been dating for more than six months; 87% of boys and 79% of girls said sexual assault was acceptable if the man and woman were married; and, one-third of acquaintance sexual assaults occur when the victim is between the ages of eleven and seventeen![19] In addition, there is the increasing use of date-rape drugs which, even though "they don't remember anything," leaves victims feeling dirty.

Another astonishing fact is the epidemic of oral sex going on in junior high and high school. According to *The Oprah Winfrey Show* (May 7, 2002), kids reported that "Oral sex is not considered sex in my school ... I don't think oral sex is as big a deal as a good-night kiss." In *Miss America By Day*, Marilyn Van Derbur makes reference to a fourteen-year-old girl who believes that 75% of the kids in her school are having oral sex.[20] The most distressing factor is that these teens do not realize that they are vulnerable to the transmission of venereal disease, or even that oral sex is a form of sexual activity.

Taking the time to ask and answer questions about what your adolescent children know, believe, and value can give the impetus to meaningful conversations that may help them to make more informed decisions. Other topics that require candid discussions are the use of contraceptives, opinions about abortion, and the risk of sexually transmitted diseases. Asking teenagers what their thoughts and feelings are about sexual issues can be a real eye-opener to just how much misinformation and mythology kids can carry around and spread to their friends. You can do so much to minimize your teen's vulnerability by talking, and more importantly, listening to what they have to say.

Echoes into the Next Generation: Transforming the Legacy

It doesn't help matters that we live in a "life-negative" culture where there is so much confusion around sexual values and behaviors. Often overlooked is the fact that sexual energy and life force energy are virtually one and the same. People who have passion for life have a flow of creative energy that feels inspiring and uplifting to be around. It is life-positive. They are considered to be "juicy"; those around them soak up their spark and creative exuberance. Instead of being the norm they stand out. Why is that? And what is creative life force anyway? Where does it originate? In Indian culture, it is referred to as "second-chakra energy" and it arises from our sexual organs. It is the arousal energy that made troubadours sing, and the great masters compose, build, paint, create theater, and write literature that delights us and endures through time. It is the energy of both creation and procreation.

Unfortunately, so much fear exists about this potent force that social and religious institutions have had a pervasive influence in damping it down. When a lid is put on feelings and sensations that are normal so that they are considered pathological instead of accepted, it is difficult for living, breathing human beings to know what to do with these feelings. Attempts to dictate what thoughts, feelings, and sensations are proper or improper is a breeding ground for guilt and shame. Thoughts are thoughts and sensations are sensations. Period! They do not need to be acted out inappropriately. When the moral judgment is removed, individuals are able to acknowledge and experience their authentic life energy freely. Without the defensive mechanisms of denial and repression, healthy decisions and expressions of sexuality are more likely. The unspeakable becomes spoken, and families can become a model for shaping healthy versus damaging behavior.

Healthy Sexuality

What does healthy sexuality look like in families? Let's look at two critical stages of child development: early childhood and adolescence. Somewhere between the ages of four and six, children feel a special bond and attraction to their opposite-sex parent. In fact, this phenomenon is so universal that the Greeks portrayed the unfortunate consequences of this *unresolved* dilemma in the plays *Oedipus Rex* and *Electra*. (Of course, with new, blended, and same-sex households, these stages may show up differently.)

Daughters, especially around the age of five, routinely fall in love with their dads, as do little boys with their moms. This is a normal, healthy stage of development. Children of this age will "flirt" with the parent of the opposite sex. This is not flirting in the adult sexual sense, but rather a practicing necessary to negotiate this developmental task. In other words, the kinds of behaviors that will later form the repertoire of adolescent, peer flirtations are first elicited and tested at home where it is supposed to be safe. This is the time when little girls will tell their fathers, "I love you, daddy; I want to marry you and have a baby with you when I grow up."

At this delicate, vulnerable age what is needed to foster healthy development is for the father to tenderly say (and mean) something like: "I love you too, sweetheart, but daddy's married to mommy. When you grow up you can marry someone special just for you, and if you want, you can have children with him. But, I'm so glad that you're my little girl and I will always be your daddy."

Many times, what happens instead is that the child's manner may be handled poorly by misreading this *truly innocent* "practicing" behavior. Instead of the parent helping the child with her emerging sexuality, the response may be more reminiscent of that of a lover, promoting in tone, actions, or words their "special" relationship. For example, playful flirtations such as "Yes, my little princess, I'll always be your prince—but let's keep it our little secret," may result in further awkward and inappropriate responses. This courting behavior often feels overwhelming to the child and may be frightening to the parent as well. This fear can lead to a squelching of appropriate touch and affection so necessary for emotional maturation.

Well-defined generational boundaries are vital for healthy sexual development. Parents need to be adults, *not peers,* to their children. Frequently these boundaries are weak in adults who were themselves sexually traumatized as children. If you are struggling with these issues, get help to strengthen your own boundaries so that you can model healthy limits, thereby transmitting healthy sexuality to the next generation. Children are supposed to lose rather than win the Oedipal struggle, with the parents' gentle guidance in accepting reality versus fantasy. They may not like giving up these romantic illusions, but they must! It is better that they accept this disappointment as preschoolers than to grow up romantic fools pursuing partners that are unavailable or worse.

Additionally, if these lessons are not learned early on, it is likely that a sudden fracture of the parent-child relationship will occur at the next important stage of sexual development—adolescence. At this time the parent is confronted with a blossoming young lady or man who looks like the spouse that he or she fell in love with some years earlier—but perhaps even more beautiful or handsome! If the parents are not comfortable with their own sexuality and warmly erotic with each other, this sudden attraction to their teenager may cause what is known as *incest panic*. Particularly in the case of father-daughter relationships, the father is drawn to his offspring in ways that the possibility of acting them out seems real and threatening. Out of this fear, he may, consciously or unconsciously, suddenly cut off physical warmth, becoming distant and cold. In this typical scenario, the daughter feels not only abandoned but also rejected because of her new and fragile sexuality and forming sense of self. Sadly, so often adolescent girls "lose" their father's affection just when they need it most.

And then there is the possibility that at different ages, the father may have actually acted out sexually with her. He may have touched her inappropriately or kissed her on the mouth with a more adult kiss. (In step-families, this vulnerability is heightened even further.) This could have frightened both daughter and father (or stepfather). And, tragically, in some cases it goes farther.

So how can these awkward but common sexual feelings be handled? If we neither wish to withdraw affection nor repress these "unthinkable" feelings, what are the options? Held in, these powerful energies can easily build like pressure in a volcano—only to be felt covertly as tension within the family dynamics. This dysfunctional undercurrent can lead to addictions and health problems including eating disorders. Acted out in sexual ways, these conflicts become perverted, leading to frigidity, impotence, and promiscuity.

Neither of the above two choices is appealing to healthy functioning. Let's take a look at a refreshing third option using the somatic (felt-sense) experiencing you learned earlier. With honesty, rather than denial and repression, coupled with compassion, you *can* regulate these forces. First of all, when these sexual sensations arise, notice them for what they are and try to accept them in a non-shaming way as part of a shared, if not universal, human experience. Next, allow these sensations to move through as waves of *pure energy*. This energy is then free to be expressed in creative outlets or transferred to an appropriate partner. These conflicts can be moved through in this transformative way in a surprisingly short time.

Breaking the Cycle of Sexual Trauma

Here is a simple case example to illustrate the importance of working with sexual feelings and sensations:

The New Father

A young father reported that he was anxious about diapering his infant son. As he was assisted in focusing on the pure sensations that arose (without thought or judgment), he noticed first some dread in his stomach; next, he noticed feelings of sexual pleasure in his genitals coupled with a sense of shame. As he continued to focus, with compassion, on these different bodily feelings, the sexual sensations turned to rage and, then, disgust within minutes as he remembered being molested by his favorite grandfather at a very tender age.

Focusing on these sensations allowed this new father to feel anger towards his grandfather for the first time. As the anger slowly dissolved, tears of liberation flowed. He was relieved to realize that he wasn't a bad person. Later, at home, he purposefully paid attention to his sensations while watching his wife diaper their son. This young man was then both pleased and amazed at how quickly the sexual sensations that were stimulated were directed towards his wife instead. And as he gazed at his little boy this time, the feelings that emerged were those of pride and love.

In summary, when parents become less afraid of experiencing their own sensations, practice appropriate boundaries, and have an understanding of what children need to develop healthy sexuality, awkwardness and tension are replaced by more comfortable familial relationships. Parents then become free to show warmth and affection to their children (at any developmental stage) in ways that are neither romanticized nor sexualized.

When puberty hits, teenagers who have received healthy models and a good dose of affection are less likely to feel inept with their own budding love relationships. They may be fortunate enough to escape the painful clumsiness that often leads to avoidance of social activity or its opposite—being compulsively driven into promiscuity in an attempt to get the love that a rejecting repressed parent was unable to give.

On the other hand, there is a strong possibility that the adolescent who has not had the advantage of growing up in a sexually healthy family may re-enact a violation of his sexual boundaries by violating the boundaries of a peer, such as in date rape or sexual harassment, or taking advantage of a younger child, such as a neighbor, sibling, or child they are babysitting. By parents providing a healthy model and supporting the task of sexual development, the cycle of intergenerational sexual trauma can be interrupted and a new legacy of life-positive energy can be passed on.

On one more note, we wish to acknowledge the reality that many successful families may be "non-traditional"—having two parents of the same sex, being a single-parent, step-family, or blended family—yet we trust that some of the ideas presented here will have relevance to your particular situation.

All families need nurturing touch such as hugging, touching, holding, cuddling, and massage. It is never acceptable, however, for an adult or older child to satisfy one's own needs for comfort, nurturance, power, or sexual gratification by exploiting a child (or anyone) who is incapable of understanding and protecting themselves against a choice they were not free, or did not perceive they were free, to make.

This chapter is by no means exhaustive. There are many wonderful books to help parents talk to their children about healthy sex, normal sexual development, and sexual assault. *No More Secrets* by Caren Adams and Jennifer Fay, which is quoted here, may be an "oldie" but it is a gem of a "goodie." Also, *Miss America By Day* by Marilyn Van Derbur gives a meticulous, personal, and far-reaching account of the long-term effects of sexual abuse. It is an invaluable guide to the prevention of sexual violation of children. The CD *Sexual Healing, Transforming the Sacred Wound,* by Peter A. Levine (Sounds True, 2003) is an audio learning series that includes various guided exercises; it is a useful companion to this chapter.

TOWARDS A
HUMANISTIC VIEW
OF TRAUMA

Introduction:
Hope for the Future Through
Prevention and Societal Change

Part IV concludes this guide with an optimistic look towards the future. Systemic change in our society's institutions would make a huge leap forward in the prevention and healing of trauma, and in our general well-being. Parts I, II, and III were written for all adults (professional or lay) who care for children. Part IV addresses the special needs of infancy, as well as provides impetus for readers who wish to participate as change agents on a broader scale. For example, people may be motivated to become activists in their communities by organizing grassroots campaigns that make the needs of mothers and babies central to the birthing process. Leaders with careers in institutions such as education and medicine may be inspired to design programs of proactive care. Certain overwhelming events cannot be avoided; however, traumatic symptoms *can* often be prevented or at least minimized.

Although all of the chapters can be useful to *all* who touch children's lives, Chapter Ten was written for prospective parents and all those who work with birthing and babies. It features guidelines and practices to promote healthy pregnancy, birth, and infant development. It also includes ways of bonding and welcoming your baby into the world with respect and dignity as you learn what babies need to thrive, rather than merely survive.

Chapter Eleven was written specifically for educators. Case examples and activities are described that can be used by teachers, counselors, nurses, school psychologists, social workers, as well as occupational, physical, and speech therapists who work in the schools. A fresh look at addressing challenging students in the new light of trauma is presented that can be especially useful for student support teams. The ideas and games can be used with individual students, small groups, or the entire class. They focus on improving both learning and behavior.

Chapter Twelve was written for educators, children's mental health organizations, and other providers who wish to be fortified with more skills to deal with community catastrophes and mass fatalities. The activities can be used with groups of students after both man-made atrocities (such as war and terrorism) and natural disasters (such as fire, hurricanes, earthquakes, floods, and tsunamis).

Chapter Thirteen concludes this book. It is targeted towards program managers, top-level administrators, and other change agents who are responsible for writing policies and procedures that can transform our health care delivery systems. Ideally it will inspire and seed ideas that can be infused into existing organizations to bring about radical improvements leading to a brighter future in patient care, especially for infants and children.

CHAPTER TEN

🌿

On Coming into the World: Birthing and Babies

When we ponder the nature of being human . . .
spirit embodied in matter . . . And when we respect
the power and knowing of every birthing woman and baby . . .
and honor their vulnerability . . . Then we help birth a
better future and a happier, more peaceful world.

– Suzanne Arms, author of Immaculate Deception I & II
and founder of Birthing the Future[1]

For in the baby lies the future of the world. . . .
– from a Mayan proverb

This "baby" chapter is meant to open your eyes to the delicate and impressionable beginnings of life—the fetal period through infancy. It suggests both personal and systemic changes to make birthing practices more family-friendly and in line with what we know is needed by babies, pregnant women, and their partners for a natural and gentle birth. Chapter Ten also addresses: 1) how to enter the magical inner world of your baby; 2) what you need to know about infant brain development and the important role that caregivers play during this fascinating time; and 3) what can be done to support a baby who has had a difficult entry into this world.

If your baby is no longer a newborn you needn't be dismayed. For the older infant or toddler who did not have an ideal birth experience, you will be heartened to learn that there is much that can be done in the way of repair. Babies and young children, although vulnerable, are also quite responsive and resilient when given the proper support. If you instinctively feel that your baby is still struggling with incomplete birthing responses, you will appreciate this chapter's practical tips to help you make a more secure bond and meet the developmental needs of your growing baby.

A Content Mother-to-Be Provides an Ideal Womb

Wisdom seen printed on a coffee mug: "The best thing a father can do for his children is to love their mother." There may be quite a bit of truth to that adage, especially during the fetal period. Studies by Stott and Latchford[2] as early as the 1970s reveal that marital discord during pregnancy can cause negative repercussions to the unborn infant. In fact, they discovered that harsh conflict between parents was closely associated with infant ill health, neurological dysfunction, developmental lag, and behavioral disturbances when parental tension was chronic. Short-term resolvable stresses did not appear to have significant long-term effects on the infant. Another pioneer in the field of infant stress and early child development, Lester Sontag, conducted longitudinal studies into young adulthood (1966). He concluded that high maternal anxiety correlated with somatic problems and personality shifts in infants that could be observed in later life.[3]

Changing Times

We live in a world of extremes. There was an era in Western culture when it was mandated that pregnant women be pampered, perhaps resting all day long, and excluded from activities that might evoke even minimal strain. Working outside the home was scorned even for non-pregnant women; in addition, women were excluded from important financial decision-making, legal contracts, and voting. If, due to necessity, they did work outside the home, women who got pregnant hid their "condition" as long as possible in fear of being fired or put on unpaid leave as soon as the pregnancy was found out. With the dawning of the age of feminism in the late 1960s and early '70s, women became "free" of such restrictions. Gains toward equality in the workplace, long overdue, were finally won.

Although the discriminatory treatment suffered by women seems silly and unfathomable now, it is good to take stock of societal changes and not "throw the baby out with the bathwater." A growing number of researchers are studying prenatal stress and gathering convincing evidence of the importance of the mother's well-being and mental health while she is carrying a baby.

Studies in the twenty-first century validate the work of pioneers on the phenomenon of "transmittable stress." In a 2004 *New York Times* article entitled "Tracking Stress and Depression Back to the Womb" (December 7, 2004), Laurie Tarkan cites a number of research articles that link maternal stress and depression to effects on the developing fetus, with some studies looking at repercussions on the child's life at four years of age. These studies have shown effects ranging from less "stress resilience" in newborns to serious behavior problems in preschoolers.

Through fetal monitoring, researchers are able to listen to movements and heartbeats of human babies. There is clear preliminary evidence that the fetuses of mothers who are stressed or depressed respond differently from those of emotionally healthy women. In addition to behavior problems later in life, "these infants have a significantly increased risk of developing learning problems, and may themselves be more vulnerable to depression or anxiety as they age" when compared to children of mothers who were less burdened by mental health and high-stress issues.

Dr. Catherine Monk from the College of Physicians and Surgeons at Columbia University studied fetal heart rate changes when women in their third trimester performed a series of stress-inducing computer tasks. *All* the women were affected with increased heart rate, respiration, and blood pressure. Remarkably, the heart rate of fetuses of emotionally healthy mothers did *not* increase, while the heart rate of babies with depressed or anxious mothers reacted to these stressful stimuli with increased heart rate.[4]

The way this works is that depression tends to heighten the levels of stress hormones like cortisol, which might make fetuses more jumpy. Chronic exposure to these hormones at such a critical time may shape an infant's adaptive responses. In these studies, depressed moms also had lower levels of serotonin and dopamine, important neurotransmitters that affect mood. Their newborns had less developed learning skills, were less able to calm themselves when agitated, and were less responsive socially, according to Dr. Tiffany Field, author of one study and director of the Touch Research Institute at the University of Miami, School of Medicine.[5] There is no question that exposure to excessive stress hormones alters the *in utero* environment. It is erroneous to believe that the fetus is buffered from its surroundings until birth.

The implications are clear. Early prenatal care needs to go beyond the "check-up." Emphasis needs to be shifted to self-care, nurturance, stress reduction, and reverence for pregnant women as a cultural priority. The mother's mental, physical, and spiritual health during gestation plays a crucial role in laying the foundation for a healthy baby. Longer-term studies make the issue of prenatal maternal mental health even more poignant. In a study published in 2002 in *The British Journal of Psychiatry,* researchers asked 7,448 women in England to assess their level of stress while they were pregnant and answer questionnaires about their preschool-aged children's behavior. Four-year-olds whose mothers reported high levels of anxiety in late pregnancy were more likely to have behavior problems, most notably attention difficulties. "Mothers who scored in the top 15 percent of the sample on anxiety at 18 or 32 weeks' gestation were generally 2–3 times more likely to have a child who scored more than 2 standard deviations above the mean in behavioral/emotional problems," according to the author of this study, Dr. Thomas O'Connor, a professor of psychiatry at the University of Rochester.[6]

Providing a Safe Haven for the Developing Baby

It is obvious that we must shift our values for the well-being of future generations. Providing the safe haven of a "good womb" experience must become a societal priority. If you are a woman who loves and wants to work, or you have no choice, it is important that you monitor your stress levels during the day. Using sensation-focused mindfulness, you can alleviate the accumulation of stress, giving you and your baby an opportunity for deep relaxation and rest. Refrain from work that puts undue pressure on you mentally, emotionally, physically, or spiritually. If there is ever a time to take optimal care of yourself, this is it!

Another fact we know from studies with fetal mammals is that the autonomic nervous system does not mature in the womb. This is a little complicated so try and bear with us. Even before the time of birth, a very primitive (unmyelinated vagal) system is the main operative autonomic component. This system, when under stress, suppresses heart rate while (over-) stimulating intestinal activity. During the stress of birth, if the heart rate dips too low and meconium is present, fetal distress is indicated. Babies who have been highly stressed during and after birth may be lethargic, lacking energy because of over-activation of this "shut-down" system. The sympathetic branch, responsible for arousal, such as increased heart rate and flailing limbs, is less developed at birth and continues to mature in the following months. When this system is over-activated, babies may seem fussy and inconsolable. The "new" parasympathetic branch of the autonomic nervous system, responsible for calming, is very immature at birth and only develops fully around eighteen months of age. The baby's maturing nervous system is dependent, therefore, on its environment to groove the neural pathways for deep relaxation, self-soothing, and building the capacity to tolerate stress and frustration.[7] After birth, infants need parents who can keep them warm, nurtured, rocked, cuddled, held, smiled at, and sung to. They need caregivers who are not stressed out, distracted, overwhelmed, depressed, or anxious. These early months shape the nervous system of the newborn and become a blueprint for the way the baby handles life's ups and downs. Marital discord, domestic violence, harshness, drug and alcohol abuse, and emotional unavailability train the brain to perceive danger even when there is none! The brain is tuned to hyper-alertness until it can no longer cope and shuts down.

Babies thrive when they sense they are safe. Family, friends, neighborhoods, and societies can strive together to support those who are raising babies to ensure a brighter future. Experienced parents can be a vital resource in helping inexperienced parents. Envision a world where all moms can have in-home volunteer helpers to mentor and lift them out of the stresses and strains that go along with parenthood. With the shrinking of the extended family, it is not uncommon for mothers with newborns to live in isolation. Support groups that begin at birthing centers and other groups like La Leche League (which gives free help to nursing mothers) can reduce this sense of separation.

Prenates and Babies
Are Sentient, Conscious Beings

Well-documented research shows that long-term memory begins even before birth![8] For example, "when mothers repeatedly read aloud a given story passage during the last trimester of their pregnancy, their newborn babies recognized that specific story passage during the first 33 hours after birth."[9] Although the study of how babies are shaped by their earliest experiences in the womb as well as during and immediately after birth is still in its own infancy, we've learned a great deal about these early imprints. Clues come both anecdotally from adults in therapy and from the stories told through the gestures and body language of babies and children. For example, a baby whose mother was heavily anesthetized during labor may appear placid and resigned after birth—mistaken for a "good" baby. Or, a baby who started her journey pushing her way down the birth canal in perfect rhythm with her mother's contractions only to be pulled out by suctioning or forceps near the end of her journey may show a pattern of behavior such as effectively beginning something and then giving up on projects or relationships just as they are coming to fruition. A baby born as an emergency cesarean-section may play out yet another story.

Wendy Anne McCarty, PhD, author of the book *Welcoming Consciousness: Supporting Babies' Wholeness from the Beginning of Life* (2004), helps us understand the exquisite sentient nature of the consciousness of babies prior to, during, and after birth. In her book, she cites many remarkable studies of children and their parents that verify with precision the accuracy of fetal and birth "stories." She has been a pioneer in both clinical practice and research in the field of pre- and perinatal psychology. McCarty teaches us how to observe and listen to the difficulties experienced by babies, toddlers, and their families during the prenatal and birthing period. From her rich work facilitating and witnessing the restoration of natural rhythms and attunements disrupted by traumatizing events for mother and baby, she teaches others how to "listen," observe, and follow the baby's lead in order to facilitate repair. This includes validating the baby's distress and assisting the baby in completing incomplete motor responses. In "The Power of Beliefs: What Babies Are Teaching Us," McCarty shares with us four vignettes from her therapeutic work that she co-facilitated with Ray Castellino, D.C., at the BEBA Clinic in Santa Barbara.[10] These birth stories poignantly illustrate the powerful impact that beliefs—from these earliest stages of existence—already have in shaping behavior. Basic principles are demonstrated that assist babies to shift potentially constrictive beliefs to life-enhancing ones. McCarty also references a classic study by Chamberlain in which he hypnotized mothers and their children separately and compared their recall of birth and post-partum experiences and found that the stories of the children correlated to a high degree with the mother's story.[11]

In addition to the discovery and effect of complex early beliefs, Edward Z. Tronick of the University of Massachusetts, Amherst, writes: "Infant emotions and emotional communications are far more organized than previously thought."[12] He explains that the infant displays a variety of appropriate affective expressions and appreciates the emotional meaning exhibited by caregivers. He postulates that transformation of negative affect into positive affect depends on frequent reparation of interactive errors; whereas negative affect development appears to be associated with sustained periods of interactive failure.

Welcome to the World!

Throughout this book, you have been learning ways to assist children when they encounter shocking and overwhelming events. A commonly overlooked stressor is the birthing process itself. Making the transition from the protective, warm, amniotic-fluid environment of mother's womb into the reality of the outside world can be a challenging event. This is especially true when there is little consciousness regarding the needs of the birthing mother and baby. Established medical practices often create an unnatural hostile environment, which can be the source of additional, and unnecessary, stress for the baby. The newborn's primal needs for emotional warmth, connection to mother, and for a response to its non-verbal communications are often largely ignored.

Thanks to the women's movement of the 1970s, together with concerned doctors and nurses, a variety of new humane birthing rituals were developed. Recognizing that the institutional environment of the typical hospital is not conducive to the comfort and nurture of mother, father, or baby, these early pioneers explored various prenatal and birthing practices. While the Lamaze and the Bradley methods prepared parents to work as a team during labor to ease painful contractions through synchronized breathing, Frederick Leboyer focused on quiet births in dim lighting and on easing the baby's transition from the warm maternal fluid by placing the babies in a warm-water tub. Training programs for midwives, practical nurses, and doulas were developed to meet the increasing demand for more sensitive home births. However, due to insurance issues and few contingency plans for emergencies, these never became mainstream methods. In the decade of the '90s, new understanding emerged regarding the consciousness of prenates and babies. Now in the twenty-first century there is a revival of interest in promoting more humane birthing practices.

Trauma Prevention from the Start: Birth As Nature Intended

Birth, as it is routinely conducted in North America, is a medically managed event usually taking place in a hospital. It is outrageous that we have gotten so far away from any sense of honoring the intimacy and sacredness of the birthing process. Instead, birth is treated as a pathological condition or as a disaster waiting to happen. With anesthesia, high-tech equipment, fear, and a "doctor-knows-best" attitude, women often lose access to their own instincts and initiative. They have been deprived of the right to engage naturally and actively in labor and birth without undue intrusion. Of course, some medical interventions are necessary for the safety of the moms and babies. When this is the case, a medical team with a compassionate attitude, aware of the consciousness of the baby, can be influential in creating a positive outcome.

Childbirth is a normal rite of passage requiring good health, emotional support, a tranquil environment with privacy from strangers, and a skilled midwife. Contrary to the modern myth that birth is too risky to occur outside of a hospital without specialized equipment, drugs, and a physician, credible scientific studies both in Europe and the U.S. show quite the opposite. In fact, what is shown is the inherent safety of a woman giving birth in the setting of her own home, if that is where she is most comfortable.

> Because labor is a complex physiological/psychological process regulated by a woman's own hormones, anything that increases confrontation is likely to stimulate the production and release of fight-or-flight hormones [adrenaline] that are well-known to inhibit or stop labor.[13]

Many hormones play a critical role in the process of labor and birth. While high levels of endorphin and oxytocin increase the likelihood of a shorter, calmer, and less painful birth, increased levels of adrenaline can create havoc. Disrupting labor may cause stress to the unborn baby, as well as a sense of panic and more painful labor for the mother.

This disruption (inhibiting labor through excess adrenaline) may have had the purpose of jolting our female ancestors to move quickly to a place of safety when endangered during the birthing process.[14] High levels of adrenaline, however, resulting from a woman's fear of medical procedures, restraint of movement due to monitoring equipment, lack of confidence, and/or lack of emotional support are detrimental to the process of birth. Unfortunately, the typical hospital setting is anything but natural. It can be intimidating and the cause of great anxiety, which is counterproductive during the birthing process.

Fortunately some exemplary models of natural childbirth exist in the developed world as well as in tribal societies. Holland, for example, has more midwives than obstetricians, with 70% of all births occurring under their guidance and one-third occurring at home. Breastfeeding is standard, and every baby and mother pair receives ongoing emotional and practical support from a Home Health Aide. Medical residents are schooled in natural birthing practices by observing experienced midwives. Sweden and Austria are examples of other developed nations that understand the importance of natural birthing practices. They also understand the precious responsibility society has to nurture the newborn's familial bonds—a factor that has the potential to reduce later violence. They understand the potent role of early bonds in shaping the baby's brain and behavior over a lifespan.

In the 2005 documentary *What Babies Want: An Exploration of the Consciousness of Infants,* Sobonfu Somé from the country of Burkina Faso in West Africa (featured among other birth pioneers such as Joseph Chilton Pearce and David Chamberlain) beautifully describes the Dagara tribal rituals for preparing the prenate, mother, family, and community for the entry of the new being.[15] (Somé is from the Dagara tribe, and her name means "Keeper of the Rituals.") The welcoming ritual includes placing village children up to age five next to the birthing room in order to answer the baby's first cry, seen as mirroring the newborn's call, thus signaling that it has arrived safely and in the right place. Dr. McCarty writes in her book *Welcoming Consciousness,* "The Dagara believe that what happens to us at birth and while in the womb actually molds the rest of our lives."[16] Emerging scientific research and clinical experience validate the accepted wisdom of these so-called primitive people.

Honoring the Miracle of Birth

The 1940s spawned an era of hospital births, along with the glorification of drugs and technological equipment capable of turning the miracle of birth into the debacle of unconscious delivery. By the late 1960s and early 1970s, the women's movement had spurred awareness of child abuse and domestic violence. Along with it came a new consciousness regarding women's bodies, rights, and treatment during labor.

Fortunately, the legacy from this era has not been entirely lost. It has been reawakened with a new respect for the miraculous process of birth. If having your baby at home is unacceptable, know that you have several other options. For one thing, birthing centers are becoming increasingly available. They have the advantage of combining the best of both worlds: creating the warmth and comfort of a "home birth," the sensitivity and experience of women trained in birthing (i.e., midwives and doulas), and the proximity of medical technology if needed.

It would be a laudable advance if professionals resolved their own birth traumas first, before participating in the birthing of others. As consciousness grows regarding early trauma patterns and birth stories continue to be revealed, perhaps more sensitivity and tenderness will emerge in the birth "industry."

Remember, You Have Choices: What To Look For

If you do choose to have a hospital birth, locate a midwife and doctor in your area who do not participate in the following unnecessary common practices:

1. **Inducing labor:** This interferes with the baby's natural rhythms and chosen time to exit the womb. Babies need time to be born and to experience the impulses to initiate. Rushed babies display the after-effects in later life by getting angry when feeling rushed or having lifelong patterns of motivational problems, punctuality, and quitting. There is a big difference between "being delivered" and "being born" (participating in our own "birth dance").

2. **Cutting the umbilical cord abruptly while it is still pulsating and pumping oxygen and nutrients into the baby:** This treats the baby as an object with no

feelings rather than a being with a range of physical and emotional needs for connection and nourishment, especially when it is so tender and vulnerable.

3. **Washing off the vernix:** The vernix caseosa was meant to be massaged into the baby's skin to support healthy immune function. It could be considered nature's first body lotion!

4. **Separating mother from baby after birth:** This is an absurd and savage practice that goes against both instinct and the neurobiology of bonding. Because of the strength of the first imprints, a newborn should not be separated for a minimum of eight hours, according to best birthing practices. Scales to weigh and measure can be taken *to* baby and mother. The less interference with the bonding processes the better.

5. **Treating birth as a medical condition with something bound to go wrong, rather than a normal biological process:** This includes the rampant use of ultrasound during gestation that may lead to sensory overload for your baby even prior to birth.

Search for birthing centers and obstetricians who support the ideal conditions for establishing conscious connections between the mother and infant. The following tips were gleaned from the Taos Birthing Conference of 2005 sponsored by Suzanne Arms, founder of "Birthing the Future," a non-profit educational organization dedicated to promoting optimal birthing, bonding, and breastfeeding practices:

- Insist on a room with privacy for intimate family and birth assistants only.
- Insist on a birthing room with soft lighting. Cloth can cover fluorescent glare.

- Get extra emotional support for the birthing mother from a trained doula.

- Use quiet, soft voices and plenty of warmth and laughter.

- Use a birthing stool to support an easier, more anatomically natural birthing position. Gravity then helps the process!

- Ensure constant proximity to mother and as much skin-to-skin contact between mother and baby as possible. Electromagnetic resonance instruments show that mother and baby's subtle heart patterns are in synchrony at a distance of at least three feet and possibly up to twelve feet. Creating a distance greater than this during the early weeks of life is disruptive to the normal biological processes. This may cause a high level of stress hormones and poor attachment.

The Danger of Drug Overuse

The routine administration of drugs during labor together with anesthesia at delivery was practiced for many years without questioning the safety of these practices to either the baby or the mother creating a frightening disconnect between women and their bodies. The sublime and womanly experience of birthing a baby in synchrony without drugs can be a transcendent rite of passage when a woman is given the proper knowledge and emotional support. During advanced labor, higher levels of endorphin are secreted, a calming hormone that serves as a natural pain reliever. Pain medications from the opiate family and epidurals (while sometimes useful and even necessary) can cause a drop in endorphin production, leading to an intolerable labor. On the other hand, women who have a natural childbirth with high levels of endorphin and the proper support may not only have less pain; they have the possibility of experiencing an ecstatic—even orgasmic birth. Also, certain drugs interfere with oxytocin secretion, which is a potent stimulator of contractions that help to dilate the cervix. Actions that disrupt a woman's hormonal balance can slow or stop contractions, thereby lengthening labor.

Apart from a disruption to the natural process of labor, in which both the mother and baby participate, the mother receives her baby in a drugged state instead of being fully present. If drugs affect the mother, they are likely to affect the baby. A study conducted during the 1970s and 1980s by Martin Richards, a physician at Cambridge University, England, found evidence that babies whose mothers were given just one 50-milligram shot of Demerol (pethidine) for pain often showed negative neurological effects for up to several years.[17] Opiates such as Demerol suppress basic physiological functions crucial to the baby's ability to breathe and suckle. At the same time, of course, drugs can save lives; it is just that they are frequently overused. The "drug culture" itself became yet another obstacle to baby-centered birth. The outrageous concept of babies born during a time convenient for the adults was spawned.

Birth on Schedule: Induction and Cesarean

As ludicrous as it may seem, along with the popularity of drugs making birth a medical event, scheduling cesareans when unnecessary and inducing labor so that the baby is "born on time" are two unfortunate practices that have become commonplace. If you think we're kidding, note that during the mid-1970s in Britain almost 90% of births were being induced as a way to ensure that all babies were born between the standard working hours of nine to five![18] Today in the U.S., it is "normal" to induce labor when a baby is a week "late." Messing with Mother Nature is more likely to create a cascade of complications. Inducing labor before the baby is ready may lead to a longer, harder labor. It is not unusual for an epidural to then be given for this unnecessary pain. With mother numbed and unable to feel the rhythms, her baby is more likely to get stuck in the birth canal. In a blink of an eye, the mother is being prepared for cesarean surgery! Much suffering due to birth and medical trauma often can be avoided simply through an act of patience that respects the infant's timing.

Another perpetrated modern-day myth is that cesarean surgery is safe. Although safer than in the past, it carries the same risks as all major surgeries! The risks to the baby are even greater. They include: side effects from the drugs given to mother (which pass quickly into the baby's bloodstream), breathing problems, trauma from the required separation from mother, more difficulty latching onto the breast and suckling, problems from being subjected to painful procedures in ICU—just in case! Birth complications are more than double that of vaginal birth—they can even be more than ten times as prevalent.[19] Without labor, babies are more likely to be pre-term. Having a cesarean surgery often results in "the domino effect" with one intervention leading to another and another and so forth.

Despite these dangers, cesarean surgery has been widely accepted as a quick and easy solution for avoiding minor difficulties or even circumventing the pain of labor and birth altogether. "The cesarean rate in the United States reached an all-time high of 25 percent in 1990. We are usually alarmed when we hear of any 'disease' or problem increasing by 40 to 60 percent. Yet the above statistics mean that in a twenty-year period, cesarean surgery increased in this country by *400 percent,* with only passing public and professional outcry," writes Suzanne Arms in *Immaculate Deception II.* Arms also reports that European research shows little significant improvement in birth outcomes if an overall cesarean rate at a hospital is higher than 7%. At Bellevue Hospital in New York City a midwife-run maternity unit has succeeded in achieving an overall cesarean rate of plus or minus 3% for the past several years, with no negative effects.[20] Any vaginal birth is generally safer, even for women who had a previous cesarean surgery. Check the cesarean surgery rate of the various hospitals in your area before making a choice if you cannot find a birthing center nearby. Be proactive. Keep your birth family-centered, not doctor- or hospital-centered.

One of the most dramatic repercussions of cesareans comes from denying the baby the "rite of passage" through the birth canal. Not usually discussed are the physiological and psychological benefits of completing the birth process that the baby was naturally prepared for and energetically mobilized to meet. The benefits of the birth canal include natural stimulation to the lungs, the sensory-motor impulses, and central nervous system. Birth is not easy! Labor involves a synchronized effort between mother and baby of contractions, pushing, and resting. When the energy mobilized to begin the downward journey never happens, the baby starts its life with impulses to move that were never met. In addition, our developmental sequences are programmed to act in a chain; each phase building on the pervious one and providing, in turn, the foundation for the subsequent developmental phase. For example, the newborns impulse to suckle may be diminished if propulsion through the birth canal is aborted. Frequently, these babies can be seen mimicking birthing patterns in an attempt to gain the satisfaction of a natural birth. This is because we are biologically hardwired to complete the pushing-out phase of birth.

Games Babies Play

Fortunately, there is much that can be done to help a baby renegotiate a traumatic birth. When a baby has been deprived of some, if not all, of the satisfaction that comes from carrying its instinctive movements through to completion, repair work can be done through your support. First of all, talk to your baby about what happened to him. Let him know that *you* know what he's been through and that you care about his frustrations. Watch for subtle, and not so subtle, signs of pushing. All you need to do is to give light but firm support for your baby's pushing movements at the bottoms of his feet and at the top of his head, providing just a touch of resistance to push up against. Or, have him push his feet against your belly, guiding him by lightly holding his ankles.

Make sure these baby games are fun for all involved. Play with the intention of decreasing stress and looking for signs of frustration and struggle followed by squeals of delight. If your baby is old enough to crawl, you can use pillows to make up tunnel and cave games. Monitor your baby's reactions. Watch for increased focus when pushing followed by signs of satisfaction and relaxed breathing. Use your imagination to create spontaneous games of engagement that meet your baby's needs for movement, contact, and support. Be sure to pace the play activity so there is a chance for your baby to rest and integrate any newly organized movements. If your baby is distressed, stop and talk to him. Trust your instincts to know when enough is enough to ensure that he is not overstimulated.

When a baby is born by cesarean surgery, induced, or pulled out by forceps, important transition movements that he or she is preparing to make never occur. Light cranial work from a certified cranial-sacral practitioner who specializes in infant trauma can be useful in helping a baby complete these birth movements. Family therapy clinics, such as BEBA (Building and Enhancing Bonding and Attachment), A Center for Family Healing in Santa Barbara, California (www.beba.org), focus on the issues that occur before, during, and after birth.

If your child is a toddler or older, play therapy can help him or her experience the pressure and sensory-motor patterns that are inherent but have never reached completion. A somatically-oriented play therapist can also help your child to express his unique birth story. This repair work may reduce the risk of entrenched behavioral patterns and later, core beliefs about oneself.

If your baby was born prematurely, she will need extra skin-to-skin contact. Infant massage shows multiple positive effects for preterm infants receiving this tactile/kinesthetic stimulation for fifteen minutes three times per day. According to Tiffany Field, PhD, from the Touch Research Institute, University of Miami School of Medicine, data analysis revealed that the massaged infants gained 47% more weight, remained in the hospital six days less, were awake and active longer, and showed better performance on the Brazelton Scale on habituation, orientation, motor activity, and regulation of state behavior.[21] Neonatal nurses can be trained in infant massage techniques, but teaching parents and grandparents to give the therapy enhances their own wellness also, helping depressed mothers, for example, to feel less depressed.

Infant massage is a common daily child-care practice in many parts of the world, including India and Africa, for all infants. In the United States the practice is gaining recognition, and infant massage therapists trained in India have started institutes with the purpose of teaching parents. For more information contact: www.infantmassageusa.org.

Sound and rhythms that re-create the womb environment can also be of great help. There are custom-built cradles with a sound device that simulates mother's heartbeat and blood circulation in the womb. (Kaiser Permanente in Northern California used them with babies born cocaine-addicted to help them settle and sleep.) This can be music to a baby's ears, especially when separation occurred too early. The reproduced heartbeat causes a calming reflex in the baby. Toy stores carry large plush stuffed animals with the sound of the heartbeat designed for a similar purpose for infants.

Remarkable Devin

Eight-year-old Devin came to play therapy with his mom with a long list of diagnoses by a variety of professionals. These included ADHD, auditory processing deficit, sensory integration dysfunction, and dyspraxia. His list of symptoms was just as long: aggressive outbursts, hyperactivity, focusing difficulties, and trouble completing assignments. Devin was reported to daydream at school and suffer frightening nightmares at home.

After taking a birth history, it was discovered that Maria, Devin's mom, had been on medication and bed rest since her twenty-first week of pregnancy to prevent preterm labor and a premature birth. At thirty-seven weeks she went off meds, hoping to begin a natural labor. After Maria's water broke, her contractions were too weak to move the labor along so she was induced with Pitocin. Due to severe pain, she was then given narcotics. There was concern about the low level of amniotic fluid, and Devin was under distress for a couple of hours before the medical staff discovered that the umbilical cord was wrapped around his neck three times. Suctioning was used, and he was blue at birth. As if that were not enough, three weeks after his birth Devin was hospitalized due to jaundice and high bilirubin levels. He was tested for a blood disorder. His mother described his condition as follows: "His red blood cells were bursting. He was diagnosed with hemolytic anemia. Weekly blood draws were taken, as Devin was held down screaming, to monitor his health."

In his first session, cheerful and talkative eight-year-old Devin drew a rocket complete with rocket-launcher and trailer. "The astronaut," he explained, "was glued inside, and it would take ten seatbelts to make it safe, and he would have to wear two astronaut suits to come out because it's so cold out there." He also drew the astronaut's lifeline, attaching it to the rocket. Next, he got our undivided attention when he announced, "The cord is the most important part."

A few sessions later, Devin was working diligently, recording a secret code with magic markers. He kept getting sidetracked, and when he lost focus he would make mistakes. After the third mistake, he melted down with an outburst of frustration. With all his might Devin scrunched up not only the page he was working on, but the entire cardboard art pad!

After his anger was validated, Devin was invited to look around the room and choose something that might help him calm down. Without wasting any time, he reached for the stack of pillows and began building a tunnel using the legs of a chair as a frame. Then he squeezed his body through it little by little. He turned himself around and proceeded with a little resistance on the top of his head. Remarkably, before he got all the way through he reached out for an electrical cord that was nearby and began wrapping it around his neck—just like the umbilical cord was wrapped! Gently, he was assisted to unwrap it and continue on his journey through the tunnel.

After coming through his tunnel at his own pace, Devin crawled over to hug his mother, who was there to receive him. With his breathing deeper and calmer, Devin silently returned to his project of secret code-making with a refreshed attitude. He kept focused until he completed his work. This time he made no mistakes! Maria reported that after that session, his frustration outbursts ended both at school and home. Later, after a four-month follow-up, Devin continued to cope with challenges free of tantrums, according to his mother.

Devin still needs some help to increase his attention span. It seems clear from observation and checking with Devin that he gets active, off topic, makes loud noises, and is driven to silly antics when he is stressed. His stress reportedly feels more than uncomfortable—it is frightening to the point of terror. Devin reports a sensation that he has no words for, but essentially it feels like "life or death" and is linked to holding in his breath and his belly. All of his peculiar behaviors appear to be a courageous and ambitious attempt to guard against feeling the sensations of terror again that he presumably felt during and following his birth.

Devin is a bright, clever, and charming boy who loves to visit and play. He has a wonderful family whose members are committed to support his healing. With his temper outbursts behind him, there is no doubt that he will, through support with his art and play, be able to tolerate more sensation and be able to relax "into himself." In this way his attention and focus will continue to increase so he can be freed of the label of ADHD with its implications that he will need medication.

The First Three Months

"At birth a baby's brain contains 100 billion neurons, roughly as many nerve cells as there are stars in the Milky Way."[22] But that's not all. Trillions of connections are continuing to build as neurons send out pathways of communication with other neurons. These connections, or synapses, do not remain static. As in the adage "use 'em or lose 'em," so too go the neural pathways. Like a topiary artist shaping a tree into clever designs by pruning away what is not needed, the baby's brain loses connective highways that are not traveled: "Deprived of a stimulating environment, a child's brain suffers. Researchers at Baylor College of Medicine, for example, have found that children who don't play much or are rarely touched develop brains 20% to 30% smaller than normal for their age."[23]

Since nerve cells are proliferating rapidly during early infancy, we must protect newborns from as much pain as possible. Pain causes the developing nervous system to grow extra nerve cells to fire and transmit pain information to the brain. Countless painful needle sticks, breathing tubes, and surgeries are given to newborns. Until recently, medical personnel believed that infants did not feel pain; they thought that their responses were merely reflexive! Open-heart surgery was performed with no anesthesia or other precautions until 1988! Babies *are* sensitive to pain, and if they are not crying it's most likely because they are in a state of shock. Studies show that children who were born prematurely (receiving multiple medical interventions) tended to report more pain in childhood and to have a lower threshold for pain than their siblings.[24] The implications are to eliminate all unnecessary medical procedures and show sensitivity during those that are indispensable by using various local and topical anesthetics, for example. If an intervention is necessary, the baby should be prepared beforehand and supported afterwards by gently acknowledging what she has been through.

What Newborns Need

It is most important for caregivers to recognize what their newborns need and lovingly provide it. For one thing, newborns need to be held. They need to mold into the inviting warmth of their parents' bodies—not into a plastic baby carrier. They are accustomed to being rocked and jiggled inside the womb; they need to be gently stimulated outside the womb as well. They need to find their way to the nipple and suckle at the breast. They need to be swaddled with a receiving blanket so that they feel "held" securely when they are not skin-to-skin. They need to be soothed with gentle and rhythmic rocking and swinging. They need to feel the stimulation of movement and play. They need to hear the sounds of their parents' voices singing and sounding to them and calling their names. They need to know that it's alright to cry for "no reason" as they are held comfortably by parents who are at ease with their baby's tears. Remember that infant tears may be a discharge and release from birth trauma.

The Roots of Self-Esteem

It is not at all uncommon for both adults and children to struggle with deeply held beliefs such as "Something must be wrong with me" or "Nobody likes me." Therapists such as Dr. McCarty, who specialize in pre- and perinatal psychology, find that clients discover that these beliefs started at the very beginnings of life. In her journal article, "The Power of Beliefs: What Babies are Teaching Us" (2002), Dr. McCarty suggests that very young babies already have established complex beliefs from their prenatal and birth experiences, and she addresses how to support them in re-patterning these embedded traumatic blueprints during infancy.[25] In her book *Welcoming Consciousness,* McCarty expands on this concept: "Two common situations that give rise to this conviction include (1) the discovery of a pregnancy in which the baby was unwanted, rejected, or a source of resentment and (2) the separation of baby and mother at birth." In our [the authors'] clinical experience with both children and adults in therapy, we too have found that many times this appears to be the case. Dr. McCarty further postulates that perhaps "our need for love, connection, being seen and welcomed is so strong from the beginning of life that we make these constrictive choices or beliefs to cope . . . that we would do anything to be connected and in a relationship."[26] One could also say that such "choices" are later translated to beliefs.

Fetal Defenses

Foster and adoptive parents often are helping babies to ameliorate patterns from a toxic womb—the result of nicotine, alcohol, cocaine, or other substances. Anecdotal reports from clinical practice have suggested, for example, that it may be possible for a client to smell the remnants of nicotine when working on prenatal issues if the biological mother smoked during her pregnancy. Nicotine causes the placental blood vessels to constrict. Clinical experience suggests that babies in the womb adapt by squeezing their little tummies as though to narrow or restrict the umbilical cord from ingesting this poison. What is supposed to be a safe place becomes a danger zone—much like a war zone as the fetus is bombarded with stress hormones and toxins. Fetal defenses are different from an adult's defenses. A baby cannot flee, it can only fight off the unpleasantness by tightening its belly, or it can twist and turn in an attempt to "get away." The imprints made during the prenatal, birth, and infancy period are strong enough to shape basic perceptions and beliefs about oneself and about the world. These adaptive patterns based on threats to survival need to be taken seriously. They play havoc with relationships in later life. When they revolve around issues of nourishment, they also have the potential for rage responses coupled with eating disorders.

Feed Me Now!

It is not uncommon to work with couples who wish to improve emotional connection and intimacy with their partners by addressing and eliminating problems of explosive rage. It is also not uncommon for these same clients to have food issues, if not an actual eating disorder. Rage and food issues tend to alternate, since one is "acting out," and the other is "acting in."

When working with the sensations underlying rage, sometimes the client discovers a sense that life-sustaining needs for food or physical contact had not been met during the fragile period of infancy. The following poignant example involves a thirty-five-year-old mother named Gemma. In situations with her husband, she tends to hold back her feelings of irritability (when she knows he's not to blame) until she cannot bear them. She describes the sensations as if her skin can no longer contain the intensity and feels like it will burst. Then she explodes, noticing that her hot cheeks feel like they are on fire. Gemma recognizes that her angry outbursts, directed at her husband, are highly exaggerated responses to not getting a perceived need met quickly enough. She did not realize, however, the early roots of her intense feelings. In the past, when Gemma was less outwardly expressive and tended to "disappear" during conflict, she had a pattern of fasting and then over-eating.

As we worked together tracking the sensations that arose on Gemma's skin, inside her chest, and around her face and mouth, she described a sense of being an infant and not being held. As she felt her heart race and witnessed the panicky feelings in her chest, she described having a sense that her life was in danger. Gemma felt the impulse to scream. Continuing to track awareness of other sensations, she described a feeling of helplessness as no one responded. Next she felt a "hard wall" that she described as "a fortress surrounding my softness that protects me from feeling pain." This hardness melted into gentle tears as Gemma continued to focus on her sensations with support in present "adult time," rather than in regressive "infant time," where automatically she defended herself against the unbearable agony.

Gemma decided to talk to her mother about her birth. She learned that in 1970 in Italy where she was born, the trend was to deprive newborns of mother's milk for the first twenty-four hours! The rich immunity substance, colostrum, which comes in first, was for some odd reason thought to be harmful. Newborn Gemma was placed in a cradle next to her mother's hospital bed. She reached over and patted Gemma's head when she cried instead of picking her up. She did this to prevent Gemma from searching for her nipple due to the superstitious beliefs of that era. As Gemma explained this during a somatic therapy session, she felt deep sadness well up inside as her tears slowly moved down her cheeks, releasing her long-held grief. As she cried, she also got insight regarding the origin of the puzzling and excessive agitation she experienced whenever someone innocently patted her on the head.

Feeding and relationships go hand-in-hand. Effective feeding supports the development of attachment, self-regulation, and healthy separation. When a parent reads and responds to the gestures, facial expressions, and vocalizations of the infant regarding timing of feeding, amount, preferences, and pacing, positive attitudes about relationships are forged. The quality of the feeding relationship is characteristic of the overall relationship between infant and parent. Trust your baby. Feed her when she's hungry; do not force-feed.

The best way to prevent long-term issues with nourishment and relationships is to make sure that babies get their initial needs met for contact. Also, breastfeeding should be on demand, not on someone else's schedule. It's heart-breaking to consider all the obese Americans in their fifties and sixties who were put on a feeding schedule of every four hours as newborns because it was the latest trend. Developmental models tended to be (and still are for the most part) parent-oriented, talking about babies as if they were unconscious and devoid of feeling. Things were "done to them" instead of "for them," and often horrendous life-long scars resulted from "doing it for their own good."

You, as the guardians of infants, can avoid these pitfalls by respecting your baby's needs. In the *Infant Mental Health Journal* (Fall 1998), Dr. Beatrice Beebe writes about the "implicit relationship knowing" between mother and baby. When the two come into resonance together, it is a special moment of meeting.[27] There is a sense of "I know that you know that I know. . . ." This quote, if kept in mind, can be a valuable guide in your developing relationship. Dr. McCarty writes that when she relates to babies at this higher level, magic happens![28]

We are just beginning to understand that there is a powerful biological basis for this "magic" of resonance. It has to do with our exquisite ability to mirror one another, not only on a physical level by imitating actions, but at also at an emotional level, thereby perceiving not only the feelings of others but their intentions as well. In the early 1990s, Italian researchers discovered that while all mammals have evolved limbic circuitry to "read" internal states, primates have the unique capacity to create an internal state that resembles that of others by observing and copying intentional external behaviors.[29] According to Daniel Siegel (author of *Parenting from the Inside Out*) and the research of Marco Iacoboni, both at UCLA's Center for Culture, Brain, and Development, it is the firing of mirror neurons that make it possible to have resonant relationships in the first place.[30]

Siegel and Iacoboni are applying this new knowledge of mirror neurons to the implications for language and social development in children. This attunement with primary emotions is the way that children develop the sense of "feeling felt." It is communicated non-verbally through facial expressions, tone of voice, and bodily postures, gestures, and actions, forming the basis for empathic connection from the very beginning of life. Understanding mirror neurons helps us understand how babies with depressed or anxious caregivers become vulnerable to these same states so quickly. In "Cells that Read Minds" (2006), Sandra Blakeslee of the *New York Times* "Science Times" quotes Dr. Rizzolatti, one of the Italian researchers who first discovered mirror neurons in Parma, Italy:

> We are exquisitely social creatures. Our survival depends on understanding the actions, intentions and emotions of others. Mirror neurons allow us to grasp the minds of others not through conceptual reasoning but through direct simulation. By feeling, not by thinking.[31]

This groundbreaking research makes it remarkably clear how important it is for parents to work on their own emotional issues and to grow increasingly conscious and mindful as they nurture and raise their very impressionable young. From infancy, children possess complex groups of "mirror neurons" that imitate, on an internal level, what they see, hear, *and* feel modeled by their caregivers.

The Secret Life of a Baby's Growing Brain

An infant not only experiences reflexive reactions but is also experiencing a sea of sensations. It has a nascent consciousness that registers what happens to it and around it, even in the womb. Yet there has been a long-held cultural belief in the West that babies lack both awareness and sensation. Ironically, it has taken modern technology to "validate" the innate wisdom of tribal cultures that honor the baby's feelings and gifts right from the time of conception.

We are just beginning to understand what instinctual peoples have always known in terms of how aware a newborn is and how its interaction with its environment changes everything. Moment by moment, the infant's sensations are shifting *in direct relationship to its caregivers' facial and vocal expressions.* In scientific terms, your baby's developing brain is doing a dance of negotiation and organization of non-verbal right-hemisphere functioning. It is now a well-known fact that these earliest interactions between mother and infant determine the actual shape and structure of the brain in humans and all mammals. This is a radically different concept from even one decade ago. Your baby's brain develops according to what you feed it, spiritually, emotionally, intellectually, and physically. The quality of your interactions, connections, bonding, nurturance, and play create the neuronal pathways that affect relational patterns for life!

Every culture has its own version of the familiar peek-a-boo game that adults, children, and babies delight in playing over and over again. In light of what we know about infant development in relation to coping, it makes sense that when the baby gets excited and has a chance to recuperate by temporarily hiding its face, a lot more is happening than just fun. Besides the baby experimenting with object permanence, she gets to expand her self-regulatory capacity for more pleasure.

Face-to-face attunement (where the baby's basic needs and rhythms are perceived and responded to) of the infant-mother pair facilitates development of the right orbito-frontal cortex, the part of the brain involved in a crucial way with increasing resilience to stress and trauma.[32] These early "mommy images," once installed in implicit memory, become the basic building blocks for self-soothing as babies mature into toddlers, internalizing mother's face as a symbol of comfort. As toddlers explore the world, moving away from mother, they carry these earliest experiences with them. If this imprint is lacking, the development of curiosity, social relationships, discovery, and learning are affected. The importance of mother in the development of self-regulation of emotional arousal cannot be overestimated. It remains life-long. When black boxes are recovered from downed airplanes, it is not uncommon to hear the pilots seconds before the crash calling out for "mommy."[33]

Match, Mismatch, Rematch, Love

Creating a bond of affection that helps your baby to develop the brain pathways for vision, feelings, language, and motor skills—as well as mechanisms for coping with stress—may seem a little like a game of tennis. The good news for parents is this: Having a relaxed rather than anxious approach works best. You don't need to be a perfect fit. Even if it were possible, such a fantasy fit is not how a baby learns to cope. Frustration and protestation are normal. A baby's perceptions, sensations, and expressions (if not frozen in trauma) are changing moment by moment because infants *live* in the moment. It is one of the factors that make them so refreshing to be around. So, what do you do if you and your baby are not in tune?

Suppose, for example, you are energized and rush towards your baby, excited to play with her. She, on the other hand, has just awakened from a nap and happens to be in a very cranky mood. Your intensity overwhelms her. No one is to blame. The critical brain-building at this stage is to repair the mismatch and come back into synchronicity. What might this repair look like? Your baby is in distress. You try to console her by holding and movement. She cries harder. You try harder. She gets more wound up.

You realize that you are not matching what she needs. You center and calm yourself and watch for your baby's cues. She is not hungry, wet, or cold. She just needs to cry. You let her know gently that it's alright that she cries and continue to hold her without trying to make her stop. After a while she stops crying and looks to engage face-to-face with you. You meet her gaze with matching intensity. She looks away and you accept her gesture with understanding. You relax and give her all the time she needs to recover, knowing that she will look again when she is ready—and wait until she initiates contact. Your job is to be there to support this process as she finds a comfortable state of arousal. You are careful not to provide more stimulation than she can tolerate.

With each successive match, mismatch, and repair your infant becomes more resilient. The window of tolerance for sensation increases, as does the ability of his or her nervous system to charge and discharge smoothly. Piaget's extensive work in child development many decades ago described a parallel process of cognitive growth in regard to frustration tolerance. He labeled the concept "periods of equilibrium and disequilibrium" in reference to skill development.[34] A baby who cannot yet crawl sees a toy and wants to touch it. He reaches out to grasp it, but it is beyond his reach. The child may experience this as confusion or frustration, which creates a state of disequilibrium. But, this very state spurs his development. He mobilizes his energy to attempt a belly crawl but is not quite able to coordinate his movements. He cries in frustration but continues to try again and again until he gains mastery. Eventually the child changes his cognitive structures to accommodate (account for) the new experience and moves back into equilibrium.

While Piaget was referring to the infant's motivation to move to the next level of organization of motor and language skills, the researchers in the field of attachment and its relationship to self-regulation report similar phenomena. But instead of these developmental milestones, we are talking about the development of emotional health as brain re-organization takes place at a non-verbal level in the prefrontal cortex. The critical difference here is that the equilibrium and disequilibrium occur within the relationship of infant and caregiver. "The more the mother tunes her activity level to the infant during periods of social engagement, and the more she allows him or her to recover quietly in periods of disengagement, the more synchronized their interaction."[35] Each time the repair is made, the infant brain organizes itself at a higher level of capability to recover from distress, which is fundamental to the infant's affective development.

The emotional presence and mindfulness of the caregiver is central to the optimal affective development of the infant. When the caregiver is emotionally unavailable, there is a price to pay with diminished tolerance for feelings. "One way the child attempts to repair this failure of mutual coordination is through the exclusion of those emotions that produce aversive reactions in the caregiver."[36]

The best trauma-prevention gifts you can give your baby are the gifts of emotional presence and somatic resonance, which is an inherent "knowing" of when the inevitable mismatch occurs and the receptivity to respond gracefully to repair it. In this way, your infant gets the message "I can be distressed, but it won't last forever—there is a way out! I may feel awful now; soon I will feel good again." This type of resonance equals love and everyone wins.

Thriving or Surviving?

In this new millennium it is time to get beyond the myth that it's sufficient to simply weigh a baby with a scale to determine its wellness! Infants suffer stress, sensory overload, physical pain, and emotional hurts. Babies cannot thrive when overwhelmed. When babies are chronically stressed, the more primitive hind brain develops extra cells, while the neocortical structures, responsible for language and social relating, grow at a diminished rate. Joseph

Chilton Pearce, author of *Magical Child* and *Evolution's End,* states in the documentary DVD *What Do Babies Want?* (2005) that it's as if the emergent brain cells must decide, "Can we go for more intelligence—or do we have to defend ourselves?"[37]

Thus the adaptive brain shapes itself for bigger and better defensive responses or, when feeling safe, to experience more pleasure, curiosity, learning, frustration tolerance, and delight. The brain literally develops in correspondence to its environment. A thriving baby is a baby whose needs are met for pleasurable eye contact, the parent's soothing voice, skin-to-skin touching, holding, movement, and play. One of the first things a healthy baby instinctively does after birth (if it hasn't been drugged or separated from its mother) is to search for its mother's face and listen for its mother's (and father's) voice. The blissful gaze between mother and infant creates a rush of feelings in the mother that turns on the infant brain. One is not possible without the other!

In Allan Schore's landmark book, *Affect Regulation and the Origin of the Self: The Neurobiology of Emotional Development* (1994), he cites numerous studies regarding the process of regulation of the infant's newly developing nervous system, beginning at birth. Face-to-face attunement of baby and caregiver was the mitigating factor that increased the capacity to self-regulate. With proper attunement in the mother-baby dyad, the orbito-frontal cortex develops properly, ensuring this "stress protection" against later traumas.[38]

What All Babies Need
for Healthy Development

Healthy infant development is all about attunement or the careful "tuning in" to your baby's needs. Since babies have no control over their surroundings, you will need to set up the environment in a way that matches your baby's needs. While some babies are overstimulated, other babies get too little stimulation and feel detached and isolated, even though others may be nearby. Babies are not passive tiny people; they learn through interactions with their surroundings.

When attention (whether from familiar people or strangers) is given to a baby, it is important to notice how that attention affects the baby. If you keep your attention balanced between your center and your baby, it is easy to take note of your baby's reaction to stimulation and adjust the focus to the amount that is just right. Often parents try hard to comfort their distressed baby by focusing even more energy on an already riled-up little one, inadvertently "pressuring" the baby to stop fussing. This can create an escalating cycle frustrating to everyone! This is most likely to happen when the parents' needs weren't understood when they were infants.

Bonding: The Basis of Emotional Connection

Bonding is a special kind of togetherness. It is a comfortable feeling of well-being that occurs within the dynamic relating of the mother and her newborn. It is a "settling in together" that includes four essential components: 1) touching skin-to-skin; 2) communication that includes both eye contact and mother's voice; 3) holding; and 4) playfulness. Babies look for their mother's face and, through touch and smell, search for their mother's breast. Secretions of prolactin (the bonding hormone) create what some mothers have described as "a rush of love" that feels divine. This face-to-face gaze with pleasant vocalizations brings growth not only to the baby, but also to the mother. What is even more astounding is how this emotional growth between a mother and her newborn is the catalyst that "turns on" the infant brain, releasing chemicals, proteins, enzymes, and other elements that actually shape both the structure and capacity of the brain.

Whether a baby perceives the world as friendly or hostile depends on the quality of these earliest interactions. Babies born to a depressed or anxious mother develop in response to those states. Babies born into a violent home develop brains that are shaping themselves for survival and defensiveness, with perception filtered to expect danger—whether or not danger is present. Babies born into safe and nurturing families develop brains with receptivity to pleasure and an eagerness to explore their surroundings, take healthy risks, and connect with others.

Bonding with Dad

Bonding with dad also begins before birth. Newborns recognize the voice of their fathers. When a baby's father is present during the birth, there is a deeper imprint with dad than is possible in his absence. The documentary *March of the Penguins* is a touching story of familial bonding at its best. The father must sacrifice his own need for food, comfort, and freedom of movement in order to protect its unhatched offspring from blizzards in weather that is eighty degrees below zero! And penguins are birds! This poignant movie shows a sad contrast to human behavior and how far we have strayed from our instinctual roots. Research confirms that genetic material is activated or de-activated by our immediate surroundings. In other words, genes are "turned on" or "turned off" by what happens in the precious and amazing loving rhythm and resonance between the newborn and the environment created by the family, especially its mother and father.

Supporting the Baby's Emotional Development

What happens if this bonding process is interrupted? Because the beginnings of life lay down the blueprints for behavior, it is crucial to do everything possible to repair injuries and promote bonding. Infants and toddlers are vulnerable for many reasons. They may want to fight or flee when threatened, even though it's impossible; they are totally dependent on others for everything, and they have no context for their frightening experiences.

Disruptions to bonding—whether caused by a mother with a mental disorder, a violent or negligent home environment, or a highly anxious mother who overwhelms her baby (for example, by force-feeding to gratify her own need to do a "good job")—cause a disorganization to occur in nervous system development. Babies rely on the stability and grounding of their caregivers to recover from periods of normal "disequilibrium" associated with learning new things. Biologically they are wired to seek and cling to their mothers, just as baby monkeys do. When the caregiver is the cause of prolonged stress or is unsafe to "cling to," there is confusion in the relationship and difficulty in the nervous system's return to equilibrium and homeostasis.

Such patterns lead to a disorganized attachment, which impedes social learning and language development. The energy of development is instead diverted to areas of the hindbrain responsible for survival. Protective and defensive responses arise to buffer overwhelming feelings. Examples of automatic responses of babies when threatened are: shallow breathing, vomiting, spitting, clenching muscles, arching the back, pushing away, biting, tightening the tummy, withdrawing by sleeping too much, or numbing out. These are the signs and symptoms of a traumatized baby. Without intervention, these babies are at risk for childhood disorders that may show up as early as two years old. Traumatized infants become traumatized children with attention difficulties, hyperactivity, eating difficulties, and learning, mood, and conduct disorders.

Less Anxious Mom and Dad = More Resilient Baby

If you feel anxious or irritated and at your wits' end because you cannot soothe your crying baby, step back—rather than towards—your infant. Then notice your own breathing, taking the time to calm and center yourself, perhaps letting your baby know in a soothing voice that you know she is struggling and assuring her that it's okay that she's upset and that daddy (after centering himself and observing his baby's cues) will rock her gently or just hold her while she's crying. Babies often cry even when their tummies are full and they are clean, warm, and dry. They discharge stress and emotional hurts by crying. If your baby has no "apparent" needs that haven't been met, it is best just to acknowledge her distress, letting her know that you are listening and accept her tears.

If you are having difficulty with the concept of supporting your baby's tears by "holding" rather than "doing," ask yourself this: If you are crying because you are overwhelmed with stress, hurt, or grieving, would you prefer that the person closest to you try every trick in the book to get you to "hush up"? Or would you prefer that they listen compassionately as your unobstructed tears flow gently down your cheeks, releasing you from pain? The greatest gift is to have another understand, rather than attempt to change, how you feel. Paradoxically, feelings change once felt.

Baby Steps: The Very First Tasks for Emotional Well-Being

The very first "task" of babies is to form bonds of trust. Since they are dependent beings, they need to sense that they are wanted and truly welcomed. Lisbeth Marcher, the Danish founder of *Bodynamics*, refers (after the work of Erik Erikson in his landmark 1950 book *Childhood and Society*) to this earliest stage of development as "Existence." To master this stage, a baby must feel that his existence is not in question. This need for a sense of "I am" and "I have a right to be here" is crucial. If there is resentment, neglect, prenatal distress, or birth trauma during this period, to be alive, to exist, may literally be experienced as dangerous. Babies in such a condition may grow up feeling empty, out of touch with their bodies, and have difficulty tolerating intimacy. Babies need to hear and feel this message in their bones: "YOU ARE WANTED!"

There are many ways you can help a baby feel a sense of security and trust that her existence is honored. These can vary from

312 — Trauma Through A Child's Eyes

making sure your newborn's neck is properly supported and fulfilling your baby's cues for comfort to the more complex work of reparation. For example, if your baby was unwanted or unplanned, it will take extra effort. Whether your baby was adopted, is in your foster care, or is biologically yours, traumatic beginnings can be repaired. This would involve talking to your baby truthfully about what happened in a soothing voice and said from your depths. You might let her know that although she was unexpected, she turned out to be a blessing and a joy—and then treat her like a treasured surprise! If you have not fully accepted her, you may need to get emotional support for yourself to help you actively bond. Making the commitment to breastfeed can be a boon here, as the bonding hormone, prolactin, is automatically released when the baby suckles.

In addition to emotional repair work between parents and baby, helping a baby release shock patterns created from both ordinary and extraordinary intrusive medical procedures is imperative if your baby exhibits symptoms. This is especially true when birth was difficult, respiratory problems occurred, and/or surgical procedures were necessary to sustain life.

As mentioned earlier, the Dagara tribe of West Africa has welcoming ceremonies at conception. After a period of post-birth adjustment, the ceremony continues as the baby is introduced to its entire community. Rituals include singing the baby's name to let him know that he is a unique and valued member with its own special place among its people.

Families and groups can make up their own rituals that celebrate this important rite of passage, with the baby being truly honored, adored, and welcomed. If you'd like to start this tradition, a wonderful resource is the earlier-mentioned DVD, *What Babies Want,* featuring among other birth pioneers Sobonfu Somé of Burkina Faso, who graciously teaches her country's welcoming customs to communities in the United States.[39]

Meeting Baby's Needs

The next stage of development begins in the months after birth and continues until approximately 18 months. This is often referred to as the "Needs" stage. The task is for the baby to learn to communicate needs and develop trust that his needs will be acknowledged. The good parent gives the message: "Your needs are OK; they do not overwhelm me. Even if I can't always meet them, I will not be upset with you for having them. I will try to meet your needs whenever possible and always when necessary."

When babies are put on feeding schedules rather than being fed when hungry, are not held, rocked, and cuddled enough, or not protected from the cold or sun, they suffer. Emotional and physical nourishment are fundamental at this point of development. Being force-fed, ignored, overstimulated by an excited or frenzied parent, and/or exposed to violence and even loud noises can cause problems later in life, ranging from eating disorders to difficulty with relationships, regulating emotions and moods, to disorders of conduct, attention, and hypervigilance.

"Me Do It Myself"—Becoming Autonomous

What parent of a one- or two-year-old child has not heard the words "No, **me** do!"? At this stage toddlers need support to be different from their parents. They need to know that they can try new things, bond with an extended family or friends, and move out into the world without fear of rejection for their efforts. They also need to know that they are not alone as they reach to explore the world but that their parents are nearby, ready to offer support when needed. In other words, they are paying attention nearby (not involved with the computer, etc.), watching and willing to extend a hand if looked to or asked for assistance. Still, the adults intervene as little as possible in the child's exploration and self-learning so that their toddler can begin to feel the exhilaration that comes with growing independence.

Again, parents need to resonate with their toddler, sensing the appropriate amount of help by noticing when she is stressed from too little help or disempowered by too much help. Your baby will appreciate your support to develop a sense of competence in exploring the world and becoming less dependent. The message to send your mobile baby is "I support you to be who you are, and if you need my help, I am here."

Clues That a Baby Is Stressed

Infants cannot flee, but they *can* and *do* exhibit defensive responses when the environment is too much to bear. Following are ten clues that reveal that a baby is stressed or overwhelmed:

- Squirming and twisting away
- Startle reflex
- Facial gestures of disgust
- Protesting through loud vocalizations
- Averting eye gaze
- Kicking or pushing movements
- Involuntary jerking
- Arching spine or tensing muscles
- Dazed expression
- "Checking out" by excessive sleepiness

It is important to note that an infant who has had a difficult womb or birth experience and/or has a sensitive temperament is likely to be more vulnerable to stimulation. Some of the behaviors listed above may be attempts to conclude an incomplete motor response from this early struggle (as suggested earlier in this chapter).

There is much that you can do to avoid losing confidence in yourself as a parent. Remember, the more tension you feel, the more likely it is that your baby's defensive responses will grow stronger. When you are stressed step back, slow down, and take care of yourself by self-soothing. Check your breathing, find your center, and let your baby know that *you* know she is frustrated. Watch for her cues, slow down to "baby time," check your intuition, and then respond to your baby's needs.

The Wondrous World of Babies

Thanks to early pioneers in prenatal and birth therapy—such as William Emerson, PhD, Wendy Anne McCarty, PhD, and Dr. Raymond Castellino, DC, RPP—we have learned a great deal about what babies want from us and what support they need to heal their wounds.

In 1993, Drs. Castellino and McCarty founded BEBA, A Center for Family Healing (Building and Enhancing Bonding and Attachment) in Santa Barbara, California. They opened the BEBA research clinic to treat early trauma during infancy by providing in-depth infant-oriented family therapeutic support and videotaping the work for future research and educational purposes. They have shared what they are learning from babies regarding their need for relatedness, respect, understanding, and support through BEBA's writings, conference presentations, and parent education groups. And they have been training other professionals to carry on this precious healing work.

Newborns are exquisitely sensitive and aware beings. They can discriminate both the scent and voice of their caregivers at birth. We now know that prenates respond to their parents, growing more active in the womb when a familiar voice speaks directly to them. Within two days a baby can recognize his mother's face! Vision is the last sense to develop. Researchers have found that the newborn experiences seeing the world a bit like viewing a faded photograph through a tube. Perhaps this lack of immediate visual acuity is nature's way of "damping down" an overload of visual stimulation to prevent overwhelm.

Unfortunately, human babies are at our mercy to rescue them from other sources of overstimulation, such as people (parents included), loud or harsh noises, bright lights, abrupt changes in activity, position, or temperature, and insensitive handling.

Much of what has been learned about early imprinting and responses comes from the stories told by the body postures, gestures, behaviors, and facial expressions of our tiniest youngsters. Another way we get to learn about early birth stories is from anecdotes chronicled later in life. Adults may enter therapy with core views about themselves and existential issues that have plagued them from the start. Psychic themes of "not feeling wanted," "gasping for air," "not being well-received," "being too much," "not enough," "never having enough time," "always doing things backwards," or "falling to pieces easily" may have their origin in anything from a cord wrapped around the neck, to being stuck in the birth canal, pulled out by forceps, having an induced birth, to being birthed by a severely depressed mom who withdraws from her newborn.

A baby stuck in the birth canal during an exhausting labor and born to a highly anxious mother will have a different "body story" than a baby born one month prematurely. A baby, who was planned in advance, thrilling his parents at the pronouncement of pregnancy, will have a different imprint than a baby who was born as the result of a failed abortion.

Was Wanda Wanted

Wanda entered therapy in her early thirties complaining of mild depression. All she could say regarding her situation was that she felt "unwanted" by her husband ever since her son had been born. She could give no clear reason for her vague yet nagging sense of dread in the pit of her stomach. She declared that her husband's behavior did not warrant her fears. Although slightly critical of her weight, he was as amorous as ever.

As Wanda explored the sensations in her gut, she remembered having these same feelings from time to time throughout childhood. She stated that her deep-seated abandonment fear—that she was "unwanted"—was not new. She described herself with low self-esteem as a child and wondered if her friends really wanted her around. Again, these feelings and beliefs seemed far-fetched when compared to her actual life. She reported that she had many playmates, that her parents were loving and that she maintained a close relationship with them.

With prompting, Wanda asked her mother to share the circumstances and details that surrounded her conception and pregnancy. Wanda uncovered the baffling mystery of her somatic confusion when her mother candidly admitted that Wanda was *not* wanted! She explained that she and Wanda's dad were content with their family of three children and not planning on more. Five years later, they were shocked to discover Wanda on the way. Resentful and depressed throughout the nine months of gestation, Wanda's mother admitted to never having fully accepted her fate until she looked into her daughter's big blue eyes for the first time. Her parents *didn't* want her—until *after* Wanda was born.

The good ending to this story is that Wanda's candid and loving conversation with her mother brought a sense of relief that began to repair her internal breach. It ended her confusion, thereby permanently altering and bolstering her self-perception.

Talk with Your Infant Now—Before She Grows Up!

Fortunately, you needn't wait until your baby is an adult, or even until your baby is verbal. Your infant is absorbing everything around her like a sponge. And she will let you know if she understands what you are saying. Talk to your baby about any difficult experiences he may have encountered in an honest but reparative way and watch his reaction. Then adjust to whatever he needs from you to feel supported moment by moment. If your baby got off to

a really bad start—for example, with emergency medical procedures or a difficult pregnancy and birth complications—you may
want to seek professional help.

Over the last four decades, a new field of prenatal and birth
therapy has developed to study and help resolve issues that arise
out of these delicate beginnings. Post-graduate schools, such as
the Santa Barbara Graduate Institute in California, have doctoral
programs in this branch of psychology. Its purpose is to help babies,
children, and adults heal the stress or trauma that may have
occurred before, during, or near the time of birth. There is much
you can do to transform a baby's bad experience, either on your
own or with the help of a birth therapy specialist. Many body workers are specially trained in "biodynamic cranial-sacral" therapy
for birth issues; and a growing breed of prenatal and somatic psy-
chotherapists get post-graduate training in schools like Santa Barbara Graduate Institute and the California Institute for Integral
Studies in San Francisco.

Being with Babies

Dr. McCarty, whose work was referred to earlier, wrote two marvelous booklets entitled *Being with Babies: What Babies Are Teaching Us*, Volumes I and II (1996, 1997). In them, she explains how
babies' "expressions are not random; rather they are intentional
and meaningful."[40] Often, what babies are telling us is quite obvious; at other times they speak in subtle ways that can be learned
by watching for their cues. The communication tips listed below
are excerpted from Dr. McCarty's first booklet (Vol. I):

Observation Checklist[41]

- Facial expressions.
- Eye contact and what babies choose to look at.

- Where they place their attention—by focusing on something or someone in their outer environment, or by focusing inside themselves with eyes closed.
- Body language and movement (very important).
- Gestures with their hands and feet.
- Level of tension and relaxation.
- Body rhythms (such as sucking, nursing, and general movement tempo).

Treat babies with the same empathy and thoughtfulness you would accord your best friend. The idea is to build safety and well-being so that your baby develops a sense of trust that you will read her cues and provide for her the sustenance and nurturance that she cannot provide for herself.

Babies *do* get traumatized and they *do* remember. Although preverbal children cannot put words to their experiences, there are well-documented accounts of encoded experiences in children between birth and two and a half years of age in books such as *Ghosts from the Nursery: Tracing the Roots of Violence* and *The Mind of Your Newborn Baby*. (See bibliography.) Their traumas show up in behavioral changes and later get acted out in their play. If your baby suddenly refuses to eat or drink, avoids eye contact or looks dazed, seems listless or cries for prolonged periods, be suspicious. Your baby may have been overwhelmed by a medical procedure, overstimulation, temperature extremes, abrupt change, parental discord, or even handling by a babysitter. Be careful with whom you leave your baby.

Dr. McCarty also recommends that you include your baby in what is happening in the moment by communicating using the following:

Communication Tips[42]

- Talk to the baby directly.
- Include them in the conversation.
- Pause and wait for their response. (This pause is essential. Babies generally process and respond at a much slower pace.)
- Acknowledge their response.
- Respond appropriately.

Remember that the baby's sense of self is profoundly affected by the mirroring of his parent, extended family, and other caregivers. Dr. Belleruth Naparstek, a leader in the healing field of imagery, stated in her 2004 keynote address during the Behavioral Medicine Conference at Hilton Head, South Carolina, "The mommy image is the basic building block of self-soothing."[43] If you keep this awareness foremost in mind, together with the knowledge that babies understand the meaning of what is being said and respond as sensory beings to thoughts, emotions, and actions, it will be easier to enter into a dialog that lets them know that they can depend on you to understand and fulfill their needs. After all, nurturance and safety are truly the essence of love.

In addition to being included in conversation, babies need quiet, softness, appropriate stimulation, gentle rocking, cuddling, eye contact, calmness, soothing voices and music, tranquility, swaddling, and firm support (especially for the neck). They also need warmth, skin contact, snuggling, and molding into their caregiver's body. They need an easy pace—not the hurried "life in the fast lane" of modern times. They need you to arrange the environment to encourage exploration, as well as rest. Most of all they need you to notice what they need by slowing *your* rhythm and pace to adjust to their cues. Adjusting to the baby's needs, rather than having the baby adjust to your needs (whether it be for play, affection, food, eye contact, or stillness) will pay big dividends in building a secure bond with baby.

To Circumcise or Not Circumcise

In *Immaculate Deception II*, author Suzanne Arms answers the question "Is circumcision necessary?" She states that the world's pediatric associations unanimously agree that there is no medical reason for it, yet circumcision is still performed on 60% of newborn males in the U.S. each year.[44] Although it may be done for religious or cultural reasons, it is most often unnecessarily performed on the basis of the widely held myth that it promotes hygiene and prevents infection. This consideration seems, at least, to be overstated.

Newborn babies feel pain. Circumcision is still sometimes performed without anesthesia. The delicate healthy skin tissue protecting the head of the penis is pulled back, crushed, and cut off. Parents are told that it is a simple procedure and the baby will get over it quickly. Ms. Arms graphically describes the screaming of the helpless infant as it is held down during this painful procedure, as well as the strong efforts of the baby boy to escape. She tells of a father going pale and leaving the room as his terrified baby with its back arched tried in vain to pull away. The baby's mother, who was left to witness her son's anguish, was quoted saying, "I'd never have allowed it if I'd known it would hurt him." Unfortunately, we have heard similar stories from mothers we have known personally.

If you are in the throes of making this important decision for your baby boy, please be warned that in addition to being painful, there are risks. The procedure may cause hemorrhage, infection, and/or unintentional mutilation. The wound may be raw for ten to fifteen days. Circumcision is most definitely painful and can leave a traumatic imprint. We have worked with men, circumcised as babies, who have sensory memories of being "medically molested." Fears associated with being touched intimately can then create issues around their sexuality.

For more information, contact NOCIRC (P.O. Box 2512, San Anselmo, CA 94979; (415) 488-9883), an organization dedicated to ending circumcision. If you must circumcise, at the very least ask for a local anesthetic to minimize pain and talk to your baby to prepare him.

ℊ

Removing the Barriers to Learning and Self-Control in the Twenty-first-Century Classroom

This chapter is a concrete guide for educators on the "why" and the "how" of helping traumatized students in the classroom setting. Teachers often recognize these youngsters as the bullies or the bullied. They may be scapegoats, unstable, avoidant, isolated, hyperactive, withdrawn, anxious, defiant, bored, inattentive, or unmotivated. Or worse, they may be violent. Astute teachers recognize them when they enter school. Some of these children are labeled compassionately as "difficult to reach"; others are labeled disdainfully as "troublemakers"; while still others go unnoticed like "ciphers in the snow."

Whether you are a neophyte or a veteran in dealing with such children, this chapter is full of examples, tools, activities, and inspiration to help you understand and reach those puzzle kids who don't fit neatly in the box. Our aim is to build a bridge between brain and body, usually ignored in public education. You will learn how to awaken students' minds for optimal learning, while aiding them in regulating their bodies.

While the number of children labeled "at risk" for failure is increasing, funding for specialized education is decreasing. Schools can no longer afford to turn a blind eye and deaf ear to their traumatized students. With fewer external resources available, there is even more need to help children access their most precious internal resource—the body's ability to self-regulate!

If policymakers are serious about the promise of "no child left behind," they need to understand how trauma affects both learning and behavior. School environments can be designed to support healthy development with creativity rather than cost. This is possible as the knowledge gap is narrowed between science and classroom practice. Rewards and punishments, anger "management" programs, guidance opportunity classes, and shuffling children from school to school don't do the trick. And traditional cognitive-behavioral approaches, while helpful with certain students, don't address the core problems when dealing with children who have trauma histories.

Classroom teachers, counselors, psychologists, nurses, and therapists (occupational, physical, and speech) can *effectively influence* the physiological and emotional responses of their students. Whether from perceptual shifts in working with traumatized students after reading this book or by using the actual structured activities recommended, you *can* make a difference. And although this chapter does not include a formal assessment tool, it can guide school psychologists to recognize students with post-traumatic stress disorder who may otherwise have been misdiagnosed with attention deficit/hyperactivity disorder, obsessive-compulsive disorder, anxiety disorder, depression, or even in some cases (as you shall see) with autism.

It would take an entire text to visit all the challenges that educators face today. Keeping a complex issue as simple as possible, this chapter illustrates how trauma affects both conduct and achievement. Typical profiles of students who may be suffering from traumatic stress are described, and various case examples presented. Suggestions and directions for activities are provided to get you started. With a little practice, you will soon be creating your own activities as you interact with your own clever students. Some activities are for teachers to use with the whole class, while others are mainly for counselors and school psychologists to use with individuals or small groups. A few suggestions are made for program design and may need the support of administration. Additional suggestions for school-wide trauma first aid after a crisis such as a natural disaster or terrorist attack follow in Chapter Twelve.

The goal is to help you identify students with trauma symptoms and to provide the tools and activities to help them thrive. When students are routinely given the time and support necessary to take responsibility for their own internal state, they can *and* do! The adults at school can teach self-regulation by: 1) Monitoring their own internal states when upset and de-activating themselves, thereby modeling healthy self-regulation; and 2) Structuring activities in such a way as to *intentionally* give guided practice in building body awareness, releasing habitual trauma-based responses, and forming alternative pathways in the brain that lead to socially appropriate behavior.

Our Misunderstood Students

Because trauma is so prevalent but so misunderstood, so too are the children who are often living in a daily state of terror. Or, even worse, they are numb and unresponsive. Already anxious, these students find that the unpredictability of classroom demands and playground events heightens their arousal to an unbearable state. What might seem like ordinary stress to another student can be perceived as a life-or-death struggle. Vain attempts may be made to gain a sense of control by blaming others or through temper tantrums. The dilemma lies in the fact that for those suffering the effects of trauma, the threshold for tolerating sensations generated internally has been compromised. Because of this it may take very little external provocation to upset them. In fact, to the outside observer, it may appear as if antecedents are absent.

Without knowing the basic dynamics of trauma, educators have (naturally) been perplexed about how best to handle troubled students. Typically, these students have been relegated to "catch-all" classifications such as conduct-disordered, ADHD, obsessive-compulsive, or even mentally ill. They are typically separated from their classmates and placed in special classrooms. Often they are labeled as "Emotionally Disturbed" or "Learning Disabled." Frustrated teachers or parents may insist on medication as well. These solutions do not resolve the underlying cause of the problem; they are akin to watering the leaves of a dying tree while ignoring its roots. And often, these placements and labels can be a huge disservice to students already suffering from overwhelming fear and rejection.

The pain of post-traumatic stress disorder was not recognized until 1980.[1] Unfortunately, when it was legitimized by the American Psychiatric Association as a diagnosis, it was also perceived as a non-reversible disease to be treated with medication and talk therapy. Those who did not fit neatly into the category of PTSD were misdiagnosed or ignored. Even worse, the behavior of students acting out the pain of their unresolved trauma was seen as willful and met with punishment. Fortunately, Dr. Lenore Terr's groundbreaking book, *Too Scared To Cry* (1990), showed empirical evidence, for the first time, on how trauma affects children. Her study of the twenty-six kidnapped students from the 1976 Chowchilla school bus hijacking dramatically highlighted the long-term effects of untreated trauma.[2] Symptoms recognized today as hallmarks of severe shock had been completely overlooked. The examining psychiatrist said that the students "would just get over it." The implications of trauma as a frozen state of helplessness had not yet been conceived. We know a lot more about trauma now. As you read the vignettes in this chapter, you may see your own challenging students in a different light. If you are working with school children, you can be assured that you are often working with the effects of trauma.

Observing the Body's Response to Trauma in the Classroom

How do your students' traumas show up? In the classroom, students' trauma "stories" are revealed by their posture, facial expressions, and energy level. Hyperarousal can be observed as guardedness, fidgeting, "restless leg," ADHD, compulsive talking, darting eyes, anxiety, agitation, distractibility, "out-of-seat" behavior, and "looking for a fight." Meanwhile, immobility and feelings of helplessness can easily be observed in a student's collapsed posture (draping one's self across the desk like a rag doll), a lack of initiative or motivation, listlessness, failure to complete work, depression, difficulty transitioning to new tasks, flat affect, and a sense of lifelessness.

A more discerning eye may be required to observe constriction. Students may show signs of muscle tension and fatigue. Or they may have somatic complaints. The most common are chronic tummy aches and headaches and/or neck and back pain. If untreated, persistent symptoms can worsen to irritable bowel and loose bowel, eating disorders, and shallow breathing; the latter prevents adequate oxygen from reaching the brain. These are the children who make frequent visits to the school nurse or are often absent.

Dissociation shows up as daydreaming, numbness, distractibility, "head in the clouds," blank stare, inattention, denial of reality, and an inability to connect with others. It may also interfere with the ability to connect with the meaning of an oral lesson or printed material (in other words, poor academics). Referrals from teachers with complaints such as "Lionel just sits there and does nothing" or "Amy stares into space" are as frequent as those for disruptive behavior, and often just as frustrating.

Beyond Academic and Behavioral Yardsticks: Assessing the Deeper Problem

Now that you've begun to think about trauma's effects on students in general, let's take a look at profiles of real students who will probably remind you of ones in *your* classroom:

1. Jordan, the third-grade boy who couldn't read.
2. Alex, an explosive seventh-grader who, unprovoked, threw a chair.
3. Ruby, a quiet eleventh-grader with chronic absenteeism and headaches.
4. Carlos, a fifth-grade boy who refused to do his work.
5. Forrest, a traumatized preschooler misdiagnosed with autism.

Each student's problematic behaviors are presented in a case format and examined in light of his or her trauma history. The examples given will be useful to all members of the student support team. The tools show how to assess students and how to design interventions and modifications that promote self-regulation. Some of the tools will help school psychologists and counselors gather assessment data. Other tools are for teachers to use in the classroom. Some students require a multi-modal approach of coordinated services among teachers, psychologists, and counselors. This fresh approach enables us to identify and help traumatized students most effectively.

Rather than looking at the obvious behaviors, antecedents, and consequences, we'll take a deeper look at what may be hidden beneath the surface. Throughout each vignette, suggestions are made to guide the school psychologist and counselor in making more discerning assessments. Activities tailored to individual needs are suggested that are simple enough to be used by teachers, aides, and classroom volunteers. The first example is a third-grader named

Jordan who perfectly illustrates what traumatic dissociation looks like at school and how it affects reading, thinking, and behavior.

Jordan: The Boy Who Couldn't Read

Jordan was referred to our school's Student Support Team in third grade because, although he seemed bright, he couldn't read. His family was loving and supportive. He was read to at home and, according to his teacher and parents, understood scientific concepts. He was the eldest of two boys and expressed no complaints. To top it off, Jordan adored his skillful teacher, who had an upbeat teaching style and provided a splendid learning environment. Jordan expressed sadness that he couldn't read. He was described as "a hard worker who tries his best." By November, Jordan's behavior began to change. As he became increasingly frustrated, he would "lose it," having angry outbursts to "blow off steam."

With no signs of mental delay, no maltreatment or neglect from home, and an optimal learning environment, one might well ask "What's the deal?" Why couldn't Jordan read? Assessing the number of vowel and consonant blends Jordan had mastered or words he could read per minute was of little value. Like a sleuth I began investigating the underlying dynamics.

I agreed to assess Jordan. Using a standardized achievement test, he read short passages silently, followed by comprehension questions that he was unable to answer. Because his word recognition skills were at an average third-grade level, I "tested the limits," going beyond the standardized instructions, asking Jordan to read aloud. He had the phonics down. But when I posed a question about what he had just read, his response was "What did you say?" Since hearing and vision problems had been ruled out by the school nurse, rather than repeating the question I asked a different one. "Jordan, what were you just thinking about while I was reading to you?" He looked at me with big, soft brown eyes. I could never have predicted his sobering response: "I was thinking that the world was going to end soon and worried that I would die." No wonder he hadn't "heard" a word! Jordan dutifully pronounced each word without emotion. Meaning was pre-empted by fear.

In Jordan's case, he was able to put his thoughts into words, but for many students, their worry is so dissociated (cut off from conscious experience) that they will shrug their shoulders and respond, "I dunno." And the truth of the matter is that, often, they don't. I closed the test book and invited Jordan to draw some of the things that were disturbing him. One of the images he drew was of himself in a spaceship far above the Earth. He pointed to the clouds saying, "I would be safe up there."

As he colored his drawing, Jordan began to share his troubles. He told me that he was a "very bad boy." I was perplexed. Both school and home reported that he generally did not have a behavior problem, and got along well with peers. His temper outbursts were not directed at anyone, and the tantrums were rare and recent. As Jordan continued to draw he made a "confession." He told me that when he was in preschool, he "threw" a desk across the room in a fit of anger. He sighed as he got this guilt off his chest. The story did not add up. It seemed like a fantasy, along with some of the other things that Jordan told me. I made a list of all Jordan's concerns, which numbered around a dozen.

At a conference with Jordan and his mother, we discussed his worries. The first item was the "thrown desk." Jordan's mother was stunned. She blurted out, "That was me! Jordan, you didn't throw a desk, I did! I was furious when I saw a bruise on your wrist; I thought someone had hurt you. I didn't exactly throw it, but I pushed it real hard!" Jordan couldn't accept his mother's response. He insisted that he did it! It took time for his mom to soothe and convince him of reality.

Jordan's story is a cogent illustration of three important points:

1. Trauma resides in the nervous system and becomes frozen in a special kind of memory (called implicit) as if stuck in a time warp. All the disturbing events Jordan listed (for example, the death of his uncle) which his mother confirmed as true had happened *four years earlier!* Other incidents were unverified. Yet he had talked about all the incidents, fantastic or real, as if they had happened the week before we met! Jordan was clearly living in the past.

2. Trauma is a violation of the protective boundaries that prevent overwhelm. Boundary "rupture" distorts a basic sense of self. A child who witnesses violence often merges helplessly with the violator, blurring the sense of who is who. Traumatized Jordan could not differentiate his mother's behavior from his own! Thus, he lived in a fantasy that he was a "bad boy." Of course, we don't know what else happened that day that may have also shaped his distorted beliefs.

3. A student like Jordan with unresolved trauma lives in a world where elements of conscious experience are split off from each other or "dissociated" from current reality. No wonder he wasn't succeeding in school. Polite students like Jordan may appear to be paying attention, but with their head in the clouds, a teacher's lesson registers like a Snoopy cartoon dialog bubble: "blah, blah, blah, blah, blah." And a simple story is merely a string of words without meaning.

Jordan's thoughts were preoccupied with the world ending, although when we first started the assessment, he had said that he felt fine. His picture revealed what his words could not. Students like Jordan are often mistakenly diagnosed with attention deficit disorder (ADD) and treated with medication to increase attention, while their symptoms of fear and jumbled thinking remain undiscovered and/or ignored. If the hidden fears are discovered, the student might be diagnosed with a mood or thought disorder. Neither solution addresses the underlying trauma.

Many compassionate teachers, like Jordan's, see their students' internal struggles but do not know what is troubling them or how to intervene. Seeing the link between trauma and learning problems clearly is the first step. In addition to an empathic connection, skills can be developed that assess the feelings and thoughts of students, not just their reading skills.

Next Steps: Beneficial Activities in the Classroom

The first step in Jordon's case has already been completed. A good dynamic assessment that uncovers trauma and how it impedes learning can lead to solutions that the typical academic skills-based protocol cannot. This requires a genuine interest in learning the child's perspective and using the simplest of tools: crayons or markers and a piece of drawing paper.

Because Jordan had been living in the past for four years, and many of his fantasies involve family dynamics, Jordan has a lot of emotional "catching up" to do. Collaboration, referral, and follow-up with a school-based mental health professional or family therapist may relieve some of Jordan's stress. But the classroom teacher can help students like Jordan too. Exercises and activities can be part of a daily routine that will benefit all students in becoming more embodied and more focused in the present. While Jordan would most likely benefit from grounding and centering to help him concentrate in present time rather than be consumed by worry from the past, a wide assortment of movement and art activities for a variety of challenging students is presented in the following pages.

In some of the activities, guided practice is given to purposely activate students with excitement and then de-activate the nervous system during the calming down, settling, and resting phase. Other activities are designed for grounding, centering, finding resources, discovering boundaries, and honoring personal space. Some will help bring back protective and defensive responses that may have been lost, such as the restoration of *healthy* aggression. There are also activities designed to help students shift out of a "bad mood," express themselves in a socially acceptable way, or de-activate a high arousal state. A few activities are included that may improve learners' visual-motor and balancing skills. All are meant to empower and restore vitality and resiliency.

Good news for educators is that the movement activities you will learn about not only improve behavior—movement has side effects: It improves learning! Physical movement creates the nerve cell networks that make it possible to learn in the first place. In fact, learning takes place as the mind and body process sensation, emotion, and thought. Billions of nerve cells link our senses to our muscle movements. The integration of this input comes through the vestibular and proprioceptive systems. The vestibular system controls our sense of balance, gravity, and motion, while proprioception gives information about our position in space through awareness of the joints as they are moved by our muscles. In addition, working both sides of the body in cross-lateral movement promotes development of the corpus callosum (essential for the two hemispheres of the brain to communicate). Neural pathways that form connections for learning are weaker for those who have suffered trauma but *can be improved* through activities that require using these pathways.

In a fabulous book for educators, *Smart Moves: Why Learning Is Not All in Your Head,* Dr. Carla Hannaford (neuropsychologist and educator) cites scientific research as well as anecdotal reports showing a clear connection between thinking, learning, and the body. Dr. Hannaford says that research explains how movement directly benefits the nervous system: "Muscular activities, particularly coordinated movements, appear to stimulate the production of neurotrophins, natural substances that stimulate the growth of nerve cells and increase the number of neural connections in the brain."[3] Movement is also necessary for efficient teaming of the eyes for focusing when reading. When the body and head move, the vestibular system is activated, strengthening and coordinating the eye muscles.

SIMPLE GROUNDING AND CENTERING EXERCISES

Grounding will benefit all of your "Jordans." One exercise that helps children feel grounded is the Tree Exercise. Most students take to this naturally. It can be done with the whole class, a small group, or individually. If you are lucky enough to have an outdoor grassy area, take the children outside so that they can experience more tangible contact with the earth.

"THE MAGIC IN ME" TREE EXERCISE

Have children stand up with sufficient space around them to move their arms like swaying branches. Read the following poem as students pretend that they are big strong trees, with roots for their feet that grow deep into the earth.

The Magic in Me[4]

We're going to play, but before we begin,
I want you to find your own magic within.
Just take some time to feel and to see
All the great things that your body can be.

Pretend you're a tree with your branches so high
That you can reach up and tickle the sky.
What's it like to be strong like a big old oak tree?
With roots in your feet and your leaves waving free?

Now you're connected to the earth and the sky
It may make you laugh, it may make you cry.
It doesn't matter when you go with the flow
With your branches up high; your roots way down low.

Hear the breath in your body, if you listen it sings.
Now you are ready for whatever life brings.

Note: Pause here to give your students time to stand up tall, stomp their feet, and feel their "roots" as they connect to the ground. Have them wave their arms, feeling themselves bend and sway with resilience as the wind blows their "leaves and branches."

It is easy to spot the "Jordans." They may be staring into space, tuned out to the directions, or lagging behind. The teacher, aide, or other adult can give these youngsters extra support by standing nearby and directing them to bring awareness to their lower legs, ankles, and feet as they make contact with the ground.

CHOO-CHOO STOMP

This exercise is adapted from Julie Henderson's book, Embodying Well-Being or How to Feel as Good as You Can in Spite of Everything.[5]

Have students form "trains" of eight to ten students by resting their hands on the waist of the person in front of them. Have the trains take very short vigorous steps, lifting their feet only a few inches from the floor and bringing them down in a satisfying thump. Move around the room with the energy and momentum of a locomotive. Have students chant "Choo Choo Stomp Stomp" or "Stomp Stomp Choo Choo," enjoying until slightly tired.

This exercise brings energy down to the feet and lowers the center of gravity to create stability very quickly. It also creates strength, presence, and attention. For variation, have all the "little trains" couple together to form one "big train" like a conga dance line. You can also have the children drop their hands so that each child can be his or her own train, moving singly.

For teenagers, a great way to ground is to put on some tribal music with a good beat and have them dance, creating their own chants.

A SIMPLE CENTERING EXERCISE

Have students stand (with or without music), feel the connection of their feet to the floor, then bend their knees to lower their center of gravity, creating a feeling of greater stability. Next have them sway, shifting their weight gently from side to side, from foot to foot. Direct their awareness to the sense of going off balance and coming back into balance by finding their center of gravity. After they have explored this movement for a while, have them repeat the exercise and share the sensations they feel in each position. Students can point to the place in their body where they feel "centered." For most, it will be in the area near the navel and about two inches inside the body. Next, students can repeat the above, this time moving forward and backward instead of from side to side. Young children can pretend to be a toy top moving about in a circle with hands on hips. As the "top" slows down, it wobbles until it finally rests, stopping completely.

The Eyes, Trauma, and Reading: Help for Students Who Can't Focus on Print

While Jordan had difficulty comprehending the words he "read," many students suffering from trauma cannot focus their eyes well enough to even pronounce words. An exercise called "Lazy 8's" improves visual tracking skills and is presented below

Disruptions in visual processing are characteristic of students who have been traumatized. For many who have witnessed or been involved in the horror of a violent attack or an accident, the wide-eyed look of terror remains as if frozen in time. Sometimes it is simply a blank expression. When the chaos is random and chronic, eyes will tend to wander to the sides to broaden the peripheral field of vision as a function of hypervigilance, or standing guard. Children who *saw* the danger coming directly at them may experience a momentary visual "freeze" at certain triggering angles as their eyes glide across a page of print. For some students, the left-to-right movement across the page becomes stressful, leading to fatigue after reading.

Being able to focus awareness on different points in space simultaneously may stimulate creative thinking, but it wreaks havoc when trying to sustain attention on words when trying to read. Often traumatized students are labeled learning disabled or dyslexic because of lack of ability to track smoothly with both eyes.

Carla Hannaford writes, "I often find that children with learning difficulties experience distress when I ask them to focus on my thumb as I move it through their entire visual field. Their eyes jump, they complain that it hurts, and they have difficulty maintaining focus. This visual stress, when the eyes don't focus effectively or track together efficiently, is due to inadequate muscular development in the eyes, often caused by lack of movement."[6]

This of course can be due to lack of stimulation when babies are raised in impoverished settings. Too much TV watching can also reduce the full range of motion of the eyes because of the small angle of movement required to track the screen. The lack of visual stimulation can also be caused by stress and trauma. Dr. Hannaford notes: "Under stress, the eyes will react by moving peripherally and the dominant eye muscles will not receive full motor function from the dominant side of the brain. This makes foveal focus and tracking across a page of reading difficult. Integrated sensory input will also be minimized. ... In European schools, children knit as part of their skills training."[7] Knitting strengthens fine motor coordination, as well as visual tracking. Dr. Hannaford goes on to recommend "Lazy 8's for Eyes" for maximal visual efficiency. This exercise is taken from *Brain Gym* activities created by the Dennisons, founders of educational kinesiology.[8]

---------------------------------- 🍃 ----------------------------------

LAZY 8'S FOR THE EYES

The goal is to improve hand/eye and eye/hand coordination. Lazy 8's are done by training the eyes on a moving thumb as it traces an invisible infinity sign in the visual field. To do this, the student holds either thumb at eye level in the mid-field of the body at approximately an elbow length from the eyes. For maximum muscular activation the movements should be s-l-o-w and conscious. Holding the head still but relaxed, just move the eyes to follow the thumb. Move the thumb directly up the center of the mid-field to the top of the visual field and then counterclockwise out, around, and down to the left side. As the thumb reaches the lower mid-field of the visual field, bring it back up the center and clockwise out, around, and down the right side. This should be continued in an even flowing movement at least three times with each hand. Then both hands should be clasped with the thumbs forming an X. While focusing on the center of the X, again follow the clasped thumbs through the Lazy 8 pattern.

A cautionary note for working with severely traumatized students: Working with the eyes can be highly stimulating. It is important to introduce this work very slowly, perhaps making only one loop at first. Stop immediately if the student complains of eye pain or fatigue. Have them rest their eyes and notice what sensations, thoughts, or images come up. Assist them with any painful feelings they may have. Do not push. Another idea to strengthen visual coordination is to have the student try "Lazy 8's for Writing" with chalk on the board or on the sidewalk, making them as large as they can. Use the eye exercises when appropriate, working up to completing the figure eight with ease three times with each hand.

Alex: The Explosive Acting-Out Student

As the passages became denser with words, Alex could not answer simple questions that "should" have been easy for a youngster of his intelligence. He hadn't even gotten to the hard stuff. Looking for clues, Alex's teacher asked him to read aloud. To her astonishment, this academically accelerated seventh-grader picked up his chair and threw it dangerously close to several classmates. He screamed with a piercing infantile sound. Then he yelled repeatedly, "Shut up! Shut up! Shut up!" Stunned, the teacher called the vice principal. After a struggle, out-of-control Alex was escorted to the office. Why would a mentally gifted middle-school student resort to screams and tantrums?

Educators and parents are baffled by students like Alex, who don't fit in any "box." When raging youngsters have grown up in the violence of the inner city, often without one or both parents, deficits of self-control make sense. But youngsters with intact families growing up free of poverty within a "good enough" environment can be puzzling. They are frequently neither easy to diagnosis nor to help. So, with best intentions, they are often misdiagnosed and broadly categorized as behaviorally disordered. If they don't improve with medication, they might end up lumped together in classes with other children who are misunderstood. So, who are these students like Alex who are volatile? Why is the above scenario so common? What makes Alex and others like him tick? Let's take a look at Alex's developmental history.

Alex was born with the umbilical cord wrapped tightly around his neck. He was also stuck in the birth canal and emerged quite blue. His early history revealed colic, frequent tantrums as a toddler, and a low frustration tolerance for imperfection as a young child. His behaviors progressively worsened. With the onset of raging hormones in seventh grade, all hell broke loose. Alex was growing up, but his nervous system remained immature. His classroom teacher, not surprisingly, thought he either had a conduct disorder or was emotionally disturbed. Alex apologized and admitted that he shouldn't have exploded; he said that couldn't help it.

Unfortunately, as any teacher knows, students like Alex are not rare. The key to knowing what makes Alex tick is in his history. His problem was written in black and white when his mother filled out the compulsory "Developmental History" form when Alex entered kindergarten—she noted his colic and tantrums at that time. He was not emotionally disturbed nor did he have ADHD. Alex's "bad behavior" was a disorder of self-regulation that was apparent as early as infancy! How can we help Alex, and how can we help teachers who have volatile students like Alex?

The first step is for the teacher to learn to recognize a student who is becoming activated before he explodes and assist him in calming down. If a student suddenly becomes explosive, the teacher needs to remain cool and follow a de-escalation procedure that he has committed to memory and practiced in advance. Using the "Guidelines for De-Escalation" described below can relieve the pressure building in the student's nervous system before it boils over. This not only is the best damage control, but it will help the other students feel safe knowing that the teacher is in control. The second step is for students like Alex to be given guided practice in "assisted self-regulation," described later in this chapter.

De-Escalating Explosive Situations

An outraged teacher does not ensure safety for anyone. The brain of a traumatized person under threat responds in a dramatically different way compared to one that is not suffering from post-traumatic stress disorder. When the "early warning center" of the midbrain registers change in the environment (for better or worse), a person with normal self-regulatory capacity experiences elevated arousal. In other words, the sensory images produce an alert state so that various responses are possible. Signals are sent to the survival brain in case a defensive response is required. Signals are sent *simultaneously* to the frontal lobes to engage socially through facial expression or words if the novelty is non-threatening, or even friendly! Functional magnetic resonance imaging (fMRI) brain scans show us that for a child who has been traumatized, the perceived threat is *not* processed through dual signals sent to the higher and lower brain simultaneously. Instead only one channel activates—the amygdala awakens the reptilian survival brain, while the higher neocortical brain activity that can think and reason lies dormant. We have a dilemma when students with trauma histories are placed with teachers who harbor their own unresolved trauma. When lizard brain meets dinosaur brain in a classroom confrontation, the showdown is not pretty. It is predictably a disaster. What all students need (especially in "Emotionally Disturbed" and "Guidance" classrooms) are teachers who can access the best of their humanity at the worst of times. Instead of a fire-breathing gila monster, students need the soothing words and calm gestures of a stable teacher who possesses self-control and confidence.

Yes, the teacher in charge has the power to de-escalate a hostile, frightened child. Words spoken in a calm, firm voice (delivered by a teacher with an upright posture) can be effective when she or he is able to have the presence of mind to utilize a step-by-step plan to help the student out of the mess, saving face as much as possible. An example would be: "Antoine, you're out of control. You got angry so fast when Maria sharpened her pencil—it took us all by surprise! It must have really startled [annoyed, etc.] you. It's okay now—it's over. We'll work together to help you settle down." After Antoine settles down, you can offer him a quieter place to finish his math. Then let him know that he must remain calm in order to go out to recess after his work is completed.

Following are some succinct tips to assist you when under fire:

Guidelines for De-Escalation

- Take a deep breath, take one step back, and ground yourself first. Let your energy settle into your feet and lower legs, feeling the support of the ground.
- Remind yourself that you know what to do because you have memorized this list.
- Adopt a soothing tone of voice; raising your voice provokes more adrenaline!
- Avoid threatening behaviors or gestures.

- State the behavior you observed without shaming or exaggeration, despite the temptation.

- Show that you understand your student by reflecting her overwhelming feelings.

- Avoid threatening punishment.

- Make a statement that shows the student that she is not alone; this will assist her in calming down.

- Make a statement that shows that the relationship between you can be repaired.

- Make a statement that gives a choice to save face.

- Make a statement that states the misbehavior without chastisement.

- Make a statement that shows the correct behavior, and/or what can repair the infraction.

If you doubt that the above guidelines will actually work or that they are too "wimpy," visit the classroom of any teacher noted for success in handling challenging students, and you will see these principles in effect. Seeing is believing! If you still don't have the confidence to de-escalate an out-of-control student, perhaps the next story will give you heart. The power of presence, tone, and words can truly help, whether spoken to a crazed student in the classroom or a violent criminal on the loose.

The Power of Cool: Carolyn's Story

When my friend Carolyn was home alone one evening, she was awakened by the sound of the mini-blinds rattling downstairs. First she thought it was one of her cats, Sinca—but Sinca was upstairs. Heart racing, she charged down the stairs in her B. Kliban cat nightshirt, thinking that her other cat had gotten into trouble. Halfway down, Carolyn momentarily froze as she spotted the intruder, wearing a ski mask, as he broke in through her window. Standing on the steps Carolyn was frightened, but she simply sat down. Instead of her arousal escalating into panic or confrontation, her calm energy became her strength. She recalls simply saying in a firm voice, "You must be really frightened to see me. Don't worry, I won't hurt you. I just want you out of my house! If you walk backward slowly and reach behind, you will be able to turn the doorknob and let yourself out." The intruder was fumbling with the deadbolt and became quite agitated. "It's okay. It sticks— pull it towards you," she said with determination. With those instructions he was able to pull the knob and let himself out. Carolyn found out later, after the police caught the intruder, that he had a knife in his possession and was a convicted rapist! The point is, with non-threatening directions on how to stay safe and save face, the crazed intruder did as he was told!

ACTIVITIES TO SUPPORT ASSISTED SELF-REGULATION, WITH GUIDED PRACTICE IN COOLING DOWN

Almost any school activity can be structured for the practice of self-regulation. Monitoring and modeling a charged (activated) and calm (de-activated) nervous system, with opportunities for self-soothing and self-monitoring, are essential. Martial arts such as aikido and other sports or games played on a mat can be modified so that "Time Outs" or "Pauses" are built in to manage activation. The trick is to assist students to become skillful in recognizing small agitations *before* they escalate. This can be taught in the following three-step process. Group support is given for a self-proclaimed "Pause" to:

1. Track activation (agitation or excitement).

2. Take 60 *full* seconds to calm and settle (allow more time if needed).

3. Re-ground and re-center before resuming activity.

MODIFIED SPORTS

Below is the outline of a structure that can be used for Modified Wrestling and Modified Touch Football (for example) that supports students during physical education in both self-assessment and self-regulation of their level of arousal. It is adapted from Dr. John Stewart's book Beyond Time Out, *with a shift in emphasis from tracking only emotions to tracking physiological sensations.⁹ An important feature is the availability of support from both adults and teammates in taking the time to calm down and self-soothe when agitated. The "activities" of resting, cooling down, and integrating this new way of behaving are the centerpiece of the skill-building.*

To facilitate tracking sensations, it is suggested that a large color-coded poster with a thermometer depicting various levels of arousal be prominently displayed. (For example: blue = calm, purple = OK, green = beginning to sense irritation or excitement, orange = feeling tense, and red = about to explode.) The group leader or coach/referee blows the whistle at regular intervals during the activity, at first having all players self-assess and report their "color" before proceeding. In another twist on Stewart's ideas, we suggest that rather than counting to ten, the adult in charge guide the students to track their sensations until they are feeling "blue" (calm) or at least "purple" (OK). Students having difficulty can be given support through extra time, pairing with a calm buddy, or receiving guidance from the proximity of a calm adult until they discharge their activation and are able to settle down. As the students become more skillful, the activity can be made increasingly challenging by adding the element of surprise. Simply have the teacher/coach blow the whistle at irregular intervals to accomplish this.

FOCUSED BREATHING

The following exercise is a simple breathing meditation developed to bring body awareness to a class of underachieving (and mostly delinquent) teenagers who failed eighth grade. It can be used, however, with elementary and high school students as well. As a prelude, the class was read a news clip about basketball coach Phil Jackson's use of meditation with the Lakers as he led them to victory. This inspiring lead-in, together with the natural fascination teens have with their bodies, made the following exercise a favorite.

1. Students are given a large "Post-It" on which they number from 1 to 5 and write the following:

    1) Inhale:

    2) Pause:

    3) Exhale:

    4) Pause:

    5) Changes noted:

2. With eyes open or closed, students simply follow their breath, carefully tracking the route, rhythm, and length of the inhale and exhale. They also notice whether or not pauses occur between the inhale and exhale. Next, they are asked to observe whether the length of the inhale/exhale is even or uneven, and what they notice about the pauses. There is no right or wrong way to do this. The exercise is designed to bring focus and awareness to the breath without attempting to change anything.

   Simply through observation, students notice how the breath changes, by itself, over time. They may also be invited to notice what happens with their muscle tension and other sensations as concentration deepens.

3. Begin with an approximately three-minute daily routine at the start of class. Work up to five to ten minutes (depending on your students' capacity) per day as a routine practice. The structure provided by the details of the five questions on the Post-It help children who are normally squirmy to focus. As students become more adept at concentration they may be weaned off using the Post-Its as an aid.

   Optional: After the breathing meditation, have students use the Post-It to make brief notes of their observations after each numbered item. See sample below.

Student Observations

   1) Inhale: Longer than exhale

   2) Pause: No

   3) Exhale: Uneven

   4) Pause: Yes

   5) Changes noted: Exhale became more even with inhale.

A CALMING EXERCISE FOR THE WHOLE CLASS: "HOOK-UPS" FROM BRAIN GYM

This is another simple and effective exercise from Brain Gym that can be used with students who are disruptive in class or having trouble calming down after a fight or verbal confrontation. It's a good idea to have students do this before asking them to talk about what happened. It takes only two to five minutes and decreases adrenaline production by bringing attention away from the survival centers of the reptilian brain.

Hook-ups are done by crossing one ankle over the other in whatever way feels comfortable. Next, the hands are crossed, clasped, and inverted. To do this easily, stretch your arms out in front of you, with the back of the hands together and the thumbs pointing down. Now lift one hand over the other, palms facing, and interlock the fingers. Then roll the locked hands straight down and in towards the body so that they eventually rest on the chest with the elbows down. This complex crossover action serves to balance and activate the sensory and motor cortices of each hemisphere of the cerebrum.

While they are in this position, direct students to rest the tip of their tongue on the roof of the mouth behind their front teeth. This action brings attention to the mid-brain, which lies right above the hard palate. This configuration connects emotions in the limbic system with reason in the frontal lobes of the cerebrum, thus giving an integrative perspective from which to learn and respond more effectively.[10]

Ruby: "Unmotivated Truant"

When visiting homes of truant students, nine times out of ten I discover that they are "shut down" and collapsed. This takes the form of either depression or chronic somatic symptoms, like headaches or stomachaches (especially with diarrhea). As I invite these truants to explore their sensations, thoughts, images, and feelings while tending to the area of their discomfort, one or more traumatic events generally emerge. When I ask the children if they have someone to talk to about their pain and fear, they invariably say, "No." And, in fact, comments like "Oh, no, we don't go *there* in my family" or "Grandma would kill me if I ever brought *that* up" are common.

While some of these students come to school infrequently, others come but ask to see the nurse or go home when it's time to do independent work. Participation with a teacher they have bonded with may bring a sense of safety. When they are given an assignment, they are left alone with inner turmoil. Coming to school already in a high state of anxiety, many of these children can find the prospect of being left to their own thoughts too much to bear. Often these students are silent and don't rock the boat. Teachers assume that they don't care about learning or they would show up. Many of these students actually care very much. They are frequently painfully shy and can't reach out, like quiet Ruby.

Ruby was one such eleventh-grader referred to me for headaches and absenteeism. In fact, she was in danger of not graduating. When she wasn't depressed, she was anxious. Remember the "panic anxiety" experienced by a large percentage of traumatized students—*the sense of imminent danger or impending doom associated with a thwarted (blocked or prevented) urge to escape. This, we believe, is the essence of trauma: the urge to escape coupled with the perception of not being able to.* Moving out of the "immobility response" (depression) can be a fiercely energetic experience, one that is often frightening. Without the support of caring adults, children brace themselves against the power of their own sensations. This bracing not only prevents completion of the activation cycle necessary to restore a sense of safety, but creates stress on the body, draining it of energy.

As a preschool child, Ruby lived in a house fraught with domestic violence that ended tragically in murder, resulting in the death of her father and the imprisonment of her mother. She was raised by her grandmother and uncles. Of course, Ruby and her siblings were tragically affected. So, too, were her grandmother and uncles. Feelings were locked away inside Ruby as a shameful family secret. I learned that the sister who witnessed the murder was being homeschooled due to chronic illness. Ruby wanted to stay home as well. She enjoyed learning and liked school. But coming to school every day was over-stimulating on good days. As the depression started to lift and her life energy returned, the repressed energy from the shocking violence and grief experienced more than twelve years earlier created panicky feelings with accompanying head and stomachaches.

When I first met with Ruby she never meant to tell me her story—but images from her past tumbled forth as she reported the sensations of her headache and stomachache. She began to tremble and shake. Tears fell, and I held her in my arms as she pieced together fragmented memories. We continued to work together twice a week until Ruby's attendance and grades improved in direct correlation to reduced anxiety. I attended Ruby's graduation the following year; she confided in me that she never would have continued to come to school if I hadn't helped her with her debilitating feelings.

Very often, the chronically absent child is suffering from trauma symptoms. Families may not want counseling because of the private nature of their pain. They do not believe it is a benefit to reveal their secrets. The good thing about sensory-based counseling (which can be done by the school counselor, school psychologist, or school-based mental health therapist) is that no family history questions need be asked. Ruby knew that when a terrible image from her family's past surfaced, she was free to say as little or as much as she wanted. She said, "I hear shuffling sounds in the next room . . . and I'm scared." But she could have simply said, "I'm scared" or "I feel like running, but I can't." She didn't need to tell me more than that. Ruby chose to tell me more because she felt safe with me. Whether she shared details beyond this was irrelevant—being both witnessed and held as she discharged her life-long shock through trembling, shaking, and tears was sufficient to relieve the symptoms that were keeping her from participating in an education she held dear.

Ruby got the support she needed because an astute and compassionate teacher referred her for counseling. While another high school teacher may have taken the stance of not "babying" eleventh-graders, one of Ruby's teachers realized how much she was suffering. A different teacher threatened Ruby with "F's" for absenteeism, but her science teacher showed her kindness and, like a good parent, got her the help she needed. Ruby looked forward to the sensation-based counseling sessions, even though they brought painful memories to the surface. As the emotions of fear and grief released, her stomachaches, headaches, and fatigue lessened. Ruby had more energy for her schoolwork.

Teachers can help students like Ruby by recognizing and referring them to counseling. Depression is often a symptom of trauma and can be experienced emotionally *and* physically. School counselors, school psychologists, and nurses can learn how to counsel students using this non-threatening sensory-based approach that helped Ruby. Using the principles you've discovered so far by reading this book is a good start in helping distressed students. If you'd like more extensive training, contact The Foundation for Human Enrichment to get information on Somatic Experiencing® Training Programs (www.traumahealing.com). If your school does not offer counseling services, a referral to a psychotherapist trained in Somatic Experiencing® can be located on the same Website, or ask the Student Support Team for a referral to an agency or therapist who specializes in treating childhood trauma. Do not ignore the quiet ones! Remember, help for Ruby started with a caring teacher.

Carlos: A Defiant Student Who Avoids His Schoolwork

Carlos' head hung down. He was failing math and in trouble at school about three out of five days a week for disruptive behavior, most of which erupted during math. He had been kicked out of class on this occasion because of resistance to starting his assignment, accompanied by an angry outburst. Whenever his teacher put pressure on him to perform, he often became defiant. She reported that he would "get up and bolt out of class." Carlos' teacher was convinced that he had attention-deficit hyperactivity disorder.

"Mood Shifting": Developing Internal Resources

Many students, like Carlos, avoid written work, especially with a challenging subject. Some are perfectionists who begin working, only to scrunch up their paper in a fit of frustration. This can sometimes be the beginning of a long bad day (for student and teacher) that they are unable to shake. Often these children live with deep shame about what they perceive as a lack of competence. For these students, the ability to shift attitude or mood seems insurmountable. Low frustration tolerance makes transitioning from one activity to another difficult as well.

When I met with Carlos, he told me that he hated math. Instead of asking him "Why do you hate math?" I began a sensation-based process with him. The following activity was developed spontaneously for Carlos, and other students like him, whose mood seems cast in despair. The process, which I call "mood shifting," helps to lift children out of a foul mood by helping them to discover their own internal resiliency:

1. Building safety: I let Carlos know that I understood that he hated math. I didn't try to talk him out of his feelings or extol the benefits of math. I also let him know that I was willing to explore his struggle with him if he wished.

2. Working with sensations, images, and emotions: I asked Carlos to imagine (with eyes opened or closed) that there was a math paper in front of him and to describe anything he might notice. The following is what he described:

He said that his mind just "goes blank" sometimes—when he gets to a difficult problem "there's a wall that comes up." I asked him to describe the sensations of the wall. He described it "like a paper shredder in his head above his left temple that happens only during math."

3. Developing resources: I asked Carlos to remember a time when he might have had a good feeling about math. He quickly responded that there weren't any. I asked him to take as much time as he needed, challenging him to find a time when he felt good about math, no matter how far back he had to stretch. It took a while to recall, but Carlos finally looked directly at me and relayed the following story:

His first-grade math teacher was having a difficult time getting her class to regroup in addition. Carlos didn't understand how to regroup in addition, either. But Mrs. Shultz demonstrated again, and this time Carlos got it. His best friend Oscar did not. His teacher asked Carlos to help Oscar. When Oscar learned how to regroup with Carlos' help, Carlos said he "felt good." Carlos lit up with a grin from ear to ear just by telling me this story. Remember, this was a story from first grade! Remarkably, his shift in posture out of shame into pride happened quite easily. His spine elongated and his chest expanded. When asked what the good feeling felt like inside his body, he said it was "warm." What a dramatic difference from the slumped position I first encountered!

Shifting from a Pleasurable Experience to a Traumatic Experience and Back Again: The Power of Pendulation

Now that Carlos' expression showed hope, I had him return to the image and feeling of the "paper shredder." He described it as looking like a square. As he focused on the size of the square, he recalled a bad experience and told me about it. He remembered a time that his older brother was "helping" him with his math homework (Father was raising the two boys alone, and older brother was forced to be in charge of his little brother after school). Carlos said that his brother, who was mean-spirited, grew impatient and verbally blasted him, calling him stupid because he didn't understand how to do the problems on his math papers. Tears streamed down his face now as his head slumped over and his torso collapsed in utter shame. After Carlos released his tears and we sat together through this painful experience, I reassured him that it was not his fault; his brother never should have hurt him with those mean words. I let him know that he was certainly not stupid. This was the first time Carlos had recalled from conscious memory the beginning of his troubles with math.

When he was ready, Carlos focused once again on the square until it almost disappeared by becoming a tiny grain of sand. I asked him to imagine working a hard math problem in his fifth-grade class. Again the wall came up. This time when he looked at the wall, he saw black. I asked him for an opposite image, and Carlos saw himself punching (an active self-protective response against meanness and humiliation) through the wall to get to the other side. Within thirty seconds he was able to see himself on the other side!

The reason Carlos was still affected after so many years is that unless the charge held in the trauma and shame of a "flashbulb" traumatic memory is released, it remains locked in the body memory, coloring and shaping the way we perceive our experiences. Carlos' painful "forgotten" experiences lost their powerful grip once the unconsciously held memories were made conscious and subsequently released. Noted researcher Bessel van der Kolk has stated, "Traumatic memories need to become like memories of everyday experience, that is, they need to be modified and transformed by being placed in their proper context and restructured into a meaningful narrative."[11]

At the 2001 "Cutting-Edge Conference on Healing Trauma: Attachment, Trauma, the Brain, and the Mind," Daniel Siegel, MD, stated that we know a person has healed from early experiences when they can weave their experiences into a coherent narrative without collapsing into overwhelm. Pleasant memories are interwoven with the unpleasant. As more pleasant experiences shape us, we realize that life is textured with varying degrees of success and failure, victory and defeat—i.e., life is not *all* good or *all* bad.[12]

When a child is shamed about schoolwork, the humiliation etches the experience deeper in memory. With few experiences to counter-balance his shame, the past became frozen in Carlos' body. This was apparent in the dark cloud hanging over Carlos, confirming for him that "nothing ever changes." When the child's internal experience doesn't change, neither does self-concept. Giving

Carlos a pleasant felt sense experience provided him with new resources to call upon for math and other stressors.

Deepening Carlos' New Resources

Next I had Carlos tell me more about helping Oscar. He immediately said, "I felt happy and proud." I invited him to take some time to notice where he felt these emotions. Without hesitation he pointed to his chest. Then I asked him to describe the feelings he was experiencing in his chest. He replied, "It's warm around my heart. It feels like I just fell into a little hole of happiness!" Carlos' facial expression changed into a broad glowing smile. Then he said, "I'm ready to go back and do my math paper now!"

Neuronal connections for pleasure and security can only be strengthened through *experiential* knowledge. When active processes of experiencing sensations are given the time to develop, a whole new type of learning takes place that optimizes brain function. Strong positive emotional experiences help students to remember what they learn. Strong pleasurable sensations lay the foundation for students to be receptive, rather than blocked, to the nurturance that teachers and counselors can provide. Witnessing and reinforcing your students' positive experiences changes the way they feel about themselves. The trick is to make sure that the *bodily sensations* (warmth around the heart and little hole of happiness) that underlie the *emotions* (happiness and pride) are given time to develop, be felt deeply, and be expressed.

I explained to Carlos that his heartfelt experience of helping Oscar and his pride in understanding the math skill well enough to be able to teach his friend would remain a part of him always. No one, no matter how mean, could ever take away this feeling because he felt it *inside* himself. This is the best kind of resource that teachers and counselors can help students develop. These personal resources are portable—they stay with students wherever they go and are available whenever needed. These internal "felt sense" experiences are what contribute to the emergent maturation of self-identity.

Carlos then agreed to try a little experiment. Whenever his mind went blank in math or he started to get frustrated, he would take some time to "mood shift" by remembering the picture in his head of his teacher asking him to help Oscar. He was asked to focus on his success at teaching Oscar how to regroup in addition. The next step was to let the feelings and sensations come back until he felt relaxed, safe, and ready to try the problem again or ask for help rather than have an angry outburst.

I checked with Carlos and his teacher periodically. Carlos still had other issues to work out. Recently he had been separated from his biological dad and was struggling emotionally. He was now living with his mother and did not like his new stepfather. He rarely got to visit his dad anymore (who had custody of him when he was younger). I asked Carlos to recall a time when he had fun with his dad, and he vividly described inner tubing in the snow together. I had Carlos visualize this experience and describe what it felt like in his body. He said that it felt good in his belly and he felt a little better. We practiced how he could see and feel a pleasant memory to shift his mood. Carlos learned that he no longer had to be stuck in sadness or anger. He had options. He called these good feelings "islands of happiness." Now he had two physical experiences implanted in his memory to help him. Soon Carlos stopped hating math, and his teacher reported that he improved dramatically with work completion, and his angry outbursts during math class ceased.

Avoiding and Recognizing a Misdiagnosis: Is It Autism or Post-Traumatic Stress Disorder?

School psychologists, speech and language specialists, teachers, and counselors: beware of hasty diagnoses. When I worked at a preschool special-education assessment center, I was struck by the high number of three-year-olds referred due to speech and language delays, coupled with marked delays in social skills and stereotypical play behavior. Many already had been labeled autistic after receiving a psychological assessment at a university or private clinic. Although some of the toddlers and preschool youngsters were clearly autistic, it appeared that *some* were suffering from post-traumatic stress disorder. A few of these youngsters had experienced traumatic birth, life-saving surgical procedures, or child abuse. It seemed that for many of these children, making such a strong diagnosis without considering trauma was premature.

Other children, who never attended preschool, were referred for special education upon being spotted by kindergarten teachers. An example was the five-year-old boy who compulsively read the same phrase. His teacher counted twenty-six repetitions before he was satisfied that he had gotten it just right—all the while rocking back and forth. He engaged in limited speech and made little or no eye contact. Parents and staff asked if this child suffered from obsessive-compulsive disorder or autism. A diagnosis of post-traumatic stress was not even considered as an option. Since the implications of trauma are generally misunderstood, this was not a total surprise.

The lucky toddlers and preschool kids who received play therapy after a premature diagnosis of autism often had a "mysterious disappearance" of symptoms such as spinning, lack of emotional responsiveness, preoccupation with objects, and difficulty in making transitions. The following story shared by my friend Patti Elledge, a speech and language pathologist, is an edifying illustration of a boy named Forrest who had been misdiagnosed. Using a combination of parent education about trauma's effects on the nervous system together with Somatic Experiencing® play therapy, Forrest was "cured" of autism (or, rather, of his misdiagnosis).

Forrest: Traumatized Preschooler
Misdiagnosed With Autism

A beautiful tow-haired boy named Forrest was just over two years old when his worried parents brought him to Patti Elledge for speech and language therapy. He had been diagnosed with autism. He certainly had "autistic-like" behaviors. Forrest was a hand-flapper, didn't make eye contact, and had limited ability to engage socially. He also had an unusual way of playing with toys and wasn't able to imitate sounds. In fact, he rarely used any sounds other than a high-pitched squeal. He didn't respond to any language—even his name! How frustrating for Forrest's family! They were exhausted because he was fussy and difficult to soothe, with his crying often ending in tantrums.

Patti noticed that Forrest entered her office with a genuine smile that communicated a sense of "expectancy" of play. It showed only through his clear, sparkling eyes. As she responded to him with offerings of smiles, toys, and interactions, it was heartbreaking to see him shut down, go "blank," and drift away. Forrest could have easily been placed in an early-intervention program for autistic children, as was recommended to his parents. This treatment plan employed rigid behavioral conditioning and strict routines for learning speech sounds and attention skills.

Fortunately, Patti paid close attention to Forrest's significant trauma history. His gestation and birth were complicated. His mother had been pregnant with twins, was highly anxious, and had been medically treated for a rapid heart rate. Late in the pregnancy, she noticed less movement of her babies. An urgent C-section was performed, but Forrest's twin had already died.

Although Forrest survived and appeared "normal," medical concerns emerged soon after birth. He had low platelet counts, hypoglycemia, and hyperbilirubinemia. Forrest's parents, against their instinctual desire to nurture, were instructed not to touch or hold Forrest because he was a "high-risk" infant. The medical issues finally resolved; he was released from intensive care at three weeks of age.

Forrest's mom and dad were both excited and anxious as first-time parents. In addition to the sudden and shocking death of one twin, they brought home a *very* traumatized infant. As they focused intensely on the surviving baby, this loving couple did all the "right" things. You can imagine their growing horror as their inconsolable infant cried into the wee hours of the night. To complicate matters, Forrest had a hernia operation at three months and was hospitalized with severe anemia at six months. He broke his arm when he fell from a swing at eighteen months, which turned out to be a frightening emergency-room experience. The doctor instructed both parents to hold a screaming Forrest down as he was x-rayed and placed in a cast. Later, he swallowed a coin and broke his leg on a play gym, further escalating a cycle of medical trauma and overwhelming stress.

Early trauma such as this can give rise to autistic-like symptoms. The combination of prenatal trauma coupled with three weeks in a *lifesaving but highly intrusive medical environment* had set Forrest into high nervous-system activation. Authors such as Perry and Porges report that elevated stress, without the calming touch of caregivers during critical periods, can have long-term effects on the developing brain.[13] Drs. Daniel Siegel and Allan Schore both also write that such a severe and ongoing dysregulation may be at the heart of the psycho-physiological state that psychologists call dissociation.[14] It was easily identified by Forrest's withdrawal and blank expression. This is a normal and predictable "energy conservation device" in the face of overwhelming terror when fight or flight are not options. It was Forrest's involuntary coping mechanism—the only one he had. "Frozen" in his defensive shell, Forrest grew into a terrified two-year-old appearing autistic to the well-meaning professionals unschooled in the devastating effects of early trauma.

It is no surprise, given the large number of newborns routinely separated from their mothers at birth in U.S. hospitals, that so many of our little ones are entering the school system with untreated trauma that lies at the heart of their language and social delays. Forrest was a classic case.

How Patti Helped Forrest

Instead of focusing on speech and behavior management, Patti set up a six-month treatment program focused on family education. Mom or Dad accompanied Forrest to each session, learning to identify calm, parasympathetic states—first in themselves and then in Forrest. Nurturing mother's fragile sense of calmness and safety was a primary goal. Therapy involved teaching the parents to track sensations, discharging *their* activation, grounding and settling. As mother became increasingly able to experience her sensations and connect with herself in a pleasurable way, she was also noticing the joy of a deeper connection with Forrest. Soon, this realization of the importance of her own calmness in helping Forrest interact became a core resource that she looked forward to improving as therapy progressed.

Prior to those new experiences of regulating her own sensations, mother had assumed that she needed "to do something." She came to realize that doing less was in fact the recipe for healing. As the family gave up their struggle and began to process their own grief in a nurturing, fun, and warm environment, Forrest began to blossom. His tantrums became an opportunity for his parents to stop and center in the deepest, calmest place within. As they provided this safe haven of tranquility, Forrest calmed down and moved towards them with more playful interactions. Rather than a "chase-and-dodge" cycle, Forrest's parents learned to follow *his* lead and *his* readiness for more interaction. His coos and babbling following a tantrum let them know that he was able to tolerate more play. He would often roll back towards them, again as a signal that he was available. Forrest began to show all the signs of connection. His eye contact and vocalizations increased, and he began to imitate. By the fifth month of therapy he was playing with toys and showing signs of symbolic play—unheard of with a true diagnosis of autism.

In order to move Forrest from traumatic freeze to social engagement, the final weeks of "speech and language" therapy focused on pretend play. With a baby doll named "Noah" and a puppet named "Dr. Kit," Forrest overcame his fear of the doctor's office. Patti accompanied Forrest to the pediatrician, and when he went still and blank with fear as he entered the waiting room, she exclaimed, "Let's run!" After racing towards the door and up the grassy knoll outside, they collapsed in gleeful laughter. After a few more cycles of exercising his flee response, Forrest showed a greater capacity to tolerate the doctor's office. This play offered him a much-needed escape route, which had not been viable in the past. The defensive orienting response of flight in this situation helped Forrest to have a sense of agency and mastery in a setting where he had previously only experienced overwhelm and lack of control. Forrest's family continued with various themes of "renegotiation" of the trauma at home, including play with a Dr. Silly puppet and a band of unruly monkeys. (For step-by-step guidance in using somatic play therapy with traumatized toddlers and preschoolers, please refer back to "The Story of Sammy" in Chapter Four.)

A Happy Ending for Forrest

Forrest is a beautiful example of repair and recovery from infant PTSD. He was clearly misdiagnosed as autistic. He is now attending a regular elementary classroom, has very good communication skills, a full range of normal emotions, and many friends. Forrest's parents are so grateful for his development that they strongly desire that this information and Forrest's story be disseminated to agencies, schools, and other families who may have a child who has been similarly misdiagnosed. If you are a school psychologist, be sure to first rule out any possibility of post-traumatic stress disorder before making a differential diagnosis of autism.

Anger in the Schools

Why "Anger Management" Doesn't Work for Traumatized Students

As discussed earlier, the triune brain is made up of three distinct parts. The neocortex is our thinking, rational brain; the limbic system (mammalian or midbrain) expresses emotion, empathy, and is responsible for the storing of experiences; and last, but certainly not least, is the instinctual brain responsible for our survival. The brain of a traumatized child has been altered. It is tuned to "high alert" and sensitive to the tiniest trigger. The trigger can be general, specific, or a mystery. The trigger may lead to a flashback. The following scene gives a clear illustration of the delicate thread by which a child with post-traumatic stress disorder hangs:

On an excessively windy day, a high school student was referred for counseling because he wasn't paying attention in class and appeared agitated. During counseling he reported that he was struggling with repeated flashbacks of being attacked that caused him unbearable anxiety. He was unaware of why he was so distracted and tense, but he did say that he felt like hurting someone but knew this would be a big mistake. After drawing a picture of his anger, he discovered that the downed tree branches scattered on the ground reminded him of the stick that he had been repeatedly beaten with (over a four-year period) by a "caregiver" whom he lived with while his mother, a refugee from the Cambodian killing fields, was struggling with major depression. The way to undo these tangled perceptual webs is to uncouple the associations that are bound by these strong instinctual defensive energies. A single facial expression, words, smells, or in this case, seeing a few sticks on the ground can set off an alarm that in a flash brings the past into the present. The way to safely release or discharge these strong and persistent stimulus-response reactions is through experiencing the sensations of how the body wanted to protect and defend itself through fight or flight, duck or cover, but was unable to do at the time.

Associations that act as triggers don't go away by *talking*. Neither do they go away by stopping to *think* about possible consequences. Once the instinctual brain gears up for survival, it has no use for words. When the almond-shaped amygdala is on alert, the language centers of the brain show little or no electrical activity. Instead, an urgent message is sent quickly to the cerebellum to act. In other words, with PTSD one is hard-wired to bypass cognition (the rational brain) when danger is *perceived*. Functional magnetic resonance imaging (fMRI) instruments have shown clearly that in those suffering from trauma, the circuitry takes a different route than for people who have not been traumatized. Rather than sending *simultaneous* messages to the thinking brain (to assess whether the threat is real) *and* to the instinctual brain (to protect itself if it is), the message speeds *involuntarily* along the shortest path possible to the instinctual brain for survival.[15]

Anger management approaches used in schools do not take this brain research into account. Once it's understood that the traumatized brain has a *distinctly different* physiology from a nontraumatized brain, it becomes clear why current methods fail. While cognitive-behavioral programs may be effective in helping students calm down when irritated or frustrated, they are of little use to a student being driven by the "survival alarm" of PTSD. Counting to ten, slowing the breath, thinking of options, talking and problem-solving are great stress-busters under ordinary circumstances. But it is naive to expect students riddled with traumatic imprints to stop acting out by "thinking" when triggered.

Alternatives to Anger Management

Students can be taught how to notice what's going on in their bodies. They can also be taught how to modulate their own arousal and how to release this charged energy in a slow, gradual manner. Examples of how teachers and counselors can help their students release chronic trauma patterns and responses are described below.

1. Strong survival energy can be directed into specific physical activities that promote healthy protective, readiness, and defensive responses. This type of release helps complete the incomplete responses from the traumatic event through the vehicle of the body's exquisite sensory-motor system. Games can be co-led with a classroom teacher and a gym teacher or other adult. The whole class can participate, with special attention given to children who need more guidance. (See games designed for this purpose later in this chapter.)

2. Deep discharge can happen when students are given the opportunity to sit with an adult when they have been triggered or shaken up. A counselor, school psychologist, nurse, or mentor can be invaluable here. This adult can learn to lead the student(s) to explore their internal impulses and sensations in a safe, non-judgmental environment with no disruptions. During this quiet sitting time, students are neither advised nor admonished. Instead they are given the time they need for their bodies to process their intense emotional experiences. It is during this time that change occurs, as students feel their involuntary vibrations, tears, heat, trembling, gurgling, laughter, release of tension, sweat, and/or shaking happen. Involuntary motor movements may also be observed, encouraged, and

slowed down. Releases such as these create shifts in perception and behavior. These releases also create a re-organization in the autonomic nervous system in a way that words cannot. And, over time, as this new brain organization is integrated, transformative changes take place as dual pathways are more easily accessed, giving the thinking brain a chance. As students discharge their high activation, they naturally begin to think, concentrate, and focus more easily. Impulsive behavior decreases, and peaceful social engagement becomes possible. The following story illustrates this process.

Trauma-Healing = Peace-Building: The Story of Tony and Mitch

The following case is an example of an instinctual reaction driven by traumatic impulses. It is also an example of the alternative approach suggested above of "sitting" with students to allow safety, quiet, guidance, and time for deep physical releases to occur. This sensory-based approach was chosen as an option rather than moving Mitch to different classes and/or sending him to an anger management group. The story that follows of Tony and Mitch shows step by step how the release of enormous tension inside both teenagers was evoked, shifting perceptions and attitudes.

Mitch was struck by a car as a pedestrian two years earlier. Since the accident, he fatigues quickly, has momentary petit mal seizures, and stresses easily. He has had occasional verbal outbursts but had never been physically aggressive prior to being hit.

One day at school, Mitch was working on a science project with classmates. Some of the students were fooling around instead of focusing. Mitch, a conscientious student, was annoyed when the unruly group ignored his attempts to get them back on task. Tony was especially uncooperative. His laughter set Mitch off. Before the teacher even realized trouble was brewing, Mitch lunged at Tony and began choking him around the neck! It happened at such speed that, according to witnesses, it was like watching a frog attack an insect by thrusting its tongue with such alacrity that it would take slow-motion photography to describe what happened. It took several people to get Mitch to release his grasp.

Mitch alarmed everyone, especially himself. His behavior did not match his self-perceptions. He described moving from a feeling of irritation to rage instantly. He said, "I really don't know what came over me," as he apologized profusely to Tony and the class. Mitch felt humiliated; Tony felt scared and angry.

Mitch had never received emotional first aid after being injured by the car. He was loaded with "charged" survival energy that never released after his brush with death, so his set point for unbearable stress was already primed. After the incident, Tony alternated between being angry and frozen. The high school counselors met and decided that maybe it would be best to place Mitch in a different group so that the two boys wouldn't have to cross paths. I proposed an alternative. I volunteered to work with each of the boys first, then possibly together to work out a peaceful solution as an option to segregation.

Mitch was eager to meet with me. A very respectful young man, he was suffering from feelings of isolation and debilitating embarrassment. He was concerned about his reputation and also wanted Tony to forgive him. He was totally willing to take responsibility for his behavior. He wanted nothing more than to apologize and make it up to him. Tony, on the other hand, responded with a hostile "What for? I *never* want to see Mitch again. He better not come near me!"

I explained to Tony how I completely understood. I also knew how terrifying it must have felt to be choked and how his body was naturally prepared and ready to fight. I also intimated that he might still be carrying these feelings. He admitted that he wanted to beat

Mitch up but restrained himself because he wanted to keep out of trouble. Tony, with some trepidation, agreed to the meeting.

Tony sat uneasily in his chair with his upper body tensed for a fight and his legs shaking restlessly. I asked him to speak first. He shared his angry feelings. Mitch admitted how wrong his actions were, that Tony did not deserve what he did, and apologized. He asked what he could do so that Tony would accept him as a classmate. Tony said, "It's too late; the damage is already done."

Up to this point, the counseling session appears typical. But what happened next was very different. Tony was asked to feel his internal sensations and work with his *physical reactions.* I asked the teens to try a little experiment. They agreed. The boys knew me from other situations and trusted me. Trust makes it safe to be vulnerable. And having a sense of safety cannot be underestimated.

Next I explained how natural and wise it is to protect yourself. When one person is attacked, the other automatically goes into counter-attack. Tony's life had been threatened and his body was fully charged for a battle that never happened. I asked him to describe what he was feeling, and he admitted to Mitch that he still felt like fighting. With gentle guidance, I asked Tony to describe the "fight sensations" in his body. He described tension in his upper body. I had him continue with the details, including specific locations. Mostly he described the incredible energy in his chest, shoulders, arms, and hands. He also felt his heart beating rapidly. Next I asked him to focus on the movements that his body would need to make to release this tension. He said it would require taking a swing or perhaps punching Mitch.

I asked Tony to take some time to look around the room and to look at Mitch, noticing if there was any danger in the present moment. Since he was not in danger, I asked him to switch his focus away from Mitch and back, instead, to the awareness of his own body's readiness to protect himself. Next, I asked him to put his full attention on completing the motions of swinging or punching or whatever physical reaction appeared naturally—and taking the time to discern which of the movements would be most satisfying. With eyes closed, he was able to determine that neither felt quite right. Instead, he felt his arms wanting to grasp Mitch's hands and pull them off his neck. With encouragement he went through the sequence (in his imagination first) and then sensed the "micro-movements" as he allowed the sensory-motor impulses to unfold (with guidance) in slow motion. Next I asked Tony to rest for a while. As he did, he began to gently tremble. I simply explained that his body was letting go of traumatic energy he had been holding in check since the incident to avoid a fight. He thought it was "weird" how his body was doing so much shaking all on its own; he did not find it unpleasant or frightening, though. These two parts (sensory-motor "unwinding" through micro-movements and release of the nervous system activation by not overriding the involuntary shaking) took about fifteen minutes each. When Tony's body released every bit of tension, he looked at Mitch and spontaneously forgave him. There was no need for me to facilitate the finale. This is why I consider trauma-healing a method of peace-building when it occurs at this primal physiological depth.

As a postscript, the boys agreed to stay in the same class group and never had a problem again. Mitch received continued support to work on the activation from his accident. This type of healing goes far beyond conflict resolution, suspension, and "anger management." It holds a promising potential for building peace in our schools as students learn to release aggressive responses in a healthy, yet satisfying manner. When a youngster's nervous system is at peace, the desire for revenge disappears.

A Word about School Bullies

Students like Alex (who threw the chair) and Mitch (who attacked Tony) display violent behaviors that are puzzling to their teachers and potentially dangerous, but these are not malicious acts. While violent outbursts may be sudden and unpredictable, malicious bully behavior has a tendency to be premeditated. Often these youngsters have been physically abused and are plagued with feelings of powerlessness and shame at school. The abused student victim unwittingly takes on the characteristics of the perpetrator and "looks for" the weaker students to torment. This can take the form of intimidation and humiliation via teasing, extortion, and/or physical assault. Of course, the weaker students usually have their own trauma histories.

After the Columbine High School shootings near Littleton, Colorado, in 1999 in which fifteen people died, lawmakers in Colorado and several other states initiated bills to prevent bullying. This was a result of the theory that the "killers had complained of being harassed, ridiculed or mistreated by other students." The same newspaper article noted that it is estimated in some studies that 15% of schoolchildren are routinely bullied in any year.[16]

While the scope of this chapter does not include extensive coverage of either bullying or school shootings, we do know a few facts. The FBI issued a report in 2001, prepared in conjunction with The National Center for the Analysis of Violent Crime (NCAVC), after careful analysis of eighteen school shootings. It concluded that: "There is no single profile of the school shooter or a checklist of danger signals pointing to the next adolescent who will bring lethal violence to a school."[17]

We also know that whatever the cause, bullies and shooters are deeply troubled. While some come from obviously traumatic situations, such as domestic violence and child abuse, others act out for less obvious reasons. After reading this book, ideally you are more aware of the "hidden" causes of trauma that play havoc with the behavior of children from loving homes and safe neighborhoods. The good news is: regardless of the cause, all schoolchildren can have healthier, more resilient nervous systems when teachers and administrators recognize traumatized students and give them the support they need to engage in pro-social behaviors.

Violence in Our Schools

While most traumatized students are not outwardly violent, various studies point to the conclusion that *virtually all violent criminals have suffered extremes of childhood abuse and trauma.* Of fourteen incarcerated juvenile murderers in one important study, twelve had been brutally physically abused, and *all* of these offenders had a history of serious head injury.[18] In *Ghosts from the Nursery: Tracing the Roots of Violence,* Robin Karr-Morse and Meredith W. Wiley (1997) present a comprehensive review of the literature regarding the prenatal and early childhood factors associated with violent behavior. They have concluded that two or more factors together create the type of violent behavior that can be modified or prevented by early interventions. For example, delivery complications and birth trauma together with maternal rejection at one year of age have been linked to later violent behavior.[19] This evidence is compelling enough to significantly alter the way we view violent behavior. However, up until now, the tools to address the traumatic roots of violence didn't exist. By default, acting-out behavior in the schools has been dealt with by punishment, suspension, and expulsion. Or, it has been swept under the musty, overburdened carpet of special education and/or the criminal justice system. Neither of these solutions is adequate, and both are costly.

In order to prevent and reduce violent behavior in our schools, we must acknowledge the crucial role that unresolved trauma plays in this arena. To quote Bessel van der Kolk from his definitive book *Traumatic Stress: The Effects of Overwhelming Experience on Mind, Body, and Society:* "Re-enactment of victimization is a major cause of violence in society."[20] Fortunately, schools can do a great deal to help.

Traumatic Re-Enactment as the Vortex of Violence

It astonishes us far too little.
– Sigmund Freud

The drive to heal trauma is as powerful and tenacious as its symptoms. Youngsters traumatized by physical and sexual abuse or emotional neglect are inextricably drawn into situations that replicate the original trauma. The urge to resolve trauma through reenactment can be severe and compulsive. The adolescent prostitute, the "stripper," "sex worker," or sexually promiscuous teen usually has a history of early sexual abuse. Children who have been beaten or witness battering may repeatedly seek abusive relationships or become perpetrators. Students from abusive backgrounds seem to be drawn together like magnets on the playground: bullies and their victims often suffer the common denominator of trauma's grip.

Re-enactment can be defined as an unsuccessful attempt *to resolve the intense survival energy mobilized for defense against a perceived lifethreatening experience.* An accurate example of violent "acting out" was depicted in an episode of the TV show *Law and Order* entitled "Subterranean Homeboy Blues," summarized below:

In the opening scene, a beautiful young woman named Laura waits for a subway train. She has a "far away" look in her eyes, and a mannequin-like rigidity in her body. Suddenly a street person appears, flails his arms wildly in her face, and then disappears. The woman's eyes follow him vigilantly, but her body remains still, almost frozen. She boards a crowded train, where two youths are acting menacingly. She pulls a gun out of her bag and shoots them both.

Six months prior to this incident, Laura, a professional dancer, had been raped and beaten by three men in a subway. Her injuries were so severe that after undergoing several back surgeries, she was forced to abandon her dancing career. In the wake of this tragedy, she purchased a revolver, intent on defending herself if the need should again arise, which, *in her perception* (warped by trauma), it did.

The Two Faces of Rage: Violence and Self-Harm, or "Acting Out" and "Acting In"

In addition to the obvious "traumatic incidents" (like the bizarre criminal act from *Law and Order*), many schools are beset with rising numbers of students raised in an emotional vacuum. Early and prolonged neglect leads to impotent rage masquerading as apathy. School shootings, shocking although no longer rare, awaken us to acknowledge a deep current of aggression and emotional detachment that plagues many young people. And this is just the tip of the iceberg. Aggression takes many other forms such as bullying, extortion, sexual harassment, "cyber-stalking," dismissive language ("dissing"), and rampant gang violence.

Just as startling is the growing number of depressed students committing violent acts directed against the self. These include self-mutilation, cigarette burns, eating disorders, hair-pulling, head banging, binge drinking, overdosing, and other forms of "high-risk" behavior. One expert on self-harm speaks of kids getting together in "cut-of-the-month" clubs. A Toronto teenager interviewed by *The Medical Post* nonchalantly stated, "Our school is *known* for cutting." Many other teens attempt or commit suicide out of quiet desperation.[21]

According to studies by Drs. Judith Herman and Bessel van der Kolk, cutting and suicidal behavior have a high correlation with early abuse and neglect (particularly sexual abuse).[22] Van der Kolk says that the childhood thought "I wish I was dead" progresses to "I can always kill myself" as the untreated injuries cause increased pain with the onset of puberty. These chronic destructive behaviors are a result of impairment in affect regulation that undermines the whole psycho-biological system. Without adult nurture there is no capacity to self-soothe. Of course, this type of conduct may sometimes be the result of other severe but mysterious underlying trauma-related wounding. Medical/surgical trauma, which by its nature invades personal boundaries, is most likely another common culprit.

The Rage of the Unparented

Gabor Maté, a Vancouver physician and co-author of *Hold On To Your Kids: Why Parents Need to Matter More Than Peers,* writes:

> Frustration is the primitive human response to not getting one's way, especially to *not having one's essential needs satisfied.* Violence is a measure of immaturity, endemic in our teen population. And immaturity has the same root as the bitter frustration that accompanies it—the unmet emotional requirements of youth deprived of nurturing adult contact.[23]

Dr. Maté credits American poet and social critic Robert Bly as aptly referring to the phenomenon of increasing violence as "the rage of the unparented." The rise in youth violence has followed a trend that Vancouver developmental psychologist (and Maté's co-author) Gordon Neufeld calls peer orientation. He explains it as the price we pay for no longer living in villages, tribes, communities, or neighborhoods where adults mentor and raise children. The extended family is, for many kids, geographically or emotionally distant. The nuclear family is itself under extreme stress, as indicated by high divorce rates. Into this void steps the peer group ... with disastrous results.

"Kids were never meant to nurture one another or to be role models for one another," Dr. Neufeld says. "They are not up to the task. It's the immature leading the undeveloped."[24] The aggressive gang ethic of inner-city ghetto youth now dictates the cultural style of middle-class young people across North America. The culture of cool disguises massive dissatisfaction and fear. For this reason, both at home *and* school, the emotional nurturance of children *must* be our highest priority.

Adolescent Elephant
"Gang Behavior" at Kruger Park

A previously unknown and inexplicable aggression aimed at the rhino population in Kruger Park in South Africa left park rangers puzzled. Scientists at first suspected human cruelty. Wrong. These random acts of violence were, however, directly traceable to human ignorance.

A *National Geographic* piece that was aired on National Public Radio featured interviews with those who solved these mysterious murders. To the scientists' surprise, it was *gangs of adolescent elephants* that did the damage! This happened only *after* the adult bull elephants had been culled in an attempt to counter an overpopulation problem. Without their fathers and grandfathers to parent them, the ordinarily playful adolescents became juvenile delinquents! "Animal managers" had inadvertently disrupted the social order of the herd.

Further investigation into these extreme behavioral changes resulted in finding that the teen males' biochemistry had been altered by the separation from their elders. Adrenaline, as well as testosterone levels, was significantly elevated. The young elephants tended to go into longer periods of premature must. It was in this state that they began their killer rampage on the innocent rhinos.

Just like elephants, teens need adult guidance to contain their behavior. Schools *can* help. One enlightened principal in Camden, New Jersey, addressed the problems of neighborhood violence, emotional neglect at home, and strong absenteeism by instituting first-period rap sessions in *every* homeroom, *every* morning![19] Yes, the first hour was set aside for kids to express their fears, hopes, obstacles, and daily grind with each other under the guidance of caring adults. Guess what! They bonded with each other and with their *homeroom* teachers, giving true meaning to that word. And they started coming to school. They were getting their needs met for group belonging and adult witnessing.

Another idea is to provide adult mentors. In the "Adopt-a-Student" Program, a teacher, parent, custodian, nurse, or other volunteer is matched with a student with similar interests from the same school. Ideally, the relationship continues for the three or four years of middle or high school. The adult is charged with providing healthy recreational activities, listening, and homework help. The key is that the match creates a good bond, is pleasurable for both, and the student receives routine contact. Because the young of any species belong under the protective wings of adults, frustration and rage can be minimized only if we succeed in restoring children's attachments to the adult world.

Grief Groups for Children in the School Setting

During my own elementary school years in the 1950s, only *one* of my classmates lost a parent! It stands out so clearly in memory because my classmate Linda's father died, leaving her mother a widow. This word was new and it haunted me. She was the *only* student I grew up with from a single-parent home. As astonishing as it may seem, in those nine years from kindergarten through eighth-grade graduation, no other classmate lost a parent through death or divorce.

How things have changed! With divorce rates at 50% or more and increases in poverty and violence, it's a sad fact that separation and loss due to death and divorce are now widespread. Drive-by shootings are rampant in the inner city. And most students experience the death of a fellow student, relative, or a teacher during their school career. These events can create ongoing instability and emotional turmoil for today's students.

Grief groups in the school setting can ameliorate the pain and isolation that these youngsters feel. Having a safe place to work through the emotional memories, to grieve, release pain, and celebrate life together can lighten a heavy load. When children share in a group, they create friendship bonds as they comfort one another. Sometimes they even encourage their fellow group members to study and finish school assignments.

When meeting with grief groups, it is important to be skillful in helping students with both grief and shock symptoms. (Refer to Chapter Eight for detailed information.) Often, the shock symptoms dominate the student's life, interrupting his or her ability to learn. While sudden illness and accidents can happen anywhere, rates of domestic violence, drive-by shootings, and death by overdose and suicide continue to rise in urban schools. It is no longer rare for a student to lose *several* loved ones over the course of one school year.

Whether a student loses a relative, classmate, friend, or neighbor, they need to complete the grieving process. Unfortunately, in our society once the funeral is over the student is usually left to grapple with both the shock and grief alone. Students need support from caring adults and compassionate grieving peers to move through this process and come to an emotional completion so they can move forward. Some people may feel that this is not the job of the schools. Funds and efforts may be focused solely on academic programs. Yet if we do not treat the emotional intelligence and well-being of our students as important, we are not educating them to be successful in life. "Character Education" is becoming a trend, but educators are missing the boat if they do not understand that character traits such as empathy, compassion, and responsibility are more likely to take hold when taught experientially, *not* didactically. Groups are a great way to achieve this type of "process" learning.

Grieving students can share a myriad of emotions, make memory books, light candles, and read letters they have written to the deceased. Listening to (and being listened to by) others going through the same deep hurt is a very powerful and moving experience. Everyone grieves at his or her own pace. But those who lose family or friends suddenly (from tragic accidents or violence) are especially vulnerable to getting stuck in shock and never moving beyond denial, which is the first stage of grieving, without this valuable help.

Enrique

Enrique is a prime example of a student who needed help to grieve fully. Three weeks before he was to begin high school, his father was killed instantly on the freeway in the family van. His mother suffered broken bones and bruises but survived. Enrique had been away at soccer camp at the time. When he started school, he was different from the other students: his skin was pale, his eyes were glazed, and polite words tried to cover a vacant, hollow expression.

When the grief group formed, Enrique joined. The students got acquainted with each other's tragedies; they learned how to listen, reach out, and share each other's pain. During the first meeting, Enrique was the *only* student who said that he was "doing OK." But Enrique was *not* OK. Not only was he unable to share his feelings, he was failing all of his classes, daydreamed in class rather than finishing assignments, and seldom returned homework. At home, he fought with his brother or moped.

During a group grounding exercise, the teens learned to sense the support from the ground and the chair, to track their breathing, and to notice how their internal sensations changed over time. When Enrique was asked to become aware of his feet and how it felt to contact the floor, at first he said that he couldn't feel them. After about a minute or two of focused awareness on his lower legs and feet, he felt tingling sensations. He opened his eyes, looked up, and said, "Oh my God, I just landed in my body! I haven't felt real since my dad died!" With that, he made meaningful eye contact with the other members of the group for the first time. Then, Enrique exclaimed, "It's like I'm connected to an inner me!"

After Enrique was able to feel what it was like to be "home" in his body, he was able to begin the grieving process. With the support of his group, he was able to cry and share a myriad of other feelings. Although his struggle was often painful, the comfort he received from his new friends helped him through. They even offered to help Enrique catch up with his late school assignments. Enrique slowly, but surely, began his recovery.

Unfortunately, many students do not get the crucial help they need. I have encountered many high school students who lost parents in elementary school and *never* got past the initial shock because they did not have the support to do so. These students were usually referred for counseling due to depression and failing grades years later. When they were interviewed, it was revealing to see how stuck they were in the past—still wishing and hoping their parents would come back.

Make Room for Rover: The Role of Dogs in Healing Trauma

There are hundreds of studies in the literature showing unequivocal evidence of the healing power of pets.[26] Dogs in particular can teach everything from good social manners to empathy. My therapy dog, Beijo, was a healing addition to the high school grief group. When a student cried, he would lean against them, bringing connection and comfort. When a student was frozen in shock, Beijo would lay down across her feet to help with grounding and containment. Most of all, his "waggily" tail and delightful disposition would cause smiles and laughter to lighten up the heaviness. Hugging him and petting his soft fur was a big resource for most of the kids.

Beijo helped in other ways, too. Students who had test anxiety would ask to complete their quizzes in "The Helping Paw Counseling Center." Beijo would lean against their leg or lie down next to them, helping the stress to melt away. He also taught lessons on prejudice. Many youngsters in the inner city assumed that *all* dogs were mean. Some were afraid of Beijo before they got to know him just because he was a dog. With a little encouragement—and sometimes by watching how gently Beijo played with other students—they changed their opinion, realizing that not *all* dogs are the same. They learned what it meant to pre-judge another creature, how the word "prejudice" originated, and how belief systems *can* change when there is openness to new experiences.

Recommendations for Teachers

Creating a Safe Classroom Environment, A Sense of Belonging, and Experiences of Competency as Resources for Your Student

What do children need to be successful in school? According to John Stewart, PhD, a developmental psychologist who is pre-eminent as a school consultant for the behaviorally impaired, *all* students need three things. In his book *Beyond Time Out,* Stewart stresses that for healthy emotional development, students *must* have:

1. An atmosphere that creates a fundamental and pervasive sense of *safety.*

2. A classroom climate where all students can enjoy a sense of *belonging.*

3. Circumstances that provide frequent and expanding experiences of *competency.*

When these three essential needs are met, a substantial reduction in the level of increased stress and anxiety (that children may associate with school) is possible.[27]

Safety First: Designing an Atmosphere of Comfort and Security

For a student to feel safe, he must experience his caregivers as having both the ability and the commitment to make sure that his physical needs are met and to keep him free from harm. This means that teachers possess the know-how to contain conflict rather than escalate it. It also means that they set reasonable limits, establish a comfortable routine, and utilize classroom space in a way that respects student boundaries. Teachers must also listen and respond to complaints about bullies and help students resolve interpersonal conflicts rather than sweeping the issues under the carpet, hoping they will magically disappear.

Many students live in a chronic internal state of anxiety (or get easily triggered into this state) before the bell rings. They may live in chaotic homes with anxious caregivers or within a violent environment. The poverty of the inner city with its tough neighborhoods serves to exacerbate the struggle for parents to meet basic survival needs. For your traumatized students, the baseline for flight, fight, or freeze is already higher than average. The biochemical engine of anxiety fuels adaptive *acts of defense against unbearable overwhelm* which are most often mistaken for *acts of defiance against the teacher.*

Youngsters who have a compromised autonomic nervous system have a lower threshold of tolerance for added stressors. Without stable affect regulation, these students can accelerate from an appearance of relative calm to panic (or rage) within seconds. The explosively aggressive student *is* out of control. When a teacher or administrator makes intimidating gestures, threatens to punish, or humiliates this already fragile youngster, fuel is added to the fire and *no one* feels safe. What this child needs most is a stable teacher who will contain him so that he does not hurt himself or others. Others in that class depend on the teacher to provide a sense of external safety. It is essential for the adult in charge to skillfully help an explosive student to regain self-control.

(See "Guidelines for De-Escalation" after the story of Alex earlier in this chapter.)

Belonging—The Strong Need for Affiliation

It's no surprise that gang members call their homeboys "associates." It accounts for both the need to belong and the need to be competent. In a way it's like a sense that they have roles to play in the "family business." All children need to feel a strong sense of belonging. When adults cannot meet this need, youngsters instinctively seek their own protection and membership by forming close attachments to their peer group.

Students who do not have a strong relationship with caregivers at home and at school have a difficult time "fitting in" with peers who exhibit pro-social behavior. Those failing academically are even more vulnerable to gang activity in order to manage feelings of numbness, emptiness, and anxiety. The impulse to affiliate with peers is especially strong after a traumatic event.

The great tsunami of 2004 in Southeast Asia offers some lessons from Thailand about belonging. Our Trauma Outreach Program (TOP) team worked at a school where more than fifty children had been orphaned by the tsunami. The students that we worked with in Thailand did not come from the inner city. Most had solid family and community ties, as well as strong spiritual connections through the monks at their village temples.

The principal of the school we served pulled these orphans out of their classes so that our team could help them with their grief. Outdoor physical games were designed to engage them in highly stimulating activities—ideally to provide a sense of renewed strength, power, and fun. And they did just that.

What happened next surprised us. The children left behind (because they did not lose a parent) became despondent when their classmates were separated from them. A few even became agitated, saying that they wished they had lost a parent so that they could participate in these new activities with their classmates! Before we noticed this dynamic, we complied with our Thai hosts to further divide the students. We honored their request to shepherd the "most severely traumatized" orphans into a separate room for small-group art activities.

The large group of students who had been energized and having fun outdoors suddenly looked and acted deflated as the classmates they had bonded with were taken away—bringing up the panic, perhaps, of the tidal wave as it swept parents and friends out to sea. Team members quickly came to the same conclusion: group affiliation fostered group healing, while separation and segregation led to fragmentation. We quickly learned our lesson and worked with the whole class the next time we visited the school. In this way the stronger students helped the more vulnerable ones by their enthusiasm, hugs, smiles, and hand-holding.

In applying these lessons we realized that inclusion comes in various forms and is vital for creating a sense of belonging in children. Our traumatized students—the ones with the greatest degree of anxiety and hopelessness—are usually the ones who are separated from the mainstream. They are segregated with others who suffer from similar problems. Because they lack control, they are typically stripped of less structured activities such as art, music, physical education, dance, and extra-curricular activities. School becomes less palatable; motivation wanes further. All outlets for creative expression that can promote a stronger self-identity or reduce stress are eliminated from the very students who need them most.

An alternative to separation of students with behavioral difficulties is to offer "guided practice" activities in self-regulation *within* the regular classroom. The supervising teacher must be trained in the principles of self-regulation and be a model of stability. *It is a must that she co-lead her class with at least one other adult during the guided practice sessions.* The classroom teacher might team with the physical education teacher, school counselor, school-based mental health workers, or aides. She might invite one or two volunteers to assist. Simple instructions regarding the purpose of the guided activities and defining the roles of the adults are all that is needed. She must be both patient and firm, appreciate the struggles of traumatized children (that they are not *bad*), and believe that with practice her students can succeed. The teacher needs a map of where her students are, where they need to go, and how to get them there in terms of the basics of "charge and discharge" (See activities at the end of this chapter).

These guided practice activities should be exciting enough to raise activation levels. Next, sufficient time needs to be allowed for slowing down to discharge activation. Finally, and most importantly, a period of time needs to be included for complete resting and settling down.

Competence

Competence is the last of the three characteristics outlined by Dr. John Stewart as essential in fostering appropriate behavior and true learning. He defines competence as: "multiple and frequent experiences which support an expanding sense of one's own capabilities."[28] Students do best when they are given challenges that are *within* their reach. They become autonomous when the goals set by teachers provide the grist to experience success after a struggle that is *not* overwhelming. The concept of "Optimal Frustration" was first presented by Heinz Kohut as a model for setting academic objectives.[29] Kohut suggests that if a child grows up with chronic exposure to *either* unmanageable frustration and challenge, *or* far too little experience of frustration and challenge, the net result will be the child's enfeeblement. Wise teachers tailor academic activities well within their students' "window of tolerance." This promotes competence.

For some students academic achievement may bring a sense of competence, but for far too many it does not. Those who are academically challenged need opportunities for competence that draw out their hidden talents. Each student needs to shine her own special light; many students also need someone to safeguard that light by providing frequent opportunities for it to shine. Every child needs at least one adult who "gets them" in order to feel safe, valued, and competent.

These two resources of safety and competence were rated and weighed (as a counterbalance) against clients' trauma histories on a "Trauma Antecedent Questionnaire" developed by Drs. Judith Herman and Bessel van der Kolk. Safety, on this survey, meant having had someone to protect you, namely, "Was there anyone you felt safe with growing up?" At a conference in 2001, Dr. van der Kolk said, "The greatest damage in trauma is the loss of the feeling of someone to protect me." Competence was defined as "being good at something—like having a talent, hobby, craft, or some other way to escape from misery." Dr. van der Kolk went on to say that the resources of safety and competence *must* be in place before therapy can be successful. He referred to the need to feel competent as "a huge issue."[30]

A Somatic Viewpoint

The most valuable competency, in our opinion, is the ability to experience and tolerate internal sensations of both pleasure and pain without becoming overwhelmed, withdrawn, acting out, or numbing out. Once traumatized students gain a greater capacity for self-regulation, they automatically possess more self-control. Once students have mastered the ability to "be with" their sensations and move out of habitual destructive patterns, they can begin to plan a future different from their past.

It is the job of educators to set up situations for youngsters to learn and practice self-regulation until they have gained mastery. Acquiring the know-how to remain grounded, centered, and contained in situations that were formerly overwhelming is an internal competence (or resource) that lays the groundwork for authentic self-esteem. An exemplary school program will include this type of mastery as a keystone for learning social behavior. Without this foundation, the need to defend a fragile ego at all costs will prevail despite straight "A's" and the most enviable talent. Bottom line: out-of-control students do not feel good about themselves.

Creating Competence Through Play and Pleasure

Educators help build competency by filling up their students' empty "sensory bank accounts" with rich experiences in movement, music, art, and interactive play. We know that new neuronal connections are built through enriched sensory experiences. Group activities that incorporate play have the added advantage of fulfilling the need to belong. Examples of school activities that build competency are programs in theater, movement and dance, martial arts classes, painting, music, exercise, journal and poetry writing (with read-alouds), drumming, and meditation.

Sometimes schools can find these resources in the community and link up collaboratively. For example, Cornerstone Theatre Company in Los Angeles offers community theater in the inner city that promotes interracial, multigenerational performances. It bridges the generation gap by giving school children a chance to be involved in the expressive arts with a broader community, including the elders from a variety of cultures.

Groups can make jewelry, do crafts, sing together, weave together, or plan activities. They can also get together to strategize ways they can make a difference or offer a community service, such as urban beautification through gardening, reading stories to younger children, or helping the elderly. Schools might also collaborate with local City Department of Recreation Programs that provide outdoor group projects and sports for youth.

Sand tray play is another rich resource for younger students.

When children manipulate objects in the sand, creating with their hands, something magical happens. Because sand tray play involves both the sensory experience of moving sand and the motor experience of manipulating tiny toys and figures with small fingers, it is a marvelous vehicle for healing trauma. As with children's drawings or other forms of therapeutic play, what is most important is the child's experience of having their world, their feelings, and their creativity witnessed by a caring adult. A child feels safe when the teacher or counselor refrains from judgments, advice, and analysis. Connection takes place without words when there is an acknowledgment of the "hands knowing how." As Carl Jung wrote, "Often the hands know how to solve a riddle with which the intellect has wrestled in vain."[31] The adult's job is to step inside the student's experience in order to join the journey at the emotional level.

Dramatic Play. Dramatic play gives children the necessary psychological distance from their problems, creating safety to express their thoughts and feelings unabashedly. Play is both natural and spontaneous. It's the easiest way that children have to communicate with each other and with adults who know how to play. An added benefit is that active play employs motor muscles that can easily evoke protective and defensive postures and movements. In turn, this may restore a sense of strength and competence that may have been lost during overwhelm. When children engage in make-believe play, self-consciousness disappears. One empowering activity to help children develop healthy defenses is to invite them to pretend to be their favorite animals. They should be encouraged to take on the characteristics and motor movements of those animals. They can growl, hop, jump, bare their teeth, spring, rattle, claw, swim, slither, pounce, and/or hiss.

Other fun ways for children to play out their authentic feelings is through puppetry and mask-making. Simple finger and hand puppets work well. As the adult interacts she can model sensation vocabulary. Children can make their own animal, people, or fantasy masks out of cardboard or papier maché. As they hide behind masks and puppets, they can act out their struggles, feelings, and resolutions. Avoid having the student re-enact his or her particular trauma. Instead, give as little guidance as necessary to help the child engage in an empowering solution. Some examples would be: confronting a fire-breathing dragon while actively dodging the flames so as to not get burned, running fast to safety, a slow-motion soft landing on pillows or rubber mats, finding a safe place to hide, winning a sword fight or battle, gently stitching up a cut or turning a certain way to avoid an accident. With dramatic play, as with sand tray, children are engaged in a sensory-motor activity that creates the opposite of feelings of helplessness and immobility.

Original Play. "Original Play" is a term coined by O. Fred Donaldson, PhD, author of the Pulitzer Prize-nominated book, *Playing by Heart: The Vision and Practice of Belonging*. It is another delightful way to involve students in pleasurable, healthy activities. A colleague of ours has used this mat play, together with Somatic Experiencing®, successfully with fourth- and fifth-graders who have attachment disorders. Original Play is a non-competitive way to engage in the creative act of play while practicing kindness and safety in all interactions. Its basic tenet is the transformation of fear and aggression into love, kindness, and belonging. It is both a physiological and psychological process combining cognitive, affective, and sensory-motor experiences while having fun.[32] Original Play is such a powerful experience that it was adopted by the African National Congress as part of its campaign to stop violence.

Research with human babies and animals unequivocally reiterates the necessity of experiencing the pleasure of play in order to improve brain chemistry. Play involves the healthy use of touch; and touch is like fertilizer for the brain. Babies who are regularly touched and played with thrive physically, display increased cognitive skills, and calm more easily. Many of our students have not had healthy touch as babies; therefore, play that involves healthy touch is essential to repair this trauma of neglect.

Modified arm wrestling, three-legged relay races, mat play such as rolling, tumbling, and "leap-frog," hand-clap play that rhythmically mirrors a partner, and other old-fashioned games that seem to have all but disappeared with the advent of computer and video games can help with the mammalian need for touch as part of bonding. There is also a plethora of research on the healing power of play with furry pets, especially the use of dogs in schools and hospital settings. (See "Make Room for Rover" on page 376.)

SILLY FUN FACIAL EXERCISES THAT RELAX THE REPTILIAN BRAIN

Julie Henderson describes a ton of fun exercises that have been studied by Paul Ekman, PhD (a professor of psychology from UC Medical School, San Francisco) and appear to make distinctive changes in physiology, thereby affecting emotion. Her book Embodying Well-Being, or How to Feel as Good as You Can in Spite of Everything *for kids and adults is filled with ways to discharge stress and agitation. She calls it "Zapchen Somatics," as it comes from an interweaving of Eastern philosophy and Western psycho-physiology.[33] Six of these delightful practices are described below.*

HORSE LIPS

With your lips loosely together, blow air vigorously between them. That's all there is to it! Repeat until your lips tickle.

How this helps: It releases the tightness around the mouth, "relaxes the brain stem," and makes you laugh. (I have actually witnessed grown-ups spontaneously making horse lips to let off steam. I also had an adult client who did this during a session for about five minutes! He reported a dramatic change of perception regarding the issue that had been troubling him.)

TALKING FUNNY

Press the tip of your tongue against your lower teeth. Relax your tongue so that it feels like it fills up your whole mouth. Now try to talk! Any topic is OK, from serious stuff to funny stuff to talking about your problems. Allow the fullest laughter you possibly can.

How this helps: According to Julie, it relaxes the tongue. As this action flexes both the palate and dura across the base of the brain to the occiput, it pumps and relaxes the brain, causing the free flow of cerebrospinal fluid, which helps us to feel freer, more relaxed, and less bound up by our circumstances. It also helps us to laugh at our stories about ourselves, breaking up old repetitive patterning.

TONGUE STRETCH

Simply stick out your tongue. Then grasp your tongue with clean fingers on the tip and gently pull as far as it will go.

How this helps: This exercise relaxes the root of the tongue and relaxes the brain stem.

YAWNING

Take a deep breath in. At the top of the breath, open your mouth wide, lift your soft palate, and make yawning sounds. If it doesn't work right away to evoke a real yawn, it means that you are trying too hard. Relax and do it again, this time without trying!

How this helps: Yawning relaxes your throat, palate, upper neck, and brain stem. It helps you to "come down out of your head" so that you can experience your sensations. It improves digestion by increasing saliva production. It also increases the production of serotonin, a neurotransmitter that tends to balance mood, calming you if you're hyper and lifting you up if you're feeling gloomy. And it helps balance the flow of cerebrospinal fluid, which helps keep the brain and spine flexible.

JIGGLING

Stand with feet about hip-width apart and knees slightly bent. Bend and straighten your knees just a little. Repeat over and over again until you find the rhythm to "jiggling." Let all your bodily parts hang loose and flop or bobble to the rhythm of your jiggle. Let your limbs shake and internal parts jiggle. Let your brain jiggle, too!

How this helps: The jiggling supports the rhythms of pulsation, which support life, liveliness, and well-being. It relaxes the joints, pumps the diaphragm, and moves the bodily fluids vigorously. Jiggling also increases energy by stimulating metabolism and loosening us up when we feel stiff or rigid.

HUMMING

While this can be done in any position, Julie recommends learning to hum by first lying down comfortably. Create a voiced sound: Hmmmmmmmmmm. Let the sound move through your body as a vibration. The key is to pay attention to the sensations of the vibration. They are more important than the sound. Allow the felt pulse of the sound (the vibration) to move throughout your whole body. The more relaxed you become, the further the sound will travel. See if it can move out into your arms and hands, down through your torso, and into your legs and feet. Let it move into your head and up into your brain. Hum and rest. Alternate between humming and resting. Eventually, as your body loosens, the vibration from the "hmmmmm" sound will move all through you!

How this helps: Sound moves by compressing and expanding whatever it is moving through. When you make the sound all through your body, the pulsation of opening and closing presses and awakens the body. Muscle, fluid, nerves, vital organs, and bone are all being massaged. As the sound moves throughout your body it dissolves blocks that are stuck, creating a wave-like pleasant feeling of all body parts being connected and working harmoniously, thereby improving body image.

Julie recommends that when you do these exercises with your class, use the following principles as a guide for optimal benefits:

- Learning takes place through direct experience of new pleasurable sensations.

- Forget a struggle to do it "right"—these activities are intended as joyful play (activating the limbic and reptilian brain), *not* thinking and planning (which activates the neocortex). STOP if it's not fun!

- Do only a little bit and then rest while staying mindful of any new sensations. Resting time should be as long as the exercise period, thereby giving the body needed time to integrate new patterns of open movement, vibration, and breath. Alternating between playing and resting in small measured increments stimulates the transference of what we learn into long-term memory.

Activities for Teachers and Counselors: More Tools for the Classroom

Restoring Safety, Belonging, and Competence after Traumatic Events

Although several activities described below may be more appropriate with individuals and small groups, most may be used with the entire class. They are divided into three basic groups:

- Art, music, and writing activities that build safety, resources, and sensation awareness

- Physical activities and games that foster healthy defensive responses, boundary setting, and group cohesion

- Balancing activities that restore lost protective reflexes, confidence, and resilience

ART, MUSIC, AND WRITING ACTIVITIES THAT BUILD SAFETY, RESOURCES, AND SENSATION AWARENESS

FEELING GOOD

1. Instruct students to draw a picture of a time when they felt (good, content, satisfied, happy, etc.) recently or before the (accident, hurricane, earthquake, injury, abuse, surgery, etc.).
2. Have them study their artwork, close their eyes, and locate the place in their body where they are able to feel the goodness. Encourage students to allow that feeling to spread and grow.

RESOURCES FOR COPING

1. Have the class brainstorm different resources that help them to cope. Write students' ideas on a large chart or board for all to see. Next, instruct students to make their own personal list of "People, Pets, Places, or Things" that help them cope. (Teachers can integrate this into a lesson on categorization by having students list headings and sort by the four categories, if appropriate, but this is not necessary.) When finished, invite them to draw a picture of something from their coping list.

(Examples are: my dog, cat, grandpa, garden, friend's house, auntie, poems, singing, playing ball, making things, swimming, mom or dad, writing letters, playing with my brother, kindness from strangers, my new teacher, God, collecting rocks, biking, scouts, hiking, drawing, reading, dancing, playing the oboe, soccer team, the corner lot, TV, the woods, the mountains, the beach, my room, under the willow tree, praying, doing math, computer games, playing pretend, my hamster, looking at the stars, grandma's feather quilt, my teddy bear, my paint set, my chemistry set, baking cookies, skipping stones, eating cookies, talking to my friends, playing tag, etc.)

2. After students have drawn and colored their pictures, have them study the resource they chose and ask how it makes them feel to look at the picture. Next, have them recall the most recent time they were with the person or pet (or did the activity or visited the place) they selected and notice how it makes them feel inside (emotions and sensations). As they close their eyes, have students describe and locate these feelings.

ESCAPE STORIES

1. Ask students to share "Escape Stories." How did they manage to finally find safety? Did someone help them or were they alone? Where they able do anything to help themselves? How did they let grown-ups know they needed help?

   Focus on two elements:
   - What the student did to survive. (Examples: moved to higher ground, made themselves look bigger so they could be seen, made themselves smaller so they weren't seen, walked, ran, hid, climbed, pushed, stood up on their tippy toes, cried for help, froze, shouted, kept quiet, held their breath, made a plan, waited, prayed, crawled, reached out, held on, pulled away, ducked, covered their head, etc.)
   - Who or what assisted them. (Examples: sister, neighbor, rescue worker, tree limb, belief in a higher power, a pet, Red Cross, luck, time, medical staff, inner strength, rope, boat, helicopter, paramedics, life vest, a parent.)

2. Instruct students to draw and color their "Escape Scene."

3. Instruct students to study their drawing and find the part that brings them a feeling they like. (Examples: powerful, strong, lucky, comforted, loved, supported, warm, brave, proud, fast, etc.) Have students locate the sensations that accompany these feelings in their bodies. Allow plenty of time to savor them and notice if the good feelings spread to other places.

NO MIRRORS

1. This is an activity involving music that was designed to provide resources to girls in a small group setting (grades 4–12); for example, it teaches them how to replace vicious gossip with support for one another. It requires the use of the CD, "No Mirrors in My Nana's House," written by Ysaye M. Barnwell[34] and performed by her group, Sweet Honey in the Rock, an internationally acclaimed a capella quintet of African-American women. First, have the girls listen to the lyrics a few times. (See sample stanzas below.) Then, hold a discussion about what the words mean to each of the girls. The girls can sing the song along with the CD.

   #### No Mirrors in My Nana's House

   *There were no mirrors in my Nana's house
   no mirrors in my Nana's house
   so I never knew that my skin was too black
   I never knew that my nose was too flat*

   *I never knew that my clothes didn't fit
   I never knew there were things that I missed*

   *'Cause the beauty in everything
   was in her eyes
   like the rising of the sun.*

2. Ask the girls to name one person who reflects their beauty back to them. In other words, who is their "Nana"? Some of the girls will have one special adult (perhaps a parent, grandparent, auntie, or teacher) or an older sister or cousin who sees their beauty, worth, and wholeness and reflects it back to them. Have the girls write the name of that person in their journals. Next, have them take turns describing how that person helps them to see themselves and their relationship to the world more clearly or in a way that makes them feel better about themselves. Some of the girls may not have a person who acts as a good mirror for them. If that is the case, have them pick a girl in the group that they trust enough to ask to become their "Nana." (In addition, you might also locate mentors for those girls.)

3. Have the girls pick a time when they felt the love for them reflected in their "Nana's" eyes, voice, body language, or actions. They can write or draw this image in their journals. Next, have them reflect on that image and notice what they feel inside themselves. Have them describe the sensations and emotions that they experience in the now as they recall the person who is the strongest resource for them. Let the girls know

that whenever anyone tries to put them down, they can call upon the power of their internal "Nana."

4. Encourage them to be "Nanas" to each other when at school. Teach them the strength and importance of girls supporting other girls rather than engaging in mean competition. Give them a homework assignment to see how many ways they can support each other between group meetings. Have them report what they gave and what they received in the way of backing, encouragement, and just being seen during the week. They can keep a log of their experiences. Discuss the feelings of both being a "Nana" and having a "Nana." The girls can share what they would like from each other as they learn to cooperate more.

SENSATION BODY MAPS

For preschool through second or third grade, have the child lie down on butcher paper while someone else traces the entire body with a marking pen. Help the child to make a coding key to describe sensations and emotions that they feel, using a variety of colors and/or markings. Children are instructed to color and mark different places on their body map where they feel different sensations and emotions using the key.

Examples of coding keys are:

- Blue = sad
- Orange squiggly lines = nervous
- Pink polka dots = happy
- Black = numb
- Purple curvy lines = energetic
- Red = hot and mad
- Brown = tight

See also the "gingerbread person" figure near the end of Chapter Eight for a sample color chart (under "Giving Emotional Support . . . ").

For third-graders and older, have each child make a "gingerbread" person shape on a large sheet of paper. Have each student make his or her own coding key on the bottom of the paper. Have them fill in their body map to indicate the location of any sensations and emotions they are feeling in the moment. Be sure to encourage the expression of both comfortable and uncomfortable feelings.

Variation

A simple version of this for very young, very shy, or learning-disabled students is to have them choose two colors for their coding key: one color for comfortable (feelings they like) and the other for uncomfortable feelings (ones they don't like). The outline of the gingerbread person can be pre-made by an adult.

TYPICAL-DAY SENSATION AND EMOTION GRAPHS

Have students reflect on today, yesterday, or another day earlier this week that seems like a typical day. Invite them with eyes open or closed to take a peek inside their body and trace their feelings (emotions and sensations) as they change from the time they awaken until the time they go to bed (or up until now if they choose today). Have them write a list of six to eight feelings. Instruct them to make sure to include both those that are comfortable and those that are experienced as uncomfortable. You might have the group brainstorm a variety of feelings as examples to heighten awareness.

Once students have made their own lists of their typical feelings, they draw a horizontal or vertical bar graph with the same number of bars as the number of feelings they have listed. Each bar is labeled with one sensation or emotion. The bars are then colored to represent how much of the day is spent with each of these feelings. For example, if the student perceives that he feels nervous most of the day, they color that bar almost full. If they are calm about half the time, they color the bar halfway. If they feel "antsy" a little bit, they color the "antsy" bar in a little bit. This is a good assessment tool both for the teacher and the student. A "check-in" graph can be made rather easily as a short-cut by providing the students with ready-made blank graphs that can be labeled and colored as a daily or weekly feelings barometer. Students who routinely experience only unpleasant feelings can be helped to find resources that bring a balance of at least some pleasurable feelings. Introduce fun activities that create a change in physiology, such as the "Silly Facial Expressions" described in the section above. "Talking Funny" and "Humming" are good examples for creating shifts. It is important for children to learn that sensations and emotions can change, despite the fact that their life circumstances remain the same.

Have students take the time to track their sensations after a fun activity, to plot it on a simple graph, and compare their own changes over time.

DRAWINGS OF WORRIES, FEARS, OR DISCOMFORT AND THE OPPOSITE

Instruct students to make two drawings on two separate sheets of paper. One drawing depicts a worry, fear, or whatever prevents them from feeling good; the other drawing shows the opposite—something that brings a feeling of comfort, hope, goodness, happiness, safety, or ease. Often, children will do this naturally; they draw a disaster like a car crash and afterwards draw a rainbow. It doesn't matter which drawing they do first. Allow individuals to decide. When finished, children can share sensations they feel when they look at both drawings, one at a time. Then they can cover their "worry" drawing with its opposite and notice how their sensations and feelings change. A modification of this is to have students fold art paper in half, using one sheet instead of two.

DRAWINGS FROM DREAMTIME

This exercise is especially useful in a one-to-one or small group counseling situation, or when students report "bad dreams" and nightmares.

Ask students to tell what they remember about their dream. Then invite them to choose one part of the dream that stands out most vividly. After they draw it, have them tell about the various parts. Pay particular attention to the inanimate objects. It is important not to interpret the dream. Rather, encourage the students to imagine or pretend that they are the various objects and creatures in the drawing as they make the images come alive and interact with each other in drama or dialogue. Listen to the meaning the children give to the symbols, and help them to embody the various characters as they work their way through to process incomplete sensations, feelings, images, or thoughts. For example, if a student draws two samurai warriors with swords walking side by side, ask him to imagine what it's like to be one of them—perhaps starting up a conversation with the other. The child can dramatize or simply report the actions and feelings of each. Be sure to notice and ask the child about the setting—desert, mountain, ocean, island, cliffs, city streets, outer space, etc. Often the child will draw both the problem and the solution in the same picture. Sometimes the solution is tiny or hidden at first—like the miniscule yellow dot that one child drew between a crack in a rock. When asked to tell about it, he said, "That must be a little ray of hope coming through."

PAST, PRESENT, AND FUTURE DRAWINGS

Traumatic imprinting tends to keep children stuck in the past. This exercise can bring a sense of movement. It can also assess how a child might perceive her future.

Have students fold a large sheet of drawing paper into thirds so that the folds are vertical. Direct them to label PAST at the bottom of the first column, PRESENT at the bottom of the middle column, and FUTURE at the bottom of the last column. Then have the students draw three pictures in the appropriate columns to represent their life as it was, is now, and how they predict it will be in the future. If a child's future looks grim and is similar to the past, work with their here-and-now feelings from the drawing that depict the PRESENT. Ask what sensations they are aware of as they look at the drawing. Guide them to focus on the sensations and watch how they change. If students feel unpleasant sensations, help them to track these until there is a discharge. When students feel pleasant or, at least, comfortable sensations, have them check to see if their perception of the FUTURE changes. If it is changing for the better, have them draw a new FUTURE picture on another sheet of paper. As they look at their latest creation, have them notice and track any different sensations and feelings that may be emerging. Exercise caution into pushing them to feel better before they are ready; allow time for feelings to transform organically.

DRAWING A SAFE PLACE

This "Safe Space" drawing was inspired by and is an adaptation of the "Fantasy" exercise from Violet Oaklander's book, Windows to Our Children.[35] *This activity can be done with individual children or groups.*

Have drawing paper and crayons or markers readily available before starting. Invite students to close their eyes as you take them on a fantasy trip. Let them know that when the imaginary trip ends, they will open their eyes and draw something that they see. Take the time to help the students relax by bringing awareness to the rhythm of their breathing and detecting any places in their body that might be tight or tense. Ask them to see what happens if they note these places without doing anything to change them. Invite them to take a deep breath and exhale slowly, making the sound Haaaaaaaaaah. Next make up a story that starts in nature, such as a path in a forest. With as many sensory details as possible, invite them to notice what they experience along the way. For example, if they are walking in the woods, they might see squirrels scampering about and the sun coming through the trees; they might smell the scent of pine trees or flowers; they might feel themselves trudging uphill or skipping down a trail or jumping from rock to rock.

When they come to the end of the trail in their imagination, they notice a mountain in the distance and decide to explore it, but it's very far away. Because this is their fantasy and all they need is imagination, they realize that they can grow wings and turn into a bird. Now they fly to their mountain. Once they land, they experience being in a totally safe place. It's their safe place and no one can take it from them. This place might remind them of a safe place they know, or it can be totally made up. It can have people in it or not; they can be real or imaginary. What's important is that the children create their place exactly as they wish. Using their imagination they make it as comfortable as can be. They can add stuffed animals or real pets; it can have bean-bag chairs or soft shaggy rugs and blankets. It can have over-stuffed chairs and pillows. The child can be alone or have people who love him or her in the scene. They can have photos or posters on the wall. They can have plants and flowers.

Invite them to create their safe place and take a look around. They can then walk around their place. (The emphasis is that this is *their safe place* and no one can take it from them.) After the students have enough time to explore it, have them find a comfortable place to relax in their space. Ask them to notice what sensations arise that let them know that they feel safe, and exactly where in their bodies they know it.

When the students have found the safety inside, invite them to open their eyes and draw what they saw when they looked around. They can title their drawing "My Safe Place" or "My Private Space" if they wish, or something to that effect. Remind them to trust what they saw and felt, and tell them that they can return to the image and the feeling whenever they desire. Students who have difficulty finding a safe place even in their imagination, of course, will need extra help. They can be paired up with other children and guided by an adult to find even a tiny place of safety. School staff must determine if a particular child feels unsafe because of past trauma or a current unsafe situation and take appropriate action to ensure the child's safety by working with family, extended family, and/or social workers and law enforcement personnel when necessary.

Physical Activities and Games That Foster Healthy Defensive Responses, Boundary Setting, and Group Cohesiveness

Because trauma overwhelms the nervous system, children who have experienced trauma often have difficulty moving between various levels of nervous system activation. They may be hyperactive and demonstrate poor impulse control, or they may present as lethargic, spacey, or depressed. Any familiar game such as "capture the flag" and jump rope can be adapted so that concepts of activation and deactivation are present. Simple equipment is sufficient, such as balls and parachutes. Students' level of excitement and competition can be provoked to arouse the fight/flight response. Activities need to be structured so that highly energized periods are interspersed with states of calmness with sufficient time for settling. During the time set aside for settling—which can be accomplished by having the children sit quietly in a circle to rest and debrief—the students are asked to check their internal sensations. Questions are asked for a show of hands, such as: Who feels strong now? Who feels weak? Who has energy? Who feels tired? Who feels hot? Who feels cold? Who feels good? Who feels sick?

During both phases (the excitement and the settling), excess energy is automatically discharged. As children "chase," "flee," "escape," "make boundaries," "run to a safe place," and "feel strength and power in their limbs and belly," they are forming new neural pathways that support resiliency and self-regulatory capacities. Sensory experiences through play are what build neural networks to repair trauma most efficiently—*not* verbal models based on cognitive-behavioral awareness. Sensory-motor input has a direct effect on the reptilian survival brain.

Using Physical Games to Assess Students and Provide Resources in the Aftermath of Trauma

When children have experienced overwhelming events they become stuck in trauma if the normal resources that protect them from danger have not been recovered. What children need in order to feel whole rather than frightened is a sense of safety, connection, grounding, and the actual experience of defending their boundaries or fleeing from danger.

The games and physical activities that follow are designed to restore lost resources while at the same time providing fun and a sense of connection with classmates. Because events that overpower happen quickly, children have few choices. **Activities to prevent and heal trauma need to include the following elements: extended time to restore a sense of preparedness, a variety of choices to select from, and the chance to discover and build new skills.**

Rationale for Activation, Discharge, and Deactivation

The best way to build confidence and competence is to help students develop their internal resources. When children are encouraged through play to heighten awareness of their body states, it is much easier to restore resilience after a mishap. Another purpose for these types of activities is to assess how each individual child is coping. It is easy to see which children are withdrawn, shut down, collapsed, and need support to come out of freeze. It is also easy to recognize the students who need support to calm and settle after having fun: for them, the return to a non-aroused state does not occur naturally so they remain hyperactive without adult intervention to re-train the nervous system.

Checking In with Sensations (Use of Paired Opposites)

When working with young children or those with language barriers or developmental delays, sensation language can be simplified. In Thailand, we used the vocabulary of paired opposites. This helps to simplify the checking and tracking process. For example, during the resting phase, name each sensation below one at a time and ask the students to raise their hand if they feel what you are naming:

SENSATIONS	EMOTIONS
hot or cold; warm or cool	sad or glad
weak or strong	fearless or afraid
energetic or tired	friendly or mad
easy breathing or difficult breathing	bored or enthused
open belly or tight belly	joy or grief
calm or excited	resentful or grateful
headache or no headache	silly or serious

The Naturalness of Games

In past decades—before the extensive use of computers, hand-held video games, and other electronic devices—children spent more time playing actual (not virtual) games. These games often taught life skills. For example, in "Mother, May I?" permission must be requested and given before taking steps towards someone else. If a playmate advanced too far or too fast, they would have to take steps backward. What a natural way to learn about manners, pacing, and boundaries. Another popular game was "Ring Around the Rosie" where students gather in a circle, hold hands, and move together singing: "Ring around the Rosie, pocket full of posies, ashes, ashes, they all fall down." All the kids fall down in a heap on top of each other giggling in delight. This group chant was used to help children cope with the bombings and burned-out buildings in England during World War II (although some say that it originated during the Great Plague when garments and bed clothes had to be burned). In either case, children released their distress through play, song, laughter, and being with each other. Other popular games like "Duck, Duck, Goose, Goose" and "Tag" give children practice in running to a designated "safe" place where no one can get them. These might seem like just games, but this older style of play seems to symbolically help kids learn how to navigate in the real world.

FOR THE LITTLE ONES: THE SLEEPING CROCODILES

This first game was taught to us by our colleague Eldbjörg Wedaa, who is the director of the Pinocchio Preschool in Bergen, Norway, a theatrical and musical school designed especially to help traumatized children have fun while learning to self-regulate. This game can be used with three- to seven-year-olds.

1. Divide the class into two groups: the crocodiles and the crocodile hunters.

   The crocodiles lie face down on a carpet pretending they are swimming or sunning themselves peacefully until they hear the hunters enter the "swamp" area.

2. The hunters are instructed to sneak up on the crocodiles, carefully stepping over them and scurrying about while the teacher plays music. The crocodiles now pretend they are sleeping. They are told to settle down, close their eyes, and get very quiet with calm breathing so they don't get "caught." When the music stops, the hunters tag any crocodile that moves even the slightest bit or opens its eyes.

3. The hunters change places with the sleeping crocodiles and play another round. Children who got "tagged" because they stirred, opened their eyes, or made noise do not trade places. They practice being "sleeping crocodiles" again. Those who have trouble settling can be coached to calm down by an adult or older student helper. (Gently place a warm hand on the student's back and breathe slowly and deeply, transmitting your calm presence to the child. Remind the child that it's time to settle down.)

SOMATIC EXPERIENCING® ACTIVITIES

The next set of activities was specifically designed for school children, using the principles of Somatic Experiencing®, by our Brazilian colleague Alexandre Duarte, who has an extensive background in physical education and various movement therapies. They are especially suitable for elementary school children; teachers are encouraged to adapt the games up or down in age suitability by increasing or decreasing their complexity. "The Parachute" activities below were used by Alé and our TOP (Trauma Outreach Program) team in Thailand after the 2004 tsunami. More classroom activities specifically used after that natural disaster (such as "Coyote/Tiger Chases Rabbit") can be found in Chapter Twelve, which focuses on disaster relief work in the schools. There are a variety of games that are suitable for either indoors or outdoors. Some are more suitable for outdoors due to space requirements for running, although any large indoor area with open space will work, such as a gymnasium, community room, etc.

THE PARACHUTE

Because the shape and size of a parachute brings children close together in a circle, it is a natural community builder. All that's required is a parachute and two or three lightweight balls that are two different colors. These activities can be used with five- to twelve-year-olds.

1. Lay parachute flat on the floor to delineate the space, and have children encircle the outer perimeter in a seated position. Next, have them make

eye contact with each of their classmates and the adults who are strategically placed near the students who might need the most containment or support.

2. Each child grabs the edge of the parachute and pushes and pulls, with emphasis on feeling the tension of the parachute and the strength of their individual muscles and collective effort. Because they are still sitting they can be instructed to notice the weight in their hips and buttocks as well as the strength in their upper arms as they pull. Make sure they are having fun!

3. Next, have them stand up and feel their feet and lower legs as they bend their knees to get a sense of their grounding and connection to the earth. With young children, you can have them stamp their feet and march in one direction as they hold on. With older children, have them bend their legs, lift the parachute, and make an elliptical movement with their arms like "stirring the pot."

4. Ask the children to notice the body sensations that they feel. Then, do a group check-in by asking, for example, "Who feels strong in their arms? Who feels strong in their legs? Who feels weak? Who feels tired?" and so forth.

5. Next, have the group (already standing up) make waves with the parachute. Instruct them to pay attention to feeling their strength. If some feel tired or weak, instruct them to feel the strength of the whole group together. As they flap the parachute, it activates their energy and level of excitement.

   Note: At this point, not all children will be able to tolerate the pleasurable activation. If this is the case, the adults will need to help them recover their energy by resting and grounding, with attention put on their feet and lower limbs. For the children who feel weak, look spacey, or complain of fatigue, headache, or stomachache, adults or more able children will need to help them. This extra support can be given by making eye contact, showing empathy, and then gently but firmly pressing their feet against the floor using your hands. If the child has a tummy ache, have them place their own hand over the place that hurts. Place your hand on top of theirs, pressing lightly to give support and warmth to the internal organs as you wait for them to relax and soften.

6. Next, have the students make waves again, but this time toss one of the balls on top of the parachute. The children work together to keep the ball bouncing up and down without falling off. To make this activity more challenging add a couple more balls, one at a time. It's kind of like the group is juggling together. Remember to have the students sit in a circle, recuperate, debrief by sharing sensations, and settle down.

7. Finally, have all the children run in place to feel the power in their legs, reground, and experience the flee response. When they stop, instruct them to make eye contact with classmates on the other side of the circle, saying "hello." Then they can all raise the parachute and run underneath, huddling together under the canopy, again making contact by saying "hello" in unison for even more bonding.

THE WOLF COMES AT MIDNIGHT

One of the factors that causes overwhelm is lack of time to prepare and protect oneself. In this game, children get the opportunity to feel the oncoming threat in small increments. As threat increases, in a manageable way, they experience extra time to prepare and choose defensive maneuvers.

All that's needed is masking tape, chalk, yarn, or something similar to make a designated half circle to represent the wolf's cave and designated safe places for the children to run towards. It's best if there is a wall behind the teacher, such as in the corner of a ball court or near the exterior wall of the classroom. The teacher or aide announces that she is the wolf and goes to her cave (or they can later appoint a child to act as the wolf). Next, the children gather around the wolf as she stands inside the half-circle with three to five feet of space in front of her. To make the game more thrilling the teacher can wear a wolf mask and/or tail. This will help to differentiate her roles as wolf and teacher.

Now the children are instructed to ask, "What time is the wolf coming?" The wolf responds in a deep dramatic voice, "THE WOLF COMES AT MIDNIGHT" while he bares his teeth. Some of the children will be trembling with excitement already. Then they ask, "What time is it now?" and the wolf responds, "EIGHT O'CLOCK."

At this point, the teacher (and aide, if available) carefully monitors the kids to see if any children are overly excited or experiencing distress. Then, the wolf turns back into a teacher and suggests that it's time to take a moment to notice how they are feeling in their body. This gives the children a chance to switch their focus from the external threat to their internal sensations, thereby fostering nervous system discharge. (Refer to the sensation questions in the box above.) They can be asked to notice their legs in particular and if they feel the urge to run.

When the children are reasonably settled, the wolf stirs the pot of activation once again. The children can now ask, "What time is the wolf coming?" The wolf answers, "THE WOLF COMES AT MIDNIGHT." "What time is it now?" "NINE O'CLOCK. YOU BETTER GET READY!"

At this time, the teacher needs to help the children to prepare a plan, rather than just run away. She might suggest that the children look around to orient to their surroundings, searching for a safe place. If a child needs a friend, he can look around to pick someone to help him escape. The teacher might suggest that the children run in place or back and forth to feel the power in their legs as they prepare to run. This step is very important because it brings to conscious awareness the power they have in their bodies to execute a plan, rather than just blindly scattering in all directions. The orientation is a crucial aspect in repairing traumatic activation, as it introduces incremental excitement, discharge, and settling. It also creates the time and space that were not available when the children were originally overwhelmed. This type of practicing builds new neural pathways in the brain that create more resiliency in the nervous system. Through play, the students become more creative in choosing and experimenting with new escape options. This in turn reduces anxiety over time.

Repeat the same process, hour by hour until you reach the midnight hour. When the children ask, "What time is it now?" the wolf replies, "IT'S MIDNIGHT . . . IT'S MY TIME." The wolf runs after the children as they scurry to their safe places.

Once everyone is safe, the teacher gathers the children close and again the focus is shifted internally as the teacher asks them to notice and identify their sensations. Once everyone is settled, it is important for the teacher to ask, "Who feels safe now?" The final step is to have the children locate where inside themselves they feel safe and what the sensation feels like.

SPIDER TRAPS THE FLIES

This exercise is designed to give children a physical sense of their body's boundaries and sense of limits. This game also helps children to become aware of being approached from 360 degrees around them and to feel the excitement and empowerment of defending their space.

Teacher designates areas approximately eight to ten feet in diameter using masking tape to accommodate groups of about ten children each. One child is selected to stand in the middle and be the spider. The other children represent the flies and surround the circle, standing just outside the designated boundary. When the child in the center is not looking, the other children step inside the circle, challenging his boundary, trying not to get caught. The spider in the middle tries to tag the children that enter his web. Those flies that are "captured" then join his team on the inside. The game ends when all the flies are inside the "spider's web." Repeat the game as often as desired.

DEFENDING YOUR TAIL

This fun game will help children to play the roles of both "prey" and "predator" simultaneously. They get to defend their own territory (body boundary) while "attacking" others.

Each child will need a "tail" approximately three feet long. It can be a three-inch-wide strip of fabric or a length of soft rope. The tail is tucked into the child's waistband at the rear. Teacher designates a boundary with a few "islands of safety" where the children can rest, such as trees, hula hoops, mats, or rubber bases used for sports. When the teacher says, "GO!" the children run after each other trying to capture the tail by pulling gently. The children are encouraged to find creative ways to defend themselves, such as sitting, dodging, turning quickly, or running to a designated safe place.

The teacher needs to monitor which children can orient and defend themselves with agility and which cannot. Some children may appear stiff, frozen, or distressed and not want to play this very active game. The teacher can help these children develop the necessary skills in several ways:

1. Educate them by whispering helpful suggestions, such as turning their head to look behind and using their hands to defend themselves.

2. Have a "buddy system" where a more able child holds the hand of another and they run away together.

3. Use the "Superhero Handicap Cards." (See directions at the end of this section.)

PAST-PRESENT-FUTURE HOPSCOTCH

When children have been traumatized there is little or no experience of the present or sense of the future. Images, thoughts, and sensations tend to be frozen in time from the past event. The child's world, therefore can become preoccupied with worry and pain from the traumatic events, especially when they are under stress. This game is designed to help children overcome being stuck in the past and to begin to explore the concept of time in a way that restores movement. In this way they can be encouraged to sequence from the past into the present moment with a new idea of a possible future. Several hopscotch grids can easily be painted or drawn with chalk. Or, even easier, the children can just pretend that the grids are there.

The teacher has the children form several lines to make the waiting time shorter. The first student in each queue moves in "hopscotch" fashion (alternating between hopping on one and two feet). The game starts by having the children name an event as they hop. If the event is in present time, they hop and land on both feet. If the event they name reflects the past, they hop backwards on one foot. If the event is in the future, they hop forward on one foot. The idea is to keep thoughts and feelings moving, rather than be stuck in the past. Each student has a turn to do the same.

Examples

- Hopping in place on both feet: "I'm playing hopscotch now."
- Hopping backwards on one foot: "Last week my hamster died."
- Hopping in place on both feet: "I'm having fun now."
- Hopping forward on one foot: "We're having a party on Friday."

If a student states only unpleasant experiences on every turn, especially for the future, suggest that she alternate between pleasant and unpleasant future images. For example, a child whose parents are going through a divorce might say: "Today my parents are fighting—yesterday they were fighting—tomorrow they will still be fighting." Perhaps the next round, if she is still preoccupied with the divorce, the teacher might suggest something the child might like to do for fun. Only give this guidance when students are "stuck" in the past or see a grim future. Encourage them to imagine some things that might make them feel better if this does not happen spontaneously.

Note for All Activities and Games

All children need to experience a sense of competence. To level the playing field for those students who do not exhibit skillful orienting and defending responses or are slower or weaker than the other children, you can use Superhero Cards to create a handicap in order to level the playing field. You will need a pack of 12 to 36 different-color cardboard cards to give out superpowers as deemed appropriate. The following are examples to get you started:

- Red Cards = Extra Time (times on cards can vary from five to ten seconds to give a child extra time to orient)

- Blue Cards = Invisibility

- Purple Cards = Extra Strength (gives permission to have a friend help them)

- Green Card = Safety Zone (student *cannot* be captured)

- Orange Card = Superhero (a card that when held up makes the approaching student weaker and slower)

These cards can be especially useful when special education classes are mainstreamed with regular education students. Add your own ideas to meet the needs of the individuals in your class. And I'm sure your students will suggest ideas for cards; if they don't, ask them to!

Balancing Activities That Restore Protective Reflexes, Confidence, and Resilience

In order for optimal learning to take place, it is essential that all children have the opportunity to freely explore their own body in space. When students have experienced trauma that involves encounters with gravitational forces and velocity, such as falls, vehicular accidents, and sporting injuries, they may have impaired access to their natural protective reflexes and balance. They are then more likely to sustain repeated injuries or be "accident-prone." Of course, children who have experienced early trauma and neglect may have poorly developed reflexes as well. Whether from developmental or shock trauma, students lacking agility or proficiency in self-defense may develop adaptive strategies that are fatiguing, rob self-confidence, and create a poor body image.

Although the primary need for healthy reflexes is self-protection, they are also necessary for brain integration. Students with undeveloped or "frozen" reflexes are more susceptible to learning problems, especially with reading and writing. Activities that improve balance and motion have a significant effect on visual processing and academics. Vision is a brain process of which the eyes are only one component. Data stored in the motion-processing and memory systems of the brain provide information that the brain uses to create the images we see.

When there are incomplete motor responses due to trauma, the information needed to create new images may be distorted due to past experiences. This is often a result of vestibular system (balance) disturbances. When a sense of balance is restored, brain processing speed and sensory integration are enhanced. Competence in these areas is of particular assistance to students diagnosed with attention-deficit/hyperactivity disorder, dyslexia, and other learning disabilities.

Restoring healthy protective reflexes and defenses that have been "lost" due to a single incident (such as falling off a bike or taking a tumble in gym class) is not difficult. And the entire class will benefit from having a teacher who incorporates simple equipment such as balance boards, bean bags, fitness balls, and balance beams into her regular physical education program. Students who have suffered trauma from falls, however, will need to increase confidence in their own equilibrium responses by having a teacher or aide guide them to test the waters in *very small increments*, allowing any activation to settle before attempting to do more. Some children will override their fears and plunge into a balance activity with bravado, only to get overstimulated or re-injured and then shut down even more. Others may be stiff and frozen in fear, resisting the equipment altogether. The teacher needs to gently "chunk" the activity down into tiny steps that will challenge the student without overwhelming her. When balance exploration is done in this gradual way, confidence will grow as fear changes to exhilaration.

Balance and self-concept improve when children spontaneously use their limbs to protect themselves. A side benefit is that when students rely more on their kinesthetic, tactile, and vestibular sensory systems, they are less likely to be overly dependent on their vision for balance. When the eyes are more relaxed and liberated from bearing the burden of vigilance, they are less likely to fatigue. In turn, reducing eyestrain promotes binocular teaming necessary to focus on printed material. Energy that was used by the visual system to aid in balance is now available for reading and writing. We also know that neural involvement increases with higher levels of challenge difficulties; thus increasing vestibular balance increases the brain's ability to process information with speed and efficiency.

SIMPLE EXERCISES TO IMPROVE BALANCE REFLEXES

ROLL-AROUND

Using a fitness (gym) ball appropriate to the size of the student, have the child kneel down in front of the ball and lean his or her entire torso over the ball with tummy facing down and arms hanging over the ball. Other students form a circle around the child and act as spotters to help him or her regain balance, if necessary. The teacher places a firm hand on the child's back and gently pushes the child forward on the ball, meanwhile observing how the child protects himself from falling or rolling off the ball. Look for how the child makes use of shoulders, arms, hands, torso, hips, legs, and feet to assist. Continue with several turns until the child begins to involve more of her body in a relaxed but alert manner. Watch for places in the body that are stiff or frozen. After a few turns if the child is still unaware of certain parts of the body (for example, she doesn't involve her shoulders), the teacher can suggest exploring what it feels like to engage the shoulders. Usually, this step is not necessary unless the reflexes are exceptionally frozen. As students become more relaxed, they spontaneously use their body more efficiently.

Variation

Push the child gently backwards or from side to side on the ball.

PUSH ME AROUND

Again using a fitness ball, have the child sit upright on the ball with feet spread shoulder-width apart for good stability. Have one student on each side of the child and lots of pillows or soft rubber mats on the floor. One student *very gently* pushes (more like a tap) the child towards the student guarding the other side. The other student "catches" the child if he isn't able to balance himself. This goes back and forth until the student is balancing easily. If the child gets dizzy or uncomfortable in any way, stop and track sensations until the child feels settled.

Variation

If the child on the ball is fairly adept at balancing, have her close her eyes for the activity to increase the challenge.

BEAN BAG BALANCING

Using a balancing device, such as the Belgau balance board sold by Bala-metrics,[36] stand on the board adjusting your balance until you feel steady. The Belgau's level of difficulty can be changed by adjusting the angles of the rockers under the board. With other balance equipment, or with the Belgau, a child can adjust the difficulty also by experimenting with the width of their stance.

Once the child feels confident that she can keep moving slightly to keep the board balanced, increase the challenge and add the skill set of visual tracking by introducing the bean bag toss. Instruct the student to throw the bean bag up in the air with both hands, trying to make both sides of the body move symmetrically while balancing on the board. This activity is designed to develop dynamic balance and to integrate both sides of the brain. Both the right and left hand and arm need to perform the same motions.

Next, instruct the student to throw and catch the bean bag with the left hand for several minutes; then reverse the activity, throwing and catching the bean bag with the right hand for several minutes. Finally, the student should throw and catch the bean bag with both hands again. As children throw and catch the bean bag, they should try to point the tip of their nose at the bean bag as it moves through space. Instruct them to let their head rock back and forth as they throw, follow, and catch the bean bag. The neck muscles, the visual system, and the vestibular system will get practice in working in synchrony.

BALL BUDDIES

This is a simple activity to improve both coordination and social skills for very young children or for developmentally challenged students of any age, such as those with pervasive developmental delays (autism, for example). All that's needed is a ball to roll and a pair of students seated on the floor facing each other about three feet apart (or closer if this is too difficult). The children are instructed to spread their legs open to catch the ball as it is rolled toward them. Each child takes a turn to roll and catch, continuing the game back and forth. As their coordination improves, adjust the challenge level by having the children move further apart. Encourage them to look at their partner to make sure that they are ready to catch the ball. This game usually results in lots of glee and laughter as it aids children in learning non-verbal communication skills, as well as shared joy.

Variation

Have older children pair with younger children to learn pacing and patience. Have regular education students pair with special education students.

ROLLER BALL

A simple game that can be played by three or more kids (four to ten years of age) has each participant roll a ball towards one of the other children. (It can be asked that the "roller" call out the name of the child that he is rolling the ball to. This is an excellent way to combine motor and cognitive functions.) As the kids do this for a while, a second ball is introduced, requiring more coordination and flexible orientation. It also builds up the level of excitement. This can be done with three or more balls, but it is necessary to ensure that the kids are not being overstimulated.

Equipment manufacturers sometimes include teaching manuals with a variety of activities for balance, visual tracking, auditory tracking, and kinesthetic awareness. An outfit called Balametrics (mentioned above) has kits with either a video or an instruction manual filled with activities for parents, teachers, and therapists. Gym balls or fitness balls can be purchased almost anywhere, from discount department stores to various mail-order yoga and fitness catalogs.

Conclusion

In order for children to thrive at school, they need to be able to function beyond a survival level. When trauma symptoms are addressed and strategies developed to intervene, students' energy is freed up to learn and to engage in pro-social behavior. We live in stressful times. Many students, whether suffering from posttraumatic stress disorder or simply overwhelmed by a fast-paced world with the pressures and tensions of everyday life, can benefit from the activities in this chapter and the next. The perspectives and interventions offered are based on sound principles of neurobiology translated into practical applications for the classroom teacher; speech, occupational, and physical therapist; counselor, nurse, school psychologist, and administrator.

The case studies were selected to serve as prototypical models for assessing children's needs and designing intervention strategies for them in light of their trauma histories—whether obvious or obscure. Jordan, Alex, Ruby, Carlos, and Forrest will probably share similar characteristics with your own students. Ideally, you can apply what you learned from the variety of challenges presented—ranging from learning problems to explosive behavior to truancy.

Because the struggle for educators to find the best practices in handling aggressive students at school is such a pervasive topic, a substantial section of Chapter Eleven is devoted to ways of working with volatile youngsters that provide enduring solutions, transforming them from the inside out. We believe that in the majority of cases, violence is the result of unresolved trauma leading to a deficit in self-regulation.

De-escalation and adult-guided "assisted self-regulation" activities have been provided for the most challenging children. However, exercises are included that will benefit the whole class by promoting optimal mental and physical health, as well as creating a stable environment, favorable to learning.

We know that trauma plays a key role in your students' conduct, whether it is acting "out" or acting "in." We also know that trauma combined with other contributing factors, such as poverty and lack of parental involvement or emotional unavailability, is a recipe for a variety of disturbances in conduct. Violence in the media and video games also contributes to the shaping of our children's behavior.

In summary, the first step is to recognize what trauma "looks like" in your students. The next is to become skillful in working with the dynamics of autonomic nervous system cycles of charge and discharge by tracking the sensations both in yourself and in your students. Once you are grounded in these skills, it will be fairly easy to use the activities described in this chapter and to adapt activities you may already be using to help *all* children grow towards sustainable self-regulation. In the effective twenty-first-century classroom, the applications of the biologically-based behavioral interventions offered in this text are critical in providing the keys to success for your challenging students.

Responding to Natural and Man-Made Disasters: Crisis Intervention at School and Beyond

In recent years, efforts have been made in some school districts to train teams of support staff to assist teachers and students in the aftermath of a critical incident such as a suicide, unexpected death, natural disaster, or school shooting. The roles and responsibilities of school psychologists and counselors have changed dramatically since the mid-eighties, when the words "crisis" and "trauma" were missing from staff meetings and school psychologist training curricula. The last few years have brought a quickening effect of tragedy, due in part to increased natural disasters caused by extreme weather, the occurrence of new diseases, school shootings, omnipresent media coverage of violence, and the advent of terrorism close to home.

In the year 2000, the National Association of School Psychologists (NASP) added a new requirement to its credentialing program. School psychologists must now acquire the skills to conduct crisis interventions. This is understandable in light of the fact that certain traumatic events that were once rare and extraordinary have become an ordinary part of many students' lives. In the wake of these changes, two crisis models have gained widespread status in the schools: 1) Critical Incident Stress Management or the "Mitchell Model," and 2) Crisis Intervention. The latter was influenced by the American Red Cross' Disaster Mental Health program, Lenore Terr's mini-marathon groups, the Mitchell Model, and other approaches. A third and more recent model gaining popularity in the schools is Structured Sensory Intervention for Traumatized Children, Adolescents, and Parents or SITCAP.[1] With the exception of SITCAP, these crisis intervention programs were easily marketed to school districts with little or no research on their efficacy.

As research becomes available, it is clear that the two early critical-incident debriefing models have, in many cases, been less than beneficial, especially with children.[2] These approaches ask victims to talk about their experiences, but there is no protocol for *processing* what gets stirred up as they tell their horrific stories. Often, this causes the terror to be *relived* rather than *relieved*.

First, Do No Harm!

Mark's Critique of Critical Incident Debriefing

Mark is an experienced hospital nurse and volunteered to participate in a demonstration session in a Somatic Experiencing® class. Working in the emergency room, Mark had witnessed horror during his entire career and wanted to work with a particularly haunting image. Forty-five minutes later, after gently working with the sensations, emotions, and beliefs that accompanied that image, Mark was free of the shock pattern that had been stimulated repeatedly with the slightest reminder of the incident. As the shock left Mark's body, his color and breathing changed. Numbness was replaced by grief over his helplessness and inability to do anything for a little child, obviously abused, that he attended years earlier in the ER. He also released the horrible feelings he held against the mother for such an act. Mark expressed a deep sense of relief that he could feel again.

After this session, Mark shared with me his experience with the debriefing component of the Critical Incident Stress Management Training. He took the course in 1996 with other emergency personnel such as firefighters, paramedics, and the police. "I still have nightmares from one of the stories that the instructor told during our training as an example," Mark reported. "It was incredibly traumatizing. I felt myself go into a freeze." Mark added that he hated to be called out on a debriefing (CISD: Critical Incident Stress Debriefing) because, as he said, "We were taught a method of patching them together [the victims] that didn't lead to resolution but instead left them raw to go off into the sunset."

He went on to describe his training. Basically, Mark was taught to debrief by asking three questions: 1) What's your name? 2) What's your job? 3) What did you see? A short education about trauma was given to normalize any reactions and off they went. There was little if any processing or integration of the awful experiences they were asked to describe! Mark did make one statement in defense of the Critical Incident Debriefing procedure—that it doesn't claim to replace therapy.

We (the authors of this book) believe that such debriefing with a lack of integration can be re-traumatizing, especially for children. And because children (and many traumatized adults as well) tend to be compliant, the first responder may not be aware that the victim is being pushed further into shutdown and dissociation.

The early pioneers in debriefing can be credited with recognizing the importance of bringing the affected people together to offer education, community bonding, and assistance. We can now build and refine a new model as we learn from the research what works and what does not. We do know that talking about the horrible thing that happened is vastly different from *processing* the images, feelings, and thoughts through the vehicle of sensations. More study and research is needed to shape the future of how assistance is delivered, especially to children.

A 2003 article in *Communiqué* (newsletter of the National Association of School Psychologists) edited by Stephen Brock, PhD, summarized some of the major findings from a conference that explored outcomes of early psychological interventions for disaster survivors. Brock also compiled a more detailed summary of available debriefing research in a paper entitled "Crisis Intervention Research and Skills."[3]

According to Brock and co-author Shane Jimerson, PhD, NCSP, in *Characteristics and Consequences of Crisis Events: A Primer for the School Psychologist,* "It was understandable [that] those early school crisis interventions were reflexive and did not have the ability for self examination."[4] Their review of the literature found that studies were conducted mostly on adults, with just a few studies including some adolescents. Results varied according to the nature of the traumatic event. Conclusions regarding debriefing, as it is currently conducted, are as follows:

1. Among adolescents and adults who suffered a minor physical injury following a traffic accident, debriefing that included the opportunity to express emotional and cognitive reactions and educate participants about traumatic stress symptoms and coping strategies did not appear to promote a more rapid rate of recovery than would have occurred without intervention.[5]

2. Critical Incident Debriefing is contraindicated as a brief (less than 60 minutes) stand-alone individual intervention for adult acute physical trauma victims. It may be applicable when used as a more involved approach and/or combined with other interventions.

3. When blood and gore were involved, subjects who were not exposed to Critical Incident Debriefing fared *better* than those who were debriefed.

4. Research was not standardized. Scholarly research is needed in order to establish empirically based best practices in our schools.

An Alternative Approach
to Crisis Intervention

Somatic Experiencing® offers a promising new model for crisis intervention in the schools and elsewhere. It was used with Thai children in the aftermath of the 2004 South Asian tsunami. Unpublished preliminary data from a one-year follow-up study conducted in Thailand show positive results. A comparison is being made between Thai survivors who were given SE® First Aid and those who were not treated. Somatic Experiencing® is also being used with survivors of Hurricanes Katrina and Rita in the United States. Those treated in New Orleans and Baton Rouge are participating in a matched study comparing subjects by age, gender, and socio-economic factors. Again, initial data are quite promising in providing evidence-based results of the efficacy of SE® (in a one- to two-session format) in disaster settings.

The emphasis in Somatic Experiencing® "first aid" is on symptom relief through the de-activation of arousal (self-regulation), rather than gathering information by having people describe a horrible event. Survivors are asked to share their post-event difficulties—not their memories. Common reactions after a disaster include: eating and sleep disturbances, irritability, spaciness, weakness in the limbs, fatigue, numbness, headaches, feeling dead, flashbacks, worry about the future, panic, and survivor's guilt. Care is taken to avoid re-traumatization by refraining from probing for the telling of the story. In contrast to other models, SE® does not ask grief-stricken, terrified people to talk about "the worst thing that happened." It is rather a psycho-physiological and educational approach. This means that support is given by listening to what the child or adult needs in order to move out of a state of shock and distress. Sensations and emotions are processed only in small increments. And the victim only reveals bits of the story as they arise spontaneously rather than being deliberately provoked.

Crisis Debriefing at School

In the following example, a group of middle school students help-lessly watched a drive-by shooting as they waited for their bus. The counselor met with the small group later that morning and a few times subsequently. One boy and one girl, however, continued to have problems and were referred for crisis counseling. After using the somatic approach, both youngsters' symptoms resolved. Curtis' story (below) is a poignant example of the details of using Somatic Experiencing® after a crisis.

Restoring Curtis' Innocence After a Drive-By Shooting

You may remember Curtis from Chapter Two. He was the middle-school boy who witnessed a drive-by shooting at the bus stop. He was referred by his counselor because he couldn't stop thinking about the event. At school, Curtis was restless and distracted; at home he was physically aggressive with his brother. When I met Curtis he told me that he didn't want to act the way he was acting. He "wanted to feel like himself again." He said that his biggest problem was the angry feelings he had each time he pictured the man who was shot lying on the ground. He also got distracted in class and had difficulty sleeping. But he shared that what troubled him the most were the brand-new feelings of wanting to hurt some-body—anybody, any random target—without understanding why.

When I asked *where* he felt the anger, he said, "In my legs and feet." Together we tracked the sensations in his legs and feet. Within a minute or two of noticing his lower body, Curtis was able to tell me that his legs wanted to kick. He also mentioned that he liked kickball and soccer and described feeling strong in his legs (an important resource). He told me that he wished he could have kicked the gun out of the gang member's hands. I had Curtis use his legs to kick a soccer ball in the same way he wished that he could have kicked the gun. He started to kick the ball with vigor. Rather than have Curtis kick fast and hard, perhaps getting wound up and enraged, I gently showed him how to make the kicking movements in slow motion. I had him describe the sensations in his hips, legs, and feet as he *prepared* to kick (what his body wanted to do to stop the violence). Then I invited Curtis to rest and notice the feelings in his legs. Each time that we followed this sequence, his legs would shake and tremble. Once this activated energy was discharged, Curtis centered himself, took a deep breath, and kicked the ball as he felt his steadiness, strength, and confidence return. He got *his* power back and lost the urge to hurt a random bystander.

After this "first aid" session to move his body out of shock, Curtis' symptoms disappeared. In a follow-up several weeks later with Curtis and the school counselor, he continued to be symptom-free. He was relieved that he no longer felt aggressive towards others for no reason. Curtis shared that he felt like himself again. Not only did he get his power back; he got his innocence back!

The major shift in this type of crisis work is that the focus is *not* on the horror of the event; rather it is on completion of the body's incomplete responses to protect and defend itself. This is what led to symptom relief and long-term transformation of trauma for Curtis.

Crisis Relief with Groups

The somatic crisis work done with Curtis could have been done with the entire group of middle school students had the counselor been trained in working with the principles of tracking sensations, nervous system activation/deactivation, and sensory-motor defensive movements. As one student volunteers to process her symptoms and gets relief, the shyer students gain confidence and ask for their turn. Below are guidelines for working with groups of three to twelve students:

1. Invite as many parents (or other caregivers) as possible to participate.

2. Seat students in a circle so that everyone can see each other. Seat adults directly behind the children in a concentric circle for support.

3. It is very helpful but not necessary to have a child-size fitness ball for the student who is "working." Sitting on the ball helps youngsters drop into and describe their sensations more easily. These balls are very comfortable and children love to sit on them.

4. Educate the group on the trauma response. Explain what the children might expect to experience both during the initial shock phase and as the shock begins to wear off in order to *normalize* their symptoms. Use the information that you have learned in this book. (For example, some may feel numb; others may have recurring images or troublesome thoughts, etc.) Explain what you will be doing to help them (i.e., that the group will be learning about inner sensations and how they help to move stuck feelings, images, and worrisome thoughts out of their body and mind).

5. Do *not* probe the group to describe what happened during the event. Instead explain to them that you will teach skills to help lessen symptoms so they might feel some relief.

6. Ask the group to share some of the trauma symptoms they may be having (for example: difficulty sleeping, eating, or concentrating; nightmares; feeling that "it didn't really happen"). At the same time it is important not to over-focus on the symptoms; this can have the effect of causing more worry and may reinforce the

feeling that there is something wrong with them. Symptoms are only discussed in the context of normalizing the victims' responses and helping to guide them towards balance and equilibrium.

7. Explain what a sensation is (distinguishing it from an emotion) and have the group brainstorm various sensation words. You might even write these down for all to see, if convenient. Explain what to expect: that they might feel trembling or shaking, be tearful, jittery, nauseous, warm, cool, numb, or they might feel like they want to run, fight, disappear, or hide. Let the group participants know that these are sensations that can occur as they are moving out of shock.

8. Work with one volunteer at a time within the circle. Have that child notice the support of the adults and other students in the group. Invite him to make eye contact with a special friend or familiar adult for safety. At any time during the session, if the student needs extra support, invite him again to take a break and make contact with a special "buddy" in the group.

9. Ask the student to find a comfortable position in the chair or on the ball. Invite him to feel his feet touching the floor, the support of what he is sitting on, and his breath as he inhales and exhales. Make sure that he feels grounded, centered, and safe.

10. Begin the sensation work as soon as he is ready. First have him describe a sensation of something that brings comfort or pleasure. If he hasn't had any resourceful feelings since the event, have him choose a time before the event when he had good feelings and describe what he feels like *now* as he recalls those good feelings.

11. The child might automatically describe symptoms, or you may need to ask what kinds of difficulties he is struggling with since the event. Then ask him to describe what he is feeling. The following are sample questions and comments to use as a guide for inviting awareness of sensations:

   a. As you see the picture of the man behind the tree, what do you notice in your body?

   b. And when you worry that he might come back, what do you notice in your body?

   c. And when you feel your tummy getting tight, what else do you notice? Tight like what? What might it look like? Can you show me where you feel it?

   d. And when you look at the rock . . . or make the rock with your fist . . . what happens next?

   e. And when you feel your legs shaking, what do you suppose your legs might want to do?

   f. When your legs feel like running, imagine that you are running in your favorite place and your [insert the name of a favorite safe person] will be waiting for you when you arrive.

   g. Or, have the child imagine running like his favorite animal. Encourage him to feel the power in his legs as he moves quickly with the wind on his face.

12. The idea is to follow the student's lead. Help him to explore, with an attitude of *curiosity*, what happens next as he notices his internal responses.

(Refer to Chapter Four for detailed information on emotional first aid for coming out of shock. If loved ones have died, see Chapter Eight for help with the grieving process.)

Restoring the Resilience of School Children After Disasters: More Lessons from Thailand

Using the tools of working with trauma described in this book, the Trauma Outreach Program (TOP) team, composed of a group of Somatic Experiencing® Practitioners, worked and played with school children in Thailand after the historic December 2004 Indian Ocean earthquake caused the devastating tsunami that swept the region (www.traumahealing.com). Another group of Somatic Experiencing® Practitioners, Trauma Vidya (contact Raja Selvam at www.traumavidya.com) helped survivors in southern India. Both teams worked to help adults, students, and teachers recover from the horrible shock and grief of watching families, homes, sources of livelihood, and animals suddenly being swept away. After treating individual adults and groups of children to assess needs, workshops were given for health workers and educators to build the capacity of local people to continue the relief work long after our teams returned home.

Suggested Activities

Directions for the games we used with traumatized school children in Thailand and in the workshops for the school staff are described below (except for "The Parachute" activities, which are outlined step-by-step in Chapter Eleven). The "Coyote/Tiger Chases Rabbit" game, "Pretend Jump Rope," "Parachute" activities, and "The Empowerment Game" were successful in helping students regain confidence while having fun. Many children who complained of headache, weakness in their legs, and/or stomachache (with depressed or anxious affect) began to recover their vitality as they had experiences of mastery during the games. Watching the children's limp bodies come to life and their precious sad faces light up with laughter and joy was a sublime experience for us.

GAMES

COYOTE CHASES RABBIT

We called this "Tiger Chases Rabbit" in Asia since the tiger is an animal that local children are familiar with. Obviously you can vary the critters while the essential game remains the same. For this activity all that is needed are two balls of different colors and sizes. This game is designed to facilitate the fight and flight responses.

Teacher and children sit on the floor in a circle. The teacher holds up one ball, saying, "This is the rabbit." Then the rabbit gets passed around the circle hand-to-hand, starting off slowly. The teacher encourages the children to gradually increase the pace. Encourage them to feel their internal sensations as the rabbit "runs" from child to child.

Teacher then introduces the second ball as Mr. or Ms. Coyote and starts the second ball chasing the "rabbit." The pace increases naturally as the children identify with the strength of the coyote and the speed of the rabbit as the excitement of the chase escalates.

The teacher can increase the complexity of the game for older children or watch them creatively make up their own rules by changing directions. The idea is not to win or lose but to feel the excitement of the chase and the power of the team effort to pass the balls quickly.

Next, the children rest and the teacher checks in, asking them to identify their sensations. (Refer to Chapter Eleven for guidance on group check-in.) Also, ask the children who feels more like the coyote and who feels more like the rabbit. Play the game again, having them switch roles so that the rabbits pretend they are coyotes and the coyotes pretend they are rabbits for a different experience.

After playing this game for a while, have the group participants stand up and feel their legs and their connection to the ground so that they can discharge activated energy through their bodies. Those who feel weak or lack energy can pretend they are bunnies and see how high they can hop. For those children who need extra support, an adult or more energized student might hold their hands, helping them to hop by sharing stamina and enthusiasm.

At the end of the play, children are monitored carefully to make sure that none are frozen or dissociated. If a child is frozen, an adult might do a grounding exercise with them until they become more present.

THE EMPOWERMENT GAME

This is a very simple game that can be played for as long or as short a time as seems productive. Its purpose is to restore grounding and a sense of empowerment and group solidarity.

The class is divided into two parallel lines facing one another with approximately twelve feet between them. One is designated Line A; the other Line B. Instruct Line A to march towards the other line holding hands and stomping feet in unison. As they march together building self-confidence, they chant, "I HAVE THE POWER! I HAVE THE POWER. YOU MAY HAVE THE POWER, BUT I HAVE THE POWER!" The students are told that both teams have equal power and this is not meant to diminish the other team's power. The idea is that Line A and Line B take turns so that the students all have a "felt experience" of their own strength and resources through movement, gesture, and voice when they work together in teams.

When Line A reaches Line B they repeat the chant marching in place, while Line B listens. Then Line A returns to their starting place and Line B takes their turn chanting, marching, and moving towards Line A, whose turn it is now to listen.

After both teams get their turn, repeat the exercise. This time have the students drop their hands with a snap and engage the power and strength in their upper body by rhythmically pumping their arms in coordination with their legs as they march and chant. As the youngsters chant, they should be encouraged to increase their volume congruent with the movement, so that they can feel the growing power of using their own voice. After both sides have had a turn, the teacher draws them together in a circle, directing their awareness to their internal sensations (as in the other games). If during the course of the game some of the children feel shy, withdrawn, or tired and don't want to play, have them hold hands with another student or an adult to give them the support to feel their own power. Any time during the course of the game, the teacher can stop to do a quick check-in with the students' sensations and feelings. Be sure to give plenty of time to rest and settle.

THE PRETEND JUMP ROPE

This game gives students an opportunity to run towards (rather than away from) something that creates activation and to experience a successful escape.

No jump rope is needed. This game is done as a pantomime. Two children or adults hold a pretend jump rope while the others line up for a turn just like in regular jump rope. First the rope is swung back and forth at a low level near the ground. You can increase the imaginary height if the child seems to desire more challenge. One by one students jump over the "rope" to safety. The reason for not using an actual jump rope is that the lack of a real one engages the imagination. It symbolizes a manageable threat coming towards them. This elicits spontaneous movements and gives children the satisfaction of a successful escape.

Note for All Activities:

The key to "assisted self-regulation" after a disaster is that the adults leading the activities are able to assess and assist those students having difficulty. While some youngsters will have trouble settling down (they will not be hard to spot!), others will complain of being too tired to continue or having a headache, tummy ache, etc. For the children who appear to be affected, the teacher must make a mental map of his students' special needs.

Here's where extra help comes in handy. These activities are best played with at least one other grown-up to co-facilitate. Teachers can invite the P.E. teacher, an aide, volunteer, cross-age peer, counselor, or even the school psychologist to assist. Several adults would be ideal. The reason for this is to ensure that anyone who may need individualized assistance gets it.

In addition, extra time needs to be given to model for the whole group how to support each other in learning self-regulation. For example, a student complaining of fatigue during the sensation "check-in" might lie down and rest her head on the lap or shoulder of a friendly teacher or classmate, while an adult helps her explore where she feels tired. If she says, "my legs," the child can rest the legs for a bit and later be given support to move her legs slowly when ready—perhaps pretending she is moving like her favorite animal. (This may include physically helping the child to move her legs alternately while lying on her back with knees up and feet flat on the floor.)

On the other hand, for the child who is hyperactive and needing help to settle, an adult or more regulated student can sit next to her, helping her to feel the ground and to inhale and exhale more slowly. A partner or an adult might place a firm hand on the student's shoulder or back as they ground themselves, communicating calmness through contact. The main idea is to normalize individual differences and teach the group how to help one another as they connect more deeply.

It Takes a Village: Katrina, Rita, and Other Natural Disasters

With the comfort of home washed away and families torn apart by the Gulf Coast hurricanes of 2005, school staff were being challenged, perhaps for the first time, to help pupils muddle through the aftermath of disaster. In an article entitled "Helping Students Cope with a Katrina-Tossed World" (*New York Times*, November 16, 2005), Emma Daly reported that elementary school students in Gulfport, Mississippi, kept coming to see the school nurse at Three Rivers Elementary School "with vague complaints: headaches or stomach pains that are rarely accompanied by fevers or other symptoms." (Actually sometimes children will even have fevers in the aftermath of trauma.) Other pupils were quiet and withdrawn. All of these symptoms, of course, are common in post-disaster situations. Most people, however, don't connect physical symptoms to trauma. Dr. Lynne Jones, advisor to the International Medical Corps regarding hurricane-affected populations, is quoted in the same newspaper story as emphasizing the importance of normalizing symptoms by saying something to the children like, "This is to be expected; if you have been through a very frightening, painful experience, the pain and fear settle in part of your body." It is precisely because the body *does* bear the burden that the model throughout this book for the prevention of long-term trauma involves the vehicle of the body's sensations and feelings, and its innate capacity to restore feelings of pleasure and competency that counter the previous ones of helplessness and disorientation. In natural disasters and other mass-fatality situations, like terrorist attacks and war, the local caregivers are personally affected as well.

"Mass disasters produce a peculiar reticence in grief—everybody is looking after everybody else," continues Dr. Jones.

Our team noticed the same phenomenon in our work in Thailand post-tsunami. Everybody has lost something, so the tendency is to suffer silently rather than burden your neighbor. Survivor guilt is a classic response to disaster. One mother has lost one child, but her friend lost all of her children and her house! She rationalizes, therefore, that she shouldn't feel as bad as she does because her friend lost even more. But such inequities of loss don't mean that one's own pain or trauma is diminished. Children are especially protective and try to spare the adults their feelings because they need to perceive them as able to cope. They will keep their pain secret rather than adding more weight to their caregivers' distress.

For this reason group support is essential for both parents and children to counteract the repercussions of isolation. In Thailand, group chanting done with the monks in the temples eased the suffering. Women formed co-op groups, working together to make crafts for tourists. Families who gather together at their places of worship are comforted by both their spiritual practices and their connection to their community. People heal people! And professionals are often best seen quietly offering support from the shadows of the periphery.

In addition to parents needing support, the local first responders, medical staff, mental health workers, and religious leaders who are in service to the survivors need support to treat their own shock and grief reactions in order to be truly helpful and avoid secondary PTSD.

Our New Reality

On September 11, 2001, the collective reality of safety was shattered in the United States. We were left with profound, unanswered questions and fears about what might happen next and what to tell our children. In fact, more important than *what* we say is *how* we speak with them about such horrible things and how we *listen* to their feelings and concerns.

Children take more from the *feelings of their parents* than from their words. Their needs have less to do with information and more with security. Children need to know that they are protected and loved. The words "I love you and will protect you"—spoken from the heart—mean more than any kind of explanation. Young children need to be communicated with through physical contact, holding, rocking, and touch. In families where both parents work, it is important to take time to phone your young child so that she knows you are still there. Predictability and the continuity of keeping a routine are important for children of all ages. The making of plans together to give them a sense that life will go on and that they will have fun again is another important thing we can do to alleviate distress for our children.

Because the media use graphic fear as a selling point, it is important to minimize children's TV news exposure—particularly during dinner and before bedtime. Of course it's best to watch the news after they are asleep. Kids three to five years of age may ask questions about things that they have heard or seen on TV. At these ages children are beginning to be able to put feelings into words, and you can let them know that it is OK to have these feelings. Drawing pictures and talking about what they have drawn and how it makes them feel can be helpful, as can the telling of stories where the hero/heroine has overcome difficult situations and been made stronger by meeting and mastering an ordeal. (Refer to Chapters Four, Five, and Eleven for detailed information on using art and story to elicit and communicate feelings.) In addition, children will often draw some new creative element in their pictures to help them contextualize what has happened. For example, one child who witnessed the planes crash into the World Trade Center and then saw people jumping out of the windows drew the scene but with a small addition—he drew a small round object on the ground. When asked by his parents what it was, he replied, "It's a trampoline to help save the people falling out of the windows."

For older children, six to twelve years of age, more direct discussions can be held. It may be important to find out where they got their information and what their specific fears are. Then you can have the family brainstorm ideas for things that *they can do* to help the people who have been affected, such as sending letters to the children who lost loved ones or organizing a fund-raiser to collect aid money. Mobilizing helpful activity, rather than being a spectator, can make a big difference.

Mass Disaster Assistance Lacking for Schools after 9/11

Educators in a mass disaster situation need reinforcement from outside the immediate area that was struck. Not only have school personnel been affected just like the children, but precious few have had training of any kind to help in such a catastrophe. American Red Cross Disaster Mental Health Coordinator Lisa LaDue was assigned to the Red Cross Headquarters in Arlington, Virginia, following the 9/11 attack on the Pentagon. Her job was to respond to requests from the metropolitan Washington, D.C., community for debriefings, consultations, and counseling. This is what she wrote during an interview in 2006:

> The common cry echoed from businesses, schools, daycare providers, parents, and teachers was unequivocally the same: "We need help so we can help our children." It became obvious that although significant effort had been dedicated to disaster planning in the preceding years, parents, teachers, families, and childcare providers were generally at a great loss to know how to help their children recover from this traumatic event. Due to this pervasive skills deficit coupled with an obvious need, children became the central focus for our Pentagon special response team.

It was only after September 2001, coming face-to-face with the glaring limitations I had as a cognitive therapist to help people recover from shock, that I had the good fortune to stumble upon Somatic Experiencing®. I embarked upon the journey to complete the training that would truly give me the necessary skills to help traumatized adults and children. These new tools would have been so valuable back then. When teachers called and asked how they could help the terrified children in their classes, we could have taught them how to organize simple games that would allow discharge of the traumatic energy. We might have taught them how to integrate art, writing, and other expressive forms with Somatic Experiencing® to help calm and settle the children's nervous systems. When parents called, exasperated with feelings of helplessness because their children had difficulty sleeping or were afraid to leave home in the morning, we might have offered education and simple guidance so that they could restore a sense of balance to their lives. Educational sessions might have been coordinated for mental health and other health care professionals in the area to receive training in this psycho-physiological approach to relieve the symptoms of acute and post-traumatic stress disorder.

Since I worked closely with the greater Washington, D.C., community for one month, I was keenly aware of the highly activated state of arousal present when the trauma of the Pentagon attack was followed by the anthrax bio-terrorism scare and, later, by the terror of snipers who killed innocent people. Parents were afraid to take their children to school; children were afraid when their parents went to work or even to the store. Whole neighborhoods were afraid to leave their homes after dark. No one seemed to know how to address the effects of terror. These incidents clearly illustrate the need for coordinated services to help children and adults regain their equilibrium in order to recover from both direct and vicarious trauma.

As the co-founder and senior advisor for the National Mass Fatalities Institute, I provide Mass Fatalities Incident Response Planning courses for communities across the nation. Through these trainings, it has become evident that government officials, community leaders, directors of voluntary organizations, educational providers, and healthcare professionals are beginning to understand the need for services that address the *terror* of terrorism and other mass disasters (man-made or natural). However, it is my experience that there is still a lack of understanding among professionals of how to achieve this. Somatic Experiencing® offers hope in restoring a sense of safety, not only for the children, but first and foremost for their caregivers and the healthcare professionals who help them. It provides a fresh approach for both adults and children to recover from events that have shaken all of us collectively as human beings.

A child's fearful face, a classroom with children demonstrating regressive, disruptive behavior, and families who find their children lacking the energy to enjoy life the way they did before are all loud warning bells beckoning us to come forth with a new service plan that addresses the physical dimensions of trauma as well as the psychological and spiritual so true healing can occur. Somatic Experiencing® is the most valuable method I have found to help children reclaim their inherent vitality, alleviate symptoms, prevent somatic complaints from becoming serious physical illnesses, and develop resilience to future threats. I only wish I had possessed these skills when I set up the Pentagon Special Response Team in D.C. after 9/11.

– Lisa R. LaDue, MSW, LISW Senior Advisor,
National Mass Fatalities Institute[6]

Transforming Societal Trauma in the Aftermath of Catastrophe: The Intercultural Baby-Bonding Project

Healthy babies are born with a complex array of behaviors, feelings, and perceptions. These elements are designed to facilitate exploration, bonding, and eventually healthy social behaviors. When infants are born into a life of stress and trauma, these babies are inhibited and exhibit fearful and withdrawn behaviors. As young children and adults, they will be less social and more inclined to violence. Healthy exploration and bonding seem to be antidotes that mitigate against violence in times of disorder, dislocation, and cultural chaos.

Just as the effects of individual trauma can be transformed, the aftereffects of war on a societal level can also be resolved. People can and must come together with a willingness to share rather than fight, and to transform trauma rather than propagate it. A place to begin is in working with the very youngest children.

Many years ago (1975), Dr. James Prescott (formerly with the National Institutes of Mental Health) summarized important anthropological research on the effect of infant and child-rearing practices on violent behavior in aboriginal societies.[7] He reported that the societies that practiced close physical bonding and the use of stimulating rhythmical movement (where babies were "hammocked" to their mother's body as she worked and walked) had a low incidence of violence. Societies with diminished or punitive physical contact with their children (and intolerance towards adolescent sexuality) showed clear tendencies towards violence in the forms of war, rape, and torture.

The work of Prescott and others (Erikson, 1950, Mahler, 1975) points to what many seem to know intuitively: birth and infancy is a critical period in terms of attachment and social relationships.[8] Children assimilate the ways in which their parents relate to each other and to the world at a very young age. When parents have been traumatized, they have difficulty transmitting a sense of basic trust to their young. Without this sense of trust as a resource, children are more vulnerable to trauma. One solution to breaking the cycle of trauma is to involve infants and mothers (and fathers) in an experience that generates trust and bonding before children have completely absorbed their parents' distrust of themselves and others.

In Norway, exciting work is now being done in this area. Our colleague Eldbjörg Wedaa, an expressive arts therapist, has collaboratively developed a program utilizing the principles of Somatic Experiencing® that takes advantage of this critical period of infancy. This approach allows an entire group of people to begin transforming the traumatic remnants of previous tensions. This inexpensive method requires only a room, a few simple musical instruments, and blankets that are strong enough to hold a baby's (or toddler's) weight.

This process of bonding with babies and intercultural exchange works as follows: a group composed of mothers (fathers too) and infants from opposing factions (such as ones with variances in religious, racial, and political thinking) are brought together at a home or a community center. The encounter begins with this mixed group of mothers and infants taking turns teaching one another simple folk songs from their respective cultures. Holding their babies, the mothers rock and dance while they sing the songs to their children. Simple instruments are used to enhance the rhythm of the songs. The movement, rhythm, and singing strengthen the neurological patterns that produce peaceful alertness and receptivity. As a result, the hostility produced through generations of strife begins to soften.

At first, the babies and toddlers are perplexed by these activities, but soon they become more interested and involved. They are enthusiastic about the rattles, drums, and tambourines that are passed to them. Characteristically, without rhythmical stimulation, young babies will do little more than try to put objects such as these into their mouth. In this instance, however, the infants will join in generating the rhythm with great delight, often squealing and cooing with glee.

Because infants are highly developed organisms at birth, they send signals that activate their mother's deepest sense of serenity, responsiveness, and biological competence. In this healthy relationship, the mothers and their young feed off each other in an exchange of mutually gratifying physiological responses, which in turn generate feelings of security and pleasure. It is here that the cycle of trauma begins to transform.

The transformation continues as the parents place their babies on the floor and allow them to explore. Like luminous magnets, the babies joyfully move towards each other, overcoming barriers of shyness as the mothers quietly support their exploration by forming a circle around them. The sense of mutual connection generated by music and songs is difficult to describe or imagine—it must be witnessed.

Next, the large group breaks up into smaller groups, each consisting of a mother and infant from each culture. The mothers swing their infants gently in a blanket. These babies generate a roomful of love that is contagious. Soon the mothers (and fathers when culturally appropriate) are smiling at each other and enjoying an experience of deep bonding with members of a community that earlier they may have feared and distrusted. The mothers leave with renewed hearts and spirits. They are eager to share this feeling with others. The process is almost self-perpetuating.

The beauty of this approach to community healing lies in its simplicity and its effectiveness. The first time the process is led by an outside facilitator. After the initial experience, participating mothers can be trained as facilitators for other groups. The primary attributes required by a facilitator are an acute sensitivity to musical timing and to interpersonal boundaries. It is our experience that for certain individuals, these are skills that can be easily learned through a combination of participatory experience and explanation. Once trained, the mothers become ambassadors of peace within their own communities.

"Give me a place to put my lever," exclaimed Archimedes, "and I will move the world." In a world of conflict, destruction, and trauma, we find one such fulcrum in the close physical, rhythmic pulsation between mother and infant. Experiences such as the one just described can bring people together so that they can again begin to live in harmony.

Trauma's impact is different for each one of us. We must all be willing to accept the responsibility for our own healing. If we continue to wage war on each other, the healing most of us yearn for will be no more than a dream. Nations living near each other can break the generational cycle of destruction, violence, and repeated trauma that holds them hostage. By using the human organism's capacity to register peaceful aliveness, even in the web of traumatic defensiveness, we can all begin to make our communities safe for ourselves, our children, and our children's children. Once we establish safe communities, the process of healing ourselves and our world takes on an evolutionary dimension.

Epilogue or Epitaph?

Non-traumatized humans prefer to live in harmony if they can. Yet traumatic residue creates a belief that we are unable to surmount our hostility, and that misunderstandings will always keep us apart. The experience of bonding described above is only one example of the many concepts and practices that could be used to address this most serious dilemma.

These approaches are not panaceas, but they are a place to begin. They offer hope where political solutions alone have not worked. The Holocaust, conflicts in Israel and Palestine, the unrest in our inner cities, and civil wars over the globe have been traumatic for the world community. They portray, too graphically, the price we will pay as a society if we continue the cycle of trauma. We must be passionate in our search for effective avenues of resolution. The survival of our species may depend on it.

Trauma cannot be ignored. It is an inherent part of the primitive biology that brought us here—a part of the human condition. The only way we will be able to release ourselves, individually and collectively, from re-enacting our traumatic legacies is by transforming them through re-negotiation. Music provides a universal, culturally accessible means to begin the transformation of these legacies through group experiences.

The Price Society Pays for Ignoring Cultural Trauma: Effects on Five Generations

Historically, when human cultures gathered in small groups and worked cooperatively for the common good, there is anthropological evidence of peaceful societies and familial groups. This was a byproduct of hunter/gatherer societies that lived with a reverence for nature, as their survival was intricately interwoven with the local ecology and dependent upon it.

When natural resources became an issue due to increasing populations and "urbanization," competition spurred the birth of agriculture. And planting gave birth to fences. Anthropologists have traced the concept of "conqueror-victim" cycles back to this crucial change. Since that time, the concept of global peace and harmony has become lost in traumatic re-enactment that started between differing social clusters and has ended up in families, individuals, and in the destruction of our natural environment.

Merida Blanco, PhD, a cultural anthropologist and our good friend, spent her life studying these phenomena. This peace-loving pioneer, who yearned to use her wisdom together with Somatic Experiencing® to heal societal trauma, died in 2004. She left us her legacy, however, in the form of an unpublished inter-generational diagram spanning five lifetimes following violence perpetrated by one social group against another.[9]

First Generation: In the first generation to be conquered, the males are killed, imprisoned, enslaved, or in some other way deprived of the ability to provide for their families.

Second Generation: Many of the men turn towards alcohol or drugs, as their cultural identity has been destroyed with a pre-dictable, accompanying loss of self-worth.

Third Generation: Spousal abuse and other forms of domes-tic violence are spawned. By this generation, the connection to its antecedent from societal trauma only two generations before has been weakened or lost.

Fourth Generation: At this stage, abuse moves from spousal abuse to child abuse or both.

Fifth Generation: This cycle repeats over and over as trauma begets violence and more trauma and violence, with increasing societal degradation, including abuse of our Earth and her natu-ral resources as sustainability is disregarded.

In addition to the diagram, Dr. Blanco left us a map that she had drawn. It showed the grown children of the conquerors living in fear of the grown children of the conquered, cowering behind locked fences in gated communities. She showed rivers of despair on her map, but she also drew bridges of hope. These bridges linked the communities once again. But, she admonished, the descen-dents of the conquerors would need to reach out to the descen-dents of those conquered to build those bridges, not with pity, nor with fear, but with mutual respect and the intention to take respon-sibility for this cycle of destruction and heal the scourge of socie-tal trauma that benefits no one.

Undoing This Vicious Cycle

With the new understanding that trauma resides, unresolved, in the nervous system of individuals and the collective nervous system of society comes new hope for future generations. As *our* generation awakens by coming home to the body, restoring our primordial rhythms that bring pleasure and flow, we can begin to change this generational "inheritance" to one of victory over intergenerational trauma. Individual trauma healing not only heals us, but our offspring as well. First we heal at the level of the personal, then at the level of family, then at the level of community, next at the level of nations—and finally at the global level. One woman from Gaza, in a joint Israeli-Palestinian project that Peter Levine and Gina Ross (FHE faculty member and founder of the International Trauma-Healing Institute) conducted in Jerusalem, said, "I realize that until we find peace within ourselves, we will never be able to find peace with each other." As more and more individuals experience profound transformation at the physical, emotional, and spiritual levels by way of the vehicle of transforming trauma through sensations and feelings, and learn to adjust their actions appropriately, seeds of new possibilities for our vulnerable planet are sown. You, as educators, community leaders, medical workers, parents, and concerned neighbors, can make a difference in children's lives—from infancy to adolescence. Whether you are a day care director, classroom teacher, counselor, nurse, school psychologist, administrator, therapist, pediatric medical professional, or political leader, you are now equipped with the knowledge and skills to influence the future.

CHAPTER THIRTEEN

———————————— 🍂 ————————————

Transforming Medical Care
for the Future: A Plan
to Minimize Pediatric Trauma

When the people are even moderately enlightened,
oppression of the body and mind will disappear.

– Thomas Jefferson

Peter's Story

My "career" in developing Somatic Experiencing® began in 1969 when I was asked to treat a woman named Nancy who suffered with myriad physical problems including migraines, a painful condition that would now be called fibromyalgia, chronic fatigue, severe **PMS**, and irritable bowel syndrome, as well as various "psychological" problems including frequent panic attacks. During this session (described in *Waking the Tiger: Healing Trauma*) Nancy began to tremble, shake, and sob in waves of full-body convulsions. For almost an hour she continued to shake as she recalled terrifying images and feelings from age four. She had been held down by doctors and nurses and struggled in vain during a tonsillectomy with ether anesthesia. As I worked with more and more people with symptoms like Nancy's, I was shocked at how many had similar experiences as young children where they were overwhelmed and terrified by invasive medical procedures. As I began to train people in the method I was developing, I also got to confront my own terrifying tonsillectomy. Like Nancy, I struggled against the doctors and nurses who held me down. Desperately I tried to escape the terror of suffocation, but was overpowered and overwhelmed with panic and helplessness. As I worked with this experience, feelings of fearfulness, "tummy aches," and betrayal that had plagued me throughout my adult life loosened their grip. For both Nancy and me, we each re-owned an innocence and vitality that had been cruelly, though unintentionally, taken from us. It was at that point that I felt impelled to do what I could to prevent children from becoming unnecessarily traumatized. And while hospitals have come a long way since the 1940s and '50s, when Nancy and I had our tonsillectomies, medical procedures performed on children still are often experienced as frightening, painful, and overwhelming.

The "war on terror" can begin by reducing the suffering endured by children unnecessarily and inflicted inadvertently by the health care system. Doctors, nurses, and allied professionals are in the business of saving lives. Devoted staff members often suffer "burn-out," or vicarious trauma, as they deal with catastrophic illnesses, injuries, and what is often a chaotic, frenzied environment. Budgetary crises and understaffing of nurses appears to be the norm. Layered on top of that is a complex "managed care" bureaucracy that can bury both health care providers and patients in paperwork. Is it really surprising that precious little time has been given thus far to consider a different approach that might reduce, minimize, or eliminate repercussions for all stakeholders?

Medical and surgical procedures are supposed to resolve patients' medical problems—not create new ones. Whether interventions are urgent or planned, dealing with them can be difficult, at best, even for adults. More often than not the procedures are tricky and frightening, not to mention potentially harmful, as one can see when asked to sign the cautionary forms prior to treatment (ostensibly to waive responsibility and stave off litigation).

Ideally, with the revelations and the model presented in this chapter, you will be motivated to participate in creating change.

The responsibility to provide conscientious care that prevents unnecessary suffering, facilitates quicker recovery time, prevents future trauma symptoms, *and* saves money lies in the hands of administrators and medical personnel in public and private health care organizations. However, remember that in this business-driven environment, the consumer often has the power of patronage.

Any health care facility can easily implement the suggestions presented in this chapter. Parents and medical staff together, united in their vision to improve pediatric medical care, can be powerful allies in bringing a new consciousness to our "systems of care." This new direction would be best if it were two-tiered: i.e., the integration of both a trauma-prevention and a trauma-treatment program into the existing model. With humanistic practices incorporated system-wide, the following benefits can be expected:

- Children who might otherwise suffer with a lifetime of illness, dysfunction, or violent outbursts following terrifying medical procedures will have a chance to grow up healthy and resilient.

- These same children as adults later in life may be less saddled with anxiety and other psychological, physical, and medical symptoms of trauma. They may be more likely to rebound in the aftermath of overwhelming experiences, because a predisposition for hopelessness and helplessness has not be imprinted due to early medical trauma.

- Children who are surgical patients would have the possibility of recovering more rapidly.

- Serious health problems, and even some violent acts, might be averted.

- The needs of the body, mind, and spirit could share more equal weight in patient planning decisions made by health care system practitioners. This would allow

the children to be given the respect and dignity they
deserve.

- Society might save incalculable sums of money in health
care costs, not to mention human suffering.

The Current State of Affairs
in the Health Care Industry

A group of researchers presented a report to the public in 2003
concerning the current state of the health care industry in the U.S.,
based on a report by Dr. Barbara Starfield of Johns Hopkins. The
following horrifying data can be found in *The Journal of American
Medicine* under the heading "Data Published in Annual Physical
and Economic Cost of Medical Intervention."[1]

IDENTIFIED PROBLEM AREA	ANNUAL COST
- In-hospital adverse reactions to prescribed drugs	$2.2 million
- Unnecessary medical and surgical procedures	7.5 million people
- Exposed to unnecessary hospitalizations	8.9 million people
- Deaths due to conventional medicine	783,936 people
- TOTAL MONETARY COST	$282 billion

Death by Medicine—a report by Gary Null, PhD (together with a
group of concerned medical doctors)—shows compelling evidence
that today's health care system is so severely flawed that it frequently causes more harm than good.[2] According to Dr. Joseph
Mercola, who reports on iatrogenic incidents and posts *Death by
Medicine* on his Website, "It is now evident that the American Medical System is the leading cause of death and injury in the U.S."[3]

We know that the body is self-healing. Unnecessary drugs often block the healing process, and needless surgery may cause complications that are pointless. The current system misses an understanding of and reverence for the body's innate healing ability, the nature of the human spirit during recovery, and the power of a patient's support system in altering stress levels and alleviating human suffering. This understanding need not minimize the many miracles of modern technological medicine; however, everything in its own place.

A Vision of Alternative and Integrative Medicine for the Twenty-first Century

The future is also now. It's estimated, for example, that 36–62% of the population is now regularly availing themselves of alternative medicine (numbers depend on the definition that is used).[4] Increased consumer demand for complementary and alternative medicine (CAM) has created a powerful incentive for hospitals to expand their services, given the fact that consumers are spending billions of out-of-pocket dollars on CAM services. Recent surveys conducted by Health Forum/AHA (American Hospital Association) of its membership provide compelling data that support this trend. In 1998, in the AHA's *Annual Survey of Hospitals*, approximately 8% of hospitals indicated that they offered CAM services that were "owned or provided by my hospital or a subsidiary." By 2004, this claim by hospitals in the U.S. of providing some form of alternative treatment had increased to 18%.[5] A study conducted at the Center for Alternative Medicine Research and Education at Beth Israel Deaconess Medical Center, Boston, reported that the use of at least 1 of 16 alternative therapies during the previous year increased from 33.8% in 1990 to 42.1% in 1997 (P < or = .001). In addition, the total 1997 out-of-pocket expenditures relating to alternative therapies were conservatively estimated at $27 billion, which is comparable with the projected 1997 out-of-pocket expenditures for all US physician services. The researchers concluded that alternative medicine use and expenditures increased substantially between 1990 and 1997, attributable primarily to an increase in the proportion of the population seeking alternative therapies, rather than increased visits per patient.[6]

More and more people are fed up with the impersonal nature of mainstream Western medicine and are no longer willing to tolerate being treated as a number rather than as a human being. Hospitals are opting for a hybrid form of care called Integrative Medicine, which often advocates the appropriate combination of ancient and modern treatments from the East and the West, as well as utilizing Native American wisdom. There is also a movement to make hospitals more humane, no matter what tradition of medicine is practiced.

One such group committed to this goal is the Planetree Alliance. This is a non-profit organization working with hospitals and health care centers to develop and implement patient-centered care in a healing environment. A coalition of seventy hospitals nationwide belongs to this network of consumer-driven care.[7] Results of this organization's practices demonstrate the cost-effectiveness of creating high-quality patient treatment experiences. Some hospitals have added Healing Touch, Reiki, and massage as the research evidence pours in on the importance of touch in health and healing. Acupuncture (frequently overlooked just a short time ago and even dismissed in Western medical circles) is also becoming more common as a complementary treatment.

A Peek at a Model Family-Centered Children's Hospital

Although few in number, attitudes and environments *are* being created that are sensitive and humane. Some hospitals working to minimize pediatric trauma are those funded by the Make-A-Wish Foundation.[8] Let's look at what they are doing to prevent trauma and make a child's hospital stay more pleasant and less scary.

One such forward-looking hospital is Miller Children's Hospital at Long Beach Memorial Medical Center in California. Directions given over the telephone to find Miller Children's given by Rita, the manager of the Child Life Program, were heartening: "Enter by the blue dolphin and go straight to the boat, where you will find a receptionist to give you a visitor badge." These words, spoken in a warm welcoming tone, gave a feeling of comfort and nurturance even before the tour of this remarkable pediatric unit. This hospital's philosophy and commitment to the total care of each child also means a commitment to their whole family. Both the child and parents are oriented about what to expect before, during, and after the medical procedures. When appropriate, the Sibling Program prepares brothers and sisters for their first hospital visit as well.

The Child Life Program was developed with the sole purpose of making the hospital experience a positive one for both outpatient and inpatient children. Child Life Specialists plan individualized and group programs that prepare children by familiarizing them with things they may experience in a way that helps lessen fear and anxiety. The Child Life Specialists use simulated equipment, books, and "Jeffrey," the life-sized doll dressed in child-friendly hospital pajamas and blue surgical cap. "Jeffrey" has a special box with EKG stickers, a pulsometer, an IV, a blood pressure cuff, and a syringe that the child gets to look at, feel, and play with. Next, the child is shown a book with age-appropriate actual photos that orient them to the hospital experience step-by-step, starting with picking out the color of some very cool pajamas (with little bear and star motifs) and slippers that they are told they can keep.

I got to witness the program in action with Daniel, a little boy who was about to have a mass removed from his neck. He listened spellbound to the story that the Child Life Specialist read to him. Next, Daniel got to touch the EKG stickers that the Specialist said were "sticky on the outside and gooey in the middle." After he played with them, she demonstrated for Daniel exactly how they would be placed on his chest and showed him a photo of another child getting the same stickers.

This orientation took place in the playroom, which was equipped with carpeted climbing stairs, a slide, and a television theater featuring shows like *Bear and the Big Blue House*. The episode playing while Daniel was being prepped was about "Doc Hog's visit to the big blue house to examine bear and all of his friends." After the preparation, Daniel got to play on the slide with his mom and dad until the doctor came in to the playroom to meet the family. When the doctor arrived, he played a few minutes with Daniel so that he would not be a stranger. Next, he patiently answered any questions the family had. He also explained the sequence of events in simple language.

At Miller, children are given their own doll to dress up in pajamas along with a medical play kit, which contains a mask, syringe, gloves, cotton, alcohol swab, band-aid, tongue depressor, and a medicine cup. There are coloring books with titles such as *Tommy's (Turtle) Trip to MRI* and *My Hospital Book*, as well as a library of videos, books, and medical internet access for parents and teens. Children are given a tour of the play rooms they will get to spend time enjoying after their treatments in order to tantalize them with something to look forward to while recuperating.

Miller Children's also incorporates state-of-the-art pain-reducing technology. For example, they have "patient-controlled analgesic" machines that operate by a push of a button. It is so safe and simple that children as young as five years old can operate one! They are controlled in such a way that it is impossible for a child to overdose on the medication while at the same time getting sufficient pain alleviation.

A non-drug pain reliever is the mobile "Fun Center" complete with TV, VCR, and interactive video games. The Child Life Program manager shared that a study conducted by the University of

Southern California in Los Angeles using these play stations monitored physiological reactions of young sickle-cell patients experiencing a pain crisis. Research results were conclusive in finding significantly reduced pain responses in children who were given the opportunity to use the "Fun Center." A benefit is that it can be used by both children and adolescents. Another program that works especially with teens (and children of all ages who may not have actively involved parents) is "The Grandparent Program." This core of senior citizen volunteers plays cards, sits, and talks with the kids, just spending caring time with them, keeping them from getting lonely and bored.

In addition to the Child Life Program, great care has been taken to make Miller Children's Hospital a delightful environment for children. Each room has a colorful mural on the wall with an ocean theme. Little kids get to be surrounded by lots of sea creatures, while teens have scenes like surfboards in the sand. There are one-to-one bedside games, pet visitations, and elaborate play rooms. They have everything from arts, crafts, and imaginative play to special video conferencing through "Starbright World" (a protected Health Care Organization) that connects children interactively online to other children, internationally, having a similar medical condition. As if that were not enough, the "Giggles" TV studio broadcasts live daily, with reception available in every room. This show features a child patient, a Child Life Specialist, and, of course, "Giggles the Clown" herself! Other child patients can call in with questions, and everyone who calls wins a prize. After the show, prizes are distributed. The TV "guest" can expect peer visitors who are eager to get an autograph from the patient "star" of the day. In addition to Child Life Specialists who prepare children and walk them through procedures, there are social workers and psychologists available to work with children who, despite best efforts, may still be traumatized. Staff is also on the alert to identify children needing specialized help during their recovery period.

Suggestions to Enhance Trauma Prevention Efforts

Although there are growing numbers of conscious medical centers doing their best to increase the comfort level of children and create an appealing environment, often the simplest but most important practices to prevent trauma remain unknown or overlooked. The good news is that pediatric trauma prevention does not require fancy or expensive equipment. The skills to prevent trauma can be made available to all workers in the health care system. The first step would be to educate them regarding autonomic nervous system dynamics that cause trauma in the first place. Because trauma symptoms come from immobility, helplessness, and the energy bound in the thwarted flight-or-fight response, it is essential to make absolutely sure that no child is strapped down and subjected to being anesthetized in a terrified state. Doctors, nurses, social workers, and Child Life Specialists need to be alert to a child's feelings and strive to lessen anxiety. The child's reactions need to be closely monitored. Body language and facial expressions often tell the story of a child's fears better than words. Perhaps the orientation to the hospital routine and the role-playing can happen the week before, rather than on the day of the surgery, so that parents can be taught to play "hospital" at home until the child is comfortable enough to cooperate.

Another important point in trauma prevention, mentioned in Chapter Seven, cannot be overstated. When a child must undergo surgery, it is vital for a local anesthetic to be administered along the line of incision whenever possible. Currently, this is not routinely done despite a growing body of research indicating its efficacy in improving rate of recovery and lessening complications.[9] Many times a local can be given without the potential risks of a general anesthesia; however, a general should not be given without a local in most cases. In addition to the quick recovery time benefit of a local anesthetic, the body registers the point of incision as an invasion, perhaps no different even than that of a vicious animal attack—*despite* the fact that the mind has been rendered unconscious in an altered state. This predicament is completely unfamiliar to an unprepared child, leaving her vulnerable to later psychological symptoms. In addition, studies have shown that where there is child abuse and family dysfunction, future psychological and medical problems are predictable.[10] These at-risk children deserve to be protected from additional exposure to stressful practices.

Taking Good Programs to the Next Level of Trauma Intervention

Miller Children's Hospital at Long Beach Memorial Medical Center is one of a network of ninety model hospitals in the United States that are family-friendly. By adding the simple but crucial recommendations described above it would be very easy to initiate change in programs such as these that put children's needs first. All it would take is the initiative to educate your local hospital staff regarding the principles of trauma prevention outlined in this book. Be sure to choose a facility that understands the crucial importance of preventing medical trauma through sensitive practices, orientation, and preparation. It is also important to choose a medical center or hospital that is willing to work as a team with parents.

Contact www.ChildLifeCouncil.org to learn more about bringing programs such as Child Life and Make-A-Wish to your community. Be pro-active in reminding them, however, that sophisticated equipment is not the essential ingredient of a trauma-prevention program. Understanding and alleviating children's fear, worry, and pain is the true hallmark of prevention. Remember that the medical community mission is supposed to serve the child and the family—not the other way around! Know, and insist, on your rights. Ultimately it is up to you to make choices and to make change happen!

Candi's Story

Candi is a young African-American Child Life Specialist intern who I met when I visited Miller Children's Hospital. She was especially curious about my work in trauma prevention and captured my attention with her enthusiasm for the career she had chosen. I listened intently to her story. You see, Candi described her younger self as an outgoing, friendly little girl who was also a dancer. When she was seven years old she noticed a mysterious and debilitating pain in her knee requiring medical attention.

Candi said that she will *never forget* her dreadful and terrifying hospital experience. The doctor was "digging and poking" around her knee until an embedded sewing needle was discovered. But embedded even deeper in her memory were the insensitive words she thought she heard the doctor say to the nurses: "If we can't get the needle out, we may have to cut off the leg." As an adult, Candi said, "I understand that they saved my life—the needle could have traveled to my heart—but I was *SO* scared. Nothing was done to comfort me. When the ordeal was over, the nurses said, 'Be sure to tell your mom what a great job the nurses did!' But they didn't."

I asked Candi how this affected her life. She told me that she has been shy and anxious ever since that day. She shared this as her motivation to devote her life to the prevention of medical trauma in children so that no child has to suffer the kind of suffering she has had to endure.

Another Positive Note, from the Foundation for Human Enrichment

Our organization, the Foundation for Human Enrichment, is becoming pro-active on behalf of *all* children (and adults as well). In 2005, we began to develop a program for health care settings called "Trauma Resources: Innovative Approaches for Optimal Recovery." Several nurses, doctors, social workers, psychologists, and other allied health professionals who have been trained in

Somatic Experiencing® have taken it upon themselves to organize and structure this effort designed to "lend a hand" in educating stakeholders and staff in medical institutions about the trauma prevention and healing methods you have learned from this book. This health division, still under construction, has a threefold purpose:

- **Intervention:** Using the Somatic Experiencing® neurobiological educational model when catastrophic injury and illness occurs.

- **Prevention:** Using the suggestions outlined here to prepare children adequately prior to anesthesia, surgery, and other medical procedures.

- **Protection:** Using the gift of this body-based approach to ease the vicarious trauma of dedicated health professionals in order to enhance the quality of their professional life; thereby reducing burn-out and alleviating shortages of such valuable personnel.

This program will be the first of its kind to provide front-line interventions that are somatically based. Resources will be developed through body awareness with the goal of not only optimizing medical outcomes, but preventing psychological complications from developing after the physical wounds have healed.

Currently, many hospital and medical centers provide excellent treatment, saving lives that previously would have been lost. The next step in recovery is to provide immediate, effective interventions to address mental, emotional, and spiritual issues. The impact of catastrophic events such as accidents, injuries, painful and life-altering illnesses, and exposure to violence or natural disasters goes far beyond immediate, visible physical damage. Trauma studies reveal far-reaching consequences affecting the individual's biology and behavior on all levels.

One such hospital that is beginning to examine the need for

services that address the emotional aspects of a patient's experience is the Children's Hospital of the University of California at San Francisco Medical Center. In an exciting collaboration with both the Pediatric Rheumatology and Rehabilitation Medicine Divisions along with two members of the Child Life Department, Karen Schanche, one of the Center's pediatric social workers, has developed and implemented an innovative treatment program for pediatric patients to reduce symptoms associated with various medical treatments.[11]

Karen has been using Somatic Experiencing® principles with both outpatients and in-patients under her care. She prepares children (four to eighteen years of age) who are in the rheumatology outpatient program to successfully cope with multiple painful joint injections during regular clinic visits without having to undergo general anesthesia. In addition to showing them how the procedure will affect them, she joins with the children to determine what they need to feel safe and comfortable, introduces them to sensations, role-plays with making boundaries, and helps them find ways to access inner resources in order to maintain a sense of being in control. Part of this process includes empowering the children to make decisions about who they want with them and how they want another person to help manage the sensations of pressure and pain that can accompany the procedure.

As these young patients use such techniques as switching their focus from painful sensations to pleasurable (or at least less painful) ones, they are more prepared to endure the pain with minimal discomfort. This allows them, then, to surrender to the anguish of the injections while maintaining a sense of control and larger purpose.

Karen reports the magical result that the majority of children are much more cooperative when receiving these injections with support, compared to when they have to undergo general anesthesia. She said that kids have made comments like "I'm not feeling nauseated and I don't have to throw up!" after undergoing the procedure using the SE® method we have been describing; and many children generally are amazed at how much better they feel without the anesthesia. But the biggest bonus is that the children are free of the psychological and physical complications that come from being restrained and drugged. Embla numbing cream and freezing spray are applied locally instead of sedation. Rather than the children feeling helpless as they are held down to experience excruciating pain, Karen empowers the children by helping them to feel their defensive responses and strength by using "push hands" or "push away" games. Some of the pushing and pressure can be done during the injections to distract them as they focus on the sensations of using their own powerful muscles. Karen often integrates SE® with techniques from Ericksonian Hypnotherapy, which uses the child's own imagery and metaphor.

Although no formal research has yet been conducted, qualitative data are being collected on the benefits of such a program in the ongoing treatment of chronic illness, and also in the area of providing clinical treatment for acute pediatric oncology patients who are receiving radiation and chemotherapy for curative and/or palliation purposes. To date, Karen has prepared twenty-seven children who are in treatment in the outpatient Rheumatology Program and seven in-patient rehabilitation patients. The child patients are appreciative, and the doctors appear impressed by the improvement in their pediatric patient satisfaction and ability to handle stressful medical procedures with less distress.

In addition to the pediatric populations described above, Karen is working with the UCSF Comprehensive Cancer Center's Symptom Management and Palliative Care Services doing research with the outpatient Urologic Clinic Programs for adults. Preliminary research has been in the form of a needs assessment and ongoing collection of data pre- and post-interventions with each patient and, when appropriate, with their immediate caregivers. Currently, grant efforts are in process for long-term funding from both private and federal sources as well as from the Cancer Center's Foundation to continue this valued service for the entire Cancer Center's outpatient programs.

While much more research is needed on approaches such as the one at UCSF Medical Center, the authors have noted from anecdotal reports that individuals who receive Somatic Experiencing® treatments before and after medical procedures usually testify to rapid recovery. This includes symptomatic relief and an ability to return to a full life, even if they have suffered irreparable physical damage.

Summary

Many people experience hospitals and medical clinics as foreign, threatening, and even dangerous places. This perceived threat is heightened when a person seeks medical care for a serious health challenge or life threat. Medical trauma is particularly significant for children. Many adults recall fears of suffocation, immobilization, and terror they endured as a result of medical treatment received in childhood.

Fortunately, as you have seen, much can be done to bring more humane and palliative care to the medical industry. Through simple modification of approaches, hospital personnel can dramatically influence the degree of safety or degree of threat that the patient experiences. Orientation, preparation with the use of role-play, help in processing "the bad news diagnosis" as it is happening, and intentional use of positive language are key examples of powerful tools that health care workers can employ to impact patient outcomes without adding burdensome duties or demands to the health care workers' load. In fact, this approach may well lighten the emotional burden due to the more positive outcomes in patient recovery time and attitude.

There are many more topics, such as prevention of burn-out in medical personnel, better preparation, less invasive medical procedures, conducting research, etc., that are not covered within the scope of this book. One topic that we feel needs to be added to augment the efforts of those leaders who have paved the way to fix our broken medical system is medical education. Health care professionals need to be trained so that they understand, like you now do, the nature of trauma. Our hope is that in the foreseeable future, all hospitals and medical centers will understand the importance of preventing or minimizing stress and shock-trauma in *all* patients—but, particularly with our most vulnerable citizens, our children.

Appendix

FIRST AID FOR ACCIDENTS AND FALLS

A Quick Reference Guide

Below is a guide to post on your refrigerator or medicine chest as a summary of the valuable tools you have learned about. Remember ... trauma is a fact of life, but not a life sentence. *"It doesn't have to hurt forever."*

1. Attend to your responses until relatively calm.

2. Keep your child still, quiet, and warm.

3. Encourage plenty of time for safety and rest.

4. As the shock wears off, guide attention to sensations.

5. Allow a full minute or two of silence, observing cues.

6. Encourage the child to rest before talking about the event.

7. Continue to validate the child's physical responses.

8. Finally, attend to the child's emotional responses.

WORKSHEET FOR LISTING SYMPTOMS

The following exercise is intended to heighten your awareness of symptoms as you observe your own child. Two commonly observed examples are listed for each category to get you started.

The examples are intended to help you hone your observation skills. It will also be helpful to share your list with a therapist if your child needs to be seen by a professional. If your child is experiencing secondary symptoms, do not despair. It is never too late to help.

Area of Development with Common Examples
(Use space below to list symptoms that your child exhibits)

1. Physical
Examples: Loss of appetite and sleep disturbance

_____

_____

_____

2. Emotional
Examples: Anger, shame, and irritability

_____

_____

_____

3. Spiritual
Examples: Feeling alone and bereft, ashamed

_____

_____

_____

4. Cognitive
Examples: Confusion and shortened attention span

_____

_____

_____

5. Behavioral
Examples: Repetitive play and aggression

_____

_____

_____

Notes

FOREWORD

1. Perry, B.D. "Neurobiological Sequelae of Childhood Trauma: Post-traumatic Stress Disorder in Children," in Murberg, M., ed. *Catecholamines in Post-traumatic Stress Disorder: Emerging Concepts.* Washington, DC: American Psychiatric Press, 1994, 253–276.

2. Yehuda R. et. al. "Transgenerational Effects of Posttraumatic Stress Disorder in Babies of Mothers Exposed to the World Trade Center Attacks during Pregnancy." *The Journal of Clinical Endocrinology & Metabolism* 90, no. 7: 4115–4118.

CHAPTER ONE

1. Jean Houston, The Possible Human (Los Angeles, CA: Jeremy Tarcher, 1982).

2. Peter Levine, *Healing Trauma: A Pioneering Program for Restoring the Wisdom of Your Body,* book and CD published by Sounds True, Louisville, CO, 2005. Also: Peter Levine, *It Won't Hurt Forever: Guiding Your Child through Trauma,* CD published by Sounds True, 2001.

3. Peter Levine, *Waking the Tiger: Healing Trauma* (Berkeley, CA: North Atlantic Books, 1997).

4. Antonio R. Damasio, *Descartes' Error: Emotion, Reason, and the Human Brain* (New York: Harper Perennial, 1995).

   Antonio R. Damasio, *The Feeling of What Happens: Body and Emotion in the Making of Consciousness* (New York: Harcourt, Inc., 1999).

5. Bessel A. van der Kolk, "Psychobiology of Post-Traumatic Stress Disorder," Chapter 11 in *Textbook of Biological Psychiatry,* edited by Jaak Panksepp, PhD (Wiley-Lisi, Inc., 2004).

6. Joseph LeDoux, *The Emotional Brain: Mysterious Underpinnings of Emotional Life* (New York: Simon and Schuster, 1998).

7. Bessel van der Kolk featured in *The Secret Life of the Brain,* A PBS Video Series, 2002.

8. Peter Levine, *Waking the Tiger,* 1997 (see note 3 above).

CHAPTER TWO

1. D. M. Levy, "On the problem of movement restraints," *American Journal of Orthopsychiatry*, Vol. 14: 644 (1944).

2. Bruce D. Perry, MD, PhD, *The Vortex of Violence: How Children Adapt and Survive in a Violent World*, published online by the Child Trauma Academy, 2000. www.childtrauma.org.

   B.D. Perry, R. Pollard, T. Blakely, W. Baker, D. Vigilante, "Childhood Trauma, the neurobiology of adaptation and 'use-dependent' development of the brain: how 'states' become 'traits'," *Infant Mental Health Journal*, Vol. 16, No. 4: 271–291 (1995).

   B.D. Perry, "Incubated in Terror: Neurodevelopmental factors in the 'cycle of violence'," in *Children, Youth and Violence: The Search for Solutions*, J. Osofsky, ed. (New York: Guilford Press, 1997), pp. 124–148.

3. M. Straus, "Cultural and organizational influences on violence between family members," in *Configurations: Biological and Cultural Factors in Sexuality and Family Life*, R. Prince and D. Barried, eds. (Washington, D.C.: Health, 1974).

   M. Straus and R. Gelles, "How violent are American families: Estimates from the national family violence survey and other studies," in *Family Abuse and Its Consequences: New Directions in Research*, G. Hotaling et al, eds. (Newbury Park, CA: Sage Press, 1998).

4. National Incident-Based Reporting System, Uniform Crime Reporting Program, 1999.

5. Murray A. Straus and Richard Gelles cited in *Violence and Childhood: How Persisting Fear Can Alter the Developing Child's Brain* by Bruce Perry, MD, PhD, The Child Trauma Academy, Department of Psychiatry and Behavioral Sciences, Baylor College of Medicine, Texas Children's Hospital, 1996.

   M. Straus and R. Gelles, 1998. See Note 3 above.

6. Carla Garrity et al., *Bully-Proofing Your School: A Comprehensive Approach for Elementary Schools* (Longmont, CO: Sopris West, 1994).

7. Sue Smith-Heavenrich, "Kids Hurting Kids," *Mothering* magazine, May-June 2001: 72–79.

   Kathleen Vail, "Words That Wound," *American School Board Journal*, September 1999.

8. Lauren Fredman, "Bullied to Death in Japan," *World Press Review*, Vol. 42 (March 1995): 25.

9. Debra Pepler's research was cited in an article by Hara Estoff Marano, "Big, Bad Bully," *Psychology Today*, Vol. 28: 50–89 (Sept–Oct 1995). Also found more recently in: Debra Peplar, Workshop material, "The Playground—The Overlooked Classroom," Ottawa-Carleton Community Forum on Bullying. April 1998.

10. *Nielsen Media Research, 2000* as reported by the © 2003 National Center for Children Exposed to Violence (NCCEV). Modified: December 16, 2005. Cited in Bruce Perry (see Note 2 above).

Other sobering statistics related to television and youth reported by the NCCEV:

> Percentage of television time children ages 2–7 spend watching alone and unsupervised: 81 (Kaiser Family Foundation, 1999. "Kids and Media @ the New Millennium.")

> Television alone is responsible for 10% of youth violence. (Senate Judiciary Committee Staff Report, 1999.)

> Hours per year the average American youth spends in school: 900. (Benjamin Barber, *Harper's*, Nov. 1993: 41.)

> Hours per year the average American youth watches television: 1,023. (Nielsen Media Research, 2000.)

See also A.C. Huston, E. Donnerstein, and H. Fairchild et al, *Big World, Small Screen: The Role of Television in American Society* (Lincoln, NE: University of Nebraska Press, 1992).

10. Bruce Perry, see Note 2 above.

11. "Come in and play," *Supermarket Business*, Vol. 55: 103 (2000).

12. C.A. Anderson and B.J. Bushman, "Effects of violent games on aggressive behavior, aggressive cognition, aggressive affect, physiological arousal, and prosocial behavior: A meta-analytic review of the scientific literature," *Psychological Science*, Vol. 12: 353–359 (2001).

13. Craig E. Emes, MD, CCFP, "Is Mr. Pac Man Eating our Children? A Review of the Effect of Video Games on Children," *The Canadian Journal of Psychiatry*, Vol. 42, No. 4: 409–14 (May 1997).

A more recent review of the literature regarding violence in the interactive media concludes that increases in aggressive behavior and thoughts, angry feelings, and increased physiological arousal may be linked to violent video games. These studies were compelling enough to lead to the 2005 adoption of "The American Psychological Association's (APA) Resolution on Violence in Videogames and Interactive Media." This Resolution advocates for a reduction of violence in all media marketed to children and youth. Source: "APA Calls for Reduction of Violence in Interactive Media Used by Children and Adolescents" (APA online press release, August 17, 2005).

> www.fradical.com/APA_news_release_on_video_games_August_2005. PDF

See also C.A. Anderson, "Violent Video Games and Aggressive Thoughts, Feelings, and Behavior," Chapter in S.L. Calvert, A.B. Jordan, and R.R. Cocking (eds.) *Children in the Digital Age: Influences of Electronic Media on Development* (pp. 101–119), Westport, CT: Praeger Publishers, 2002.

C.A. Anderson and B.J. Bushman, "The Effects of Media Violence on Society," *Science,* Vol. 295: 2377–2378 (2002).

B.J. Bushman and J. Cantor, "Media Ratings for Violence and Sex: Implications for Policymakers and Parents," *American Psychologist,* Vol. 58, No. 2: 130–141 (2003).

D.A. Gentile, P.J. Lynch, J.R. Linder, and D.A. Walsh, "The Effects of Violent Video Game Habits on Adolescent Aggressive Attitudes and Behaviors," *Journal of Adolescence,* Vol. 27: 5–22 (2004).

14. Victor C. Strasburger and Edward Donnestein, "Children, Adolescents, and the Media: Issues and Solutions," *Pediatrics,* Vol. 103: 129–139 (1999).

Note: For assistance in video game selection, the Entertainment Software Rating Board at www.esrb.org can help you weed out inappropriate titles. Another helpful resource is "A Parent's Guide to Video and Computer Games" by Kevin Simpson, which is an online article found at www.Parentcenter.com.

15. Marilyn Van Derbur, *Miss America By Day: Lessons Learned from Ultimate Betrayals and Unconditional Love* (Denver, CO: Oak Hill Ridge Press, 2003).

16. Vernon Wiehe, *Sibling Abuse* (Thousand Oaks, CA: Sage Publications, 1997), p. 59.

17. Dr. Bruce Perry, *Violence and Childhood: How Persisting Fear Can Alter the Developing Child's Brain* (2000). Available at www.childtrauma.org.

18. Robin Karr-Morse and Meredith S. Wiley, *Ghosts from the Nursery: Tracing the Roots of Violence* (New York: The Atlantic Monthly Press, 1997), p. 91.

L.W. Sontag and R.F. Wallace, "Study of fetal activity: Preliminary report of the Fels Fund," *American J. Diseases of Children,* Vol. 48: 1050–1057 (1934).

Also cited in: *Birth and the Origins of Violence: Featured Paper* (1995), an unpaginated paper by David B. Chamberlain, Ph.D at www.birthpsychology.com. Dr. Chamberlain is also the author of *The Mind of Your Newborn Baby* (Berkeley, California: North Atlantic Books, third edition, 1998) and is one of the organizers of the First International Congress on Pre- and Perinatal Psychology.

19. Inge Bretherton, "The Origins of Attachment Theory: John Bowlby and Mary Ainsworth," *Developmental Psychology,* Vol. 28: 759–775 (1992).

More attachment information is available at www.psychology.sunysb.edu/attachment/

This Website is a resource of New York University at Stony Brook (SUNY) and the New York Attachment Consortium. It is a library of researchers' publication lists and online articles that include attachment measures for infant-mother, childhood, and parenting and marriage research.

CHAPTER THREE

1. Dr. Lenore Terr, MD, *Too Scared To Cry: Psychic Trauma in Childhood* (New York: Basic Books, A Division of Harper Collins Publishers, 1990), pp. 159–161.

2. Dean G. Kilpatrick, Ronald Acierno, Benjamin E. Saunders, Heidi S. Resnick, Connie L. Best, Paula P. Schnurr, "Risk factors for adolescent substance abuse and dependence: data from a national sample," *Journal of Consulting and Clinical Psychology*, Vol. 68, No. 1: 19–30; quote on p. 23 (August 2003).

3. Gerald Huether, personal communication, 2004.

4. Marilyn Van Derbur, *Miss America By Day: Lessons Learned from Ultimate Betrayals and Unconditional Love* (Denver, CO: Oak Hill Ridge Press, 2003).

CHAPTER FOUR

1. Antonio Damasio, *The Feeling of What Happens: Body and Emotion in the Making of Consciousness* (New York: Harcourt, Inc., 1999).

2. Joseph E. LeDoux, *The Emotional Brain: Mysterious Underpinnings of Emotional Life* (New York: Simon and Schuster, 1998).

3. Robert Fulford, D.O., personal communication, Summer session, New England College of Osteopathic Medicine, Biddeford, Maine, 1980.

4. Lenore Terr, *Too Scared To Cry: Psychic Trauma in Childhood* (New York: Basic Books, A Division of Harper Collins Publishers, 1990), p. 235.

5. Eugene Gendlin, *Focusing* (New York: Bantam Books, 1981).

CHAPTER FIVE

1. Peter Levine, *It Won't Hurt Forever: Guiding Your Child through Trauma*, CD published by Sounds True, 2001. Rhymes composed by Peter Levine, with Lorin Hager and Maggie Kline. Instructional pamphlet by Maggie Kline.

2. Bessel A. van der Kolk, Alexander C. McFarlane, and Lars Weisaeth, eds. *Traumatic Stress: The Effects of Overwhelming Experience on Mind, Body, and Society.* (New York: The Guilford Press, 1996).

CHAPTER SIX

1. Robert Fulford, D.O., personal communication, Summer session, New England College of Osteopathic Medicine, Biddeford, Maine, 1980.

2. Judith Acosta, LCSW, and Simon Prager, PhD, *The Worst Is Over: What to Say When Every Moment Counts (Verbal First Aid to Calm, Relieve Pain, Promote Healing and Save Lives)* (San Diego, CA: Jodere Group, 2002).

CHAPTER SEVEN

1. D.M. Levy, "On the problem of Movement Restraints," *American Journal of Orthopsychiatry* 14 (1944): 644.

2. Found online at the magazine's Website.

3. K. Yashpal, J. Katz, and T.J. Coderre. "Effects of Preemptive or Post-Injury Intrathecal Local Anesthesia on Persistent Nociceptive Responses." *Anesthesiology* (1996).

   C. Michaloliakou, F. Chung, S. Sharma, "Preoperative Multimodal Analgesia Facilitates Recovery after Ambulatory Laparoscopic Cholecystectomy," *Anesth Analg*, 1996.

   S. I. Marshall and F. Chung, "Discharge Criteria and Complications After Ambulatory Surgery," *Anesth. Analg.* Vol. 88, No. 3: 508 (March 1, 1999).

4. Kaczynski's mother and Dahmer's father were both personally interviewed by Peter Levine via telephone.

5. Susan Brink, "Soothing the Littlest Patients: Doctors Focus on Easing Pain in Kids," *U.S. News & World Report, Inc.*, June 12, 2000. www.usnews.com.

6. *Ibid.*

CHAPTER EIGHT

1. William Steele and Melvyn Raider, *Structured Sensory Intervention for Traumatized Children, Adolescents and Parents*, Volume I of the Mellen Studies in Social Work Series (United Kingdom: Edwin Mellen Press, Ltd., 2001), p. 155.

2. Judith S. Wallerstein, Julia M. Lewis, and Sandra Blakeslee, *The Unexpected Legacy of Divorce: A 25-Year Landmark Study* (New York: Hyperion, 2000). The exact quote came from a debate between Dr. E. Mavis Hetherington, who wrote *For Better or Worse: Divorce Reconsidered* with John Kelly (New York: Norton, 2002), and Dr. Judith Wallerstein, who conducted studies reported in *The Unexpected Legacy of Divorce*. This debate was reported on by Mary Duenwald in *The New York Times*, p. 1 of a 3-page article (see note 2 above).

3. Dr. E. Mavis Hetherington and John Kelly, *For Better or Worse: Divorce Reconsidered* (New York: W. W. Norton & Company, Inc., 2002).

4. Vicki Lansky, "Divorce: 10 Things I Learned" (Oxygen Media, 2001). www.oxygen.com/topic/family/fammtrs/divorce10_20011109.html.

5. Judith S. Wallerstein, Julia M. Lewis, and Sandra Blakeslee, *The Unexpected Legacy of Divorce*, p. 216.

   C.M. Heinke and I. Westheimer, *Brief Separations* (New York: International University Press, 1965).

J. Soloman and C. George, "The Development of Attachment in Separated and Divorced Families: Effects of Overnight Visitation, Parent and Couple Variables," *Attachment and Human Development*, Vol. I, No. 1: 2–33 (April 1999).

6. E. Mavis Hetherington, "An Overview of the Virginia Longitudinal Study of Divorce and Remarriage with a Focus on Early Adolescence," *Journal of Family Psychology*, Vol. 7, No. 1: 39–56 (June 1993).

7. John W. James and Russell Friedman, *When Children Grieve* (New York: Harper Collins, 2001).

The Grief Recovery Institute, www.grief-recovery.com

In U.S., contact P.O. Box 6061-382, Sherman Oaks, CA 91413. Telephone: (818) 907-9600.

In Canada, contact RR#1, St. Williams, Ontario, Canada N0E 1P0. Telephone: (519) 586-8825.

8. Elizabeth Kübler-Ross, *On Death and Dying* (New York: Macmillan, 1969).

CHAPTER NINE

1. Marilyn Van Derbur, *Miss America By Day: Lessons Learned from Ultimate Betrayals and Unconditional Love* (Denver, CO: Oak Hill Ridge Press, 2003).

2. Anaïs Nin, author and diarist (1903–1977).

3. Alfred Kinsey et al, *Sexual Behavior of the Human Female* (Philadelphia: W.B. Saunders, 1953).

4. Children's Hospital National Medical Center, Washington, D.C. (www.safechild.org), 2006.

5. Harborview Medical Center, Harborview Center for Sexual Assault and Traumatic Stress (Seattle, WA, 2006). www.depts.washington.edu/hcsats/pdf/factsheets/csafacts.pdf.

National Committee for Prevention of Child Abuse, "Basic Facts About Sexual Child Abuse."

The following statistics are from the National Incident-Based Reporting System (NIBRS):

Sixty-seven percent of all victims of sexual assault reported to law enforcement agencies were juveniles (under the age of 18); 34% of all victims were under age 12.

One of every seven victims of sexual assault reported to law enforcement agencies was under age 6.

40% of the offenders who victimized children under age 6 were juveniles (under the age of 18).

The data are based on reports from law enforcement agencies of twelve states and include the years 1991 through 1996. (Bureau of Justice Statistics www.ojp.usdoj.gov/bjs/, 2006)

6. Groth, 1982; DeFrancis, 1969; Russell, 1983. As reported by the Children's Hospital National Medical Center, Washington, D.C., Website, (www.safechild.org), 2006.

7. Caren Adams and Jennifer Fay, *No More Secrets: Protecting Your Child from Sexual Assault* (San Luis Obispo, CA: Impact Publishers, 1984).

8. Vernon R. Wiehe, *Sibling Abuse: Hidden Physical, Emotional, and Sexual Trauma* (Thousand Oaks, CA: Sage Publications, 1997), p. 59.

9. *Child Adolescent Psychiatry Journal*, Vol. 35: 1 (January 1996).

Criminal Justice Source Statistics (2000, Table 4.7, p. 362).

10. J.V. Becker and E.M. Coleman, *Handbook of Family Violence* (New York: Plenum Press, 1988), pp. 197–205.

11. William Holmes, MD, and Gail Slap, "Sexual Abuse of Boys," *Journal of the American Medical Association*, Vol. 21, No. 280: 1859 (December 1998).

12. Quotation by Dr. Leigh Baker, author of *Protecting Your Children From Sexual Predators* (New York: St. Martin's Press, 2002); taken from Marilyn Van Derbur, *Miss America By Day* (Denver, CO: Oak Hill Ridge Press, 2003).

13. Caren Adams and Jennifer Fay, *No More Secrets*.

14. Susan B. Miller, *Disgust: The Gatekeeper Emotion* (Mahwah, NJ: The Analytic Press, 2004).

15. Studies by Bessel van der Kolk and Judith Herman cited at Cape Cod Conference on Trauma with van der Kolk and Peter Levine, July 2001. (As reported by van der Kolk in his lecture and Powerpoint presentation.)

16. Marilyn Van Derbur, *Miss America By Day.*

17. Jan Hindman, *Just Before Dawn: From the Shadows of Tradition to New Reflections in Trauma Assessment and Treatment of Sexual Victimization* (Lincoln City, OR: AlexAndria Associates, 1989), p. 87.

18. Jennifer Freyd, *Betrayal Trauma* (Cambridge: Harvard University Press, 1996), p. 190.

19. American Medical Association, "Strategies for the treatment and prevention of sexual assault" (Chicago: 1995).

20. Marilyn Van Derbur, *Miss America By Day*, p. 409.

Suggested listening (audio program) for this chapter: Peter A. Levine, *Sexual Healing: Transforming the Sacred Wound* (Louisville, CO: Sounds True, 2003).

CHAPTER TEN

1. This quote is from one of Suzanne's "Birthing the Future" bookmarks. Suzanne Arms is the author of *Immaculate Deception II: Myth, Magic & Birth* (Berkeley, CA: Celestial Arts, 1994) and founder of "Birthing the Future" a non-profit organization to support the child-bearing woman and share the finest world wisdom about ancient, traditional, and contemporary childbirth beliefs and practices. Information and products can be found at www.BirthingTheFuture.com.

2. D.H. Stott and S.A. Latchord, "Prenatal Antecedents of Child Health, Development, and Behavior," *Journal of the American Academy of Child Psychiatry*, Vol. 15, No. 1: 161–191 (Winter 1976).

3. L.W. Sontag. "Implications of Fetal Behavior and Environment for Adult Personalities," *Annals of the New York Academy of Sciences*, Vol. 134: 782 (1966).

4. Dr. Catherine Monk, "Fetal Heart Rate Reactivity Differs by Women's Psychiatric States: An Early Marker of Developmental Risk," *Journal of the American Academy of Child and Adolescent Psychiatry*, Vol. 43, No. 3: 283–290 (March 2004). Cited in source #4, above.

5. Dr. Tiffany Field, "Maternal Depression and Increased Fetal Activity," *Journal of Obstetrics and Gynaecology*, Vol. 21, No. 5: 468–473 (September 1, 2001). Also cited in source #4, above.

6. Dr. Thomas O'Connor, "Maternal antenatal anxiety and children's behavioural/emotional problems at 4 years: Report from the Avon Longitudinal Study of Parents and Children, *The British Journal of Psychiatry*, Vol. 180: 504 (2002).

7. Stephen W. Porges, "Neuroception: A subconscious system for detecting threats and safety," *Zero to Three Journal*, Vol. 24, No. 5: 19–24 (May 2004).

8. D. Chamberlain, "Reliability of birth memory: Observations from mother and child pairs in hypnosis," *Journal of Prenatal and Perinatal Psychology and Health*, Vol. 14, No. 1-2: 19–29 (1999).

   D. Chamberlain, "The significance of birth memories," *Journal of Prenatal and Perinatal Psychology and Health*, Vol. 14, (1-2): 65–84 (1999).

   D. Chamberlain, *The Mind of Your Newborn Baby* (Berkeley, CA: North Atlantic Books, 1998).

   P.G. Hepper, "Fetal memory: Does it exist? What does it do?" *Acta Paediatr* (Stockholm), Suppl 416: 16–20 (1996).

9. This particular study was cited in the following book:

   Mark L. Howe, *The Fate of Early Memories: Developmental Science and the Retention of Childhood Experiences (Washington, D.C.: American Psychological Association, 2000).*

10. Wendy McCarty, *"The power of beliefs: What babies are teaching us,"* Journal of Prenatal and Perinatal Psychology and Health, Vol. 16, No. 4: 341–360 (2002). This paper is based on a presentation to the 10th International Congress of APPPAH held in San Francisco, December 2001.

11. D.B. Chamberlain, "Reliability of birth memories: Observations from mother and child pairs in hypnosis," *Journal of the American Academy of Medical Hypnoanalysts*, Vol. 1, No. 2: 89–98 (1986).

    D.B. Chamberlain, "The significance of birth memories," *Journal of Prenatal and Perinatal Psychology and Health*, Vol. 14 (1–2): 65–84 (1999).

    D. B. Chamberlain, "Birth recall in hypnosis," *Birth Psychology Bulletin*, Vol. 2, No. 2: 14–18 (1981).

12. Edward Z. Tronick, "Emotions and Emotional Communications in Infants," *American Psychologist*, Vol. 44, No. 2: 112–119 (February 1989). Direct quote on p. 112.

13. Suzanne Arms, *Birth Today: Myth and Fact* (Bayfield, CO: Birthing the Future, 2004), p. 3. Part of conference materials given to participants attending the Taos, New Mexico, Birthing the Future Conference, February 2005.

14. www.childbirthconnection.org (an evidence-based maternity care nonprofit organization).

15. Documentary by Debby Takikawa (narrated by Noah Wyle), *What Babies Want: An Exploration of the Consciousness of Infants* (2005). Contact Beginnings Inc., A Resource Center for Children and Families, P.O. Box 681, Los Olivos, CA 93441. Telephone: (800) 893-5070; www.whatbabieswant.com.

16. Wendy Anne McCarty, PhD, *Welcoming Consciousness: Supporting Babies' Wholeness from the Beginning of Life—An Integrated Model of Early Development* (Santa Barbara, CA: WB Publishing, 2004), p. 64.

    This e-book (ISBN 0-9760658-5-1) can be found at www.wondrousbeginnings.com or write to 2022 Cliff Drive, #306, Santa Barbara, CA 93109.

    See the Bibliography for other titles by Wendy McCarty, as well as W. Emerson, R. Castellino, and D. Chamberlain, for more information on the life influence of the womb experience.

17. This study was cited in Suzanne Arms, *Immaculate Deception II* (Berkeley, CA: Celestial Arts, 1994), p. 85.

18. *Ibid.*, p. 84.

19. *Ibid.*, p. 91.

20. Suzanne Arms, *Birth Today: Myth and Fact*, Bayfield, CO: Birthing the Future, 2004, pp. 2–3.

21. Tiffany Field, PhD, "Massage Therapy for Infants and Children," *Developmental and Behavioral Pediatrics*, Vol. 16, No. 2: 105–111 (April 1995).

    F. Scafidi, T. Field, S. Schanberg, et al, "Massage stimulates growth in preterm infants: a replication," *Infant Behavior Development*, Vol. 13: 167–188 (1990).

22. J. Madeleine Nash, "Fertile Minds," *Time* magazine. Special Issue: How a Child's Brain Develops. February 3, 1997, p. 50.

23. *Ibid.*, p. 51.

24. R.V.E. Grunau, M.F. Whitfield, J.H. Petrie, "Early pain experience, child and family factors, as precursors of somatization: a prospective study of extremely premature and fullterm children," *Pain*, Vol. 56: 353–359 (1994).

    R.V.E. Grunau, "Do early experiences of pain have long-term consequences: evidence from the clinic." Paper presented at the Fourth International Symposium on Pediatric Pain, July 1997, Helsinki, Finland.

    R.V.E. Grunau, M.F. Whitfield, J. Petrie, "Children's judgments about pain at age 8–10 years: do extremely low birthweight (<1000) children differ from full birthweight peers?" *J Child Psychol Psychiatry*, Vol. 39: 587–594 (1998).

    Fran Lang Porter, PhD, Cynthia M. Wolf, PhD, and J. Philip Miller, A.B., "Procedural Pain in Newborn Infants: The Influence of Intensity and Development," *Pediatrics*, Vol. 104, No. 1: p. e13 (July 1999).

    (From the Department of Pediatrics and the Division of Biostatistics, Washington University School of Medicine, St. Louis, MO)

    A. Taddio, J. Katz, A.L. Ilersich, "Effect of neonatal circumcision on pain response during subsequent routine vaccination," *Lancet*, Vol. 349: 599 (1997).

25. W.A. McCarty, "The Power of Beliefs: What babies are teaching us," *Journal of Prenatal and Perinatal Psychology and Health*, Vol. 16, No. 4: 341–360 (2002).

26. Wendy Anne McCarty, *Welcoming Consciousness*, p. 53.

27. Beatrice Beebe, "A procedural theory of therapeutic action: Commentary on the Symposium, Interventions that Effect Change in Psychotherapy," *Infant Mental Health Journal*, Vol. 19, No. 3: 333–340 (Fall 1998).

28. Wendy Anne McCarty, *Welcoming Consciousness*, p. 62.

29. Giacomo Rizzolatti and Laila Craighero, "The Mirror-Neuron System," *Annual Review of Neuroscience*, Vol. 27: 169–192.

30. Daniel J. Siegel, MD, and Mary Hartzell, M.Ed., *Parenting from the Inside Out* (New York: Jeremy P. Tarcher/Penguin, 2004), pp. 76–77.

    M. Iacoboni et al, "Cortical Mechanisms of Human Imitation," *Science*, Vol. 286: 2526–2528 (1999).

31. Sandra Blakeslee, "Cells That Read Minds," *The New York Times* ("Science Times" section, online), January 10, 2006.

32. Allan Schore, *Affect Regulation and the Origin of the Self: The Neurobiology of Emotional Development* (Hillsdale, NJ: Lawrence Erlbaum Associates, 1994).

33. Dr. Robert Scaer, Behavorial Medicine Conference, Hilton Head, South Carolina, December 2004. Authors' personal notes from the conference.

34. "Periods of equilibrium and disequilibrium" is a theme that runs through Piaget's work. The Swiss-born Piaget wrote in French; he died in 1980. Some English translations of his work include:

    L. Smith, *Critical Readings on Piaget* (London: Routledge, 1996).

    P. Mussen (ed.), *Piaget's Theory: Handbook of Child Psychology*, 4th edition, Vol. 1 (New York: Wiley, 1983).

    Also, the Gesell Institute of Human Development cites Piaget's theory of "disequilibrium/equilibrium" in their series of books for parents. An example follows:

    Louise Bates Ames, Clyde Gillespie, Jacqueline Haines, and Frances Ilg, *The Gesell Institute's Child Development from One to Six* (New York: Harper & Row, 1979).

35. Allan N. Schore, Department of Psychiatry and Biobehavioral Sciences, UCLA School of Medicine, "The experience-dependent maturation of a regulatory system in the orbital prefrontal cortex and the origin of developmental psychopathology," *Development and Psychopathology*, Vol. 8 (1996), p. 61.

36. Diana Fosha (Adelphi University), "The Dyadic Regulation of Affect," JCLP/In Session: *Psychotherapy in Practice*, Vol. 57, No. 2: 227–242 (New York: John Wiley & Sons, Inc., 2001). Quote p. 233.

37. Joseph Chilton Pearce, speaking in the documentary DVD by Debby Takikawa, *What Babies Want* (see note 17, above).

38. Allan Schore, *Affect Regulation and the Origin of the Self*. See note 34.

39. Debby Takikawa, DVD, *What Babies Want*.

40. Wendy Anne McCarty, PhD, *Being with Babies: What Babies Are Teaching Us*, Vol. I (November 1996), p. 4.

    Write to 5662 Calle Real, 221, Goleta, CA 93117; they can also be purchased at www.wondrousbeginnings.com.

41. *Ibid.*, Vol. 1, p. 4.

42. *Ibid.*, Vol. 1, p. 5.

43. Dr. Belleruth Naparstek, Behavioral Medicine Conference, Keynote Address, Hilton Head, South Carolina, December 2004. Authors' personal notes from the conference.

44. Suzanne Arms, *Immaculate Deception II* (Berkeley, CA: Celestial Arts, 1994), p. 187.

CHAPTER ELEVEN

1. The designation of PTSD was the result of psychiatrists and psychologists working with returning Vietnam veterans as well as perpetrators/victims of domestic violence and child abuse. A team of field researchers further investigated and promoted the APA (American Psychiatric Association) listing of post-traumatic stress disorder in the diagnostical and statistical manual for the first time in the 1980 edition.

2. Lenore Terr, *Too Scared To Cry: Psychic Trauma in Childhood* (New York: Basic Books, 1990).

3. Carla Hannaford, *Smart Moves: Why Learning Is Not All in Your Head* (Arlington, VA: Great Ocean Publishers, Inc., 1995), p. 102.

4. "The Magic in Me" poem was written by Maggie Kline and Peter Levine and excerpted from: Peter A. Levine, *It Won't Hurt Forever: Guiding Your Child Through Trauma* (Audio Learning Program) (Boulder, CO: Sounds True, 2001). Contact www.soundstrue.com or call (800) 333-9185. The company is presently located in Louisville, CO.

5. Julie Henderson, *Embodying Well-Being, or How to Feel as Good as You Can in Spite of Everything* (Napa, CA: Zapchen, 1999). See Zapchen@aol.com or call (707) 258-8594.

6. Carla Hannaford, *Smart Moves*, p. 103.

7. *Ibid.*, p. 190.

8. Paul E. Dennison and Gail E. Dennison, *Brain Gym*, Teachers Edition, Revised. (Ventura, CA: Edu-Kinesthetics, Inc., 1994). Further information can be obtained through the Educational Kinesiology Foundation, P.O. Box 3396, Ventura, CA 93006-3396; telephone (800) 356-2109 or (805) 658-7942.

9. John Stewart, PhD, *Beyond Time Out: A Practical Guide to Understanding and Serving Students with Behavioral Impairments in the Public Schools* (Gorham, ME: Hastings Clinical Associates, 2000), pp. 148–149.

10. Dennison and Dennison, *Brain Gym*, p. 31 footnote. See note 8 above.

11. Bessel A. van der Kolk, Alexander C. McFarlane, and Lars Weisaeth (editors), *Traumatic Stress: The Effects of Overwhelming Experience on Mind, Body, and Society* (New York: The Guilford Press, 1996), p. 429.

12. Daniel Siegel, MD, speaking at the "Cutting-Edge Conference on Healing Trauma: Attachment, Trauma, the Brain, and the Mind," held in San Diego, California, in 2001. Author's personal notes.

13. B.D. Perry, "Childhood Trauma, the Neurobiology of Adaptation and 'Use-Dependent' Development of the Brain: How 'States' Become 'Traits'," *Infant Mental Health Journal*, Vol. 16, No. 4: 271–291 (1995).

    S.W. Porges, PhD, "Physiological Regulation in High-Risk Infants: A Model for Assessment and Potential Intervention," *Development and Psychopathology*. Vol. 8: 43–58 (1996).

S.W. Porges, PhD, "The Poly Vagal Theory: Phylogenetic Substrates of a Social Nervous System," *International Journal of Psychophysiology*, Vol. 12: 29–52 (2001).

14. Daniel J. Siegel, *The Developing Mind: How Relationships and the Brain Interact to Shape Who We Are* (New York: The Guilford Press, 1999), p. 319.

Daniel J. Siegel, MD, and Mary Hartzell, M. Ed., *Parenting from the Inside Out: How a Deeper Self-Understanding Can Help You Raise Children Who Thrive* (New York: Jeremy P. Tarcher [Penguin], 2003), p. 106.

Allan N. Schore, *Affect Dysregulation and Disorders of the Self* (New York: W.W. Norton & Company, 2003), pp. 212–216.

15. "The Secret Life of the Brain: Post-Traumatic Stress Disorder," video produced by the National Science Foundation and aired on PBS. To order call (800) 336-1917.

16. Michael Janofsky, "Bill on Student Bullying is Considered in Colorado," *The New York Times*, March 18, 2001, Section A, p. 10.

17. "The School Shooter: A Threat Assessment Perspective," FBI Report in conjunction with The National Center for the Analysis of Violent Crime (NCAVC), 2001. To contact them, you may write to: Federal Bureau of Investigation, Critical Incident Response Group, FBI Academy, Quantico, VA 22135.

18. D.O. Lewis, J.H. Pincus, B. Bard, E. Richardson, L.S. Princhep, M. Feldman, and C. Yeager (Department of Psychiatry, NYU Med Center), "Neuropsychiatric, Psychoeducational and Family Characteristics of 14 Juveniles Condemned to Death Row in the United States," *The American Journal of Psychiatry*, Vol. 145: pp. 584–589 (1988).

19. Robin Karr-Morse and Meredith W. Wiley, *Ghosts from the Nursery: Tracing the Roots of Violence* (New York: The Atlantic Monthly Press, 1997), p. 299.

20. Bessel A. van der Kolk, Alexander C. McFarlane, and Lars Weisaeth (editors), *Traumatic Stress*, p. 11. See note 11 above.

21. Gabor Maté, MD, "Are Violent Teens Suffering 'the Rage of the Unparented'?" (Toronto: Canada, *globeandmail.com Insider Edition*, December 18, 2004, p. F7).

See also Gordon Neufeld and Gabor Maté, *Hold On To Your Kids: Why Parents Need to Matter More Than Peers* (Toronto, Ontario, Canada: Knopf, 2004).

22. Reported by B. van der Kolk, Cape Cod Institute, conference entitled "Trauma, Consciousness, and the Body" (Bessel van der Kolk and Peter Levine Presenting), Eastham, MA, July 23–27, 2001. Authors' personal notes from the conference.

23. Gordon Neufeld and Gabor Maté, *Hold On To Your Kids*. See note 21 above.

24. *Ibid.*

25. This homeroom tactic was discussed in an interview conducted on TV a few years prior to publication of this book, but the authors can only reference it anecdotally now. (Apologies!) A great idea is nonetheless worth sharing.

26. For example:

Kali Miller, PhD, *Animal-Assisted Therapy (AAT): The Healing Power of the Four-Footed Co-Therapist, Research Supporting the Benefits of Human-Animal Interaction & Methods for Successfully Incorporating AAT into Present Settings,* Copyright 2003, Medical Educational Services, Inc., 2004 Highland Ave., Suite C, Eau Claire, WI 54701, (715) 836-9900, pp. 28–33.

Contact Kali Miller (Conference Presenter for AAT) at Corinthia Counseling Center, Inc.,185 N.E. 102nd Ave., Portland, OR 97220; Telephone (503) 251-1952.

A.M. Beck and A.H. Katcher, "A new look at pet-facilitated therapy," *Journal of the American Veterinary Medical Association,* Vol. 184: 414–421 (1984).

N.M. Bodmer, "Impact of pet ownership on the well-being of adolescents with few familial resources," C. Wilson and D. Turner (eds.), *Companion Animals in Human Health* (Thousand Oaks, CA: Sage Publications, 1998), pp. 237–247.

J.L. Hanselmann, "Coping skills interventions with adolescents in anger management using animals in therapy," *Journal of Child & Adolescent Group Therapy,* Vol. 11, No 4: 159–195 (2001).

K.M. Hansen, C.J. Messinger, M. Baun, and M. Megel, "Companion animals alleviating distress in children," *Anthrozoos,* Vol. 12, No. 3: 142–148 (1999).

27. John Stewart, PhD, *Beyond Time Out,* pp. 15–18. See note 9 above.

28. *Ibid.,* p. 18.

29. Heinz Kohut, *The Restoration of the Self* (New York: International University Press, 1977).

30. Cape Cod Institute: "Trauma, Consciousness, and the Body" (Bessel van der Kolk and Peter Levine Presenting), Eastham, Massachusetts, July 23–27, 2001. Authors' personal notes from the conference.

31. C.G. Jung, *Structure and Dynamics of the Psyche,* Collected Works, Vol. 8, second edition (Princeton, NJ: Princeton University Press, 1969).

32. O. Fred Donaldson, PhD, *Playing by Heart: The Vision and Practice of Belonging* (Deerfield Beach, FL: Health Communications, 1993); www.originalplay.org/playing_ by_heart.htm

33. Julie Henderson, *Embodying Well-Being.* See note 5, above.

34. Ysaye M. Barnwell, *No Mirrors in My Nana's House* (a book & CD) (San Diego, CA: Harcourt Brace & Company, 1998).

35. Violet Oaklander, *Windows to Our Children* (Moab, UT: Real People Press, 1978), pp. 3–5.

36. Balametrics offers equipment such as balance boards and sensory integration tools for educators, parents, and therapists. Visit their Website at www.balametrics.com or call (800) 894-3187 or (360) 452-2842. To write: Balametrics, Inc., P.O. Box 2716, Port Angeles, WA 98362, or email: info@balametrics.com.

CHAPTER TWELVE

1. J.T. Mitchell and G.S. Everly, *Critical Incident Stress Debriefing: An Operations Manual* (Ellicott City, MD: Chevron, 1996); and by same authors, *Critical Incident Stress Management: The basic course workbook* (Ellicott City, MD: Institute of Critical Incident Stress Foundation, 1996).

   S. E. Brock, J. Sandoval, and S. Lewis, *Preparing for Crises in the Schools: A Manual for Building School Crisis Response Teams,* second edition (New York: Wiley, 2001).

   W. Steele and M. Raider, *Structured Sensory Intervention for Traumatized Children, Adolescents and Parents (SITCAP)* (New York: Edwin Mellen Press, 2001).

   L.C. Terr, "Mini-marathon groups: Psychological 'first aid' following disasters," *Bulletin of the Menninger Clinic,* Vol. 56: 76–86 (1992).

   American Red Cross, Disaster Mental Health Service I: Participant's Attachments. Washington, D.C. (1994).

2. Stephen E. Brock, PhD, "Crisis Management Research Summaries," NASP *Communiqué,* Vol. 31, No. 8: 40 (2003). Published by the National Association of School Psychologists, Bethesda, MD.

3. *Ibid.*

4. Stephen E. Brock, PhD, NCSP, and Shane R. Jimerson, PhD, NCSP, *Characteristics and Consequences of Crisis Events: A Primer for the School Psychologist* (Sacramento, CA: California Association of School Psychologists, 2002).

   The NASP *Communiqué,* which referenced both Brock articles (Notes 2 and 4) in Vol. 30, No. 4 (December 2001), also featured an article titled *"Best Practices in School Crisis Prevention and Intervention:* Interview with the Editors," including Stephen E. Brock, Philip J. Lazarus, and Shane R. Jimerson, editors of the book entitled *Best Practices in School Crisis Prevention and Intervention.* See www.nasponline.org to link to NASP Crisis Resources for parents and teachers.

5. L. Conlon, T.J. Fahy, and R. Conroy, "PTSD in ambulant RTA victims: a randomized controlled trial of debriefing," *Journal of Psychosomatic Research,* Vol. 46: 37–44 (1999).

6. Interview with Maggie Kline, July 25, 2006. Contact this organization at: National Mass Fatalities Institute, Lisa R. LaDue, MSW, LISW, Kirkwood Community College, 6301 Kirkwood Blvd. SW, Cedar Rapids, IA 52404. Telephone: (319) 398-7122.

7. J.W. Prescott, *The Origins of Human Love and Violence* (Newport Beach, CA: Institute of Humanistic Science, originally 1975; most recently published 1995). Contact the Institute at 1829 Commodore Rd., Newport Beach, CA 92660.

8. *Ibid.*

9. Merida Blanco, PhD, wrote for numerous publications and for various advocacy groups.

CHAPTER THIRTEEN

1. Dr. Barbara Starfield, Johns Hopkins School of Hygiene and Public Health, "Data Published in Annual Physical and Economic Cost of Medical Intervention," *The Journal of American Medicine* (2003).

2. Gary Null, PhD, Carolyn Dean, MD, N.D., Martin Feldman, MD, and Debora Rasio, MD, *Death by Medicine*, published online at www.garynull.com (November 2003). This article is posted with the permission of Nutrition Institute of America, Inc. (NIA, Inc.), www.NutritionInstituteOfAmerica.org.

3. Joseph Mercola, D.O., "Drugs and Doctors May Be the Leading Cause of Death in the United States," Issue 394 (January 15, 2003), eHealth News You Can Use @ www.mercola.com.

4. P. Barnes, E. Powell-Griner, K. McFann, and R. Nahin, "Complementary and alternative medicine use among adults: United States, 2002," *CDC Advance Data Report #343.* Reported May 27, 2004. Available at nccam.nih.gov/news/camsurvey.htm.

5. National Center for Complementary and Alternative Medicine (CAM) as reported at www.cam.nih.gov (May 2004); and the National Center for Health Statistics, from the National Institutes of Health Survey (NHIS) Annual Study, 2002 Edition, posted at cdc.gov./nchs.

6. D.M. Eisenberg, R.B. Davis, S.L. Ettner, et al, "Trends in alternative medicine use in the United States, 1990–1997: results of a follow-up national survey." *JAMA*, Vol. 280, No. 18: 1569–1575 (1998). Study conducted at the Center for Alternative Medicine Research and Education, Department of Medicine, Beth Israel Deaconess Medical Center, Boston, MA 02215.

7. Go to www.planetree.org and click on "finding a hospital." It's also a good link to a medical video library.

8. Make-A-Wish Foundation is a national organization with a different Website and address for each state. The main web address is: www.wish.org to locate their affiliates in each state.

9. K. Yashpal, J. Katz, and T.J. Coderre, "Effects of preemptive or post-injury intrathecal local anesthesia on persistent nociceptive responses," *Anesthesiology* (1996).

C. Michaloliakou, F. Chung, and S. Sharma, "Preoperative multimodal analgesia facilitates recovery after ambulatory laparoscopic cholecystectomy," *Anesth. Analg.* (1996).

S. I. Marshall and F. Chung, "Discharge Criteria and Complications After Ambulatory Surgery," *Anesth. Analg.*, Vol. 88, No. 3: 508 (March 1, 1999).

10. V. Felitti, R. Anda, D. Nordenberg, D. Williamson, A. Spitz, V. Edwards, et al, "Relationship of Childhood Abuse and Household Dysfunction to Many of the Leading Causes of Death in Adults," *American Journal of Preventive Medicine*, Vol. 14, No. 4 (1998).

11. Phone interview conducted on July 14, 2006. Karen Schanche, MSW, LCSW, is a clinical social worker/psychotherapist who works as part of three multi-disciplinary teams at the University of California at San Francisco Medical Center: the Pediatric Rheumatology and Rehabilitation Medicine teams, and the Cancer Center's Symptom Management and Palliative Care Outpatient Service at the Comprehensive Cancer Center of UCSF. She can be reached at (415) 455-4915 or via email: karen.schanche@ucsfmedctr.org; or kschanche@earthlink.net.

Bibliography

Acosta, Judith, LCSW, and Simon Prager, PhD. *The Worst Is Over: What to Say When Every Moment Counts (Verbal First Aid to Calm, Relieve Pain, Promote Healing and Save Lives)*. San Diego, CA: Jodere Group, 2002.

Adams, Caren, and Jennifer Fay. *No More Secrets: Protecting Your Child from Sexual Assault*. San Luis Obispo, CA: Impact Publishers, 1984.

Anderson, C.A., and B.J. Bushman, "Effects of Violent Games on Aggressive Behavior, Aggressive Cognition, Aggressive Affect, Physiological Arousal, and Prosocial Behavior: A Meta-Analytic Review of the Scientific Literature." *Psychological Science*, Vol. 12: 353–359 (2001).

Anderson, C.A., and B.J. Bushman, "The Effects of Media Violence on Society." *Science*, Vol. 295: 2377–2378 (2002).

Baker, Dr. Leigh. *Protecting Your Children From Sexual Predators*. New York: St. Martin's Press, 2002.

Barnwell, Ysaye M. *No Mirrors in My Nana's House* (book & CD). San Diego, CA: Harcourt Brace & Company, 1998.

Becker, J.V., and E.M. Coleman. *Handbook of Family Violence*. New York: Plenum Press, 1988.

Bowlby, J. *A Secure Base: Parent-Child Attachment and Healthy Human Development*. New York: Basic Books, 2000.

Bowlby, J. *Separation: Anxiety and Anger*. New York: Basic Books, 2000.

Brazelton, MD, and T. Berry. *Touchpoints: The Essential Reference, Your Child's Emotional and Behavioral Development*. United States: Addison-Wesley, 1992.

Bretherton, Inge. "The Origins of Attachment Theory: John Bowlby and Mary Ainsworth." *Developmental Psychology* 28 (1992): 759–775.

Brink, Susan. "Soothing the Littlest Patients: Doctors Focus on Easing Pain in Kids." *U.S. News & World Report, Inc.*, June 12, 2000. www.usnews.com.

Buckley, Sarah J. *Gentle Birth, Gentle Mothering*. Anstead, Queensland, Australia: One Moon Press, 2005. See www.sarahjbuckley.com to order this book or learn more about this Australian MD and author.

Bushman, B.J., and J. Cantor, "Media Ratings for Violence and Sex: Implications for Policymakers and Parents," *American Psychologist*, Vol. 58, No. 2: 130–141 (2003).

Calvert, S.L., A.B. Jordan, and R.R. Cocking, eds. *Children in the Digital Age: Influences of Electronic Media on Development.* Westport, CT: Praeger Publishers, 2002.

Castellino, R., with D. Takikawa and S. Wood. *The Caregivers' Role in Birth and Newborn Self-Attachment Needs.* Santa Barbara, CA: BEBA, 1997. Available through Castellino Training Seminars, telephone: (805) 687-2897.

Castellino, R. "The stress matrix: Implications for prenatal and birth therapy." *Journal of Prenatal and Perinatal Psychology and Health,* Vol. 15, No. 4: 31–62 (2000).

Castellino, R. Paper presented at the 10th International Congress of The Association for Prenatal and Perinatal Psychology and Health, December 2001, San Francisco, CA.

Chamberlain, D. "The expanding boundaries of memory." *Pre- and Perinatal Psychology Journal,* Vol. 4, No. 3: 171–189 (1990).

Chamberlain, D. "The mind of the newborn: Increasing evidence of competence." In P.G. Fedor-Freybergh & M.L.Vogel (eds.), *Prenatal and Perinatal Psychology and Medicine: Encounter with the Unborn, A Comprehensive Survey of Research and Practice.* Park Ridge, NJ: Parthenon, 1988.

Chamberlain, David B., PhD. *The Mind of Your Newborn Baby.* Berkeley, CA: North Atlantic Books, third edition, 1998.

Chamberlain, D. "Prenatal receptivity and intelligence." *Journal of Prenatal and Perinatal Psychology and Health,* Vol. 12 (3-4): 95–117 (1998).

Chamberlain, D. "Reliability of birth memory: Observations from Mother and Child Pairs in Hypnosis." *Journal of Prenatal and Perinatal Psychology and Health* 14, no. 1–2 (1999): 19–29.

Chamberlain, D. "The Significance of Birth Memories." *Journal of Prenatal and Perinatal Psychology and Health* 14, no 1–2 (1999): 65–84.

Damasio, Antonio R. *Descartes' Error: Emotion, Reason, and the Human Brain.* New York: Harper Perennial, 1995.

Damasio, Antonio R. *The Feeling of What Happens: Body and Emotion in the Making of Consciousness.* New York: Harcourt, Inc., 1999.

Dennison, Paul E., and Gail E. Dennison. *Brain Gym.* Teachers Edition, Revised. Ventura, CA: Edu-Kinesthetics, Inc., 1994.

Donaldson, O. Fred, PhD. *Playing by Heart: The Vision and Practice of Belonging.* Deerfield Beach, FL: Health Communications, 1993.

Doubleday, Jock. *Spontaneous Creation: 101 Reasons Not to Have Your Baby in a Hospital,* Vol. 1. "A Book about Natural Childbirth and the Birth of Wisdom and Power in Childbearing Women." E-book available from www.spontaneouscreation.org.

Emerson, W. "The power of prenatal and perinatal experience in maximizing human potential throughout life." Paper presented at the Prenatal and Perinatal

Psychology Conference, Newport Beach, CA (January 1989).

Emerson, W. "Psychotherapy with infants and children." *Pre- and Perinatal Psychology Journal*, Vol. 3, No. 3: 190–217 (1989).

Emerson, W. "The vulnerable prenate." *Pre- and Perinatal Psychology Journal*, Vol. 10, No. 3: 125–142 (1996).

Emerson, W. (Audiotape) *Shock, A Universal Malady: Prenatal and Perinatal Origins of Suffering* (1999). Available from: www.Emersonbirthrx.com.

Emes, Craig E., MD, CCFP. "Is Mr. Pac Man Eating our Children? A Review of the Effect of Video Games on Children." *The Canadian Journal of Psychiatry*, Vol. 42, No. 4: 409–14 (May 1997).

Field, Tiffany. "Maternal Depression and Increased Fetal Activity." *Journal of Obstetrics and Gynaecology* 21, no. 5 (September 1, 2001): 468–473.

Fredman, Lauren. "Bullied to Death in Japan," *World Press Review*, Vol. 42 (March 1995): 25.

Freyd, Jennifer. *Betrayal Trauma*. Cambridge: Harvard University Press, 1996.

Garrity, Carla et al., *Bully-Proofing Your School: A Comprehensive Approach for Elementary Schools*. Longmont, CO: Sopris West, 1994.

Gendlin, Eugene. *Focusing*. New York: Bantam Books, 1981.

Gentile, D.A., P.J. Lynch, J.R. Linder, and D.A. Walsh, "The Effects of Violent Video Game Habits on Adolescent Aggressive Attitudes and Behaviors." *Journal of Adolescence*, Vol. 27: 5–22 (2004).

Goer, Henci. *Obstetrics Myths vs. Research Realities*. New York: Bergin and Garvey, 1994.

Goer, Henci. *The Thinking Woman's Guide to a Better Birth*. New York: The Berkley Publishing Company, Penguin Group (USA), 1999.

Hannaford, Carla. *Smart Moves: Why Learning Is Not All in Your Head*. Arlington, VA: Great Ocean Publishers, Inc., 1995.

Hepper, P.G., "Fetal memory: Does it exist? What does it do?" *Acta Pœdiatr* (Stockholm) 416 (1996): 16–20.

Hetherington, E. Mavis. "An Overview of the Virginia Longitudinal Study of Divorce and Remarriage with a Focus on Early Adolescence." *Journal of Family Psychology* 7, no. 1 (June 1993): 39–56.

Henderson, Julie. *Embodying Well-Being or How to Feel as Good as You Can in Spite of Everything*. Napa, CA: Zapchen, 1999.

Herman, Judith Lewis, MD. *Trauma and Recovery*. New York: Basic Books, 1992.

Hetherington, E. Mavis, and John Kelly. *For Better or Worse: Divorce Reconsidered*. New York: Norton, 2002.

Hindman, Jan. *Just Before Dawn: From the Shadows of Tradition to New Reflections in Trauma Assessment and Treatment of Sexual Victimization*. Lincoln City, OR: AlexAndria Associates, 1989.

Holmes, William, MD, and Gail Slap. "Sexual Abuse of Boys." *Journal of the American Medical Association* 21, no. 280 (December 1998): 1859.

Huston, A.C., E. Donnerstein, H. Fairchild, et al. *Big World, Small Screen: The Role of Television in American Society*. Lincoln, NE: University of Nebraska Press, 1992.

Houston, Jean. *The Possible Human*. Los Angeles: Jeremy Tarcher, 1982.

James, John W., and Russell Friedman. *When Children Grieve*. New York: Harper Collins, 2001.

Karr-Morse, Robin, and Meredith W. Wiley. *Ghosts from the Nursery: Tracing the Roots of Violence*. New York: The Atlantic Monthly Press, 1997.

Kilpatrick, Dean G., Ronald Acierno, Benjamin E. Saunders, Heidi S. Resnick, Connie L. Best, and Paula P. Schnurr. "Risk factors for adolescent substance abuse and dependence: data from a national sample." *Journal of Consulting and Clinical Psychology*, Vol. 68, No. 1: 19–30 (2003).

Kohut, Heinz. *The Restoration of the Self*. New York: International University Press, 1977.

Kübler-Ross, Elizabeth. *On Death and Dying*. New York: Macmillan, 1969.

Leboyer, Frederick. *Birth Without Violence*. New York: Fawcett Book Group, 1990.

LeDoux, Joseph E. *The Emotional Brain: Mysterious Underpinnings of Emotional Life*. New York: Simon and Schuster, 1998.

Leitch, Laurie. "A Post-Tsunami Diary," *Psychotherapy Networker*, Vol. 29: 62–69 (Nov-Dec 2005). Laurie Leitch was a member of the FHE's TOP team that went to Thailand to do SE-based relief work.

Levine, Peter. *Healing Trauma: A Pioneering Program for Restoring the Wisdom of Your Body* (a book and CD); *It Won't Hurt Forever: Guiding Your Child Through Trauma;* and *Sexual Healing: Transforming the Sacred Wound,* (the latter two are primarily audio programs). All available from Sounds True, Louisville, CO.

Levine, Peter. *Waking the Tiger: Healing Trauma*. Berkeley, CA: North Atlantic Books, 1997.

Leo, Pam. *Connection Parenting: Parenting Through Connection Instead of Coercion*. Deadwood, OR: Wyatt-MacKenzie Publishing, Inc., 2005.

Levy, D.M. "On the problem of movement restraints," *American Journal of Orthopsychiatry*, Vol. 14: 644 (1944).

Marano, Hara Estoff. "Big, Bad Bully," *Psychology Today*, Vol. 28: 50–89 (Sept–Oct 1995).

Marshall, James. *George and Martha*. New York: Houghton Mifflin Co., 1972.

Marshall, S.I., and F. Chung, "Discharge Criteria and Complications After Ambulatory Surgery." *Anesth. Analg.* 88, no. 3 (March 1, 1999): 508.

McCarty, Wendy Anne, PhD. *Being with Babies: What Babies Are Teaching Us, An Introduction, 1.* Goleta, CA: Wondrous Beginnings, 1996. (Available through www.wondrousbeginnings.com.)

McCarty, W.A. *Being with Babies: What Babies Are Teaching Us, Supporting Babies' Innate Wisdom, 2.* Goleta, CA: Wondrous Beginnings, 1997. (Available through www.wondrousbeginnings.com)

McCarty, W.A. "How our earliest experiences in the womb and at birth affect us now." *The Energy Field*, Vol. 5, No. 1: 1 (2004).

McCarty, W.A. "Keys to healing and preventing foundational trauma: What babies are teaching us." *Bridges—ISSSEEM magazine*, Vol. 13, No. 4: 8–12 (2002).

McCarty, W.A. "Nurturing the Possible: Supporting the integrated self from the beginning of life." *Shift: At the Frontiers of Consciousness*, Vol. 6: 18–20 (2005).

McCarty, W.A. "Supporting babies' wholeness in the 21st century: An integrated model of early development." *Journal of Prenatal and Perinatal Psychology and Health*, Vol. 20, No. 3: 187–220 (2006).

McCarty, W.A. "The CALL to reawaken and deepen our communication with babies: What babies are teaching us." *International Doula*, Vol. 12, No. 2 (Summer 2004).

McCarty, W.A. "The Power of Beliefs: What babies are teaching us." *Journal of Prenatal and Perinatal Psychology and Health*, Vol. 16, No. 4: 341–360 (2002).

McCarty, W.A. *Welcoming Consciousness: Supporting Babies' Wholeness from the Beginning of Life—An Integrated Model of Early Development* (eBook). Santa Barbara, CA: WB Publishing, 2004. (Available through www.wondrousbeginnings.com)

McCarty, W.A. *What Babies Are Teaching Us: A Collection* (eBook). Santa Barbara, CA: WB Publishing, 2005. (Available through www.wondrousbeginnings.com)

Michaloliakou, C., F. Chung, S. Sharma. "Preoperative Multimodal Analgesia Facilitates Recovery After Ambulatory Laparoscopic Cholecystectomy." *Anesth Analg* (1996).

Miller, Susan B. *Disgust: The Gatekeeper Emotion*. Mahwah, NJ: The Analytic Press, 2004.

Neufeld, Gordon, PhD, and Gabor Maté, MD *Hold On To Your Kids: Why Parents Need to Matter More Than Peers*. Toronto, Ontario, Canada: Knopf, 2004.

Monk, Catherine. "Fetal Heart Rate Reactivity Differs by Women's Psychiatric States: An Early Marker of Developmental Risk." *Journal of the American Academy of Child and Adolescent Psychiatry* 43, no. 3 (March 2004): 283–290.

Oaklander, Violet. *Windows to Our Children*. Moab, UT: Real People Press, 1978.

O'Connor, Thomas. "Maternal Antenatal Anxiety and Children's Behavioural/Emotional Problems at 4 Years: Report from the Avon Longitudinal Study of Parents and Children." *The British Journal of Psychiatry* 180 (2002): 504.

Pearce, Joseph Chilton. *Evolution's End: Claiming the Potential of Our Intelligence*. New York: HarperCollins Publishers, 1992.

Pearce, Joseph Chilton. *Magical Child: Rediscovering Nature's Plan for Our Children*. New York: Dutton, 1977; reprinted by Penguin Books (Plume) in 1992.

Perry, Bruce. *Violence and Childhood: How Persisting Fear Can Alter the Developing Child's Brain*. The Child Trauma Academy, Department of Psychiatry and Behavioral Sciences, Baylor College of Medicine, Texas Children's Hospital, 1996.

Perry, Bruce D., MD, PhD. *The Vortex of Violence: How Children Adapt and Survive in a Violent World*, published online by the Child Trauma Academy, 2000. www.childtrauma.org.

Perry, Bruce D. "Incubated in Terror: Neurodevelopmental factors in the 'cycle of violence'," in *Children, Youth and Violence: The Search for Solutions*, J. Osofsky, ed. New York: Guilford Press, 1997.

Perry, B.D., R. Pollard, T. Blakely, W. Baker, and D. Vigilante. "Childhood Trauma, the neurobiology of adaptation and 'use-dependent' development of the brain: how 'states' become 'traits'." *Infant Mental Health Journal*, Vol. 16, No. 4: 271–291 (1995).

Porges, Stephen W. "Neuroception: A Subconscious System for Detecting Threats and Safety." *Zero to Three Journal* 24, no. 5 (May 2004): 19–24.

Prescott, J.W. "The origins of human love and violence." Newport Beach, CA: Institute of Humanistic Science, 1995. (1829 Commodore Rd., Newport Beach, CA 92660)

Rothenberg, Mira. *Children with Emerald Eyes: Histories of Extraordinary Boys and Girls*. Berkeley, CA: North Atlantic Books, 2003.

Sapolsky, Robert M. *Why Zebras Don't Get Ulcers: An Updated Guide to Stress, Stress Related Diseases, and Coping*. New York: W.H. Freeman & Company, 1994.

Scaer, Robert. *The Trauma Spectrum.* New York: Norton, 2005.

Schore, Allan N. *Affect Dysregulation and Disorders of the Self.* New York: W.W. Norton & Company, 2003.

Schore, Allan N. *Affect Regulation and the Origin of the Self: The Neurobiology of Emotional Development.* Hillsdale, NJ: Lawrence Erlbaum Associates, 1994.

Siegel, Daniel J., MD. *The Developing Mind: How Relationships and the Brain Interact to Shape Who We Are.* New York: The Guilford Press, 1999.

Siegel, Daniel J., MD, and Mary Hartzell, M.Ed. *Parenting from the Inside Out: How a Deeper Self-Understanding Can Help You Raise Children Who Thrive.* New York: Jeremy P. Tarcher/Penguin, 2003.

Smith-Heavenrich, Sue. "Kids Hurting Kids." *Mothering* magazine, May-June 2001: 72–79.

Soloman, J., and C. George. "The Development of Attachment in Separated and Divorced Families: Effects of Overnight Visitation, Parent and Couple Variables." *Attachment and Human Development* I, no. 1 (April 1999): 2–33.

Somé, Sobonfu E. *Welcoming Spirit Home: Ancient African Teachings to Celebrate Children and Community.* Novato, CA: New World Library, 1999.

Sontag, L.W., and R.F. Wallace. "Study of Fetal Activity: Preliminary report of the Fels Fund." *American J. Diseases of Children,* Vol. 48 (1934): 1050–1057.

Sontag, L.W. "Implications of Fetal Behavior and Environment for Adult Personalities." *Annals of the New York Academy of Sciences* 134 (1966): 782.

Steele, William, and Melvyn Raider. *Structured Sensory Intervention for Traumatized Children, Adolescents and Parents,* Volume I of the Mellen Studies in Social Work Series. United Kingdom: Edwin Mellen Press, Ltd., 2001.

Stern, Daniel N. *The Interpersonal World of the Infant: A View from Psychoanalysis and Developmental Psychology.* New York: Basic Books, 1985.

Stern, Daniel N. *The Motherhood Constellation: A Unified View of Parent-Infant Psychotherapy.* New York: Basic Books, 1995.

Stewart, John, PhD. *Beyond Time Out: A Practical Guide to Understanding and Serving Students with Behavioral Impairments in the Public Schools.* Gorham, ME: Hastings Clinical Associates, 2000.

Stott, D.H., and S.A. Latchord, "Prenatal Antecedents of Child Health, Development, and Behavior." *Journal of the American Academy of Child Psychiatry.,* 15, no. 1 (Winter 1976): 161–191.

Straus, Murray A. "Cultural and organizational influences on violence between family members," in *Configurations: Biological and Cultural*

Factors in Sexuality and Family Life, R. Prince and D. Barried, eds. (Washington, D.C.: Health, 1974).

Strasburger, Victor C., and Edward Donnestein, "Children, Adolescents, and the Media: Issues and Solutions." *Pediatrics,* Vol. 103: 129–139 (1999).

Terr, Lenore, MD. *Too Scared To Cry: Psychic Trauma in Childhood.* New York: Basic Books, A Division of Harper Collins Publishers, 1990.

Tronick, Edward Z. "Emotions and Emotional Communications in Infants." *American Psychologist* 44, no. 2 (February 1989): 112–119.

Vail, Kathleen. "Words That Wound," *American School Board Journal,* September 1999.

Van Derbur, Marilyn. *Miss America By Day: Lessons Learned from Ultimate Betrayals and Unconditional Love.* Denver, CO: Oak Hill Ridge Press, 2003.

van der Kolk, Bessel A., Alexander C. McFarlane, and Lars Weisaeth, eds. *Traumatic Stress: The Effects of Overwhelming Experience on Mind, Body, and Society.* New York: The Guilford Press, 1996.

Wallerstein, Judith S., Julia M. Lewis, and Sandra Blakeslee. *The Unexpected Legacy of Divorce: A 25-Year Landmark Study.* New York: Hyperion, 2000.

Wiehe, Vernon R. *Sibling Abuse: Hidden Physical, Emotional, and Sexual Trauma.* Thousand Oaks, CA: Sage Publications, 1997.

Yashpal, K., J. Katz, and T.J. Coderre. "Effects of Preemptive or Post-Injury Intrathecal Local Anesthesia on Persistent Nociceptive Responses." *Anesthesiology* (1996).

Zand, Walton, and Roundtree. *A Parents' Guide to Medical Emergencies: First Aid for Your Child.* Avery Publishing Group, 1997.

CLASSIC BOOKS FOR BIRTHING AND NURSING

Bradley, Robert, MD. *Husband-Coached Childbirth.* New York: Harper & Row, 1965; revised 1981.

Dick-Reed, Grantly, MD. *Childbirth Without Fear: The Principles and Practice of Natural Childbirth.* New York: Harper, 1959; revised 1972.

Leboyer, Frederick. *Birth Without Violence.* New York: Fawcett Book Group, 1990.

Montagu, Ashley. *Touching: The Human Significance of the Skin,* third edition. New York: Harper & Row, 1971.

Torgus, Judy, ed. *The Womanly Art of Breast-Feeding.* Franklin Park, IL: La Leche League International, 1987.

ADDITIONAL RESOURCES

Alliance for Transforming the Lives of Children. This is an evidence-based source of information for parents on consciously conceiving, birthing, and nurturing children at www.atlc.org.

The American Association for Pre- and Perinatal Psychology and Health (APPPAH) has published a small booklet/guide entitled "One Hundred Books (and videos too) from 1977–1997 in Prenatal/Perinatal Psychology and Health." It can be ordered from APPPAH, 340 Colony Road, Box 994, Geyserville, CA 95441. Telephone (707) 857-4041; fax: (707) 857-4042. APP-PAH's Website: www.birthpsychology.com.

Balametrics offers equipment such as balance boards and sensory integration tools for educators, parents, and therapists. Visit their Website at www.balametrics.com or call (800) 894-3187 or (360) 452-2842. To write: Balametrics, Inc., P.O. Box 2716, Port Angeles, WA 98362, or email: info@balametrics.com.

BEBA (Building and Enhancing Bonding and Attachment): A Center for Family Healing, Santa Barbara, CA. Specializing in early infant trauma and family therapy, through publications, conference presentations, video, and parent education groups. Website: www.beba.org.

Birthing The Future, P.O. Box 1040, Bayfield, CO 81122. Telephone: (970) 884-4090. This is a non-profit organization to support the child-bearing woman and share the finest world wisdom about ancient, traditional, and contemporary childbirth beliefs and practices. Information and products can be found at www.BirthingTheFuture.com and www.Castellinotraining.com.

Calm Birth, a Childbirth Method for the 21st Century. See www.CalmBirth.org or email to info@CalmBirth.org. The practices transform the birth process and imprint a peaceful beginning on both mother and child. "The positive impact of this on society can't be overestimated," says Christiane Northrup, MD.

Castellino Prenatal and Birth Therapy Training at www.Castellinotraining.com.

Childbirth Connection is an evidence-based maternity care nonprofit organization. Website: www.childbirthconnection.org.

William Emerson (pioneer in pre- and perinatal trauma); articles, videos, and conference transcripts found at www.emersonbirthrx.com.

Collected Works I: The Treatment of Birth Trauma in Infants and Children. Petaluma, CA: Emerson Training Seminars, 1997, 2001, 130 pages.

Collected Works II: Pre- and Perinatal Treatment of Children and Adults. Petaluma, CA: Emerson Training Seminars, 1999, 220 pages.

Shock: A Universal Malady—Prenatal and Perinatal Origins of Suffering. Petaluma, CA: Emerson Training Seminars, 1999. (Includes six CDs and a 30-page booklet.)

Elora Media: Children's books, videos and music to enrich creativity. Website: www.eloramedia.com.

Foundation for Human Enrichment. 7102 La Vista Place, Suite 200, Niwot, CO 80503. Telephone: (303) 652-4035; Fax: (303) 652-4039. The FHE, founded by Dr Peter A Levine, is a non-profit, educational and research organization dedicated to the worldwide healing and prevention of trauma. Professional training in Somatic Experiencing® is provided, as well as outreach to under-served populations and victims of violence, war, and natural disasters. www.traumahealing.com.

International Trauma-Healing Institute (ITI), 269 South Lorraine Blvd., Los Angeles, CA 90004. Contact Gina Ross, Founder and President of ITI, at www.traumainstitute.org for trauma outreach, prevention, and healing in the Middle East and worldwide.

Lisa R. LaDue, MSW, LISW, Senior Advisor (Co-founder and former Director), National Mass Fatalities Institute, Kirkwood Community College, 6301 Kirkwood Blvd. SW, Cedar Rapids, IA 52404. Telephone: (319) 398-7122. Website: www.nmfi.org.

Peter A. Levine, *Healing Trauma: A Pioneering Program for Restoring the Wisdom of Your Body,* book and CD published by Sounds True, Louisville, CO, 2005.

Peter A. Levine, *It Won't Hurt Forever: Guiding Your Child through Trauma,* CD published by Sounds True, Louisville, CO, 2001.

Peter A. Levine, *Sexual Healing: Transforming the Sacred Wound,* CD published by Sounds True, Louisville, CO, 2003.

Dr. Belleruth Naparstek, *Successful Surgery,* an imagery CD to prepare for medical procedures; available from www.healthyjourneys.com.

TOUCHPOINTS, Ed Tronick, 1295 Boylston, Suite 320, Boston, MA 02115. Tel: (617) 355-5913. Early education for professionals in emotional and behavioral areas.

Trauma Outreach Program (TOP) is an FHE program that serves victims of trauma through outreach, education, training, and research throughout the world. It was created post-tsunami in 2005 in Thailand. TOP is working with survivors of Hurricanes Katrina and Rita. Website: www.trauma-healing.com.

Trauma Vidya was created after the Indian Ocean tsunami and to provide relief to those in India suffering from symptoms of traumatic stress through education, training, treatment, and research. Contact: Raja Selvam, Founder (FHE Senior Faculty) at www.traumavidya.org.

Wendy Anne McCarty, PhD, R.N., Prenatal and Perinatal Psychology and Energy Psychology Consultant. Santa Barbara Graduate Institute; Co-Founder & Primary Therapist, BEBA; Co-Creator & Founding Chair, Prenatal & Perinatal Psychology Program, Author, Researcher, Educator for Professionals and Families. Global Private Practice by phone, supporting Professionals and Families to prevent, identify, and heal stress, trauma patterns before and during pregnancy, birth, and infancy, as well as repair core patterns from this period during childhood and adulthood. To contact Dr. McCarty: wmccarty@wondrousbeginnings.com. For more information and to purchase Dr. McCarty's publications, visit www.wondrousbeginnings.com.

ZERO TO THREE, Matthew Melmud, Director, 734 15th St., Suite 1000, Washington, D.C. 20005. Telephone: (202) 638-1144. Education for professionals in emotional and behavioral areas.

Index

About the Authors

Peter A. Levine received his PhD in medical biophysics from the University of California at Berkeley, and also holds a doctorate in psychology from International University. He is the developer of

Somatic Experiencing® and founder of the Foundation for Human Enrichment. He teaches trainings in this work throughout the world and in various indigenous cultures. Dr. Levine was a stress consultant for NASA on the development of the space shuttle project. He is a member of the Institute of World Affairs Task Force of Psychologists for Social Responsibility and serves on the American Psychological Association's Presidential Initiative on Responding to Large-Scale Disasters and Ethno-Political Warfare. Peter's current interests include making his work available to underserved populations. He is the author of the best-selling book *Waking the Tiger: Healing Trauma* (North Atlantic Books), available in eighteen languages, and the book and CD *Healing Trauma: A Pioneering Program for Restoring the Wisdom of Your Body* (Sounds True), as well as the audio learning series *It Won't Hurt Forever: Guiding your Child through Trauma* and *Healing Sexual Trauma: Transforming the Sacred Wound*.

Maggie Kline has been a marriage, family, child therapist for over twenty years and is a retired school psychologist. She uses Somatic Experiencing® in individual and couples psychotherapy. She integrates Somatic Experiencing® with art and play when working with children and teens. Maggie is a senior Somatic Experiencing® instructor and consultant for the Foundation for Human Enrichment, teaching Dr. Levine's method. She assisted him in developing the Sounds True audio programs for healing childhood and sexual trauma. Maggie co-authored the article "It Won't Hurt Forever—Guiding Your Child Through Trauma" (*Mothering* magazine, Jan.–Feb. 2002). She also volunteered to lead the first FHE-sponsored trauma outreach relief effort in Thailand following the 2004 Indian Ocean tsunami.

Before becoming a clinician, Maggie was a master teacher for Long Beach Unified School District, a school counselor, and a parent. Her rich and varied background in working with children from diverse cultures and of all ages, from preschool through high school in regular and special education, brings clarity to the practical steps outlined in this book to prevent and heal the symptoms of overwhelm and trauma.

Foundation for Human Enrichment

The FHE is a nonprofit, educational and research organization dedicated to the worldwide healing and prevention of trauma. Professional training in Somatic Experiencing® is provided, as well as outreach to under-served populations and victims of violence, war, and natural disasters.

Somatic Experiencing® (SE), developed by Dr. Peter Levine, is a short-term naturalistic approach to the resolution and healing of trauma. It teaches mechanisms to regulate and discharge the high levels of energy arousal associated with defensive survival behaviors, making it possible to return to normal in the aftermath of highly "charged" life-threatening experiences.

Contact us at: Foundation for Human Enrichment
7102 La Vista Place, Suite 200
Niwot, CO 80503
Telephone: (303) 652-4035
Fax: (303) 652-4039
www.traumahealing.com.